NOTES ON LIFE

NOTES ON LIFE

by
THEODORE DREISER

edited by
Marguerite Tjader
and
John J. McAleer

THE UNIVERSITY OF ALABAMA PRESS
University, Alabama

191

D77ln

182728

Foreword

IN HIS PASSIONATE INTRODUCTION TO *Notes on Life,* JOHN Cowper Powys, a friend closer to Dreiser by temperament and genius than most mortals can be, has given the key as to how this work must be judged. It is not a finished philosophical study, but a vast brooding reaction to the Universe. It remains only to describe the *Notes* as Dreiser left them, the reasons for this selection, and the background of his search for facts and insights.

The origins of all *Notes on Life* are to be found in four special boxes numbered 402 to 405 in the Dreiser files for *Notes on Life* in The Rare Book Collection, Charles van Pelt Library, University of Pennsylvania, Philadelphia, Pa.

The original material consisted of eleven boxes of pages filed in manila folders, plus subsidiary information, representing roughly some five-hundred-thousand words. Much was duplication, for manuscript had sometimes been copied by typists, using as many as a dozen carbons, when Dreiser was not sure under which heading he would finally place his many variations on the chapter themes.

Dr. Neda Westlake, in the *Library Chronicle* of the University of Pennsylvania (vol. 20, no. 2), has described how the Dreiser material, including the *Notes on Life,* came to the Rare Book Collection. There, a young scholar, Sydney Horovitz, intrigued with the *Notes,* undertook to sort and rearrange them. We can thank him for separating the main, creative writing from secondary material. He started to compress the work into an outline of his own; however, he took ill and could not finish the task.

We have since returned the work to Dreiser's final outline of fifty-one subjects divided into two parts, as printed in the *Library Chronicle* mentioned above, except for a change in the sequence of the last five headings, in the interest of coherence.

Because of a close working relationship with Dreiser, over a period of eighteen years, I felt not only qualified but compelled to work for the publication of these *Notes on Life,* knowing how earnestly he desired to see them completed and brought out as a final statement of his personal philosophy. In 1927, I had met him at a small literary party and he had at once pressed me into his service. He taught me how to edit, read, and report on manuscripts as well as answer letters. He then had two secretaries, each one with more than she could handle. I worked part time, until I left for Europe. Later I returned to work full time for Dreiser when he was one of the editors of *An American Spectator,* among other interests. He had already begun to work on *Notes on Life.* In the meantime I had written a novel, for which he furnished a foreword. In 1937, encouraged by my work with Dreiser, I started a magazine of the arts, *Direction,* to which he contributed material and advice. I assisted him occasionally until he left New York in 1938. In 1943–44, I moved to California at Dreiser's request to help him finish *The Bulwark,* for which he was under contract, and then, hopefully, to continue with *Notes on Life.*

After Dreiser's death in 1945, I was determined to leave as full a record of my association with him as possible and to encourage publication of the philosophical material already completed. The first result was my book *Theodore Dreiser, A New Dimension* (Silvermine Press, Norwalk, Conn., 1965). I then obtained permission from the Dreiser Committee of the University of Pennsylvania, custodian of Dreiser's literary rights, to embark on the work of editing the material Dreiser had set aside for *Notes on Life.*

Certainly, I knew his intentions for this book and believed in its value.

Dreiser had been collecting material for his *philosophy* during some twenty to thirty years. His intention was to form his *Notes* into finished chapters, such as that on *Individual Creative Power* or *Transmutation of Personality* included here. Three subjects listed had been published in his *Hey Rub-a-Dub Dub,* "a book of the Mystery, and Terror and Wonder of Life" (Boni and Liveright, 1920); this volume must be considered a forerunner of his *Notes on Life,* although his thought here shows further distinctive development.

Because of his full, tumultuous life, which ended so suddenly, Dreiser did not complete his project, yet he had poured so much of his time and interest into its preparation that even shorter essays and fragments are rich in insights and powerful Dreiser language. Many essays of two, three, or more pages can well stand by themselves. Indeed, some not included here were sold to magazines. In making a reader's selection, we have used all the longer pieces, excluding only the few already published, and chosen the shorter essays most appropriate or colorful to illustrate the chapter topics.

A third category of selections is the shorter *note,* sometimes a paragraph or two, sometimes only a few sentences. A difficulty in choosing these is that they were often typed in six, a dozen, or as many as twenty copies, with many headings, filed under as many chapters, with comments added to suit various subjects, as illustrated here under the headings *Time* and *Weights and Measures.* Many of these shorter notes have been included for their variety or poetic quality that adds a lighter touch to more ponderous expressions. Dreiser's style is often lyric as well as forceful; his writing has been left intact, not edited, but printed exactly as he wrote it—not always true of his work as published hitherto!

Where an obvious word had been omitted by Dreiser in writing by hand, it has been added, enclosed by editor's brackets. The same is true if a phrase or word has been added for clarity. Punctuation has also been emended, but only when necessary for clear meaning. Very long paragraphs have sometimes been broken up. In all cases, the editors and publishers have made only those changes essential for clarity or coherence.

For many of these *Notes* the original handwritten manuscript has been found. This is indicated by the mark [*Or*]. In cases where Dreiser worked over a typescript and put in corrections in his own handwriting, we have used the mark [*W*]. The initials T.D. or Dreiser's full name has been left just as in the original. Explanatory statements in connection with certain *Notes* are also enclosed in editor's brackets. Scholarly comment and bibliographical material appear as end notes to this volume.

Passing on to a wider consideration of Dreiser's main themes, we leave the reader to identify them in his own way, but will say only that each subject is well represented here, although some excellent material has necessarily been left aside (for some later complete edition).

Delightful essays on the life of birds, fish, spiders, butterflies, and other insects would make a volume in themselves. Representative pieces of this kind have been included under nearly every heading to illustrate Dreiser's love of nature. The same love is seen in his fascination for the stars and celestial phenomena. Dreiser's mind constantly passed from minute observations to the contemplation of matters which stagger the mind—or, as Dreiser would say, the *man-mechanism* barely equipped to deal with them.

Concerning the background of Dreiser's interest and research in scientific fields, it should be observed that, just after publication of *An American Tragedy*, he started seriously exploring human behavior and the latest theories of physiologists and psychologists. "I've written novels," he said to me once, "now I want to do something else." His greatest success had not satisfied him. His restless, inquiring temperament had always sought to probe the depths of experience, and he felt on the verge of discovering new truths. He read the latest scientific books, plodded in and out of libraries and laboratories, talked for hours with far-out philosopher friends, like Charles Fort, or with established biologists, such as Calvin Bridges, who had won the Nobel Prize for his work on heredity.

It was Bridges who allowed Dreiser to observe his work during the summer of 1929 at the Marine Biological Laboratory at Woods Hole, Massachusetts. Eight years later, in 1937, he spent another month with Bridges at the Cold Spring Harbor research center, peering for hours through microscopes. Contrasting with this, when in California, he was allowed by scientist friends to look through the giant telescope of Mt. Wilson Observatory.

Dreiser engaged a special secretary to work with him on the *Notes*. She was Harriet Bissell, who reports as follows:

I went to work for Dreiser in October, 1935. He was living in the Mt. Kisco house. I got the job through answering an ad in the New York *Times* and was chosen from about 500 applicants. I had graduated from Smith the previous June. . . . I was to take care of his files and began by reorganizing them. I was to study books which he would give me, with an eye to picking out ideas and illustrations for his book on philosophy. He had already collected and sorted a large amount of material. . . . He had a vast reading background, but not nearly as vast as that required by his subject. He was a slow reader, but one who understood what he read. . . .

I was not the only researcher who read and marked passages for him. There were at least two others I knew of who worked on and off, reading and marking passages and discussing philosophy and science with him for the purposes of this book. Unfortunately, I recollect only one name, Yvette Szekeley. . . . [I might add my own name here. M.T.]

All of this was supplemented with interviews which he solicited with various scientists. There were not a great many of these—Harvey Lemon was one. He was closely connected by friendship and common interest with Calvin Bridges, Simon Flexner, and other very considerable scientists, and with them he felt free to check his conclusions. This access to a few illustrious, mature scientific minds enhanced his comprehension of what science is about. Dreiser was a very skillful, courageous interviewer and a diverting, fascinating conversationalist, listening carefully to everything. He would insist until he was satisfied with the answer. He was welcomed by scientists, and these conversations were very productive from the point of view of his book, because he could jump over the laboratory and get to conclusions in this way. . . .

Today we have to admit that the general trend of science has not disproved Dreiser's thesis, but rather confirmed it. . . .

Enormous files on the book existed when Dreiser left for California in December, 1938. On looking over the material which you have, I notice that there must have been more added in California later on. . . .

[Some of this late material was still in handscript when I found it, inserted between typed pages. MT.]

During the three years, we worked in New York as well as at Mt. Kisco and a month or so at Noroton. Moving all the material back and forth was practically impossible and so Dreiser was often without all his files and his books. He also turned to other projects from time to time. All of this delayed and hampered work on the philosophy book. . . .

I believe the selection of material is representative. You may have left out some nuggets but since I don't remember any, I am trusting to my strong impression of the general drift which you certainly have captured.

Dreiser often said that Harriet Bissell had proved to be an extremely able assistant, and that he admired the brilliance of her mind. So it is fortunate that she has gone over these *Notes* with me and given valuable editorial advice. Thanks are due her, not only for her help at the present time, but also for her work in the past.

I am also very grateful to Dr. Neda Westlake for her faithful guardianship of the Dreiser Collection, and her assistance and confidence as a member of the Dreiser Committee, together with Professor Scully Bradley and Professor Robert Spiller.

I am deeply indebted to John J. McAleer, whose encouragement and editorial cooperation has lightened the burden of responsibility which I feel for launching this last work of a major writer, known as a novelist, but now appearing in a new role. Professor McAleer, of Boston College, himself an English scholar and experienced author of a critical biography of Dreiser, has brought a fresh eye to the final editing of these *Notes*, helped to check references and facts, and furnished important end notes for this volume.

We are both grateful to Professor Frank Muhlfeld, scientist and oceanographer, holder of many degrees, who teaches the course *Frontiers of Science*, a part of the Excel program of Fordham University at Lincoln Center. He has read this manuscript for scientific accuracy. He feels that, although new information is now available in various fields which interested Dreiser, such as electricity or space phenomena, Dreiser's over-all impressions as a layman confronting the marvels of science are valid today. His imagination and interpretations make a unique contribution, not to science-fiction, but to science literature and philosophy.

To conclude, if there seem to be repetitions of theme or motif in these *Notes*, even under their disparate headings, this was Dreiser's way of composing his literary music. He liked to turn an idea over and over in his mind, viewing it from many angles and expressing it in various ways, to persuade rather than to argue, to create the vast and sometimes nebulous atmosphere of a mysterious reality beyond what he felt to be the unreality of many of our established values and conceits. Also partaking of that super-reality is Dreiser's haunting sense of beauty and awe. These were found in his novels, but now it is as if he had become his own protagonist in a cosmic love-story of unity with nature and the Creative Force.

MARGUERITE TJADER

Introduction

Was Theodore Dreiser a great novelist? Was he a great artist? Was he a great thinker? And if he were all these things was it the greatness of his personality that accounted for this pre-eminence among other writers of our time? It seems impossible to treat any problem of this sort without being confronted by all the teasing entanglements of word definitions. But if we are not scientists or professional metaphysicians, we just have to plunge ahead using ordinary words in their ordinary sense, adding something of our own, no doubt, to the popular meaning here and there, but not wasting our reader's time by defending, or even explaining these additions.

The sympathetic reader, for whom we are writing, will naturally pick up his oar with us and pull forward whether against the wind of popular opinion or with it.

We know pretty well what we mean by a "great artist" in regard to painting and sculpture and probably in regard to music and play-acting, but I fancy most honest readers will confess they've had their moments of confused difficulty when applying the ticklish and tricky word "art" to literature. The difficulty is due, I expect, to the fact that by using *words* rather than the simpler mediums of color, form, sound, or gesture, we have in the sphere of immediate sensation moved further away from reality, while in the sphere of mental association, we have moved nearer reality.

Now the mystery of human personality, followed by its kindred mystery, the difference between one personality and another, remains the important thing in the case of everything we call art; but it seems to me that more emphatically than anywhere else, except perhaps in the case of the clown, the mystery of personality dominates the written word.

And we have, I feel, every reason to be suspicious the moment we hear critics separating the concept "art" from the concept "personality" and especially so when the conclusion arrived at is not only that there is such a thing as impersonalized or what they call "objective" art, but that such art is superior to the commoner kind where the author's personality reveals itself in every line.

It is impossible to deny that there are a few supreme writers—such as Homer and Shakespeare and Cervantes in his *Don Quixote*—who become "medium" writers for the human race itself; but in their case, the mystery of their private selves is swallowed up in a larger mystery, a mystery that makes it only too easy for the debunkers of human genius to deprive them as individuals of the glory for which they cared so little, a mystery for which the tiresome word "objective" remains totally inadequate and that—like the deity to his worshippers—is more, rather than less personal and might even be called super-personal or multi-personal; while these "objective" artists are sub-personal to such a point that from their work even the very magic of the inanimate seems to have been expelled.

In his novels, from the first to the last, as indeed in every scrap and fragment he wrote, Dreiser is a thinker, and a thinker, moreover, with a living, growing philosophy of life, that had he lived to be a hundred would have remained incomplete and unfinished. And this is the case because his philosophy was the expression of his ever growing and developing personality.

I have not encountered, and I doubt whether anyone who reads these lines has encountered, a human personality to whom the word "cosmic" could be as appropriately applied. I purposely use this word here to convey in a rough, casual, and popular sense, the volume and magnitude of his nature. Philosophically speaking, the word is far too orderly and carries with it too much of the notion of the systematic to suggest his special habit of thought. He was too personal to have ever possessed, or even desired to possess, a rounded-off and completed system of the universe. As with Walt Whitman, his world, strictly speaking, was not a universe at all. It was a multiverse. Dreiser *required* a fluctuating, wavering margin of the ragged-edged and the un-limited; and his imaginative view of real reality was still in process of creation. As Walt Whitman says of himself, he "contained multitudes." There *had* to be with him, to satisfy a certain primeval and elemental chaoticism in his nature, a dark abyss of unformulated, unfathomed, unregulated, uncharted, illimitable *welter* round every separate dimension of the multiverse he apprehended. For the world within himself as he felt its pressure when he sank into himself was a multiverse rather than a universe. His personality mellowed, grew gentler and tenderer, as he grew older but it never lost a certain destructive, explosive force. This force, however, was not a *catalytic* power. It did *not* remain integral and intact while it effected startling and significant changes in all with which it came in contact. It evoked such changes; but *it* also changed. He had moods, quests, obsessions, possessions, re-possessions, revelations, intimations, superstitions, psychic avoidances, occult attractions, atavistic repulsions, together with strange primeval proclivities and weird elemental aberrations.

There is no gainsaying it, although to orthodox pietists, ecclesiastical fanatics, and vindictive moralists, Dreiser appeared as a ramping materialist; to those who really knew him he was an awestruck mystic, a thunder-struck medicine-man of cosmogonic television. I have met in my day and time various remarkable men of genius, including among others, Charlie Chaplin and Thomas Hardy; but what, I think, made Dreiser unique was the presence in him of some terrific psycho-magnetic force for which there is at present no adequate name. This force was both creative and destructive. Some would call it spiritual. I prefer to use the simpler expressions "magnetic" and "psychic." But whatever it was, it radiated from him like what theosophists call an *aura*.

Like Fyodor Dostoievsky, Theodore Dreiser was the sort of realist whose most ghastly, lurid, murderous, bloody-pooled, spider haunted, cobwebbed background had *another background* behind it, which receded into a different kind of horror and a different kind of redemption, and the same is true of the massive Balzacian appendages of worldly glory he loves to depict; heavy furniture, tasteless ornamentation, and "trig" costumes. Behind even this we can hear the great pulsing "om . . . . om . . . . om . . . ." of the systole and diastole of our unfathomable life-dimension!

There was in Dreiser's soul something akin to his power, both for creation and destruction, of this breaking up of the atom which perturbs so many. In whatever sphere his mind functioned, it carried with it our nuclear severance and a sort of *psychic-fuse* capable of causing a series of violent explosions among the mental-elements of the "status-quo." His imagination was ceaselessly experimental and explosive. One weird cosmic world followed another, expanding the bubbles, under the demiurgic impulse of his electricity-charged, cloudy ponderings.

From the Vulcanian smithy of his brooding fancy, all manner of "Lost Atlantises Regained" rose up. Out of the protoplasmic ooze of ultimate being, they rose, conceptual worlds moving upon inconceivable orbits and plunging into gulfs of unimaginable chaos! To expect a cohesive, logical, rounded-off "corpus" of philosophic thought or any definite metaphysical system from a mind like Dreiser's is like asking for apples from a Scotch Fir. Some of the deepest thinkers in the world have resembled him in this and have had no system to offer. Where is the "system" of Pythagoras, or Heraclitus, or Da Vinci, or Montaigne, or Rabelais, or Goethe, or Nietzsche, or Walt Whitman? Indeed it is not concealed from some among us that logical and rounded-off systems of thought like that of Spinoza, and, even more so, of Hegel, are in their essence contrary to the evasive reality of life and nature.

There was something in Dreiser's cosmogonic personality that not only responded in a manner that was almost terrifying to the elemental mysteries of our Dimension but that seemed to respond to Powers and Forces beyond our Dimension. And it is this awareness in him that adds so special an atmosphere of vibrations, reaching us from far away, to those descriptions in his novels

of the decline and fall of certain unlucky persons with the particular sort
of fatal weakness in his characters that seems to excite some mysterious sadism
in the wanton concatenations of blind chance. And if these malign elements
in a chaotic multiverse strike the haunted sensitivity of Dreiser's mind as
actual demonic forces hunting down the weak and the unwise and the
ill-constructed, so also in some manner, only in a reversed direction, do certain
other forces in nature, not less beyond the level of the ordinary material
sequences of cause-and-effect, inspire with a sort of monstrously superhuman
cunning Dreiser's successful free-lances and anti-social pirates.

His mind was predominantly attracted by the chemical changes and mutations
of the elements. It was not only that such chemical phenomena haunted
him. They obsessed him. They were a mania with him. He was always seeing
humanity in relation to the mysterious movements and transformations of
the various atomic and electric events and occasions and energies and impressions, apprehended by our senses and worked over by our conscious minds,
that we accept as the palpable shapes and textures of the visible world.

For Dreiser the psychic world and the physical world were never divided.
He was always seeing mountains as men and men as atoms, and men and
mountains and atoms as transitory bubbles in an unfathomable flood of Being,
of which there was neither beginning nor end, and where reality was always
turning into illusion and illusion into reality!

In his own words—and when he is in these cosmogonic moods his words
gather to themselves a particular kind of rhythm that makes us think of
both Whitman and Melville—"transmutation of personality is positively the
outstanding law of life, so much so that even the mountains and plains,
to say nothing of the cities and the hamlets, change men, transmute them
from one thing to another. Thus the Himalayas, being unlike any other mountain
range for size, change those nearest them. For, unlike any other mountain
range, they present jagged undulations of enormous height, and they seem
to speak to men in deep tones, although occasionally they speak with the
roar of their avalanches. And yet, at the same time, they so loftily ignore
man as something puny and unimportant. And they have nurtured and made
sure the most important of humble men on our globe. In fact, their overpowering
effect has made many men too humble, so that even today they try to efface
themselves from an earth looked down upon by clouds that sit on the thrones
of Gods. . . . "

It is strange to think that this great occult spirit, so constantly haunted
by that planetary *awe* in the presence of the insoluble mystery of life which
Goethe regarded as the essence of all poetry and all religion should have
been spoken of by many as a "materialist." If such he was, it was in the
sense of turning so concentrated an eye upon "matter" that "matter" beneath
that gorgonian stare turned into something uncommonly—even uncom-
fortably—like "spirit"! You would hardly expect a mind so obsessed by the

chemistry of things to speculate after the following fashion; but these, again are his own words, and with these I will bid my old friend farewell, at least, as we say, "protem":

"For, if when you die the atoms or electrons of which you are composed should disintegrate, which would mean that they would change into pure energy, and if—and this is a purely speculative idea of my own—this energy should, for some reason, coagulate as a force, you would, thereby, become an immense power or unit of energy capable (assuming that thought is a phase of energy, which may now believe), although bodiless, of continuing to think—imagine the possibilities of observation, conclusion, interest—assuming that there were endless other such disembodied and yet *thinking* units of energy to be observed by you!—perhaps even confer with! Imagine! . . ."

John Cowper Powys
Corwen, North Wales
August 31, 1946

NOTES ON LIFE

PART I

Mechanism Called the Universe

THE RAW MATERIALS FOR THE ONWARD AND UPWARD URGE FOR WINGS were in the flaming sun long before it gave off the hot masses which eventually cooled into the earth and other planets. Some billions of years ago this planet was still a nude, lifeless, sterile thing—a world of howling storms, hot rains, and boisterous oceans beating on dead rocks and sands. Even then, it is believed that there were cycles [See Dr. Johann Keeler] of comparative dryness, which paleobotanists have traced for fifty million years to the present day.

If a modern chemist could have visited that sterile world of so long ago, he would have found that then, as now, whenever certain chemical elements were thrown together, they produced predictable compounds. This was, and is, *the Eternal Law of Nature,* and it was just as true in that world as it is in the chemical laboratory of today.

That hypothetical chemist, billions of years ahead of his time, would have reported the finding of all the simple natural compounds of today and would have noted and described the *rare formation of compounds highly complex.* He would, for instance, have detected hundreds of protein molecules akin to the infective agent in poison ivy today, or in the tobacco mosaic today called viruses—molecules so alive in some respects and so dead in others that, even today, the scientist does not know whether to regard them as dead or alive.

And later another chemist would have come upon elaborate chemical structures called genes, capable of secreting about themselves sensitive cytoplasm to form primitive, transitory cells. And still another chemist, prowling around in the slightly less dim past, would probably have eventually found a gene molecule that possessed in its chemical structure the creative genius of synthesizing another gene like itself. It must be understood that this very early world was like a tremendous chemical laboratory, with chance and other forces mixing the various chemical elements and compounds to form new compounds. It was as if the various elements and compounds making up the earth, when it was cast off by the Sun, were in vials and jars in a laboratory, and a careless giant hand was mixing and remixing them.

‡ ‡ ‡

Doesn't mechanism imply something that is not mechanical—the other half of something we call mechanical but out of which mechanism comes.

‡ ‡ ‡

As clouds appear by reason of moisture rising from a warmer to a colder level and disappear again as moisture sinks from a colder to a warmer level, why should not matter-energy, in other words the visible universe, because of some invisible change in the vasty ether, appear and again disappear? But in what cycles of time?

‡ ‡ ‡

The appearance of life, its endless varieties of flora and fauna, would suggest—considering the tremendous push of force they represent—a compulsion or determination to self-expression, particularly since nothing appears to die. On the other hand, the universe *is*, and it does not seem reasonable that it should need a will to live—more likely, a will to change.

‡ ‡ ‡

The word mechanistic, deriving as it does from our crude machinery and used in connection with the stupendous and baffling and beautiful thing we call the universe, is, of course, nothing more than a very crude and inadequate attempt to emphasize the idea of regularity of motion as well as of form in connection with all of the forms and motions we call life. And how necessarily inadequate any such general term would have to be. For even applied to some great human manufacturing plant of our day such as General Electric, General Motors, United States Steel, Aluminum Limited, Vickers Limited, which the world sees today with its quite staggering variety of products, you have something which does not even partially suggest the immense variety, color, strangeness, and often, beauty of the products of the nonetheless mechanistic system behind them all. And how much more inadequate when used in connection with this vast, strange thing the universe, the varieties of the products of which are not even dimly known as yet—and more, which to us, as we are now constituted or created, can not possibly be known. That they ever can be known—that is, that a created or evolved phase of a mass of life or matter-energy can ever know the whole of it—constitutes a problem which Einstein's relativity points to as non-solvable.

But should that, or can that, detract from the sum of the wonders and delights of life as we know it or have known it—or of its terrors, pains, and irritations? As I see it, nothing argued or shown in and through problems dealt with in this work could be further from such a result.

Consider in the first place that the words *mechanism* and *mechanistic* are but partially descriptive of the process—not at all of the result. The result! Dare I, dare any minute unit of this vast, incomprehensible thing, speak of the result or venture to assume that it will not be maintained in its power and glory, its joy and its pain, its terror and its delight, forever and forever? Poets have sung, dreamers have dreamed, philosophers, thinkers, doers, leaders of men have been, have marveled, have wept and prayed and sung or cursed for want of more of that than they had of it—not less. True, it has been written, "Curse God and die." But how many have? And why? Was it not for the reason above given? Think of the great in heart and mind who have sung of what *is*—good and evil: Homer, Euripides, Sappho, Dante, Omar, Shakespeare, Shelley, Swinburne, Keats, Goethe. And if these, and Jesus and Buddha and St. Francis and Lincoln, saw so much, need we complain of this vast organism that can only be sensed, by no means grasped, by us in the terms of energy and law—the vast bleeding, dreaming machine called life? [*Or*]

‡ ‡ ‡

Taken in itself, *compulsion (motion) is the lord of all things*, except, possibly, that which compels compulsion. And as to the nature or the why of that, who is to know? The laboratories as well as the philosophers would like to know that. But whatever it is, or from whatever it is that it emanates—mind, space-time, or ether—compulsion is still the lord of all, or at least, all that is apprehended by man is the result of compulsion—both construction and destruction, creation and dissolution or decay.

The problems that confront and trouble man in connection with it are: (1) the mystery of the reason or reasons for himself as a mechanistic and wholly uninformed part of the process, and (2) the question as to the necessity of the elements of conflict and pain in connection with the process, and (3) the seemingly predetermined and arbitrarily arranged period of duration for not one but all forms of organic or inorganic energy or matter—be it photon or atom, or cell, man or animal or vegetable, earth or sun, or solar or sidereal system or island universe, or a universe of island universes. For, as he now knows, all are composed of the same matter-energy and subject to the one law of motion, effective in its cycle of affirmation, both creation and dissolution, construction and decay—out-pouring from space-time (possibly) and returning into it again.

And how numerous and varied and peculiar and even pathetic have been [man's] speculations in regard to the same. [*Or*]

T.D.

‡ ‡ ‡

An illimitable quantity of anything—assuming all of it to be the same thing, of the same substance, not a composition or a combination of two or more things, and assuming also that it lacks the attribute of power, and by inference the mind and hence the will to transmute itself into any other thing—would be without significance or meaning. It would have none of° the attributes of life as we know it. For to attain meaning as man senses that word, there would be required of it the power plus will—two attributes of what man senses as *mind* and, more, *creative mind*—to change or transmute itself not only as a whole, which would leave it in the same meaningless condition as at first, but into at least two or more things whereby the fact, if not the knowledge, of contrast or variety could be introduced into the total of itself. But in order to have not just the fact of contrast or variety but knowledge of the same, there would need to be introduced into this mass a sensory perception of the same—in other words the attribute of sensitivity. And sensitivity being the first or chief attribute of mind, it follows that in order to have variety or contrast in nature and by the same token limitation, without which there could be no variety or contrast or form, there would have to be mind—not only sensitive but creative, which fact would seem to me to suggest, if not verify, the first assertions of Genesis, i.e., that

In the beginning God (or Creative Mind) created the heaven and the earth. And the earth was without form, and void; and darkness was upon the face of the deep; and the Spirit of God (or Life) moved upon the face of the waters (or deep). And God said: Let there be Light; and there was light. . . . And the evening and the morning were the first day.

‡ ‡ ‡

No so-called individual or organism lives to or by itself alone. All are intimately and, what is more, mechanistically connected with the *universe* as a whole, and for that reason and that reason alone are capable of functioning in any manner in which they do function. Cut off or even reduce even so much as a portion of any of the elements known to Science as parts of the universe or, for that matter, a portion of the earthly-evolved air, water, food, heat, light, color, sound, sensitivity, taste, smell or smells of the planet, or any of the exterior things with which these same deal, and the endless organisms that infest this earth are not only likely but eventually certain to perish.

‡ ‡ ‡

No one need be told that the nature or source of matter-energy, as the scientific term for the same now stands, is anything that man wholly grasps or understands. How it appears, acts, results under certain conditions has been in part—no more—observed or partially observed. The rest is mystery. Yet, because of what has been observed, it is possible to state that it both integrates and disintegrates itself not only as matter in an astounding variety of forms, but also as energy—electricity, magnetism, light, heat, sound, their waves and transmutations—and these in turn have either the power and the *will* to integrate themselves into such forms as photons, electrons, protons, neutrons, atoms, molecules, elements, and their major unifications such as suns, planets, island universes, and the like or are compelled by some law, the source of which man knows nothing, so to do. *They are. And they function.* As the Bible puts it, speaking for an awe-induced reaction in one of the elder prophets to the universe around him: "I am that I am."

‡ ‡ ‡

If the creative force that has projected all matter and energy into space and directed the various forms matter and energy have taken with a view to evoking admiration of itself on the part of its endless variety of creatures, it can be reasonably observed that insofar as man and the other evolutionary forms here on earth are concerned, it has been in no hurry so to do. To illustrate. The age of the earth is fixed by some at least at 2 billion [now at over 4 billion] years. Yet there are no traces of any life in the rocks which were once shores or under surface sands of a Primal sea that covered all the land older than 600 or 700 million years. [Life forms now estimated to go back over 2 billion years] Of these, the oldest well-preserved fossils are the trilobites, belemites, and ammonites, which are related to the cuttlefish, octopus, and nautilus of the present day. These fossils may be seen in any slab of limestone. Yet the first vertebrates appeared only about 400 million years ago, as forerunners of the fishes and of the amphibia. The occurrence of the latter indicates that by this time land had begun to appear, probably as extended swamps. At about the same time, insects made their first appearance, plants began to appear and later trees. Then came the first reptiles, but only some 200 or 300 million years ago, and they seem to have developed into the huge monsters now constructed in our museums.

The first forerunners of the mammals seem to occur about 150 million years ago. There also appeared some strange birds which looked like flying reptiles but had feathers (Archaropleryx). Plants with flowers made their appearance—also placental mammals, in which the embryo is nourished from a separate organ called *placenta*, which does not exist in the mammals indigenous to Australia. Then followed modern birds and, finally, man, the one creature that, in prehistoric but not truly ancient days by any means, developed awe and the sense of beauty that inspires awe and the feeling that this creative force desires worship and, according to some religious theorists, demands it.

But if this were really true, what a curious procedure on the part of a universal force that has built a universe during possibly an infinite period of time—a universe of most tremendous and involute processes far beyond the conception of man even now. And yet *only now* after taking endless periods of time in which to evolve endless creatures which it permitted to live without awe or worship, it is now assumed, at long last, [that] it has come to demand awe and worship of man, the most recent, and as to durability, possibly the least certain of its creations to endure. And, furthermore, a creature little better in its conduct or qualities, let alone reverence, than billions of the other of nature's creations that have been and gone. This creature also imagines concerning itself that it is the possessor of a soul. Also a hereafter graced by the privilege of basking in the presence of this most high creative energy in whose physical presence it now actually *is*. Whether it will continue to be in any other form than this is yet to be shown. A remarkable fantasy, to say the least. [*Or*]

T.D.

‡ ‡ ‡

Stars and so island universes are made of unions of elements—the units
of the several elements, 93 all told, being attracted, gravitationally we say,
although it might well be emotionally, the one to the other. Who knows
what gravitation is?

Whether known or not, it brings about the union of electrons, positive
and negative, as well as protons into atoms, and these in their turn, combinations
or unions of minute matter which we call elements. Insofar as man and
human life are concerned, atoms here, under special solar and so terrestrial
conditions, combine into molecules to make protoplasm or protein. These,
in turn, combine to make cells which under creative direction—material
or immaterial, or wisdom, as we think of it—combine to make textures suitable
in the animal, vegetable, if not mineral kingdoms, to make smaller and larger
organs—blood cells, flesh cells, bone cells, phagocytes, hormone entities even,
and genes. Also hearts, livers, lungs, bony structures, arms, legs, skulls, feet,
as well as hearts, livers, minute bones and muscles, kidneys, spleens, gall-bladders,
eyes, ears, noses, tongues, and so on. Yes, union and re-union of materially
or immaterially directed organisms or units of energy, however minute, bring
about these contrasting, yet organically and socially harmonized, differentia-
tions, plus their associate functionings in larger and larger groups, until you
have suns and island universes. That they are socially sympathetic is obvious
since they function together to bring about a great spectacle, responded
to by man, but as probably responded to in some sensory way by every
living and moving or seemingly stationary thing throughout the entire universe.

Mind?

Universal mind?

Most likely.

For, if we are so constructed as to respond to it as mental, why not all
else, which we know to be the forebears of ourselves?

‡ ‡ ‡

In *The Secret Doctrine* Madame Blavatsky explains in great detail every
step in the process by which spirit "evolves" or changes until it reaches
the point where it takes physical form. It is, of course, a metaphysical not
a scientific or demonstrable procedure. Yet today, of course, we transmit
rock into silk, gold into magnesia, wood pulp and some non-food-like chemicals
into protein or meat. In other words, we rearrange the atoms of one phase
of matter so as to evoke or provoke another phase of matter, for instance
gold broken down into magnesia, a phase of which (carbonate of magnesia
for one) is edible. Today, also, science like nature now also proceeds in the
opposite direction—that is, from the material to the immaterial, i.e., refines
matter in many instances until it changes to electrical energy, just as sickness
and death change man into—what? Five or six pounds of ash made up of
various universal elements, and?

‡ ‡ ‡

The universe, in its immensity and variety, demonstrates that Life as man knows it, or any part of it, either its matter or energy or the two as one, must be at once solid and diffuse—ranging in these two ways from the incomprehensibly minute energy particle or quantum to the incomprehensibly massive and seemingly solid volumes of the white suns and island universes. So much so that it suggests space or ether as a substance from which all the rest take their rise. For in no other way can the endless variety of form and substance—the inconceivably small moving in and through the immense, and the inconceivably immense moving in and through the inconceivably minute—[function and] *be.*

‡ ‡ ‡

If the various universal elements and the chemicals into which they can be broken down are as endless as they appear to be, and a portion of them, with solar and sidereal light added, can, on this minute earth, bring into the vision and so the sensitivity of man all of the innumerable forms he is already dimly aware of, what possible approximation of the further creative powers of these same, as they might manifest themselves in the endless reaches of space, could be made by man with his limited sensory capacities, added to those, maybe, by various chemical and physical aids he has and is devising?

‡ ‡ ‡

As a rule you only detect the presence of *energy* as and when it presses or influences matter in some way. You do not see light unless it strikes a particle of some kind. Nor do you see the energy in wind unless and until it waves a flag, shakes the tree, rolls the waves of sea or lake or pool, or when it moves a car or your arm or foot, or blows up a mountain. In other words you see what it does—not it—or what it is. For what it does is not what it is, nor final proof of what it can do.

‡ ‡ ‡

Its [the Universe's] process or processes may be organic like those of a flower or tree; its island universes flowers on a tree of universal energy. And by the same token, life here on earth—evolved (evolutionary) life—may be an organic growth like a tree or a flower—its seed, protoplasm or the salts and chemicals of elements that, with water, constitute the same. [*Or*]

Necessity for Rest

Is this a law of the Universe: Is gravitation not the pulling but the *pulled* vase—the inability of the pulled object to resist—a phase of rest for it? [*Or*]

‡ ‡ ‡

The rationalists and encyclopedists of William Blake's day (1757-1827) believed in a mechanistic, accidental, chaotic world. Blake, however, anticipated modern philosophers and physicists in his view of the Universe as, materially, a thing of order and pattern, in which the microcosm was of the same substance and *worth* and worked in the same way as the macrocosm. Like the poem of a modern seems his quatrain, always quoted:

To see the world in a grain of sand
And a heaven in a wild flower;
Hold infinity in the palm of your hand,
And eternity in an hour.

[*Or*]

‡ ‡ ‡

In the universe, consider the great suns and the little ones, those totalitarian bodies, the island universes and then the comets, planets, satellites, asteroids, star dust, the photons, electrons, cosmic rays, atoms, and elements—all are governed, it is believed, by immutable law. And all are contemplated with awe as integral parts of an enormous power that is the source of our being and our fate. Nonetheless, as among man and animals, one is still free to consider their state and fate, for, according to our physicists and chemists, their states and fates are greatly varied. Thousands of millions of galaxies though there be, or may be, all are aging, all are moving outward from some primary common center, all are dissipating the stupendous frenzy of atoms, which each sun and each sidereal system represents, separating and speeding away from their source, and hordes of them from each other, all at the rate of 186,000 miles per second. But to where? Endless space? To become what? Ether? That indistinguishable something called space-time? Science does not say positively. There may be a reassembling process, reintegration. But just how is not known.

But meanwhile man is permitted to study his relationship to this vast process and its relationship to us for, as Max Planck has asserted, "We ourselves are a part of nature and therefore part of the mystery that we are trying to solve." That is, the identical elements that make up the island universes and suns and solar systems, that occupy what we speak of as space-time—their photons, electrons, atoms, and rays—make up our solar system, our planet, our protoplasm, and us; and as such, we are an integral part of it and it is a part of us. And it follows from that that we alone "individually," as we mistakenly say, are not trying to solve its mystery, but rather it through us (the mechanisms which it has created or at least which have come to pass through it) and *we* through or because of *it* (the motivation of us which it provides) are seeking to grasp the mystery not only of it, our creator, but of ourselves as a part of it—a fantastic procedure as you must see. For as a part of it, why should we know, sense—sense the oneness of it all and all of the processes of it all. Why be delimited as machines, or animals, or men, or planets, or insects, or germs, or again as suns, planets, island universes, atoms, rays, electrons, protons, when in truth we are all one and the same thing divided—almost illimitably divided, as one might say, in this, to me at least, fantastic way. Why electrons, protons, atoms, building themselves up or being built, as you please, into all of these things. For in every single cell of our bodies, or those of all flora and fauna, are trillions of these same electrons, seeking union with the atoms and molecules of our body, just as they are seeking union with the stampeded and stampeding atoms of the thousands and millions, not of suns, but of galaxies of suns—and all in a frenzy of motion, driven by gales of light. And all attracted to or repelled by each other, repeatedly smashed and broken and rewelded into new forms. Sometimes annihilated as atoms, as photons even, but never as the basic something out of which they must have come, yet the nature of which is unknown as yet.

What atoms of the great sidereal system evolving through space, through millions of light years; and joining up here and now with a farmer ploughing in a cornfield, with the shares of this plough, the bridle of his horse, his horse, the horsefly biting the horse, the bee winging industriously past his ear, his old straw hat which he looks upon as decaying, rotting, but which is only rotting as a hat, not as atoms or molecules by any means; and fixing themselves in the soil, the nitrates of the air; and helping to form the flesh of the potato, the greenness of the bean, the whiteness of the corn, the redness of the tomato, in short the substance or nutriment of men, animals, insects, trees; and then going from these to where? Driven again to what remote sidereal service.

Well such, in part, is the identity of man with this outer immensity. But there is something more interesting still, something which to me at least tends even more than the above—the oneness of this stupendousness of this cosmic energy with his littleness, not only of man, but of the littleness of those atoms, electrons, protons, photons, which, contrasted with himself, are so infinitely much smaller than is he—to humanize this outer immensity and bring it nearer to man. And that is its subjectivity, not only to law, but to contrast, the same law and the same contrast that at times so belittles, as well as dignifies, not only men and bacteria, but these giant suns and their governing island universes or sidereal systems.

How vast the island universe! Thousands of millions of suns, interspaces with star dust, galactic clouds, films of atomic wanderers, fragments of broken worlds, and dissipated and frozen giants that before their final wreck and dissipation as asteroids turned in black or red-black loneliness and death. Man, who has claimed mind and thought, judgment, and decision for himself, is yet in his littleness not willing to grant to these anything equal let alone superior to his own imaginary decisions and indecisions, superiorities and inferiorities, moods and vacuities, weariness and accretions of power, elations or despairs, angers and affections, tortures and degradations, vasty elations, and betimes, overwhelming forces and fancies. But if these hold for the minute creatures of forces called man, bees, wasps, adventuring and warring germs, and their oft-times conquering antibodies, how about those vast, dark giants of temperatures so low as a thousand degrees who must yet voyage, loaf, perhaps tramp in disgrace and despair among the glittering millions who in their youth and strength, their newness to timeless space—the great universe of which even they are minute nothings—can boast of their surface heats or irradiations of thirty, fifty, seventy thousand degrees of heat, of radiant energy. What ho! Out of my way tramp-failure! Old-timer! Am I not he, the central sun of Orion? Am I not Sirius? Beltair? Will you be eaten by me? Move then? Swing about me as a slave, a prospective meal until such time as I shall need you for myself. For behold, I am a diamond spider of the heavens, and I have spread about me my gravitational net of force. Blunder into that and you are lost. You are mine. This is a sidereal jungle. And I am a raging lion in a galaxy of prowling lions and tigers.

And yet the irrevocable aging that goes with such stupendous strength! These too in the wild frenzies of their youth, the orgies of adventure and accumulation and self-satisfaction, still dissipate that on which they feed and of which they are—timeless energy. And force them (and behold) it will stay, it will not be confined, any more by them or by you men. Born of energy, yet must they die for the want of it. Ask not why. Ask only how, for that you may know. Even as we may know. To be—to manifest themselves, as blazing suns and sidereal systems they must blaze or dissipate their energy. And as with man—fly, gnat, germ—so with them. Is it not written of man "three score years and ten" shall be the length of his days; and of the horse, twenty-five years; of a dog, fifteen; of an ant, fifteen; of a fruit-fly, six; of a gnat, twenty-four hours. Of Sirius? What? Arcturus what? Never mind. It is written in law if not words. Of a sidereal system, an island universe, the same. Blaze as they may. Rush and turn in timeless space in endless light years—yet it is written. In the beginning was the void, and darkness. And God breathed upon the face of the waters. And He said, let there be light. And there was light. Man says of this—religion! Illusion. But of matter-energy, space-time, island universes, suns, he writes "perhaps energy began as in whorls of ether, as whorls begin where there are unequal flows of water?" At any rate, they were not, and then they were. But once made, they were but made to end. And others to take their place. For plainly they end and others do take our place.

Why?

We cannot say why?

How?

That—we already know.

Yes, even we Know.

As the Hindus so grandly phrased it—"Brahma is in all things. He is also without."

But there are other phases of this greatness, littleness, which bring the totality of the universe so near, with its smallest factor, be it worm or gnat or germ or man, and that is that no one of these can exist, neither putrescence nor glowing wholeness, sickness or health, power or weakness, disgrace or honor, but with and through and by its elements, its light rays, its integrations and disintegrations of these minute factors of itself, its protons, and electrons and atoms as well as its totality—all space and time, all matter and energy.

All are blood and brother, father and daughter to the lowliest as well as the greatness. For what is an island universe but an accretion of atoms. And what is the lowest and (to bring in man as witness as well as measure) its, to him (perhaps to nothing other), meanest or most offensive creation—cancer germ, or murder-fever, plague virus, or gluttonous lust—but some compound or dilution of its own deathless energy or substance. "I and my father are one" cries the new testament of Jesus. And the laboratories of science can say no less, confirming by chemical and physical experiment that which all, had they eyes to see and ears to hear, could see and hear of themselves. . . . [Or]

The Stars

The stars of the universe, as well as the galaxies or island universes to which they belong, are in motion. These island universes are said to contain one hundred million or more stars each. The island universes, as well as their constituent suns, rotate and may have orbits in which they move. Possibly the orbits have orbits. Some are three million or more light years away. And the light which reaches us from them is supposed to travel in a straight line. But, if all individual suns are not only rotating but traveling in orbits in their galaxies, and the galaxies themselves are rotating as a whole, and possibly (I do not know) also pursuing galatic orbits, and if then by any chance these galatic orbits move as a whole through space, how can it be said that this light travels in a straight line? How could a straight line of light from any of these moving and so remote stars come straight to this earth, which also has been complicatedly moving for so many millions of light years? And if not, what would be the nature of its path? Again, how could we possibly know the present position or whereabouts of the particular sun or galaxy from which the light arriving here today—three million light years later—came?

THEODORE DREISER

‡   ‡   ‡

How the giant stars of no greater density than that of a light smoke or that of a laboratory vacuum holding but two or three minute particles of dust can nevertheless maintain an orb formation is one of the problems of knowledge. Also, how it comes about that these almost immaterial suns when related as binaries (twin stars) can nonetheless pass, the one through the other, without alteration of form? Lastly, apart from the comparatively few particles of matter which thus outline themselves as giant orbs, can it be that some immaterial and so invisible force constitutes the remainder of these orbs and supplies the unifying force?

Mechanism
Called Life

I HOLD THAT LIFE AS WE SEE OR SENSE IT WITH OUR SEVERAL senses—in other words, the physical aspect of the world with all of its flora and fauna as well as its universal aspect—is no more than a mechanism through which something that is not a mechanism, but that can, at will, embody or disembody itself mechanistically, expresses itself and that we, along with all things so embodied or expressed, are an integral fraction of that primal essence: "In the beginning was the Word and the Word was made flesh"—or stone or oxygen or hydrogen or protoplasm or suns or sidereal systems. [*Or*]

T.D.

‡   ‡   ‡

Life is not a substance, but a mechanical phenomenon; it is a dynamic and kinetic transference of energy determined by physico-chemical reactions and their mode of association and succession—their harmony, in fact—which constitutes life. [*Or*]

The Breath of Life

What is the breath of life? It is energy radiation from all things to all things, the energy of each thing from each thing registered by all other things and vice-versa, a constant interflowing exchange of such radiations—flower to tree, flower to insect, flower to man or animal, or sun or moon or distant star and vice-versa. All things act and react. All are part of a universal something that brings that about. They register each other and these registrations, more or less, of each thing by every other thing constitutes all there is to so-called individuality, personality, thought, creative energy, and so on. And without this totality broken up into all these things that thus register the radiations of each other, which are provided by the Universe as a whole—what Emerson called the Oversoul—there would [be] nothing: no life, no individuality, no thought, no beauty, no love, no hate,

14

no pleasure, no pain—nothing. Something which we react to and describe as the Universe has provided all that. But how or why we do not know. It is. And our share in it in some brief form and for some brief period, we call Life. And its interruption or conclusion, we call death. But whether death is annihilation or something very different, who or what is to say? Sufficient unto the hour is the seeming thereof. And without *seeming*, what evil or harm or even good can be? What . . .

T.D.

‡ ‡ ‡

Water lily buds burst open as the direct light of the morning sun strikes them. Morning glories, opening with the early gray of dawn, close when the heat of the morning sun begins to absorb too much of the moisture that makes their delicate textures displayable. Moon flowers burst open with the same force as water-lilies when the heat of the day ceases and the cool and moisture of the evening reaches a point where their textures are impinged upon and forced to absorb more (moisture) than their restraining green covering can resist. [*Or*]

T.D.

‡ ‡ ‡

The old doctrine of tooth and claw is not complete. There seems to be and is a constant struggle—no equilibrium is lasting. But the image is also one of Life constantly flowing into new forms. The forms may wage war or arrange an armistice. But life does not make war against itself. It makes life, builds it, and contest appears to be one of its necessary processes. The bacteria which carry disease through the human body are not trying to kill—they are trying to live. [*Or*]

Making One Hand Wash the Other

Bacteria consume atmospheric nitrogen and, either by dying or discharging it as waste matter, fix it in the ground where it becomes food for plants, which in turn are consumed by men and animals. Apparently all of the mechanisms built by nature to provide the spectacle called life are compelled to do many things besides being (existing). In fact, their existence appears to depend on utility—service. No utility, no life. But [it] is apparently rarely, if ever, conscious utility on the part of the creature so used. [*Or*]

T.D.

The Mosquito

Fabre succeeded even in making the mosquito interesting, if not welcome. That lively itching you feel after you have given a mosquito a blood transfusion is caused by a tiny droplet of a transparent fluid of a venomous nature which the grateful fellow leaves with you.

Think of the physical and chemical arrangements, as well as knowledge, which must have preceded the manufacture of the mosquito's body and, in turn, its body power to manufacture the "tiny droplet of transparent fluid of a venomous nature" which acts so painfully and sometimes destructively upon another biologic organism—an organism also built by nature. In itself, the life cycle of a mosquito is one of the most complicated physical and chemical engineering feats to be witnessed in nature—equal in genius or miracle wisdom to that which produced the hydroids. [*Or*]

T.D.

The whole drama of life is performed in a very restricted zone, quite near the surface of our small planet. Even bacteria disappear in the upper reaches of the atmosphere, and other life extends downward only to the limits set by the ocean depths.

‡ ‡ ‡

Process is more real than *bodies*. The life process or Creative Energy (the electro-magnetic theory of matter and radiation) or Diety must be considered to be a part of the process or *The* Process rather than an external creator. In that sense, all that is good or evil, as you choose—good and evil or contrast become necessary factors of the creative process or electro-magnetism or Diety.

"Brahma is in all things. He is also without." [*Or*]

‡ ‡ ‡

Exhibitionism—setting things forth to be seen, one thing materially impressing another—is the eternal law of what we call evolution. All existence is toward more and more of that—the universe mirroring itself to itself. As Benjamin DeCasseros once put it "whatever is, aspires to mirrors." Certain it is that all life appears to desire to see and, more, to be seen—at least by its mate. Certainly among men, the instinct to command attention, exploit the ego, to act, to lead others is nearly universal. [*Or*]

‡ ‡ ‡

Every living being, and even man himself, is but a transformer of energy, changing the energy derived from the earth and air and sun into mechanical motion, nervous energy, and heat. . . . [*Or*]

The Creator and His Working Materials

Human history is a series of spectacles and has nothing to teach man except that man is a creature of attitudes. He—or the atoms, electrons, molecules, elements, and their integrations of which he is a composite—strikes various attitudes, now barbaric, now religious, now philosophical, republican, communist, tyranical, nomadic. His revolutions, celebrations, hero worship, wars, morals, religions, renunciations, self-glorifications are all attitudes or attitudinizings—the natural posings of the Great Impresario called Nature, God, Matter-Energy, Mechanism, who or which is working, creating (using) as stage materials our *atoms*, molecules, their elements, protoplasms and the

likely telepathy—to say nothing of such internal procedures as swallowing, digesting, developing energy, and so on. But although these—some of them, at least, in part—explain the *how* of life, they do not explain the *why*. It is more like seeing a man holding a piece of wood to a band saw and finding that the saw cuts the wood and later that the saw is driven by an electric motor. And still later, that there is a wire connected with the motor that may have something to do with the saw's whirling beltwise. Still later, that the wire leads away somewhere to a power house in which are certain large machines running, with which the wire is connected. Also that the machines are doing something. Next, that they are called dynamos which are driven by steam or water power; also that this steam phase is the hot vapor phase of water, the expansion of which in a steam box moves a piston to and fro, which piston so moving turns a wheel, which drives the motor of what is called a dynamo—the mechanical device in the power house which converts the mechanical energy made by the steam into a thing called electrical energy, which is developed by the induction of currents generated by the compelled relative motion of conductors and magnetic fields arranged in the machine in such a way as to contact each other at high speed. But what is electricity? An imponderable and invisible agency capable under different circumstances of producing light, heat, chemical decomposition, and other physical phenomena.

Can the eye see it? No. Can the nerves feel it? Yes, but fatally, if in too great volume. Can it be detained in a vessel? For a very little time—a few days, no more. Can it be transported? Yes, over a wire or in a properly devised case—an insulated box. Will it cure anything? It is thought to stimulate tired muscles, but no one is sure. It is also thought by some to be life itself—the body or force of the organized totality of energy called *Life*.

And what is magnetism? A property possessed by various bodies, such as lode-stones or steel, of attracting or repelling each other. And how does it do that? We do not know. Can you see it? No. You can only see what happens when it is cut off, and a body, which it has been holding up or pulling, falls to the ground. Can you feel it? You can feel the pull of it on another body, but not it, unless the pull is it. And what is that? Magic? Well, magic is a word to describe doings and results such as surpass human understanding, [which] cannot be explained by it.

Is there no more to be said about it? *No!* [*Or*]

Necessity
for Repetition

Is IT THE DUTY OF ENERGY TO BUILD AND THEN *REPEAT* THE things that it builds?

T.D.

In order to have life as we know it, there must be sensation, registration of sensation, and repetition of registration of sensation, in order that there may be durability or memory of sensation. Thus, in order to be remembered from generation to generation, there must be repetition of ideas—the sensations they evoke. Also, to have these repetitions or generations, there must be repetitions of generations of all creatures—either that or one unchanging and undying generation. But there is no such thing as an undying and unchanging generation, on the contrary, there are only changing and dying generations and, to offset that, repetitions of them. Yet, unless these are willed by something, no one can say why. However dying and repeated generations require that ideas must be repeated and repeated. The new generations must be introduced to everything. Hence, all implements favorable to the maintenance of this process must be repeated—building, clothing, types of food, grains, animals for meat, etc.; or else life will disappear—the life represented by these generations and these reactions. Days must be repeated; weeks, months; the seasons; day and night must be repeated. Heat and cold. The two sexes. Love, hate. In fact everything from stellar galaxies to germs.

It follows, of course, that in order to have repetition, everything must be ended, for repetition implies that something has not only begun but ceased.

Such a process as this implies immense order as against disorder or chaos and more *"mind"* than man ever dreamed of.

‡   ‡   ‡

Consider the thing called attention: something that holds the so-called mind, or rather the entire electrical composition called man or animal. It is an amazing mechanical fact that this electrical organism of ours that we call a *living* body—that is, responding body—and that can and does register so very many different impressions per second will not long endure the repetition of anything—whether a single note of music, the tick of a clock, a prolonged cry, the drip, drip of water on anything, a restatement of an idea, the same kind of a book, the same person or set of facts first presented and then represented and re-represented, the same piece of music played over and over, the same moving picture or play. The effect is always practically described by man at least as boring, wearying, hum-drum, unendurable. And this applies to too many years in the same place, too many and too few of the same people in the same house, same street, same town.

Even engines or dynamos seem to weary of too continuous running or whirring and break. Too many laws confuse and bore the public; a too long continued celebration, the same; a retold joke or tale of any kind. Once is plenty—enough until it is completely forgotten. The same with a war, the skill or worth of a given hero, the same beautiful face, unless for some psychic provocations, not easily determined and yet if real enough, it keeps a repetitive freshness.

No one, no thing must attract so much attention that it forces itself on the human mechanism too long. Things, all things, must at least go for a time, and regularly, if they wish to remain for a time. Nothing can permanently stand the presence of anything else, be it what it will. And this appears to be an innate and qualifying characteristic of all matter as well as mind—of matter-energy—if not the something out of which it comes—if there is any other thing than itself from which it derives. [Or]

T.D.

‡ ‡ ‡

If you study a lightning flash, one that branches out in many directions as do most lightning flashes, you will well see that it resembles a river system—a river with all of its tributaries. Also a lung system—a trachea with all of its branches; also a blood system (veins and arteries, with all of their branches); also a central nervous system with all of its branches; also the root system of a tree as well as the branch system above. For in all of these transportation systems, nature appears to have but one basic plan. Man, copying nature, constructs a railway system, a road system, a bus system, an aeroplane system. And all, as they grow, branching as above, appear to copy this system. Is there no other way to do—or is there?

Does nature lack creative power? If not, why so much repetition—is it lazy?

‡ ‡ ‡

Is the universe free or conditioned, creative or repetitive?

Any river with its branches—the Nile, Congo, Amazon, Mississippi, Volga, Danube—is like a leafless tree in which the sap collected from the rains and soil, instead of flowing up, is flowing down. . . . Both are quite the same in design, as is, also, the nervous and arterial systems of men, animals, insects and all plants. The air passages of all lungs imitate, or at any rate, are the same as these rivers and tree structures or plants. So, too, are the upward or outward spreading branches of a mother lode of gold, silver, copper, and some other metals shut up in the earth by heat. So too is water shot upward through a hose by pump pressure. So too smoke or gases pouring out of any chimney or gun-mouth. In fact, the particular form appears to be useful—and in so far as the earth is concerned, its general structural procedure is concerned—an unescapable design, something that willy-nilly has to be; that is, as if the creative process either does not know or cannot find any other way to proceed in these matters.

‡ ‡ ‡

The necessity for repetition suggests the mechanical limitation of the life forces themselves, matter-energy, space-time, plus the myth of free will and of individual creative power in connection with any of their products or evoked organisms. For with those, go form, which means limitation of size plus limitation of duration, which is necessary to change, plus limitation as to color (those of the spectrum), and of degree of heat and cold, to say nothing of the limitation of complexity as opposed to simplicity. Unescapable limitation in all ways (save, possibly, that of the duration of its totality) of the universe or its source appears to characterize the universe and all of its life products as we know them.

‡ ‡ ‡

If life is not a mechanism, why, in the vast majority of instances, an exact repetition of every other case—the arranged and unvaried process of conception, birth, absorption of existent exterior material; that is the implication of houses, streets, roads, methods of living, the presence of the sun, moon, stars, trees, flowers, vegetables, fellow beings, and animals. Then the consciousness of the sexes, of the individuality of one's own sex as opposed to the other; in other words, the sudden and amazingly glandular reactions to form and motion in the opposite sex, precisely the same reactions in all—male and female—and all evoked by not just one face or one form but a thousand faces and a thousand forms—literally, millions—the seemingly singular and always thrilling contact and union of two in "love" or desire, being nonetheless a matter of propinquity, occurring anywhere and everywhere on the earth where the sexes come in contact: in the igloo, the kraal, the tepee, the King's palace, the log cabin, the rich man's palace, the simple home, the jungle, the island, the train, the ship. And after that, the same process for all, over and over again—sexual union, conception, the new creature, the struggle for existence by all. The compulsion toward sin rallies social adjustments (that is) to more helpful social organization in order to make the struggle easier, or more agreeable: the endless annihilation in connection with the process and the *endless repetition*—no more than a cog or unit of the process permitted (and that by the very nature of the mechanism) to endure for roughly, at an average for, [not] more than 70 years or to achieve (average) [not] much more than any other achieves in the matter of strength, food, love, acclaim. And finally, all passing into the limbo of the forgotten. [*Or*]

‡ ‡ ‡

An island universe is limited in form just as much as is a solar system, which is part of an island universe. And since there are countless island universes that look—as one physicist describes them—like pin-wheels, and [others] like (when viewed from their periphery) platelets or buttons, and all solar systems resemble our own solar system in arrangement or limitation of form, and it, in turn, resembles the central nuclear-electronic system of the atom—or it resembles the solar system—an inference can be made to the effect that the universe, insofar as its various forms are concerned, is repetitious; also, that these repetitions of given forms, to the extent that they are repetitions, lack individuality; and hence, that repetitions of form are not only common to the major but the minor as well as the minutest inventions or creations or compulsions of nature; and that we, as one of its repetitious forms, have that repetitiousness in common with the rest of its forms—wherever, and in consequence are identified or (as to customs or principle) identical with one of its creative principles or compulsions. And to that extent we are a part of it, just as, to that extent, a portion of it is in each of us. [Or]

‡   ‡   ‡

The fact that not just some one thing but everything has to be repeated and repeated endlessly to be what is called a *reality* is proof positive that the so-called memory of man is nothing more than a mechanism devised to register and re-register whatever is, in order that for him or it—the mechanism—it can continue to be. No endless or fresh re-iteration or any re-registration of anything, no memory of it.

Thus a bird, to be known as a bird at all, must have wings and air to fly in or on, and a beak and claws, or at least recognizable modifications of the same, else for man—the registering mechanism—no bird. Ditto the fish, the elephant, the tree, the dog, the cat. The sun must rise and rise and rise endlessly during the evolution of man or insect or bird in order to be a sun. It must repeat the roundness, its yellowness, its heat, its setting or temporary absence over and over, and these must be registered by man as repetitions or there will be no memory after a time of any sun. Ditto the sea and the waves of the sea, the pressure of the wind, the shape of a given tree or flower or fruit, or cloud, or whatever. No repetition, no re-registration, no memory. Most distinctly and effectively it ceases to be—like the great auk, or the endless forms and circumstances that have been but are no more. Without repetition or re-registration of their presence over and over, all things become at first mere memories, then fables, then mere rumors, as for instance, the rumor of the Giant Rock in the Arabian nights, the one-time flying dragon, the giant sloth, or dinosaur; although by now— because of traces in rocks and caves, foot prints in ancient stones or forgotten sea beds or their one time shores—we find them to have been real. They were because, once, their presence and design were registered and re-registered daily, hourly, momentarily by some mechanism designed to register them, whether sloth, or bird, or animal, or man, or the mud in which they walked when they ceased thus to be registered by other things—all memory of them by other things ceased. They were as though they had never been. In fact, they passed even as the early forms of themselves so long repeated and registered and re-registered by others like them passed; that is, because of that lack of registration, etc. In other words, the so effective words of the Bible, as that time to which "the memory of man runneth not to the contrary." In other words, memory is nothing more than the constant re-registration of all things by all other things. And when these *seeming* things die or dissolve and so lose the energy power to register themselves optically, aurally, or in any other sensory fashion, they are truly ended, and with that ending all memory of them also.

Material Base of Form

FORM PLAYS SO GREAT A PART IN OUR SENSE OF LIFE. AS MUCH as anything, it tends, or seems, to establish our sense of reality. It evokes so many emotions or reactions. But consider how without the eye—sensitivity to light, and without light, which to our eye has no form, but which illuminates form and makes it visible—how formless for the most part [life] would be! True, with our hands we could feel some forms, so sense them, but how few. More, color, [which] nearly always accompanies *form*, would be absent. Not only that, but without light, which itself is material and probably has form though we cannot see it, matter would not exist. For matter is built up of energy, which is light, and since without matter there could be no *form*, you have form depending for its existence on something that basically has scarcely any form at all, or none—at least it cannot be seen as form by man.

T.D.

‡ ‡ ‡

Form—although nothing but a boundary defining matter—is not only limited and varied by all of the external forces affecting matter, but also by the internal pressures and internal limitations of matter. Gas pressure inside a balloon or a sheep or a planet like the earth, or water pressure inside a water (or other) melon, or the pressures of the fires and gases at the bottom of a volcano, or wind on water or a sail or a cloud will change and incidentally limit or extend form. In fact varieties of form are as endless as the forces operating on matter internally or externally, since form is nothing more than the invisible and, in so far as weight is concerned, imponderable outline of matter. In other words, it is outlined matter that you see and think of as having form. What is form then? Matter or an idea?

Nonetheless, outlined matter can be graceful or ungraceful to the registering mechanism called man as well as most animals and insects—which introduces the idea of beauty or force—probably to all not specifically attracted by odors or colors.

‡ ‡ ‡

It would seem as though some engineer-genius had worked out endless designs for natural forms—animal, vegetable, mineral—first to insure not only variety but appreciative or antagonistic sensory response, the one to the other, with a view not only to interest but to social activity in various ways. Not only that, but the same engineer-genius seems to have been moved to contrive endless methods for the reproduction of the endless species or designs, often out of or within themselves or by way of the split sex mechanism—male-female—or in the energy field—positive-negative device—a dual mechanism which consists of a half that acts and complimentary half that is acted upon. Compare the sex process of the opossum with that of the spider, butterfly, whale, fish, bird, tree, germ, and man.

‡ ‡ ‡

It (Life) makes its own forms, then responds to them. You make your own pie and then eat it. Motion (that is matter-energy) develops some form of change and then enjoys it. Without the will to change—no new form, without the new form—no sense of change, no enjoyment of itself.

Protective Coloration—Imitation of Design

Ceylon boasts some of the most astonishing insects in the world—the "walking leaves." Their bodies are shaped and veined like leaves. When in danger, they simulate the quiver of foliage, and to make the similarity even more striking, their feet look very much like a leaf's ragged edges.

There are among others the spiny stick insect of Borneo, also the walking stick. Here it is that an insect copies the form rather than the color of a vegetable. Brightly colored tropic birds are thought to be imitating flowers and leaves. The grouper family of fishes change their color at any time to suit their environment and so conceal themselves. The nightmare insect of Central America is accused of cowardice or fear, since, although terrifying in form, it is harmless. Here again form appears to be intentionally used to conceal fear. There are others like it.

The Japanese used frightful masks to frighten the enemy. Not that they were entirely cowardly. Rather that they wished to add to their strength by using *form* to weaken the enemy. So, also, did the Chinese and many Asiatics. Farmers use scare-crows to frighten birds from their fields. Here again form is used to imitate strength and suggest danger. But all this, especially in insects and animals, implies not only thought on the part of the user or the creator of the user, but implies understanding and the presence of the emotion called fear in insects and many creatures not supposed to have emotions, in short, mental processes of a high order. [*Or*]

T.D.

‡ ‡ ‡

Below the familiar rocks of the earth's surface is probably a thick shell of hot, rigid material resembling very weak glass, on which the continents rest and on which at intervals of geologic time they have slipped, like great pontoons on the waters of a port, according to this new picture of terrestrial events. Earthquakes, volcanoes, and new mountain ranges all probably owe their origin to physical forces within the earth which force horizontal displacements of great continental blocks of the earth's crust.

These mighty forces, which are at war changing the face of the earth, may be divided into two sharply opposing armies which will never make peace as long as our globe endures—the army of erosion, which is forever striving to reduce to flatness the irregularities of the surface by the leveling of the land and the army of mountain building, continually on the move to thwart erosion by crumpling and elevating rocks wherever the crust of the earth is weakened by erosion. [Or]

‡　‡　‡

If the process of erosion, lashed on by the whip of gravity, were to continue unchecked to its logical end, the earth would become a nearly perfect sphere, and a universal ocean about 9,000 feet deep would spread uniformly over the whole globe.

Does this explain the roundness of all the endless suns in the Universe? What becomes of the law of contrast, equation, etc. in this case? Why aren't some of them square, hexagonal, octagonal—maybe no pressure on each other, for one thing? But why no pressure? Why this liberal distribution in space of matter? [Or]   T.D.

‡　‡　‡

Form in almost all cases is related to use. It is the best form for a given end—like that of a cloud to float; a green leaf to offer a surface to the sun and so capture its rays; a rhinoceros to charge; a lion or cat to leap and bend about a given object; a snake to go on its belly and again encircle its prey; a fish to swim in water; a bird to fly; a worm to make its way through matter; a mouse to scamper fast, hear much, travel silently; a kangaroo to leap and carry its child in a pouch; a duck to paddle and swim. But to say that nature adjusts means to ends is to say that governments devise laws to govern; ship builders build ships to sail upon the ocean; that a lawyer studies to be a lawyer; a doctor to be a doctor and not a blacksmith.

However, in men that is accounted for by the existence and use of mind. When nature does it, it is thought of as a mechanical process—something that just comes about without intent or direction on the part of anything. In fact, because ants, flies, worms, fleas are small or minute, we refuse to think of them as having responsive mechanisms within them such as we call our "mind"; though their procedures, in so far as their structures and environments permit, resemble ours. At best we say they have minute minds, or that what they do, if not what they are, is the result of environment. However, the same environment produces many kinds or forms of living things, so that it is impossible—without the addition of matter-energy and time and space and direction, which underlie all things—to account for either the forms or their environments.

No time, no space, no matter, no energy, no duration—no environment or forms. Yet all of these look to be mind-governed processes. And since they do not appear to make themselves any more than we appear to make ourselves, we are confronted by an orderly mental process at once strange, amazing, beautiful, and wonderful, which, nonetheless, having no sensory equipment wherewith to grasp it in its entirety, and although we are creatures of itself, we decline to endow it with mind, even though we grant mind to ourselves!

‡ ‡ ‡

Form, as all know, is a vital factor in love—the forms or designs of the desired bodies of the dual sex mechanism composed of a man and a woman. To be sure, in all instances those designs must be *informed* with whatever qualities or characteristics or charms the lover or desirer of the other most compellingly reacts to. At the same time, that it may represent or be informed with qualities or reaction patterns which the desirer fears or even detests is also true. In nearly if not quite all instances, it must contain the highly compulsory hormones which fever and bring about the union of the two halves of the sex mechanism—the male and the female.

Interestingly enough, the form of the female half of the mechanism appears to be the more urgent and prized of the two: and thus by both male and female, the female prizing her youthful form, seemingly for itself as well as its compulsive force upon the male, actually perhaps entirely for its compulsive force upon the male; the male admiring it for the same reason—the compulsion it holds for him, the pleasure it suggests and provides. The male form has its charm not only for women but for men—in the case of the former, for what it suggests not only in the way of pleasure but protection, subsistence, the source of desired children, of possible distinctions with which the female can be associated, such as fame and wealth. For other men, where it approximates the current male physical ideal because of what it suggests in the matter of valor, health, its appeal for women, its power to respond, enjoy, endure. However, these last are as often compounded with envy and hatred as with pleasure and admiration.

But the *ideal* form associated almost exclusively with youth in both sexes cannot suffer impairment and retain the force or yield the satisfaction which the word *beauty* implies. It may, by changes, evoke other desired or respected or painful or disagreeable reactions in other men and women: such as that of strength, peace, humility, dignity, etc.; or on the other hand, those of weakness, irritability, homeliness, ugliness, gloom, and even terror or horror; but never the full youth—and sex—beauty effect. Any least change from the practical perfection of that as it applies to sex reproduction is certain to detract and in most instances irritate or pain by reason of the contrast offered to that brief, evanescent norm.

And here form comes in—the problem of form as that relates to sex in nature—the chemical and physical compulsions, which, via the sexes and in connection with the evolutionary chain here on earth, bring about the reproduction and continuation of all animal and insect species. For form in this connection is closely involved with the problem of beauty; i.e. whether beauty—or the man. A male's reaction to form in the female which he looks upon and has named beautiful is primarily beautiful, whether just as form it is a definite and compelling force or is [so] merely as a fractional part of a combination of forces which in the English language we have been moved to name beauty.

In the first place, I would like to know whether there is a word for beauty as we use that word in all languages, or whether or not it is absent in some, or of a different signification in others. It may be that in some tribal languages there is neither word nor symbol signifying beauty as we understand it.

Personally, I deduce that form is but a fraction of the concept or reaction. For while it is true that the form of a woman—the roundness of the breasts, arms, thighs, torso, neck, head, hands, feet, etc.—is conventionally assumed to make a definite whole and to affect the male as a whole, nevertheless, as a form it is certainly a composite of these and other things, and the parts as well as the whole are as frequently registered separately as collectively. Who needs to be told that the thighs, the torso, the breasts, a "trim ankle" or foot, or arm or hand or the head separately as well as collectively mean something? Yet also its mouth, nose, ear, cheeks, chin, and the neck and shoulders that support it are distinct forms and as such are registered separately, also frequently commented on by the artist or lover or passerby, and, as individual forms of beauty, remembered or reacted to violently by what we term desire, love, lust, or admiration.

But these particularized forms, either assembled in the body as a "whole" or considered separately as forms, are still beholden to other forms and chemical and physical factors or conditions for their individual or assembled effect as stimuli. For instance, there is the eye: a form as well as a mechanism for discharging energy either generated in the body or assembled there and redischarged according to additional stimuli from without, as for instance, the look of hate or dislike evoked by some exterior object, or of affection or pleasure or desire also.

Problem of Form

The form things take furnishes direct evidence of the mechanism of life. For you must know that the man machine senses forms and registers them without pre-knowledge of their existence, at least in a conscious sense. They are. They appear, very suddenly, before the eyes of the newborn child. As a child you looked upon a formful world—faces, hands, rooms, trees, grass, animals—a world of forms. But were you vastly startled? Were you unduly afraid? Not always. Yet why not? Had nine months in your mother's womb conditioned you to a world now sensible to you or, by some nervous or glandular exchange, caused you to specifically sense what was without? Or did the old atoms and electrons of you working in your new cells know all of what you were to see and feel? It is not impossible. It really should be true. But what is truer is the fact that the forms that were to environ as well as to condition you—making you, as previously they had your ancestors for thousands of years, reflections of their passing reality—were so old that they were even before your ancestors. Think of the age of the rocks, of the millions of years in which there have been animals on the earth, that the sky has known clouds, the billions of years in which space has known the sun, the moon, the stars. Think of the countless seasons of growing trees and grass. And these were here to make possible for you, when you came, to have the reactions (otherwise called your thoughts) that you were to have; and all these thoughts, mere reflections of themselves, these forms, or, if you will, of the forces of nature, which previous to their being, had brought them into being!

Forms, forms, forms . . . and forces, the *Ancient of Days,* bringing about their alterations and reactions, and actually achieving forms that react or feel as though they lived of themselves, and yet are only constructions and reflections of endless primeval forces that progressively construct and reflect or "live" through them.

Why should there be such a variety of forms? And why should there appear to run through them all a kind of unity, as if they were all expressing some one thing? Creative energy, say. And why should it be that everything appears in some form or other? Even the most shapeless thing we know—a liquid or a gas or vapor, or protoplasm, the ancestor of all earthly organisms—takes a form when the forces which surround it are equalized so that it is free (when motivated by other forces) to form now this, now that. Why are so many forms round? Why are large bodies round? And why are some forms crystalline and angular? Why should blown snow in cold regions take the form of a Christmas tree, as it does very frequently? Why does a snow crystal have its fragile complex design and the beauty of that? And why should Vitamin H crystals sometimes appear like snow crystals? And why such forms as the eagle, the blue-bird, the rhinoceros, the wart-hog? Or that of a geyser? Or a bird of paradise?

How very mysterious are these forms! The endless, ceaseless mystery of them, within and around us. And yet it seems to us now as if they were all constructed on one principle and permitted by one thing! And yet the wonder and mystery of them remains.

One of the strangest things about form is that anything we see, whether leaf, man, tree, hand, star, sun, seems to be at once a single isolated form, while in reality it is a part of a larger form. Our body, of which we are conscious as a whole, is really made of thousands of smaller forms. And although we still seem only conscious of our body, we are yet parts of society, of churches, of vacation parties, of schools, of nations, of the human race, of the animal kingdom, of the earth, and innumerable larger forms. And the same kind of relationship could be set out for any other form, whether star, or flower, fish, or grain of sand. Perhaps if we think of forms in this interrelated way, we can realize how immense is the true environment of any form and how much a form is dependent for existence on this environment.

Well then what is form? Is it something apparent to our eyes alone? Or is it something which goes beyond the possibilities of our senses and is deeply imbedded in the very heart of things? Is it both ways? What is the common characteristic that a group of atoms in a molecular form has with the group of people in a legislature, or with the electrons and protons in an atom, or with any group of cells in a human body or in a plant? Surely it is not merely shape, or symmetry, or limits, or proportion, or rhythm, though all these things may be present. Is it not rather a unity of action and reaction among the members of any one of these groups? Are not the parts so tied together that all act and react within the particular harmonious limits of that form?

Consider a family group for instance—a father, a mother, and three children. The father plans to take some of his savings and buy some stocks. But one of the children falls sick, and a very expensive operation is necessary, so that the money must be used for that instead of for the stocks. If the father were independent of that particular form, the family, he could have invested the money anyway. But he is not independent of it, and before taking any such steps, he must consider the limits of activity he has as a member of this form—the family form. Remember, you can take a picture of a family as a form.

Or suppose you cut a flowering plant. Although it may be only the stem which is cut, the flower and the leaves will die. That is because the whole plant is a form. Its parts are interdependent, and what happens to one, will affect the whole. You might say here that a leaf might be cut off the growing plant and that the loss of that leaf would not destroy it. But that only proves that the parts of some forms are of relatively greater or lesser importance to its being. For instance a child in a family might die without destroying a family. Whether the family will continue after the death of the child depends on the relative importance of the child to the family. An atom may lose an electron and still be an atom or a tree its leaves or a branch or even many branches and still be a tree.

But any change, whether of the essential or non-essential parts of any form, whether it be the loss or addition of a child to a family, a leaf to a plant, an electron to an atom, that change alters the appearance and so the individuality of that form. Its integrity as a form of forms may survive many changes. As a general rule, the greater the variety and number of forms which a large form includes, the less are its limitations as to existing as a whole. Think, for example, how many races of men have disappeared or are disappearing from the earth. Yet the form of the whole human race exists still. And think of the earth, how many changes have occurred to it since it fell out of the sun (if it did fall). Still its integrity as earth is still intact.

However, what is really happening to every form, large or small, from minute to minute, is change. What we call the integrity of a form, its permanence, its inviolability, is only a *seeming*, special to our limitations as human beings. Look around you, at the books, the table, the people, the animals, clocks, plants, everything in fact. Do they grow old, wear out, break, become "eye-sores", die? They certainly do more. A man is born, grows old, and dies. Yet is his form the same form at seventy that it was at birth? Is that wrinkled face, are those tired eyes the same ones of fifty years ago? No, the child died many years ago when the man became an adult; and the form that we at last admit is ended in our idea of death, has it not in reality died innumerable times, from minute to minute, year to year, generation to generation before it finally vanished into the formless? And is it not the same with all forms, whether of the so-called living or dead? Each little change in an old form creates a new one and ends the old one. Books rot, trees grow, the clock ticks, ice melts, the lamp breaks. Changes of form are always sudden, if we notice each little change. Only we do not. The change must come within the range of our senses first for us to notice it. But to consider forms as constantly changing, whether we are sensitive to the changes or not, helps us a great deal to realize how interrelated, how chain-like, is the whole series of forms.

The more minutely we examine form, the closer we get to the individual form, the more we notice how very impermanent any form is. And the farther we get from the individual form—to large aggregates of individuals—the less change *we* note. However, the large form itself must change in time, if *all* its parts are changing. As for instance, a state or form of government. It may begin, as did the United States, with thirteen states and between three and four million people and grow and change not only by the increase of human units, as from three to a hundred and thirty million, or maybe in the course of time to two, three, five hundred million, but also by the processes of invention, gas, electric lights, telegraphy, telephone, automobiles, airplanes, railroads, good roads, bus lines, newspapers, magazines, government buildings, battleships; in short a vast number of things which were not here when it was born, change the nation as a whole. In connection with the United States, even its physical form has changed from a strip of land on the Atlantic Ocean to the breadth of a continent. Yet it has not changed any more, if as much, as all men change between birth and death. Yet both and all other things are no more than semipermanent forms. They last, to be what they first were, *for a time only,* be it rock, or flower, ocean or pool, solar or sidereal system or—if we can believe the physicists—the universe itself. [*Or*]

The Factor Called Time

Brevity of duration (time) makes for interest
in so strange a spectacle as life.

TIME IS THE INDISPENSABLE FACTOR IN LIFE, EVOLUTION, KNOW-
ledge. And the lack of duration in time is the full explanation of the ignorance
as well as the curiosity of man in regard to nature and *life*.

With so little time and his so limited faculties for sensing space, time,
matter, and their endless energy expressions, it is not possible for him to
"know" more than very limited aspects not only as to time, but as to number,
form, motions, and characteristics of all those forms and their movements
which his very limited senses permit him to sense and, more effectively,
register.

However, it is entirely possible with the increasing development of techniques
of various kinds—syntheses, condensations, theorems, formulas, to say nothing
of radio, telegraph, telephone, aeroplane, telescope, microscope, and what
not else—for man to multiply the value of the very little time that he has.
So much so that, given a highly organized and sensitive registering mechanism
such as some humans chance to be the results of, a day or a year's study
or travel today can readily be the equivalent of ten or fifteen years of study
or travel or investigation a thousand years ago; just as labor saving devices
in the manufacturing world—the eccentric cam, the traveling crane, electric
cutting and welding, the moving platform—make possible such an amount
of production as could not possibly (have) been achieved in a hundred or
thousand times the hours, days, weeks a thousand years back. So that, in
this sense, time is a myth also, since its length or value depends upon the
nature of the organisms and the sensory as well as material skills at their
command in such portions or measures of it as their own duration in it
permits. [*Or*]

‡ ‡ ‡

Isaac Newton distinguished between *sensuous* time and absolute time and space. Sensuous time and space he regarded as relative and as a distance between things and events which we can sense and measure. [*Or*]

T.D.

‡ ‡ ‡

Time—the knowledge of it by sensate creatures such as man and animals and its service or utility to them—is not anything of their invention or creation. It is a reaction on their part to the fact of duration in connection with all created things of which they are sensible and so aware. The duration of day and of night, of the changing seasons, of summer heat and winter cold, of the growth and duration periods of all creatures about them, animal and vegetable, the appearance and disappearance of individuals coming from far places and again departing—all these would establish time as a factor in the life of man, but not by any process of thinking or inventing on his part at any point. That it arrived in his consciousness is due to his chemo-physical sensitivity—his compulsion so to react to all other chemo-physical phenomena about him. [*Or*]

‡ ‡ ‡

In connection with *Time*, there is this to wonder about. All creatures live for a period, the period varying with the species and to a degree with the climate or medium—water, air, earth. Also, their arrival time of mating, hive, hole, or nest building, the period of depositing their eggs in some other creature, and day of death is also fairly relatively spaced. For these seem to be affected and so arranged for by temperature. Man, more sensitive to weights and measures, i.e., periodicity, speaks of those periods as periods of time—one month, three months, ten days, etc. But what is time as applied to these creatures? Is it anything more than sensations relating to the duration of given mechanisms? But since the duration of mechanisms varies so greatly under heat, cold, sunlight, waves of force, etc., the significance of time as anything more than an uncertain, or relative, local measure of days here on earth becomes obvious. Besides, earth time is not sidereal or space time. [*Or*]

‡ ‡ ‡

Nature, in the labor of producing a pine or an oak wood, appears to man to manifest no *haste*. But what man knows the real energy and intensity and hurry and care that may be there. [*Or*]

T.D.

‡ ‡ ‡

The May fly becomes an adult, molts twice, lays eggs, and dies—all in the course of an evening. [*Or*]

‡ ‡ ‡

Consider the snail, the fishworm, the turtle, oyster, clam, all grubs, the processionary pine worm and then such things as wild ducks, gulls, etc., that outrace ships or trains. Speed—the *time factor*—is *what* in their lives? How much more or less do they live because of it? [*Or*]

                                                                                    T.D.

‡ ‡ ‡

In general, men experience the present, or life, in its totality for them without ability to estimate its content. And *when* it has become the past, it is even less understood. [*Or*]

                                                                                    T.D.

‡ ‡ ‡

Whatever moment passes is over forever. Its disappointments cannot be made up in the future anymore than happiness can transfer its own miraculous quality to the future. It is not time that passes but one's self, really. [*Or*]

‡ ‡ ‡

The man in the street says, "We are always getting away from the present moment," the moment of sensory stimulation from one or another person or many exterior sources. But the truth is, the present moment is getting away from us. Down-pouring stimuli from all conceivable sources are being registered by our frail and passing sensory organs. But they are being registered by endless other persons and things and not in the same way. Also, these exterior stimuli are pouring in every other direction, whether there be sensory organs of any kind in their path capable of registering them or not, and they do not return. Such being the case, they either pass or are stopped and held—like electrons or photons or light particles are held by atoms in their path. But this spells change of everything in and to man as well as nature. And he has no power to do anything but react to stimuli. So he changes, but not voluntarily. Since all things, including man's sensory organs, have but a brief duration in time, it follows that they cannot endure as sensory pictures in man or nature. They fade and pass. All things do. Only the continued origination and distribution of stimuli from somewhere keeps life extant—for *life* read *all matter-energy*. They are and must be extended in space and time in order for life to be. And because of that, life is constantly passing from appearance to invisibility.

‡ ‡ ‡

The concrete highway was edged with a mat of tangled, broken, dry grass, and the grass heads were heavy with oat beards to catch on a dog's coat, and foxtails to tangle in a horse's fetlocks, and clover burrs to fasten in sheep's wool; sleeping life waiting to be spread and dispersed, every seed armed with an appliance of dispersal, twisting darts and parachutes for the wind, little spears and balls of tiny thorns, and all waiting for animals and for the wind, for a man's trouser cuff or the hem of a woman's skirt, all passive but armed with appliances for activity, still, but each possessed of the anlage of movement.——John Steinbeck, from *Grapes of Wrath*

Note the time factor in all this, how a season of warmth must be counted on—time for growing, time for waiting to catch a favorable wind and for traveling on it, time to sink in the ground before killing frosts.

[The quotation above is typical of Dreiser's way of having a particular thought typed in the center of a page with room for comments above and below. He would then consider using it under various headings and add comments accordingly. Sometimes a whole page would be filled with his small handwriting above and below the original *Note.*

In this case the comment is short and appropriate to the heading *Time,* but under other headings, the same quotation has rich and varied comments. An interesting study could be made of these variations on a theme, almost comparable to the same expression used in music. See also same *Note* under *Weights and Measures. Editor's Note*]

‡ ‡ ‡

The phrase *the march of time* means nothing, for *time* does not march. What "marches" or changes either position or character in space is *matter in motion,* in the sense that motion means movement of bodies of matter great or small in relation to other bodies of matter great or small in space. Without at least visible or detectable bodies of matter in space (detectable by man for instance), no change of position on the part of either could be detected, unless doing so, it could be contrasted with another body in space somewhere. In the matter of motion, where this refers to internal movement or change of position of the atom or electron or constituent parts of a body or mass of matter, again motion can only be detected as between particles or parts—that is, the constituent members of the whole. One lone atom or particle isolated in space could not to the human eye or mind, at least, record either change or movement.

But now, since *time* is nothing more than a measure of movements—minute or great, fast or slow, as between one or many bodies or measures of masses of matter, moving among or near, to or from each other—it is these thus detectable movements which give rise to the illusion of time, which of course has no existence apart from them, any more than it has any existence apart from matter. No matter, no time; no space, no time. No motion, no time. But given matter, motion, and space, and the illusion of time—that is, the illusion of seconds, minutes, hours, days, weeks, months, and years—can arise. But they are not real—merely measures of many movements of many things— among them, matter and motion or energy in space. [*Or*]

T.D.

‡ ‡ ‡

The sensations of order, stability, peace, which frequently encourage the inexperienced to feel or assume that these same are durable or even partially durable, depend for their existence on the factor called time. For instance, a creature that lives but a little while, such as a midge, fly, fruit fly, or mosquito, might think, if it thought or could think as a man does, that order, peace, stability were quite durable, enduring as they might for its life. But a man or an elephant or an ant, to say nothing of a planet, sun, island universe, each living or enduring for a much longer period, could reach no such conclusion. All sorts of disturbances, dangers, accidents would have in these relatively greater periods of time opportunity to occur—storms, earthquakes, drouths, intense heat, intense cold, ice ages, heat ages, failures of food supplies, disease, wars, enemies, sicknesses, individual attacks, thefts, and what not—so that apart from the seeming non-existence of these things to a gnat, a snow fly, a fruit fly, a short-lived fish or bird, their disturbing presence would be all too manifest, the lives of their observers or victims all too lacking in peace, security, stability.

You can see how this works when you consider how to man, nature, the earth's surface, as he finds it when he arrives here, its so-called "eternal" hills and peaceful woods and fields, lakes and seas appear to him at times as havens of peace, quiet, safety, in short, as durable, comforting, and preserving. And so they may prove for a little while. Yet, only so. For the story of the earth is nothing if not a tumultuous process of change, coupled with disaster and often agony. Neither land nor water has ever looked twice the same. Titanic forces, of which the fiery volcano and the death-dealing earthquake are examples, have endlessly battled, slowly but surely transforming the globe. He who wrote of the everlasting hills knew nothing of their history. The forms and the face of the earth have altered since yesterday, are changing now, and will change, removing almost all signs of the past. There is no pause, even the briefest, in the endless shifts, removals, erections of new forms. But in connection with this, it is only time, duration in time, which will permit a human being or animal organism of a few years of life to sense this, either directly and forcefully, or if not that, then by report—yes— tradition, oral or written. But without repetition in fact, so that the tradition may be re-enforced, revivified, even these fade, and the illusion of peace, of changelessness, for many remains or would, were not the repetition and change ever present. [Or]

T.D.

Space—Time

In the phenomena of motion, space reveals itself as a tremendously powerful regulator. A railroad train is hurrying at excessive speed, guided in its motion by two straight tracks of steel. Nothing happens until it comes to a sharp turn—the train goes off the track, the cars tumble over and are bent and twisted. What was the cause of this powerful action? Was it not the tracks that guided the train? To a certain extent they did, but space itself had prescribed a track of its own. When the tracks curved sharply, the track prescribed for the train by space itself was obstructed, a conflict arose between two mighty powers, and in the heat of the combat, heavy steel was bent and human lives were lost. One of the mighty powers in this conflict was the innocent-looking "nothingness" we call empty space. It was the external, physically active space that here revealed its power; our mental space only served as a framework for the registration of the events and made possible the preservation of the pictures in our memory.

‡ ‡ ‡

Time is a definite factor and force in the Universe just as is space. Also heat and cold. Its reality as a force is due to limitation of the duration of matter and energy which are impressed on the evolved sensitivities of man and have caused him to remember and measure (in so far as possible) and name the same. The limitation of the duration of matter and (or) energy as witnessed and registered by man (the evaporation of water, the decay of metals and wood and stone, the changes that accompany the birth, growth, decay of everything from suns to men and plants) have caused him not only to think, but to labor in order to make the best practical use of the duration or time of anything. Not only that it has evoked in him the most respectable of reactions—the emotions of sorrow, pity, joy, which have accompanied the birth, growth, decay of everything, himself included—for along with and among these, he has had his day and seen it, as well as all else that has accompanied him, pass from him.

In sum, time, or duration, is something that is willed on all matter-energy by an immaterial something which permits them to be, or it is an unwilled aspect of an uncreated mechanical process which has all the grandeur of a by-man-imagined Creative process which is above and beyond the immense machine—or is it. [*Or*]

T.D.

The Factor
Called Chance

THE ONE FACTOR WHICH SEEMS TO BE OPERATING ALWAYS IN the universe and which seems by its appearances to positively refute a lawful, mechanical interpretation of nature is chance, coincidence, the exceptional character of many things and events. Sometimes we think we have "luck" or that we are "unlucky." Some people seem to be favored by fortune and others consistently oppressed by it. We say "there's always a chance." Or we wish people "good luck." We seem to be convinced that there is some arbitrary, omnipotent spirit at large, to whose bad or good graces we owe the inexplicable happenings of our lives. This factor of chance runs through everything. You, for example, may tomorrow meet someone who will play a determining role in your life. Or you may get $1000 from some source that you couldn't name now. Or you may be run over by an automobile; or you may be infected by some disease; or your house may be burnt down. To chance, anything is possible, it seems. See how it seems to have affected the course of history. [*Or*]

‡ ‡ ‡

When we look at or register the world around us, there appears to us to be two kinds of events—the usual or expected kind and the unusual or unexpected kind. We "expect" certain things to happen, and we don't expect other things to happen. Why should this be so? Because obviously, it makes little or no difference to nature what *we* expect. We can make our generalizations and our laws and rules, by which we more or less "order" nature to proceed, but still we find very unusual and very unexpected things happening right along, in our own lives, in the lives of others, among plants and animals, among the stars, and so on.

For instance, we have our life insurance companies, who have figured out mathematical laws to fit many observations of death as it is correlated with other conditions, like age, sickness, accident, and so on. And in spite of this, it always seems very unusual when you or I are involved in an accident or are sick. Although it may be that for nature, the fact of our being sick or well, dead or alive, in an accident or safe at home in bed may be equally usual, or unusual. And the same may be said of the strange coincidences which happen every now and then and which seem to be so very influential in the life of the individual or of nations or of the world in fact. For instance, in Athens, during the reign of Pericles, when the Athenians were being besieged by the Lacedaemonians, a great plague broke out: the population was almost universally affected; there were a great many deaths; the army and navy were made almost completely ineffective; the government, social relationships, all were demoralized, since no one thought that he would be alive to receive justice. That such a plague should arrive at just such a time of war, to a people of such abilities and distinction seems to us one of those strange, unusual events in nature. However, it may be that such an event is no stranger or more unusual than that Johnny Smith, an obscure child of eight years of age, should come down with measles on the very day that he and William Jones were to settle an argument concerning some marbles.

Somewhere, we may assume, and it may be true, that for each individual male or female, there exists the right environment, or stimuli, for his particular temperament. Also, somewhere the most harmful environment or collection of stimuli. And either—should he chance to meet up with and be controlled by it— would be or prove his fate. By the one, he would be greatly furthered, developed, made most effective, by the other least so, his natural powers whatever they might be would be frustrated or destroyed. And this is the element of chance that faces all. Or consider, for instance the difference of fortunes involved in being born an American, a Chinese, an African savage, a Hindoo, an Esquimaux, a German, Frenchman, or Englishman. The varying environments and consequent social viewpoints and opportunities, intellectual, financial, social, physical, etc.

What can be said with surety of ourselves? Do we know the hour of our death? Do we know what diseases will attack us? Do we know the names of those we will meet? Can we prophesy with certainty any single event in the future accurately as to time, place, or magnitude? and the events of each one as likely or unlikely as those of that day when you felt that some unbelievably malevolent fate had chosen you for special unkindness. The importance of the subjective, limited abilities, dislikes and desires of ourselves in considering chance in nature cannot be overestimated. It is our own defect of judgment to find many things alike and a few unusual. . . . Our own temperament is the arbitrary criterion for coincidence or chance.

By all this I mean to point out three facts as a basis for considering what chance is: first, that in nature only individual events or things are produced; second, that they are each one equally unlikely; and third, that it is our own temperaments which prevent us from constant awareness of the first two propositions.

With these three facts in mind, it will be comparatively easier to understand how nature can appear to be law-abiding and include exceptions at the same time, how our lives can appear to be ruled by laws which are at base made up of innumerable chance occurrences, and how, finally, chance itself may be the only law to which there is no exception.

‡ ‡ ‡

In astronomy, when scientists consider the motions of the stars, the large-scale movements of the universe, there seem to be few chance occurrences. The stars rotate, revolve, radiate, and so on according to the well-known laws of mechanics and energy, based on observations and verified by more observations. Here we find again and again the same set of conditions identified with the same set of subsequent events. If we found an exception, we would say, in effect, that the same set of conditions could give rise to another series of events, and our law would have to be modified. Whatever took place following the initial set of conditions would be a probability and not a certainty. Suppose, for example, that the earth, instead of revolving around the sun for the next hundred years, should go out of its course, and wander around in the planet Neptune's orbit, and then wander back to its present orbit and continue as before. Would this prove that the law of gravity was no good, that the earth thus arbitrarily upset the order of the universe? If we said that this law was subject to probability, then we are saying that the same causes can give rise to different effects. But how can a law be a probable law? A law that is only probable is a paradox in terms. Would it not be better to say that the law is absolute, but that the exceptions which make the law seem probable to us are really other laws of which we know nothing? In other words, that instead of introducing the loose concept of probable results following on certain causes, it would be better to say that unknown causes obviate through their own laws, the laws which we do know.

However, in astronomy there seem to be few exceptions to the known and observed laws. As we approach the consideration of small scale events and things, there seems to be an increasing amount of exceptions, of chance happenings, of laws which are probable rather than certain in operation. For instance, the seasons of the year in their succession one after the other seem to follow a more or less certain law. But when we consider the laws involved or suppose two children are brought up in the same atmosphere, the same environment, with the same training, if this external environment were all that was to be considered, the children would be alike. When we say that on account of the fact of like environment it is probable that the children will turn out to be somewhat alike, what we are saying is that there are other causes which we do not consider.

Suppose we come even further down in the scale to very small events and things—atoms. Here we see that any law which we know of is even more probable in its operation. We cannot predict anything certainly about an atom. Here chance seems to predominate. No law, whether of energy, mechanics, thermodynamics, or whatever, is sure to operate in any case. Here, then, also it would seem that instead of laws which operate with a large degree of uncertainty, it would be better to assume that there are a number of causes which are operating according to their laws but which we do not know. [*Or*]

‡ ‡ ‡

Chance may be in most cases only another name for our ignorance of causes, and therefore a factor having no reality, except for us or other limited, reacting mechanisms. This seems to be true in cases such as that of an automobile accident, when a rainy day (which we admit has a cause) coincides with the presence of some persons in an automobile (having a cause) on a dangerous turn in a road (having a cause) when the driver of the car is out-of-sorts (having a cause, either sickness, or emotion, or some such thing) and thus is not as good a driver as usual. All the factors in the accident have causes, and if all the factors had been known, the effect would have been predictable. The fact that we do not know all the causes beforehand (such as that there would be this dangerous turn in the road, or that the driver would not be able to perform as efficiently as usual, or that it would be raining, etc.) makes the accident look like chance (something unpredictable). [*Or*]

‡ ‡ ‡

Marcellus Hammond, 29 year old Negro "fire-eater," died today of first and second degree burns suffered here yesterday when flames from a blazing torch which he was about to extinguish in his mouth ignited his grass skirt at an afternoon carnival performance. [Newspaper Clipping *Editor's Note*]

‡ ‡ ‡

A cat goes prowling for a bird. From an unseen, observant, prowling boy comes a stone which ends the cat's dream of a bird breakfast. But herein lies not only surprise for the cat but instruction and so development. [*Or*]

‡ ‡ ‡

A young tiger, driven by hunger, decides to visit a plain where zebras are and by stealth of approach cut out one from the herd and kill it. The killing is nothing—a leap and a neck breaking bite. En route he is seen by a pack of wild dogs who encircle him and proceed to wear him down. Here is the factor called *chance,* itself basic in the element of surprise or interest, which is absolutely necessary to the chemical-physical concoction that we know as life. Without these elements, reason for action would cease. And without action, no change. And without change, no life as we know it. [*Or*]

‡ ‡ ‡

Hybrids, the rare crosses between existing varieties of plants and animals, are often the pioneers of evolution, for it is from hybrids that new and different strains of plants and animals develop. But often, because nature is so wasteful (mass production) in its bounty, these "differing" varieties are worthless, mere novelties of life comparable to the giants or the dwarfs and freaks of the side show at the circus. (Factor called Chance) Yet because the hybrids are pioneers, there is always the chance that some new and valuable plant or animal (man for instance) will develop. And this is, plainly, the goal—the jackpot in the gamble of evolution, which plant breeders are now playing. [Or]

‡ ‡ ‡

The entire spider family with its webs and traps (to say nothing of the entire human family), its evolutionary divisions and species is nothing if not an illustration of the operation of chance and, at the very same time, an excellent and exact illustration of the law of cause and effect; so that we can truly say that any effect springs from a given cause and, more, that there is no such thing as a cause without an effect. At the same time, it is also true that involved with the probability of a given effect is the element of chance. That is, the cause of a probable effect can be arranged for or determined, although the probability of a given effect within a given time cannot always be even approximately indicated. In other words, any effect in connection with a pre-arranged cause may be indefinitely postponed, may not even occur. The truth of this can be indicated in this way.

All spiders build webs or traps to catch their prey or food. It is statistically true that given a number of spiders, an equal number of webs or traps, and the existence of a number of insects, some insects are likely to fall in webs or traps. In fact, if it were possible for a spider or a human being to know the exact operations of the entire universe in advance, it would be possible to say which insect at what time in what way would fall into what particular spider's web or trap. But since such prevision is seemingly not granted to any life form, there intervenes the factor called chance.

The remote cause of such a factor as chance in this case is (1) that nature here on earth has evolved spiders and insects, (2) that spiders, in order to live, prey on insects. It is also true (3) that insects, in order to obtain their food or reproduce themselves, either fly or jump or both and that in order to trap them, spiders have evolved webs or traps and usually placed them where an insect is likely to pass.

But with all such causes for a given effect arranged for—and in the face of the fact that unless the effect does take place, there will be no spiders, since they cannot live without food—still it is not possible to assert that any given spider will trap any given insect or that throughout its life will trap even one insect, in some cases, will not die from lack of ability so to do. Therein lies the chance factor. Nonetheless it is true that billions of spiders do live and reproduce themselves by trapping insects in their webs or traps. Also, that billions upon billions of insects are so trapped. Yet that any given insect will so die, or any particular spider trap any particular insect at any given time, or at any time at all—no, it is not possible to so assert. And thus it is that the factor called chance intervenes. Also, that the law of averages which can say that, given so many spiders with so many nets and so many insects flitting about seeking to eat and reproduce, it is certain that an average of so many insects will be trapped and eaten by an average of so many spiders. The last is a statistical law and it can be verified. The other is the proof of the factor called chance.

T.D.

Weights and Measures

IT [LIFE] IS NOTHING IF NOT A CONSTANT AND CAREFUL WEIGHing and measuring of everything in an orderly and seemingly most thoughtful manner. The great care suggested if not actually present can be illustrated in thousands even millions of ways. For instance—

‡ ‡ ‡

You see an insect skipping gaily over the surface of a pond, of any water. Cork and wood float. None-the-less, except for the surface tension of the water, the insects would sink. Surface tension of water is the pull between its surface or top layer of atoms or molecules. The pull makes of these surface atoms a kind of net or floor that will hold up the weight of some insects as well as a floor will hold up a man or a ton of furniture. [*Or*]

T.D.

‡ ‡ ‡

The fact that your height is what it is, that you stay on the ground rather than float in space, that you can and do fall on occasion and rise with some difficulty is due to the law of gravitation and is not a function or compulsion of that mythical thing spoken of as your will. The fact that birds fly and that fishes swim, that flowers grow and bloom, that their stalks bend in the wind, and that their petals float lightly and gracefully to earth are all physical as well as chemical compulsions, really problems in chemistry and physics (one might as truthfully say engineering problems), which have all been solved by something, or just are or were—never having been created, but have always existed, if you are willing to accept that. [*Or*]

T.D.

‡ ‡ ‡

Weights and Measures are primary in all mechanical designs intended to serve a given purpose—"weights":

The concrete highway was edged with a mat of tangled, broken, dry grass, and the grass heads were heavy with oat beards to catch on a dog's coat,

45

and foxtails to tangle in a horse's fetlocks, and clover burrs to fasten in sheep's wool; sleeping life waiting to be spread and dispersed, every seed armed with an appliance of dispersal, twisting darts and parachutes for the wind, little spears and balls of tiny thorns, and all waiting for animals and for the wind, for a man's trouser cuff or the hem of a woman's skirt; all passive but armed with appliances for activity, still, but each possessed of the anlage of movement. ——John Steinbeck, from *Grapes of Wrath*

Consider the seemingly carefully calculated weights of these things—of a seed, for instance, that is to be carried high and far by delicate threads of floss arranged after the fashion of a parachute, also the choice of durable and light (in weight) material.

Certainly beauty of effect in any form must involve considerations that are related in intent or necessity to measurements of various kinds—that is, weights and measures.

[This is a duplicate of quotation used under *Time*, but comments are different, to go with the subject *Weights and Measures*. This is typical of Dreiser's variations on a theme, as explained under *Time*, page 36. *Editor's Note*]

To Where

But why weights and measures—the endless multiplicity of things and the necessity of their weighing and measuring if we are to have life as we know it? To be sure, if you find it good—that is agreeable, a pleasant or happy adventure which you are sorry to part with when you die—you have at least no critical reason for inquiry however much you may wonder and would like to know. On the contrary, if you are ill or unhappy during the major portion of your life or its entirety, you have reason for wondering why anything should have stirred as life in space—bringing into being, if it was not always in being, the endless galaxies with which astronomers attempt to deal.

For it is obvious even to ignorant man (or is it) that it need not and might not have been. That is, instead of matter-energy disporting itself after the fashion that it has and does in space, why not the primordial immaterial so arrestingly suggested by the Bible? "God is Spirit." "In the beginning God created the *heaven* and the *earth*—and the earth was without form and void and darkness was upon the face of the deep."

Or, rejecting that and accepting the terms of modern physics, might not one ask: "Why matter-energy ever?" Why not just space, empty space, without even the measuring implement *time* that goes with matter-energy but not with endless space and without even any creative impulse inhabiting the same, anywhere. In which case there would be nothing to weigh or measure, neither space nor time, nor matter, nor energy, nor any of the endless divisions into which these are now broken or arranged and which must be measured and weighed in order that we can have any sense of this thing called living. [*Or*]

‡   ‡   ‡

We, ourselves, are nothing if not weighing and measuring instruments. Every move that we make, every measure of anything that we take suggests what? Our bed is to be so long, measured by our length; our teaspoons and tablespoons are to be so large, hold so much, measured by our mouths, how wide the same, how much the space enclosed by the lips and cheeks and our throats will hold. Our houses and rooms and cities and streets and roads and trains are designed or measured according to, as we say, our needs and requirements, our comfort, pleasure, health, strength. For our use and service, all of these—each and every one—require accurate measuring and weighing. Nothing that we use or wear or lift or carry or place dare be too heavy or too light, too long or too short, too high or too low, for we are not giants or pygmies, and if we were, consider how different all things would be. You can sense all of this when you contemplate a dwarf or a giant in real life—how almost useless or at odds everything is for them. No chair, bed, table, knife, or fork or plate or cup or glass that we use is suitable to their use, capable of easy, that is, comfortable, use by them. Nor any shoe or hat or glove or dress or suit. They cannot even do with the same amount of food or water—must have more or less; also of air and heat; although light, that inexplicable something that, via our eyes, guides and makes possible all *our* measuring and weighing as well as the building and using of such devices as we have for so doing, may and again may not be quantitatively and qualitatively as necessary as to us—most likely not, since you have only to think of eyeless fishes, moles, vines that travel, measure, build, bind without eyes. And again there is the world of the exceedingly minute insects and still more minute bacteria and those still smaller creatures of the viruses (one-tenth of a millionth of a millionth of an inch in size), which cannot be seen by ordinary light waves at all, but by those of the much smaller electron particle, which is possibly that by which they function, and if so, of which they use less—light being weighed and measured to their need!

So, as you see, at no point, in connection with anything, any function or procedure, whether in or outside of man or any creature or creation—whether that be a sun, or an island universe, or an electron or particle of star dust, the farthest reaches of space in which they move, or any minutest portion of the same—nothing is beyond measure or weight or the balancing of the same, nothing without form save that which is beyond all form—space-time— but which includes it. And to know ought of them, we must weigh and measure or in some esoteric way apprehend at least something of their weights and measures, or we know nothing. For weight and measure are words—our words—indicating to us alone certain unescapable and unchanging attributes of their being and ours. For we well know ourselves to be part of this immense something that, whether it must or need not, does so present itself, to us at least, as something that has weight and measure as well as form and number, the same seemingly indissolubly united in one great whole—an immense variety of matter and energy functioning in what after endless ages of evolution we are moved or motivated to work and so speak of, though we understand them not, as space and time. And the law of all this and of our being *in it*, as we now know, is that to know ought of it all, we must weigh and measure with the senses and organs with which we are provided and those extensions of the same which we call our tools and scales or yard sticks or cloud chambers or counters or numbers or symbols or words and the alphabets that precede the words—these endless varied expressions or extensions of this great something which we call the universe, or matter-energy in space-time, and which show to us by and through the sensibilities or sensitivities with which its forces or laws have provided us, not through anything of our own which is not a creation or expression and so extension of it, of all its varied excellencies: its beauties, energies, majesties; its sounds, colors, forms, numbers.

Indeed, of its numbering and weighing and measuring, we are endless and minute, perhaps worthful, perhaps worthless expressions or extensions chemically and physically related and, we would *like* to think, of some worth. *He marks the sparrow's fall.* And in pursuit of that *like*—a chemical or physical evocation of nature in us, not anything of our own creating you may be sure—we return in our searches, scientific or emotional, to such straws of comfort as evolving and seeking man (evolved and made to seek by nature, remember, not by ourselves) has left us in proverbs or poetry—the cries of love-haunted, love-seeking man. *The very hairs of your head are numbered, He weigheth the waters, He made a decree for the rain, Behold the nations are counted as the small dust of the balance.* And we find, true enough, that chemically and physically, the sparrows fall is truly marked, for its electric, atomic, and chemical structure as well as the evolutionary and hereditary processes which have functioned and still do along with the same are reasonably well known. So, too, the metabolism of its conception, growth, and death. So that its arrival and departure can truly be said to be marked or governed by nature—every hair, feather, bone, vein, muscle, and the cells, molecules, atoms, and electrons that constituted it have their place and duties arranged for in advance. So that the sparrow as its fellows, the birds of its own species and all related species so richly and vividly and beautifully varied, come and go, season after season, and, what is more, are measured as to time, as to season, as to size, as to form, as to color, as to weight and duration, they and all other things of the cosmic as well as the protoplasmic chain. Hence *What is man that Thou art mindful of him* can more logically be made to read—What man or worm or insect or sea or solar or sidereal system can be excluded from this great legal or mechanistic Whole? It is one—its elements, its systems, its light, its atoms, electrons, protons, and particles of the same—all is one—many in one—and one in many—each for all and all for each—the same laws governing all. Yet whether as a whole or in part *it need be* or has the power or looks to the power *to will so to be or not to be,* that, man does not know.

But a curious thing in connection with all this, in so far as man is concerned— man the odd and yet certain chemical and physical extension of all this evolved here on this earth—*is this:* that in him, as has been said before, has been evolved or evoked this curious mood or desire, emotional in texture, to be permanently and indissolubly related, not merely as the chemical and mechanistic structure that he is, to this other immensely great chemical and physical mass the universe, *but as a spirit or essence,* which betimes he feels himself to be, differentiated as such and yet and still *integrally* and indissolubly united with another and greater something which he conceives to be *the* or *a Creative Essence or Mind,* inhabiting, enduring in, and directing this larger matter-energy complex or mechanism—the Universe. Feeling himself to be a *unit,* although evolutionally, chemically, structurally, texturally, and legally surrounded by and joined to endless *units* of a like character (as like as two electrons, two atoms, two molecules, two cells), still, he desires to be dealt with separately and individually as a unit—a *man,* a *mind,* or essence, deathless and changeless. And this in the face of all evolution. And he broods as to that, the uncertainty of it. Doubts and sorrows. And regardless of the immensity and complexity of all that is—his mechanistic weights and measures in connection with it and all its varied forms—still he desires, grieves, so intensely wishes to be what he cannot be (or can he?). Actually, he would like to be related to it, as child to parent, birdling to mother, ward to guardian, a legitimate and desired offspring, not a lone, desperate, unrelated particle, meaningless in energy, in time, in space, in mind or being, if such there be. Wherefore the voices of the poets and dreamers of all ages, the elder and later prophets and saints of the bibles and the religious of the world call to him as living voices utterly lovely poetic realities: *God is a spirit. You shall worship him in spirit and in truth. In my Father's House are many mansions. This day shalt Thou be with me in Paradise. Come unto me all ye who are weary and heavy laden and I shall give you rest. Oh, come, all ye faithful.*

And yet in fact, irrevocably threading through all that he is and does, uniting him chemically and physically with all immensity, building him as machines are built, that is, evolutionally constructing his body, his so-called mind, his chemical and physical reactions and moods, the electrons, protons, atoms, molecules, and their many elements that also make the endless suns and systems of endless space are laws, laws, laws, weights, measures, form and number, order, light, heat, cold, time, space, energy, all contributing and permitting, in a given and especial environment. And under fixed rules as to *order* as set over against or opposed to *disorder,* harmony as opposed to disharmony, strength as opposed to weakness, knowledge as opposed to ignorance, limitation as opposed to the illimitable, rest as opposed to labor— *behold the endless process* that is producing him hourly, momentarily, himself and, likewise illimitably, *all things.* But always via weights and measures. And yet he grieves that he may not be one such forever and ever.

THEODORE DREISER

The Mechanism Called Man

Man and the Universe

STRANGELY ENOUGH, MAN OCCUPIES IN SUCH A MIGHTY UNIVERSE a place of singular interest and honor. For he is the biological, *the living being* on the surface of a tiny planet capable of exploring the tremendous universe around him. [*Or*]

‡ ‡ ‡

It is to be remembered that the various organs through which the nature-environment-heredity operates are ages old. Before man had a mental operation worthy of the name, he was still being mechanistically and so unconsciously directed in all these physiological ways. It was the "unconscious" that developed the machinery of the "conscious." [*Or*]

‡ ‡ ‡

Man is really a formula or synthesis of forces walking, talking, eating. As such, and like any fairly well made machine, he endures for a few decades. In America, about forty-five years. But the forces constructing him are, in so far as science can determine, eternal. Although in him they are not constant. That is, the formula called man, by man, is being slowly altered. Once it was protoplasm. Before that, something much less complicated. Later, it was a fish or a bird, an ape. Now it is what we see, but still changing. How much the mechanism is to be altered in the future no one can guess. Your share as a so-called individual in this vast process is, roughly, forty-five years. [*Or*]

T.D.

‡ ‡ ‡

That he is a mechanism can be shown in endless ways. One very convincing one is this. His sufferings—the storms of stimuli, good and evil, pleasant and unpleasant, torturing or comforting, good or ill—are invariably written upon his face and body. Look and see. A ditch digger has a ditch digger's body. A tortured soul—male or female—one whom life has disappointed,

defeated, anguished, has written on his or her face that which he or she
has endured. The machine is marked, worn. Its face, body, hands, feet show
these marks. Look at the eyes, the lines about them, the mouth, the cheeks.
It is often a worn and broken machine—worn by registered stimuli, those
and nothing more. . . . [Or]

‡ ‡ ‡

Animals undoubtedly feel, think, love, hate, "will," and even "reason",
though (as man sees it) in a more imperfect manner than men. Insects—unquestionably the spider, ant, and bee—the same. Do they do all these out of
themselves or are they motivated as man is motivated? If he has mind, so
have they. If they are mechanisms, so is he. Either nature is mental or there
is no mind anywhere—only an inexplicable mechanical process. [Or]

T.D.

‡ ‡ ‡

Cattle in herds, deer, sheep, cows, when subjected to driving rain or icy
winds or intense cold will pack—turning rump to the unfavorable direction
of the wind. They will also "boil" or ferment after the fashion of any liquid
subject to heat. That is, the coldest—those at the periphery or point of cold—will
automatically force themselves toward the source of the greatest warmth,
the center of the pack, whereas the warmest, because of warmth, contend
less and so give way until they in their turn are at the periphery when
once more the cold will drive them toward the center.

But the atoms of a kettle of water will do exactly the same. Apply heat
at the base and the heated atoms will move toward the colder surface while
the colder atoms will sink to the region of heat. Warm air will rise and
cold air will fall to the source of warmth. Likewise a crowd of men. . .
[Or, unfinished]

‡ ‡ ‡

Man, operated by nature, not by himself, is not and probably never will
be an entirely logical being. He is and will be influenced in his decisions
not only by his *nature-manufactured* desire for food, drink, and sexual satisfaction, but by nature-evoked emotions in regard to peace, beauty, change,
the origin of life, and so on. These—because of the pleasure they provide
or promise, the help they offer, bring about his desire to survive. They also
help bring about his willingness to struggle and even die (!) for, often, so
little as the illusory promise of them. But death is not often, in fact rarely,
contemplated by him as an immediate certainty, rarely even an imminent
one. Mostly he imagines that he will not die yet, and mostly death comes
as a surprise. He really is not going to die even in dying! So he often goes
about fantastic matters which have nothing to do with peace, security, comfort,
his future subsistence—in fact many irrational things. And for him, often
enough, those irrationalities are the ones that provide him his greatest pleasures,
cause him to feel that life is so wondrously worth-while. But they have little
to do directly with economics, valuable forms of government, order, security,

etc., which in other moments he will tell himself are the most important of all.

Think of the millions who have thrown their lives away in futile contests—to recover the tomb of Christ; to drive out the "unbeliever" [or believers] in Allah or Mohammed; to make the world "safe for democracy;" or to make a self-centered egotist an Emperor or a King! [*Or*]

‡   ‡   ‡

Man is driven constantly, without surcease. Even in sleep. For even in sleep, memories (registrations) of experience are stirred and synthesized as dreams. That mechanism, the brain, appears even in sleep to be set in motion by stored registrations, possibly the latest and most vivid of the preceding hours, and even in sleep proceeds to harmonize at least some of them with some older ones. Thus synthesized, they appear as dreams of personalities, conversations, places, periods, and in play or book fashion, just as they are synthesized by the brain in waking life.

But in its so-called waking hours, how much more forceful and constant the life drive! Clocks tick, whistles blow, bells ring, traffic sounds, and the noise of the world's compelled motions are in the ears, upon the eyes, upon the nerves of all! Yet all are mechanistic! All are compulsions—not *calls* to action. And because of them—the subsistence or satisfaction they provide, the ills they provoke or aid in avoiding, custom, as well as fear of criticism, distaste for dirt, fear of disease, even law, acting as compulsions—the body has to be cleaned and arrayed and, more (the chemically motivated organs of the body, its food consuming, heat generating necessities compel live action) supplied with food as well as constant registration, as well as reflection of stimuli.

The stomach—that furnace of the body—must be filled. Its chemical activities must be set in motion by food, for without the combustion and energy distribution of food, the cells soon set up their particular food demands, and the nerves carry these to the brain mechanism, only there to be met in many instances, in so far as man is concerned, by past registrations of steak, chops, potatoes, coffee, or whatever the food of the country and the time may be, together with, on occasion, enticing as well as soothing registrations of restaurants, waiters, music, which in their turn and via their fusion in the brain effect the activity or labor of the body, such labor, be its nature what it will, that will provide what the body needs. And this may be pocket picking, acting, clerking, shoveling snow, or organizing or operating, or defending corporations or companies, or caring for the halt, the lame, and the blind.

But whatever the nature of this labor or activity may chance to be, it in its turn is most frequently encouraged or enforced by the gravitational pulls of the pleasure processes, which, of course, are among the most powerful of all. And in their turn again, these can be and frequently are added to and re-enforced not only by social custom and taboos which sanction and encourage them, but as often by the wheedling or complaining of dependents who desire to share happier states than are theirs, and such as others can afford them. But all of these things in combination and as compulsions to life are to be repeated and repeated and repeated, unless interfered with and checked or ended by forces extraneous or antipathetic to some or all of their factors.

But always in life, as you can see for yourself, action in man is initiated and compelled by forces outside of him—the very forces that have constructed and now motivate him. And also ended by them. In fact, through his actions, his words, his complaints, even his purely mechanistic resistances and cries (all expressions of strain in and upon the organism by exterior stimuli), you may know that this is so. "It is beyond me." "It will kill me." "It hurts!" "We will have to wait and see how it turns out." "We will have to wait and see what so and so does." "I am compelled to." "Great pressure is being put upon me." "There is nothing that I can do about it." "Man proposes; God disposes." These and endless other vocal or sound reactions to pressure, strain, unsynthesizable compulsions show man, if not all animals and vegetables, flora and fauna, to be what he is—an energy-driven machine, responding to and in turn causing responses and compulsions in others, just as a driven wheel will drive other wheels.

But not by any discreet and dominating and directing will within the organism. But rather by the union and compelled cooperation of many internalized as well as external forces and their mechanisms, all plainly generated by some general force which we call nature or the universe or matter-energy or God. But whatever it may be, inducing and compelling endless varieties of action, in all parts or phases of its universality, yet not by reason of any delegated wills or souls, but by the entire mechanism constructed by and adjusted through itself and its compulsion or Will.

T.D.

‡ ‡ ‡

If you wish to see how utterly dependent the man-machine is upon exterior stimuli for consciousness of anything, consider a man on a desert island, as for instance, Defoe painted him in *Robinson Crusoe*, or a man held in solitary confinement in a cell, as Dumas painted him in the *Count of Monte Cristo*, or as you may note, the ordinary city-dweller, transferred from the closeness and activity and confusion of the city to the comparative, if not always today, complete solitude of the mountains or of the desert. Any one who has had experience of any of those will report, as many have already, not so much the depressing effect of the alteration of the character of the exterior stimuli as the reducing of it so that the reactions are not only changed but limited.

In consequence, in the case of the individual in cell solitude, you have prison pallor (due to lack of sunlight), reduction of appetite, and more, where books or papers as well as conversation are excluded, the increasing deleterious effect of nervous inertia, so much that in the instance of individuals who

have lived a full or exciting life in the world are likely to go mad and
not only that, but die.

All prison records of whatsoever land or period testify to this. Do but
exclude the ordinary social or mental stimuli of the world, and, though food
and rest be sufficient to maintain life, the physical and nervous machinery
rusts and decays. And even though, before death or insanity, you should
choose to restore the inhibited one to the world and his former supply of
normal stimuli, the recovery of his normal physical or nervous reactions and
operations is by no means guaranteed. The human mechanism, even though
no more than temporarily insulated against normal contacts or stimuli, can
be greatly and even fatally altered.

Man is a machine, depending on exterior stimuli for his operation, or internal
functioning.

T.D.

‡ ‡ ‡

Decrease the calcium in the blood by half. Convulsions, coma, then death
follow. Double the calcium. The blood thickens so that it can scarcely flow.
Heaviness, indifference, unconsciousness mark successive stages of the mind's
dethroning. Death at the end. Reduce the amount of sugar in the blood
ever so little. There is a feeling of gone-ness. In the worst cases, there is
a blotting out of the mind. Then death. Increase the sugar a few milligrams
to the cubic centimeter and fear seizes the mind, fear of the slightest domestic
disturbance. Double images form. Speech is thick. There are illusions. Again
the blood may be slightly alkaline. Acidify slightly. Coma follows. Meaning
that what we call mind, registration and synthesis of stimuli, ceases. Make
the blood a little more alkaline. Convulsions foretell the end. Or, again,
take water from the blood. We collapse. Add water. We suffer from headaches,
nausea, dizziness. In short, change anything about the blood—the amount
of oxygen, carbon dioxide, a score of chemicals—and always the mind ceases
to function as it has been functioning.

That it can be restored to customary function is obvious. Even an insane
person can [sometimes] be restored to sanity by the "sugar explosion" process.
But the point is that man is a mechanism. Also a formula or compound.
He is a machine like an engine, for if you feed the boiler of an engine
too little coal, its steam will fall below that pressure which, released into
the steam box or cylinder, causes it to run. Overheat the water in the boiler,
and the boiler itself, unless the heat pressure is reduced or the steam allowed
to escape, will explode. The engine will die. But remember that the engine
did not build itself, and man did not build himself. And if man, stimulated
by the forces of nature, can build and regulate his engine, it is possible
that nature, or such phases of it as have devised or evolved man, can not
only build and regulate man, at least for so long as (1) he serves some purpose
(not now exactly clear to man, if clear to nature) or (2) so long as the conditions
which permit these natural forces to devise and maintain man here do not

change so much that his appearance, even if devisable, is not possible. Nature builds nothing save for a little while. Great suns last for a time only. Island universes longer, but not forever. An earth like ours cosmically achieves but a brief moment.

Consider, too, that in any organism old things have to be torn down and replaced. Whether for the better is a question. Old men go and younger men overtake their place. Old nations do the same. And old, so-called, races of men or animals or insects or types or species of vegetation are but cloud forms of matter that pass or change with each breath of temperature or social storm. That is, natural or environmental changes overtake them. The child changes to a man and then to a senile dessicated figure of what was a man. All organs the same. Doctrines and theories arrive, are amplified, and decay. Who can say that man will endure, or even such possible changes of him as may come and change. For all may go—even the last change which might have nothing in common with all the long changes of types or forms that had preceded it.

Consider in connection with this the endless time throughout all nature which has been and still is devoted to destroying and rebuilding, destroying and rebuilding. It has been called a Will to Live. But on the part of what? *What is?* And to what end? Change? But is change an unmitigated pleasure or pain? Who among men is to say? Man cannot speak for the universe. Yet as for himself, he appears to fear the changes that hurt or that end him. And to enjoy those that pleasure or entertain him. But what other end than pleasure? Any? Was the universe made for pleasure? Or man? And how many ask why? Or are capacitated even to "think" why? [Or]

‡   ‡   ‡

It is in accordance with the course of our development—the laws of our evolution—that external compulsions are gradually internalized. A special mechanical function (some call it mind, intellect, soul, others a central nervous system in association with an unconscious or sympathetic system or, as Freud puts it, man's superego) is, even as the organism or mechanism is being built, set up within it. Its purpose is plain. It is to correspond with and receive, assort, and refer to particular reaction or experience and habit store rooms or centers the various external stimuli or compulsions which originally brought it into being and still maintain it. Also, if the life forces mean anything, it is these external stimuli which are its sense of being as an organism or machine. In proof of which I offer that every child and man as well as every animal and vegetable—in short, all flora and fauna—present to us greatly varied but nonetheless convincing models of this synthesis of external and internal forces—the second internalized by the first, and in no other way.

Consider first the worm Gastrula, which before it was a worm was nothing more than an oval of associated cells surrounding a water filled center, but the oval gradually cupped by exterior forces, and then this cup form, drawn together at the top, formed a stomach. Presto, a worm! Next consider Jacques Loeb's fishes, which when the formula or synthesis called seawater in which they come into being as structures is changed in any way—that is, when some of its salt or lime or gold or other element is removed—the fish nucleus, aided as it was by these previously undisturbed forces, can no longer build the fish as it was previously built. For each element removed or weakened, some structural phase of the fish disappears—a fin, a part of the tail, an eye, some of its characteristic markings, etc. And only until the removed element is restored is the fish restored. This is equally true of the frog, the chicken and other animals, including man.

For remove some element from either the water or food he uses, as for instance, iodine from water, or lime, or sodium, or one or another of the phosphates, and, in the first instance, that of iodine, you have goitre, and in the second, soft bones or rickets. In fact, all the natural external elements now known as vitamins being in any way disturbed, weakened, or with-held, you have a modified organism, that is, one afflicted with beri-beri, scurvy, weak eyes, obesity, idiocy, pernicious anaemia, and what not. But restore these in their proper amount and the animal is restored physically and functionally.

And as for social (also constantly referred to as "mental" or "intellectual" qualities inherent in the "ego," "mind," or "soul") qualities, you have precisely the same functional picture. The biologic (psychologic and physiologic) studies presented to the world under the title *Behaviorism* constitute an enormous volume of proof which can only be touched on here. Nonetheless, and to clarify this quickly, your attention is called to the fact that the life patterns which the infant, the child, and the man see or respond to—those exterior stimuli called life, beating or playing upon the internalized sensory mechanisms evolved or constructed by life and inherited at birth—are those which shape not only many of his physical characteristics but most decidedly his reactions or responses and so general appearance and conduct.

Consider the men, women, and children of the various differentiated tribes or races of the world, their especial tribal or racial appearances and reactions or conduct, and in turn the subjection of these to climate and the geologic formations called scenery or land, plus the action patterns necessitated by the food resources by which they manage to exist. Is not a Hindu to be told from an American? A German from a Mexican or an Eskimo, a Negro from an Englishman, Chinaman, Frenchman, or Arab, or vice-versa? But why? No American will be born of Chinese parents. No Negro of the white or yellow or red races of the world. Nor will their physical or facial formations be the same, nor their color, nor their actions and reactions based on their so-called thoughts, but really based on the above listed varieties of variations of exterior stimuli playing on their internalized responses to the same.

The Negro of an African tribe will conform in his physical and action patterns to those of his tribe. In sum, his body will resemble their bodies, his actions, their actions—in short, his so-called thought, their so-called thought. Ditto, the Indian, the Frenchman, the German, Italian, Jew, Eskimo. And no single action, formation, response, or method of procedure of any member of any tribe or race or even most nations in any direction will vary greatly from that of his tribe or nation. And when it does, its causes can be traced. Also, it brings about his tribal, national, or racial ostracism, as you well know. He is not longer counted one of them. He is an alien or variation.

Also, it is for these same reasons—from such particular environmental conditions, all of them purely mechanistic—that we respond to and absorb and accept whatever social, religious, moral, ethical, or antisocial, antireligious, antimoral compulsions which are holding in the race, tribe, nation, climate, or social and economic condition in which we find ourselves.

Every child in any land presents us the model of this mechanistic response— Pavlov's conditioned reflexes. It is only by these same that it becomes the differentiated type that it is. In other words, for racial, or national, or social, or religious, or educational, or the so-called cultural or moral purposes or characteristics of any people or tribe, these conditioned environmental or exterior stimuli are absolutely necessary. And without them is neither differentiated race or nation or state of mind. And by mind, I mean action pattern. In short, according to what the individual is environmentally subjected to, those social patterns about him and the impact of which he cannot sensorially escape—so is he.

Do you wish a Thuggi? Sexually unite a Thug male and female and subject the child of the same to the Thuggi environment or action pattern, those tribe compulsions which characterize the Thuggi and which are exterior to him and circumambient. Do you wish an Englishman? Go to England and unite an English man and woman and subject their child to the English environment. For a Chinaman, retain a Chinese child in the Chinese atmosphere—otherwise no Chinaman. Ditto the Negro, Frenchman, Eskimo. Remove them—even at 10, 12, 15 years of age—and by degrees you will see them change, physically and mentally, economically, socially, or ideologically, as we say. In sum, we—all of us, animal, bird, fish, worm, man—are sensory machines, operated from without, and function according to the mechanistic patterns of the world or region or tribe or climate in which we move, by which, for good or ill, we are conditioned, motivated, compelled, and restrained.

Man and Superman

No one can tell what an opportunity or situation will bring out of him—what lacks, what wealth. Even now I have the strangest feeling of life within lives (George Fox, John Woolman). What is a state or nation or a race but a traditional life that is above each individual life and that, via heredity as well as the impact of the living examples of this hereditary influence on the other living examples about them, is being constantly transferred by one generation to another generation, although each generation on its arrival knows nothing of its coming character or nature until it arrives here and, by the super-life that brings it into being, is fitted into as well as drilled into what it is to be.

Thus, the character of any state or theory of social procedure is transferred to coming generations in that state just like the improved character of each new model of an automobile is transferred to each new generation of cars—that is, each year's new model of a car: thus, an English state or theory of social procedure is transferred to new English generations; so too is it with each new generation of Germans, Negros, Jews, French, Esquimaux. Their states or social or racial procedures are imposed upon them before and after birth. In sum, their all is transferred on and on, to generations that consider themselves as individual, separate, different—new.

Actually above, though not wholly apart from man, since he is an organism through which this larger thing, in part at least, functions, may be something else, something like we are to the cells and atoms that compose us—our bodies as over and above theirs—although each one of them has its seemingly separate being just as each one of us has ours in this larger thing that regulates us, and of which we are a part. Yet its body, like our bodies in relation to these cells of ours, may function only in part through us, in part through elements and forces above us and it—its life or feelings in part separate from ours, in part identical with ours, like the emotions we say we have as though we were one solid thing yet which sweep each cell and molecule of us separately.

To illustrate this duality as it relates to the possible being above us, we may, as human beings, think of our love for each other—our passion racially or nationally or tribally speaking for cohesion at one time or moment and again our passion for separateness, "individuality," which concerns us as human beings, not our cells, and yet in which our cells may or may not share or take part. We do not even know enough about them chemically and physically to know that. But such being the case, the super-creature, whatever its nature, in which we may be as cells, may have also moods and passions, fears and braveries in which we as its composing units may or may not share. How otherwise can we explain our meaningless, senseless wars and quarrels which bring death to millions of us at a time yet to which we are fomented by forces above us—not by ourselves ever. Again, there is our awe of space and time and beauty, which we do not create but which is evoked in us by our environment—in short, our external world which our individual cells certainly cannot share as we share these things, for our cells cannot ride in cars, look through telescopes, see with our eyes, and yet most certainly the effects of these on us as "individuals" they do share as a part of us. Our bodily "thrills" from "head to toe" prove that.

So this other thing, this super-creature, may in part be something separate from us, something with its own life, and at the same time be united with us and so, in part, achieve through our lives a part of what it is, does, desires, and enjoys. On the other hand, it may be that it, in part, does, desires, and enjoys things of which we know nothing or ever can. That super-human part of it may be a thing which few of us sense and which none of us can understand, but which at times we still feel via our mass rages, hates, awes, etc., as well as our strange sense of unity each with the other, plus our unity in this other greater thing which reacts to still much greater things than we can ever sense. [Or]

THEODORE DREISER

Physical and Chemical Character of Man's Actions

AT BIRTH, THE INDIVIDUAL IS ENTIRELY AN *HEREDITARY* PRO-
duct. Immediately after birth, this hereditary product is either in harmony
or in conflict with his environment. Images and example and after these,
moral teachings, social procedure, and tabu, the struggles for possession, and
the rejections for want of this or that come to be registered by the mind
mechanism, to be compiled, synthesized, and contrasted with what results
few if any—not even the creature doing the registering—can predict or,
when they occur, understand.

‡ ‡ ‡

Consider the unconscious. Most of the physical processes of our body,
almost its entire functioning, are unconscious from birth to death, and yet
we consider ourselves alive. For instance, we were *alive* when the forces
of the unconscious were constructing us in our mother's womb. But where
is the knowledge of it? And where was it at that time? Yet decidedly we
were alive—just as the tree is alive in the nut, the plant in the seed.

‡ ‡ ‡

To judge of the chemical and physical reactions which control both the
movements of men and animals, indeed all flora and fauna, one need only
study the reactions of crowds among men, herds among animals, flocks among
birds, schools among fishes, drifts among insects, and the pollen of weeds
and flowers. In the first place, why do animals move in herds, birds in flocks,
fish in schools. Reasons are offered: protection offered by the mass, ease
of defense, ease of reproduction, ease of leadership, which is of a chemical
and physical character. Thought as an independent, non-evoluted force motivating and protecting the individual or the herd, school, crowd is non-existent.
The instantaneousness of crowd, herd, school, and flock action is proof positive.
Not thought, but some chemical reaction to stimuli in each and all, and
whether protective or fatal, useful or useless is what governs the actions,
flights, defenses, quietudes of each and all.

T.D.

‡ ‡ ‡

The central nervous system only serves as a protoplasmic connection between the skin and the various organs and glands of the body. Exterior nerve ends are no more than photo-electric cells upon which play exterior stimuli corresponding in force or significance to the light ray which is the motivating force of the electric eye. Light and not even light entirely but its interruption, constitutes the "intelligence" of the electric eye and all that it regulates. Exterior stimuli activated by light constitute the seeming intelligence of the activities of the human being and all other material entities on earth.

In this connection, it is interesting to note that any least disturbance of chemical or organic function within the human body at once interrupts or blurs the clarity and force of all exterior stimuli, thereby destroying what is known as consciousness or the "human mind."

But mind, in that sense, is a synthetic phenomenon, easily and visibly duplicated in billions of organisms called men. In other words, you are therefore not dealing with a single individual mind anywhere which has specific and distinct mental characteristics but rather billions upon billions of evolved or constructed stimuli-receiving organisms, which, in contact with the same stimuli such as that assailing the central nervous system of the men organism here on earth, respond in a like manner and result in what is known as the human or race "consciousness" or "mind." But is a radio "conscious," or is it made seemingly conscious by exterior stimuli? But at best it is a mass *"mind"* or mass consciousness—nowhere individual. And man, as such a stimuli-receiving and reacting organism, is in no case notably different to any similar stimuli-registering organism or implement, be it worm, insect, fish, bird, reptile, radio receiver, or electrically operated telephone, telegraph, wireless, or other electrically operated system or machine.

Heredity

Heredity is nothing more than a record of protoplasm's (or the physical forces working through it) struggle to adjust itself to as well as maintain itself in various and varying ways and forms, amidst various and varying types of environment. No environment, no protoplasm, for it could only be a variant of forces operating as environment. By the same token, no protoplasm and no environment, no heredity since heredity is protoplasm's own record of its struggle with environment—its successes and failures at adjustment. Its failures have ceased, or will. Its successes endure, endure so long as they, by changing, can adjust themselves to an ever changing environment.

T.D.

‡ ‡ ‡

The map of heredity prepared by Calvin Bridges on which he traced the genes and chromosomes of fruit flies (drosophila) and the characteristics of and in the fly that these determined seems clearly enough to indicate a process of structural procedure on the part of something—*nature* (for want of a better word)—in so far as the fly and its actions here on earth are concerned. But that does not prove that the *original something* out of which the processes that produced the fly derive is mechanistic or was mechanistically derived; but, only that the process or processes that this original something uses *are*, or appear to be, mechanical. Hence, this permits one to ask, is *the something* out of which such mechanical processes arise and in which they function, but which itself is not mechanical, mind? If not, what is it?

THEODORE DREISER.

‡ ‡ ‡

All medicine is an illustration of the chemical and physical reactions of man to exterior stimuli and, what is more, clearly illustrates the identity of his current character and action. Not only with the past influences of evolution and heredity and the environing influences of the universe itself but more specifically with the infinitesimal atoms and molecules of the elements which are basic in all foods and chemicals or drugs and medicines which man consumes, sick or well, and of which he is organically composed.

Indeed, in recent days rapidly increasing knowledge, such as that concerning the chemical, and so atomic, constitution of vitamins and hormones or gland extracts, to say nothing of all the food he consumes, shows man to be nothing more than a synthesis of chemicals and their elements, which in their turn are not only common to the universe at large, but more: as, basically, arrangements of atoms and molecules form not only the building units of which man is composed, but the building or mechanism he is, and which same, in turn, respond, mechanistically as they must to those other forms of energy— light, heat, electricity by which all organic forms on earth are operated. So wholly is this true that current medical science is prepared to write, and has written (Dr. Minot? of the Harvard Medical School): "Nutrition intimately concerns the welfare of man, and his place in future history will depend in no small part on what he decides to eat." And he might have added "To drink," and more "To respond to physically and chemically."

T.D.

‡ ‡ ‡

But assuming that I speak of my mother as a machine—and now sensorially reach to her as such—how does that alter her value to me as my mother? How detract from the loveliness of her character and the sensory charm of her for me—a charm which made a nervous and troubled youth not only bearable but even beautiful? A mechanism she surely was, as are you and myself. But confronting the fact merely heightens the wonder and the beauty of this purely mechanistic whole called life. Think of it—a machine so artfully compounded and constructed chemically and mechanically as to behold with mechanical eyes a purely mechanical world and universe and react to both in such a way as to register sensations of beauty, grandeur, enthusiasm, gayety, or if for the nonce the scene be stormy, dark, fearsome, fateful, then with sorrow, gloom, anger, despair, even the desire for cessation, and death.

Consider a machine that can cry, laugh, brood, rejoice, that mechanically responds to friendship with true friendship, that can hug a baby to its breast and live for its welfare, that can work (as can a father) in the thought and for the reason of another's welfare—a son's, daughter's, wife's—getting joy out of the partial repetition of its life in another. Think of the wolf-machine, that for reason of the welfare of its cubs and the mother of the same, goes forth to kill—and with danger to its own life in the labor. That before satisfying its own hunger will drag the prey to its lair and wait while first the cubs and then their mother eat, repressing until then its own need. And you, a machine chemically, and me.

T.D.

‡   ‡   ‡

A normal-eyed man driving an automobile at forty miles an hour against an on-coming car with glaring headlights will travel thirty or forty feet before he accustoms himself to the conditions. If he is night-blind—that is, unable to make the usual visual adjustment between light and darkness in the above number of feet—then he may go 150 feet or even 200 before he does so. A person so afflicted finds it hard to see anything at all in passing directly from a bright spot into a dark motion picture theater. Even normal eyes adjust themselves to darkness only after some minutes. But good day-vision is no proof that the eye is able to adjust itself to sudden change.

But the trouble is due to chemical and physical maladjustment which can be remedied chemically or surgically. Thus, 96 percent of those who are afflicted with kidney stones, 95 per cent of those who have liver trouble, 35 per cent of those with diseased sinuses are night-blind. Also women in advanced pregnancy and others who suffer from colds, grip, and other infectious diseases.

Since 1925 it has been known that adjustment of vision in the dark depends on *visual purple*, a substance in the retina on which images are formed. Visual purple is ordinarily rich in Vitamin A. Night-blindness is connected with a deficiency of Vitamin A. Rats deprived of Vitamin A develop night-blindness and recover after the vitamin is administered. It has also been found that in cirrhosis of the liver there are deviations from normal sight. The liver is a store house for Vitamin A, and if it develops cirrhosis, it fails to supply the vitamin necessary for normal vision. Huge doses of a concentrated form of Vitamin A restore the eye-sight of eye *cones* which register bright light as well as the dark registering *rods*, those where the visual purple registers—magnias are much improved. It is a chemical and physical process as you see and has nothing to do with "mind," unless mind is a series of self-adjusting chemical and physical processes.

Mechanism
Called Mind

SO-CALLED MINDS ARE ALIVE. THEY ARE INSTANT AND MOVING. They are dynamic and not static. And while it is probable that mental processes are mechanical, the data to prove this are not yet accumulated. [*Or*]

‡ ‡ ‡

Our "minds," as all know, are subject to fears, acknowledged or hidden; jealousies, the same; prejudices; worries; plus other emotions and depressions, most frequently traceable (not always so). But if you want to see how mechanistic all this is, ask yourself, "Fears of what? Worries about what? Emotions in regard to what? Depressions due to what?" And see how related all are to definite material or physical or social facts, states or conditions; even the so-called unexplainable depressions, like the crying of the one year old babies in Paris, which was found to be due to magnetic or electrical storms in the circumambient atmosphere. [*Or*]

‡ ‡ ‡

The affectionate admiration or awe or wonder or pleasurable response excited in children or young people is not brought about by any decree or instruction on the part of anyone. You are not taught as a child to admire the sun or the moon, or the stars or the rippling water, or leaves or the grass. You do—automatically, instinctively. Warmth and a bright day comfort you, but no previous instruction on the part of any one that brings that about. The mystical and chemical structure of your body, with the production of which you had nothing to do, brings that about. [*Or*]

‡ ‡ ‡

From the early counting machine, Mr. [Raymond F.] Yates (*Machines Over Men*, Frederic A. Stokes, 1939) turns quickly to show us the amazing exploits of Dr. Bush's Differential Analyzer. You place a problem (an intricate problem, not just a sum) in one of the machines, do a little something with the gears and levers, and out comes the answer: "From a maze of 13,000 separate parts rolling along on 1000 ball bearings comes the quick, accurate answer to engineering mathematics that would require days of pencil biting. Next to automatic telephony this is," says Mr. Yates, "the crowning achievement of the machine mind."

But back of the machine is the man's mind that made it, and back of the man's mind was the evolutionary processes that evolved it. And back of the evolutionary processes were matter-energy-space-time. And back of matter-energy-space-time—? [Or]

‡   ‡   ‡

All ethnology, geology, zoology, biology, botany, history, painting, sculpture, architecture, letters, exploration, and what not demonstrate that mind is nothing more than a sensory registration of endlessly repeated and most often related stimuli from matter-energy sources and structures compelled, directed, and controlled by whatever evokes, directs, and controls matter-energy.

The so-called associative processes of man's or an animal's so-called independent mind, which selects, arranges, and seemingly compares inpouring related stimuli with differing groups of related stimuli is not willed or otherwise independently effected by man, but is due to existing chemical as well as physical attractions and repulsions, or affinities and oppositions, which characterize the various elements—their varying electrons, atoms, molecules, which automatically arrange themselves according to not only such environing influences as hold at the time but their past experiences and tensile as well as (possibly) emotional pull affinities. [Or]

‡   ‡   ‡

When the dynamic interplay of our chemisms, the sensational and emotional reactions of their various chemical and physical constituents sometimes conflict in such a way as to produce what we call mental disturbances—that turmoil that indicates a non-adjustment of parts to a whole or, as we say, strife between self-preservation and a hostile environment—that maladjustment may sometimes as easily be relieved by philosophy, psychology, law, and sometimes force or social example as by medicine or surgery, but never by anything which is not a chemical and/or physical outgrowth of the total mechanistic process called Life, as all of the above are. Evolution shows that.

More, in the animal world, without medicine or doctors, written law or human language or schools or hospitals, progeny are conceived and born, fed, trained, and brought to maturity; and the genus or species, whatever it is, is kept in good working order.

That buildings are not built, philosophies not written, music not composed, songs sung is no proof that life on that animal level is not as worth-while as it is with man, as interesting, intense, dramatic. As a matter of fact, taking "civilized" man as we see him today in factories, slums, "on the dole" [welfare] perhaps as many as five percent equipped with the means or freedom, to say nothing of the courage and energy, reactive capacity, to enjoy their lives, one earnestly wonders as to their superiority to the denizens of the jungle.

These last may flee at the first sound or turn and prepare to attack, but at least they are prepared to do one or the other, and they have fewer social obligations or restraints. Also boredom or despair, the speculative ennui as of the botched and the restrained is mostly spared them in their intense and intent existence. They have something to do and vital fires driving them. Those that do live, live vividly, which is more than can be said for the most of men. [*Or*]

T.D.

‡ ‡ ‡

All that we call living things—the protoplasmic family, like the natural energies, light, heat, and derivatives of the same, out of which they spring—are insistent, urgent, all too frequently savage in their seeming lust to grow, be, express themselves. They either crowd and struggle like weeds, trees, fish, herds, flocks or they bite, sting, rip, and devour like the creatures of the jungles or like men in war. Be it no more than a bacillus, so greatly feared by man, an alga, a harebell, a gnat, or a flea—to say nothing of these others, the bacilli and viruses—they present the fact of struggle of existence and, more, self expression—to grow, flutter leaves as a tree, walk, run, spin as a spider, play, dance, gleam under the sun—the while they defend their seeming *right* so to do.

But what is that right? No more than the variety of mood or urge of the forces—primarily for earthlings, sunlight, moonlight, starlight, and derived forces, which are but expressions of them—the hundred or more acknowledged elements under the will or urge or whip of light and heat which at the same time are forming them so to do and be.

Yet mystery of mysteries, the totality of these struggling, flashing, urgent forms, once that strange state dreamed of as consciousness, but which is no more than mechanistic or environmental direction and control (the hypnotic illusion that apparently springs from any synthesis of forces) is achieved, then in this dream of consciousness (reaction) and because of the unescapable stimuli of that which compels and permits them life, they dream the question *why*? Why am I? How is it that I have come to be? Why is my stay here limited? Why this struggle? These pains? Why am *I* hungry? Why should *I* be? Why is it urgent to live longer? Sense more? Know more? And all the while unconscious of the obvious fact that the seeming *I* thus asking is only one of endless *I*'s of the same pattern and reactions, and each thinking of itself as a separate and distinct thing and as individually asking why! But all merely compelled or permitted to ask this, in order perhaps, to establish this illusion of individuality and reality in a created thing—a thing which at best can be but a mode of escape for a totality of force that is perhaps weary and even intensely so of its oneness, and finding escape—and dare we dream rest—in this multiplicity of form and content and acted harmony and disharmony as against a boring oneness which only an endless period of multiplicities vivified by struggle and contest could make acceptable—like sleep after a toil-full day. [Or]

T.D.

‡ ‡ ‡

Sensation—that which manifests itself via matter and energy and space and time, but even so and only as (1) sight (color, form, distance, nearness, large or small size, quantity, few or many, ugly or beautiful); (2) hearing (all degrees and qualities of sound, sweet, harsh, distant, near, sad, gay, cheerful, ugly); (3) feeling (degrees of heat, cold, heavy and light, weariness and strength); (4) taste (sweet, sour, pleasant, or unpleasant); (5) odor (pleasant or unpleasant)—cannot operate or *be*, as humans understand those words, save in the presence of and via the first four—matter, energy, space, time.

Nor in the absence of the five or six senses—seeing, hearing, tasting, smelling, feeling, which last would have to include telepathy as one of its powers or sensations. But again, *mind* as we know that word—meaning thought, expression, sensation, hearing, feeling, etc.—could not *be* in the absence of sensation, which in its turn could not be without matter, energy, space, time.

But neither could matter, energy, space, time *be* for man nor any evolved creature of the protoplasmic chain without sensation, which proves that mind, or thought, is either the totality of all of these substances and sensations operating as a one and permitted by sensation (an inherent quality of all matter-energy in space-time) or that there is a super force which evokes and provides all of these things to the end that *"mind"* may function as it does.

If so, mind, plus the entire structure that supports it, is the direct and willed expression of this super power; or it is the unwilled and if so a mechanistic and yet mindless product which is still like and has the appearance to man of mind. [Or]

T.D.

‡ ‡ ‡

With respect to the origin of impressions of sensation, physicists, chemists, biologists, psychiatrists, and psychologists are not quite in accord. They seem, from the earliest of them to the latest, not to be able to decide whether they are direct sensory reactions to external stimuli affected by distinct exterior objects, or are, or that plus some chemico-physical powers of the evolved physical body, its central nervous system and cerebral cortex, plus, if we listen seriously to Sir Oliver Lodge, as well we may, a possible (and this relatively apart from our biologic or protoplasmic body with its chemico-physical controls) still more subtle etheric body of deathless duration which coordinates our physical body and at the same time may be or provide the "mental intelligence" which provides the interpretation—be that interpretation advantageous, disadvantageous, or indifferent. If there were such a thing, which I personally doubt, it might aid in explaining *instinct, telepathy, premonition,* and other now seemingly mystical but unquestionably factual powers.

Seemingly, of course, the immediate antecedents of sensations are changes in the nervous system—those which take place between the nerve ends and the brain and with which our "feelings" are said to have no sort of resemblance. Nevertheless, those changes effected in the nerve plasm by exterior objects after they stimulate the nerve ends may well be of a no more serious or discoloring or misinterpreting or disruptive character than are any of the antecedent physical changes which sometimes precede or lie between the outside object and its effect on the exterior nerve ends. To wit: Take the transportation of an idea originating in the brain of a Professor in India and written and mailed or telegraphed at Madras. Its destination is the brain of a professor of economics of the University of Havana. Now consider that it begins as an idea or fact in the brain in India and ends as such in a brain in Cuba. If it should read "Your brother Henry Smith died here today" and the message lodges in the brain of Professor John Smith in Cuba, it will be exactly the same thought or fact or impulse as was originated in the Professor in Madras, but by him transferred first by telegraph to Calcutta, then by cable to London or San Francisco, then by cable from London to Cuba, or from San Francisco to Miami and thence by cable to Cuba. In either case it would pass from brain to pencil or pen, from pen to ink, from ink to paper, from paper plus messenger to a telegraph office, from telegraph office, messenger, paper in combination to telegraph operator, his brain, then his fingers, then his typewriter, then to a telegraph instrument, thence to a receiving operator at Calcutta, his brain, his fingers, thence to a cable instrument, thence as electrical waves along a cable under the ocean, then as clicks of a telegraph key to a paper in London or San Francisco, various dots and dashes, then as dots and dashes to the ear and eyes of still another telegraph or cable operator, thence to still another cable operator, his ears, eyes, brain, fingers, and as symbols to another cable instrument, its flashes and wave impulses, and finally under water again or over land to a cable office in New York or Miami, and in either case and lastly, under water, as wave lengths or dots and dashes, to Havana, and so via the same process as troubled the professor in India to the brain of the professor in Cuba and always at every point it has been energy. But what different kinds of energy. What odd forms it has taken, and yet registering as it began as certain electrical or chemical reactions in gray matter, about which we know nothing. And though it has taken many forms, still the final form is not unlike the first form. Maybe it has come in another language and had to be translated, but the import remains the same—unmodified by all the different things the energy has been and the places it has been. Hence, a long chain of intermediate changes may not change the nature of a primary impulse. It may register as it left, the same thing at both ends. [*Or*]

‡   ‡   ‡

The fact that it does not register as correctly as a photoplate or a photoelectric cell or that there is not and has not been a sufficiently correct synthesizing of the environment of life on the part of billions of evolved organisms throughout time but only a slow and unbroken improvement of registration of data is at least considerable evidence that man and all animals, insects as well as vegetation, are slowly but surely evolved or constructed organisms intended, after a limited fashion, to function or react harmoniously in their given environments. The processes by which the universal mind or machine, operating mechanistically, has achieved this have by now been definitely outlined by *the science* or mechanistically correct reaction of such special organisms or men known by and to man as scientists, "thinkers," inventors, philosophers—yet all of them, in themselves, nothing more than advanced mechanistic achievements of the universal mind or machine. For it is a demonstrable fact that in all space-time, as these are "known" or registered in and by man, there has been no such thing as an *individual* anywhere—only types. And today it is clear that only variations of type in number, not singly as individuals, is what *is*, whether intended or not; and, more, that this result is mechanistically unescapable and so inevitable under universal law as man senses—or rather is constructed and so compelled to sense or respond to such law, is not now and never has been any such thing as individual knowledge or thinking; any individual or creative power or free will, nor any individual possession, or responsibility. Nothing anywhere has there seemingly ever been save foreordained reaction and registration, which same has automatically given rise to the spectacle known [as] Life.

Furthermore, this *life*, in consequence of its electro-chemical and physical controls or limitations, is no more intelligent or interesting or beautiful or good or evil or continuous or durable than as the creative force—whose electro-physical and electro-chemical procedure is traceable in and through all forms and motions—permits of. That these same appear or register themselves on, *in and through* these evoked and evolved mechanisms or creatures as *good* and *evil*, *desirable* or *undesirable* is obviously not due to the mechanisms or creatures, but to the force or forces evoking and evolving them at the same time that they operate in and through them. As Christ said: "By their fruits ye shall know them."

And it is now easily demonstrable that by the fruits or reactions or compelled procedures of all things, mechanistically and correctly registered as these are by all other things, and not otherwise, that they are known to themselves and to all others. Hence deductively—that is by purely compelled and unescapable reactions—it is to be seen that so it is that they are or must be known or related to the creative or mechanistic forces, whether these be one in many or many in one. "I and my Father are one." Wherefore the endless variety of life which is nonetheless registered by its endlessly varied mechanisms as variety in unity is by the same token perforce compelled to register that greater *unity*—also itself as an unescapable expression of it. [*Or*]

‡ ‡ ‡

Synthesis—so important in science, invention, all historical, sociological, economic, and other writing, and in mathematics—is obviously a great and indispensable factor in all evolutionary processes. The joining and harmonizing of one thing with another is the prime characteristic of the material universe as a whole, as well as of each least disparate atom of the same.

Could the object—assuming an object admissible in what is assumed to be an eternal process—be other than that of achieving cooperation; and, more, in almost endless additional minor aspects of itself, co-operation. [*Or*]

T.D.

‡ ‡ ‡

The assumption is that the human mind is a device which is capable of registering and synthesizing usefully and pleasantly—or, on occasion, destructively and unpleasantly to others, however pleasantly or at least painlessly enough to itself—the many inpouring stimuli from without, whether that "without" be considered nature, or the universe as a whole, or our particular solar system, or the earth and its innumerable organisms and structures, which we call life, society, the state, and its people, or whatever. Often enough, as we know, this particular device called the human mind, as well as some animal minds and even some vegetable organisms—the sensitive plant, for one—appears to be capable of what we describe as "grieving" (a dog whining and pining because of the absence of its master) or even "breaking," as for instance when one goes "insane" or "runs amok"—"jangling", as the poet worded it, "like bells out of tune."

But if there were such a thing as a pure essence—wise and undisturbed, inhabiting, as was once thought, some chamber or sanctuary of the brain, a "spirit" or representative and as such an essential part of some detached, eternal, creative, and controlling essence—could this be? Could eternal, prescient spirit, presiding over the actions and "thoughts" (for me, read "reactions") of an organism the actions and reactions of which it has in its charge, and via the rumored if not fabled "still, small voice" guides and directs; could it be so shaken or disturbed or puzzled—its mechanical vehicle being thus unduly set upon and shaken by inpouring exterior stimuli, as to lose its power to either advise or direct—and at last, because of some rupture of a portion or all of the machine it controls, begin to grieve and commit suicide or by degrees grow old, inadequate to the job, and eventually die? But if so, then this central spirit or soul would most certainly be like the engineer in the cab of an engine, the driver of a car in his car, the aviator in charge of his aeroplane, the captain in charge of his ship, and, as such, responsible for all the doings of the body—its upkeep, repair, conduct, or labors, where or where not it might go, do, etc. All told, a large order for a spirit or soul and requiring not only great wisdom but complete authority—otherwise, no responsibility, and if not, no great reason for grief, despair, rage, hate of or pleasure in or because of these seemingly non-self-directed seizures of the body or mind called love, hunger, thirst, sorrow, joy, etc.

For this, as you see, is a spirit or soul, the particular and separate agent or extension of an all-wise and powerful creator, set in its particular place to guide one of the Creator's many mechanisms or creatures—any, really, from atom to bacteria, to man, to planet, to sun, to solar system, to island universe, etc.

I repeat, a large order. [*Or*]

Mind

You must know from your own personal experience that what you can do for yourself physically, with your hands, with your physical strength, with your body as a whole, is little—almost nothing. We have the phrase—so indicative of the limitations of the physical body—"a hewer of wood and a drawer of water."

But turn from mere physical effort to the mind mechanism and see what power and speed the forces which use it as a means of registration possess and what they, through it and other mechanisms more or less like it, accomplish.

Not the mind mechanism itself, but the forces which use it as a machine, these are the things which "inform," inspire, cause to move, to do, to imitate, in short, cause to be all, not a part of, but all of that which we see and think we are.

Think only of millions upon millions and billions upon billions of machines like ourselves that, throughout the thousands and millions of years, have operated with power or wisdom, however little or however much, and so caused all and each to grow, to do, to be, more and more or better and better machines.

Think only of the "thinker" or mind-controlled machine who or which first began to respond to the need of such a thing as a wheel! Or that other who began thinking out the lever! Or the mind-directed machine that was first moved by it to think of fire as a servant; or flint as a source of fire. Or that other who was first impelled by it to throw a stone or a spear; or to think of the bow as something which would throw the spear or arrow! Or of the machine that was impelled to think of the pit as a trap! Or the dam as a detainer and container or trap for water, so needed in dry places! Or of the shell or horn or the gourd as a drinking vessel!

And then think of all the millions who were later helped by these earlier impulses or inspired, not knowing that they were mere reflections of exterior creative forces.

So called Mind is not freed power. It is free power acting through a mechanism called mind, and it is not limited by its mechanisms of whatsoever kind. It evolves them and then merely uses them as a coign of vantage or implement through and by which it proceeds to spy out or direct the creation of the thousands and hundreds of thousands of things which have served to multiply its strength and powers, not those of the machines or bodies called man except as they are useful to it as tools.

And by the magic which it is (this vast creative energy)—unquestionable
and indescribable—it spells, or seems to, both good or ill to its mechanisms,
for it presses ever forward, throwing away its old tools or laying them aside
with supreme indifference, the while it makes new and better ones. The
new among its machines help it to destroy the old, even though these were
of itself. Man has will! Man thinks! Man dreams of a better world! What
nonsense—Nature is the force, the will, the dream.

But as to how this comes about?

Proceeding where? Operating how? Controlling how? Or controlled?

We speak of God or Nature or the Creative Force. And at times we fear,
and respect, and obey, and even, where we are not always motivated, as
most often we are, *love*. For we are of It and Its tools. Its mirror. And
Narcissus-like, It appears to survey and admire and enjoy Itself through Its
self-made mirrors. [*Or*]

                                                                      T.D.

Is Cosmic Law Mind?

To man, the mechanism evolved as he is to register in limited ways both
matter and energy (matter-energy), form is material, for it can only be (to
man) an indication or expression of the presence of matter or energy or
both when described as matter-energy. So, too, is color a phase of matter
and energy (matter-energy) and not to be known apart from them by man.
So, too, is sound, which is plainly a phase of matter-energy and, as such,
distributed by nature.

So, too, is odor, feeling, or sensation. So, too, are cold and heat—or at
any rate, these are attributes—conditions of matter-energy. So, too, are all
the endless variations of the same. On the other hand, all the limiting and
so seemingly directing phases of matter-energy and its attributes—the laws
or compulsions of physics and chemistry—appear to indicate something that
is not so much matter or energy (matter-energy) as a super something, immaterial
and imponderable, that throughout all man-recorded time evolves as well
as operates and directs all matter-energy to such ends as man can register
or see. And with them and through them, man himself and before him—but
not before them, these laws, I mean—all his pre-evolutionary ancestry from
protoplasm to himself.

But what are these laws? Mind? Or the manifestations of some gigantic
mind behind, or mayhap, within—that is integrally a part of (or let us say,
the *same as*) matter-energy and that with which it may be inescapably joined,
space, as well as time or duration. It might be. If so, man, the matter-energy,
space-time evolved mechanism, might be registering in some small part some
of the visible material as well as sensorially all but immaterial aspects of
his creator—its very body and essence or spirit or mind; its laws, motions,
form, color, weight, measure, heat, cold, tone, mood, beauty, and duration—
in other words, the Universe—man's God.

How other?

For it now looks (or men and all creatures react as though it so looks) that these several attributes or phases of matter-energy—form, color, sound, odor, motion, feeling, hearing, tasting, plus the seemingly fixed phases of cosmic law, those that govern in physics and chemistry—may be, if not actually are, nature's only means of expression. Certainly they appear to man not to change and are now by man at least calculated mathematically backward as well as forward for billions of years. More important is this, that, the above being the case, man and all creatures and all phases of universal life are but the conveyed and environmentally arranged consequences or doings of matter-energy, plus its attributes, as described above (space-time, form, color, sound, feeling), plus again its laws, chemical and physical, the same either willed of itself or willed upon it by something beyond it again but capable of bringing it into being and causing it to function as it does. But to say this is merely to remove the creative process or force, as man knows it, backward by one.

However that may be, it follows that all man's so called "thoughts," "acts," "moods," sensations, desires, angers, lusts, hates, loves, and what not and those of all sentient creatures are but the matter-energy, space-time conveyed and assembled (automobile parts-wise) forces and attributes as above described. And either he, as well as the process that produces him, is mechanistic—incapable of any other form of procedure, as it, if not he, is mental and capable of alterations and changes which may alter and change him or not, as it chooses. In either case, the evolutionary process on earth, to say nothing of those visible to man in galactic space, appears to be due to matter-energy impulses, structurally ordered or induced and resulting in what man sees or thinks he sees—the cosmos, its matter and space-time, the sun and its planets, the earth and its evolutionary processes and creatures, and, at long last, his own ordered and manufactured self.

As to all this, he may well exclaim "the Lord (the Cosmic process) liveth and reigneth, blessed be the name of the Lord!" or "I am in my Father and my Father is in me." For assuredly not only all good and evil, but sorrow and joy, love and hate, strength and weakness, ignorance and wisdom, even faith and non-faith, or rather the chemical and physical laws and reactions which produce the same and his so-called mind—or electro-chemical sensibilities, which is better and truer—have the same source, and they are not of man's creating or ordering or concluding.

T.D.

The Emotions

YOU CANNOT CREATE AN EMOTION. YOU CANNOT EVEN DESCRIBE it. You can say you *"feel blue,"* or *depressed, sad,* or *angry,* or *gay,* or *doubtful,* or this way, or that. But you must remember that those words are only words or sounds evolved in you by past as well as present experiences of the things they attempt to express—like Ouch! for instance which signifies *pain* or a *pinch,* a *burn,* a *jab* with a pin. But the pain itself—is that adequately expressed by "ouch," or "oh," or "ho," or "God?" Isn't it better expressed by a tortured face, a bent and strained or swaying body, a fearsome, agonized look in the eyes, an upward tossing of the arms, a groan (which is no word), a sigh, or by sudden unconsciousness as in fainting? And yet can you say that even those things adequately express what is being felt by the one who is experiencing them?

They do not. And language does not, *ever,* properly or effectively present a deep emotion. It is its own and almost only expression, causing action or inaction as the case may be, but needing no word to be *understood* by the person experiencing it. It is always so real and different from material things like houses, dogs, cars, forms of any kind that it has to be described or pictured for others—that is, symbols found for it, word, or sound, or color symbols—but not for the person enjoying or suffering it. It may be that it is the very essence of energy or matter-energy, which expresses itself through all forms, colors, sounds, or movements in general. [*Or*]

T.D.

‡ ‡ ‡

Consider love—how it changes the individual who has never experienced it, causes him or her to halve his or her life with another. The world is not the same as before, not until love dies and not even then. One is haunted by the memory and the need of love.

‡ ‡ ‡

A genuine emotion will find expression for itself if it be no more than by a gesture or gestures, an eye-glow, a flood of tears, a tremor of the lip or of the body, or by physical weakness, faintness, a wordless moan or groan. And would not these long observed and reached to optically or by wave emanations from one perturbed body or another evoke expressions in other ways—by crude drawings, then labor-saving hieroglyphs, then letters, then words compounded of letters, then books, pictures, statues . . .

‡ ‡ ‡

A defeated love passion can endure as a reducing, defeatist stimuli for years, producing various mental states and disturbances as well as actions—for instance, travels, walks, the seeking of companionship with others; also murder, suicide; sounds (Shakespeare, Michaelangelo, Milton, Rosetti); moods, plays, poems (Hardy, Balzac, George Moore, myself, Shelley, Keats); paintings (Rosetti); and death via pining and day-dreaming. [Or]

T.D.

‡ ‡ ‡

One riddle to the sex-driven, sex-magnetized or lured young male is the female. For him she is a vision of delight compounded of agreeable form, motion, color, gesture, laughter, song. In her, the shape of his head, hat, nose, or the curl or flatness of his hair may well register as not only beauty but perfection. Be these values, registrations, magnetic pulls, what you will, they are in each, mechanistic, chemical, and physical forces reacting the one upon the other. That the synthesis of these forces, uniting and culminating in the sex act, bring about a third physical or mechanistic mystery called a child solves nothing, tells nothing of the varieties or the nature of the energies at work in this way. For they remain mysteries to the man, the woman, and the child even when the mechanistic process involved becomes relatively clear or plain, as to some, they have. For the processes themselves tell nothing of their ultimate nature or intent, whether or not, for instance, they are blind or will compulsions. Their results, the man, the woman, or the child, come and go mysteries to themselves and to all others, as we all know. And as for anything yet revealed, they may be mysteries, even unconscious processes, to the [very] forces which bring them into being. [Or]

T.D.

‡ ‡ ‡

Think of the male and female forms. Each allergically is desirable to the other. But in youth, a member of either sex, responding to the sex compulsion or love desire toward his or her opposite of the complementary sex, is not at first thinking (that is reacting) to any particular individual of the opposite sex. On the contrary, and generally throughout life, unless a given individual of one sex has already impressed him or herself on a member of the opposite sex, there is no definite concept in the mind of either of the exact boy or girl, man or woman, that is desired. On the contrary, and almost invariably, there exists a wholly depersonalized concept or type or symbol, usually highly idealized beyond any possible realization of what the desired opposite should be. Thus it is that, along with the unescapable changes that accompany the life cycle of any creature that so often brings conviction, complete or partial, of one by the other, the same being almost invariably mutual. The trouble therefore lies in the primary absence of any physical or mental counterpart of that which was pictured or preconceived by either.

But that picturing was not personally willed by either. It was and remained a chemical and physical phantasm or illusion, alluring both to a certain relationship with one who could seldom hope to personalize it. As for the subsequent "tested" or experienced "reality" which each feels that at long last he or she may know, that also, either in the worst or best aspects, remains a plexus of half truths or total misconceptions, often enough a complete myth, which death alone dissolves.

T.D.

‡ ‡ ‡

We look upon butterflies as the most harmless, as well as the most conspicuous and attractive, of all those very numerous creatures known as insects. But, actually, according to Austin H. Clark of the U. S. National Museum, many male butterflies are exceedingly jealous and aggressive, flying viciously at each other and at insects or even small birds that cross their path or invade their particular domains. Usually this belligerent spirit is aroused by intrusion of any insects into these assumed domains of theirs—a strip of roadside, a section of wooded road, or the vicinity of a particular branch of a tree or bush—that a certain male regards as his rightful property!

Some kinds have special dueling grounds to which they retire when in a fighting mood. But many others fight whenever they chance to meet. . . . Such a fight, of course, is possibly a game of bluff, since butterflies are so delicate that they would quickly incapacitate themselves if they met, or could meet, in rough physical combat. Yet they do so bluff each other. Plainly courage and combativeness are not things invented by the butterfly. Millions of them from generation to generation have the same courage as that possessed by men and other animals and creatures to struggle and obtain and possess. Man calls it an evolved and inherited instinct. More likely it is a carefully compounded chemical reaction to another compounded state built in to the female. Also, it evolves a carefully constructed form, plus, very likely, a color scheme which, via the eye and through it chemically, [acts] to cause the opposite organism as a whole to respond with an intense impulse to unite and so produce the species. This is by no means the "mind" of either male or female butterfly operating independently to achieve this, but instead the creative force of the universe as a whole. [*Or*]

Concerning Love

Love is always such an exacting thing—so greedy and savage, like a great hunger. And every lover wants all or nothing, even though giving all is not in his or her mind by any means. Gimme, gimme, gimme. And without true consideration of the extreme necessity of balance and proportion. Or even of diplomacy. A lover will throw back nine-tenths of a loaf rather than see one-tenth of it withheld. Each sees his or her side of the picture so clearly and emotionally, the other's with the eye of a prosecuting attorney, a sentencing judge, and a miser. "I will have all or nothing"—although I doubt if the he or the she ever lived who had *all*. Or if so, had it justly. And if one had *all*—all of the time—how soon would it pall and bore? Marriage that results in children furnishes no illustration of the "all or nothing" argument, for the "all" of a home and children involves the introduction of a compensating element in the form of [the] children—children that interest and attract and bind in ways not open to the unmarried lovers or married lovers who have no children. Besides, where there have been previous marriages, previous social and property arrangements, previous experiences where with to compare and contrast the latest love with earlier ones—oh, me!—how difficult it is for the latest one on either side to seem, let alone be, all that the first and ideal lover should be. And the more so because the desirability in most cases on each side has been impaired. And moreover, it is so hard for any lover to think, let alone dwell on such a possibility, or condition, or fact. It is heart cramping and, at times, heart breaking—even fatal—and all the more so because of our need of an ideal love is by then greater, because more informed as to what a lovely love should be—also, more cynical about the possibility of fulfillment.

And yet, in spite of such things, we still on occasions do meet the one we want and most eagerly wish we might have. But not as young lovers. Life by then has both instructed and abused the seeker and dreamer of love—horribly done so. Each—before the 2nd or 3rd or 4th ideal appears— thinks of possible compromises on his or her part. "I must not expect this or that, anymore—demand this or that—be as fierce as naturally I am or would be." And so—And so—And so. . . . Each struggles on, wishes. Dreams of an ideal mind or temperament; a generous and forgiving heart—one that will not demand *all*, or at least, if demanding, not expecting more than under certain special conditions is humanly possible. However, that such dreams come to anything ultimately is not for me to say. One observes and studies and wishes, and yet, at long last finds one-self alone, empty-handed, wishing. Any one of us at long last may be one such. For myself, I wish not—dream not.

Love and Hate

You say, when you feel that attraction or love compulsion, that you are in love, and, more, that you are loving someone. If that one, he or she, responds to the same degree to you, then he or she is in love also—is obsessed or attracted or compelled to join with you. But assuming, for instance, that one is more or less intensely drawn than the other, then there are two separate kinds of love—two different quantities, or degrees, or qualities—which difference is certain to affect unfavorably or favorably one or both, but to what degree is not anything which can be easily measured or determined other than by subsequent results.

Certain it is that if intense attraction is experienced by one and not the other, then, according to the different temperaments of each (nothing that can in the human organism be accurately determined), any degree of emotional reaction, including emotional transmutation, can follow. That is, love—or desire or passion—can turn to intense hate, even destructive or murderous hate, or to self-pity to the degree that sorrow for oneself—unendurable sorrow or longing—can end in sorrow eliminating self-destruction. Or, in the defeated one, it can turn and, in addition, reduce itself or disguise itself to itself as dislike or contempt, by which transmutation its original quality as a bliss-yielding desire can be caused in itself to vanish.

Or it can be intensified as to cause the victim of the attraction to desire to obliterate the indifference of the other by death, or to prevent a future love evocation of passion in it by another, or to tear it from a rival attachment or desire for another, or, stranger still, to evoke a hope of satisfaction, even a conviction of the same, which is to follow the blending in death with the opposing human substance (its form, color, temperament, emotional or mental reactions, voice). Lastly, there is the amazing mental or emotional evocation or aberration (if such it be) or conviction, following upon the frustration of such love bliss on the part of two, by persons or conditions or belief of whatsoever nature—public or private—whether these same be due to poverty or disease on the part of one or both or public or private customs or beliefs, religious or moral or theoretical, to which their mutual desires seemingly run contrary at the time, that peace or bliss or both are to be found for both, in simultaneous death.

These same passions or compulsions, when frustrated by conditions or persons or laws or taboos can drag out an unchanging vitality through years to death. Or, by degrees, by unescapable contact with the environing energies of life, they can be worn to thin threads or filaments of their original force and finally obliterated either by time or individual deterioration or death. [*Or*]

T.D.

‡   ‡   ‡

An emotion, whether one of fear or anticipation of a delayed bliss or a necessary benefit or a threatened danger as in war or social strife of any kind between individuals, can and does cause ulcers, indigestion, paralysis, nervous collapse, insanity. But an emotion is described as—even though it be not one—an idea. What it really is, is a stimulus emanating or, for detectable and definable reasons, imagined to be emanating from a friendly or an inimical source. The same then can be and probably is a ray of energy. But what is the nature of energy? Is it traveling hate or love, sorrow or joy—any one of these things traveling at the speed of thought or light? If so, is the space surrounding human beings, as well as that surrounding birds, animals, insects, thick with such traveling energy? And can this energy be described as traveling mind? If so, it must be thick with emotions, for mind is nothing if not degrees of emotion, very weak or very strong.

We know certain space paths are thick with *radioed* emotions in the form of words and sounds, songs, messages of pleasure, fear, love, hate, etc. Also that telegraph and telephone wires and cables are such space paths. Light that comes from the sun, and when not too strong or weak, may be looked upon by human beings, animals, trees, etc., as radioed pleasure—from the sun. But is that mental? Is moonlight mental? If not, why are their *effects* on men and some animals looked upon as mental, since they are said to evoke emotions? We speak of telepathy, psychic emanations, waves malicious and favorable, animal or elemental magnetism. Are these things real? If so, is the universe or all space a field of traveling mind? If so is it not mental? [*Or*]

THEODORE DREISER

Sex Love

Pleasure, like pain or the energy that brings about the same, can be condensed; or, at least, there appear to be forms of energy stimulants which, in inconceivably minute quantities and not unlike the vitamin and auxin crystals in the plant and animal world, succeed in stepping up various forms of pleasure as well as of pain. On the pain side, the venoms or acids of bees, wasps, spiders, scorpions, various kinds of insects, and snakes, as well as the thorns and the pollen of various plants to which many people are allergic (poison oak, poison ivy, poison dogwood, poison sumac) can, with the exceedingly micro-scopic quantities of the same, which they can communicate in various ways, bring about the greatest nervous agony, not only to human beings but to animals, birds, other reptiles, and insects. On the other hand, a quite minute crystal of heroin injected into a pain-racked body will dispel the same and replace it with an allover body sensation of comfort and even pleasure—even an ethereal ease. So, again, with morphine, opium, hasheesh, and other drugs.

On the pleasure side, the sex sensations produced in the male by a beautiful female form or face, or, in the female by those of the male, are really chemo-physical extensions and sublimations of the past racial experiences of the two sexes, the one with the other in reproductive process, so violently enforced by nature on both. Chemically and electrically this energy or sex sensation in both sexes has been condensed by nature into the two complementary sex organs, where the resulting sensation produced in both the male and the female organ by the brief contact, the one with the other, and this, more chemo-electrical than structural and over a very limited area in both instances, is of such an intense character as to suggest either an enormous concentration of electrical (nervous) force in some vitamin or hormone, or, of an arranged physical contact, in those areas of the two organs, of the very atoms of the molecules on the dendrites or nerve ends functioning there—and so of the production there by friction of a form of energy that seems electrical and yet may not be—energy that either directly communicates to the nerve ends of both organs the sensation of delight or ecstasy, or a force that communicated to a particular brain center in each person is converted or transformed into the sensation described as ecstatic. Yet obviously this sensation is not a thought in itself. It is, on the contrary, a nature-evoked force which gives rise in the mechanism called mind to a sensation which requires physical and chemical expression in the form of actions and sounds which, via the slow evolution of the race, has given rise to words as well as pictures and sounds or music, if you choose, intended to describe or indicate to others the nature of this sensation. And hence all those phases of the arts and/or letters which deal with this phenomenon.

Passed on from generation to generation of men and women, this sensation has directly and indirectly given rise to much lesser expressions or tinctures of its primary fire or delight as poetry, painting, sculpture, decoration, the dance, music, song, the drama, the novel, and their shadows, the moving pictures. Also love, dreams, courtship, marriage, children, life. Yet basically it appears as a form of locally concentrated energy more electrical than otherwise and traveling with the speed of energy yet evoked in two differently constructed bodies by not only the registration of form by the eye, but by the inherited hormones of those bodies which are invariably excited when the structures and chemicals and so temperaments of given males and females are sufficiently accurately balanced to permit such excitation.

However, this fever of energy or sensation resulting from the contact of the two sex organs is not thought but sensation, and it is only after the fact of sensation that so-called "thought" is evoked—thought of it as delightful, desirable, the evocation of it as beautiful, good, what not, indeed the whole evolutionary process by or through which it has appeared as good. But is the sensation electrical? And is electricity sensitive and so mental?

‡ ‡ ‡

Love is an invisible, imponderable, attractive force. It is the antonym of hate, repulsion. In chemistry it is called atomic affinity and is the basis or activating force of every chemical action; therefore, the very foundation of existence. For if the Creative Force, as we know it, is basically matter-energy—atoms, ions, or electricity and therefore God—the Creative Force is electrons, ions, protons, atoms, etc. harmonized and working together.

In chemistry, these *phases* of matter-energy are called or are described as having atomic affinity and are therefore the base or activating force of every chemical action and therefore the foundation of existence. Thus, because hydrogen loves oxygen, we have water and so on up the scale through the most complicated chemical reactions and the power of reason, love; attraction is the activating principle.

Gravitation is the attraction or love of matter in mass; magnetism and electricity are manifestation of the primary force. In biology, it is the attraction of the opposite sex, the common or garden variety of which, and very often by some, is considered to be contaminated by passion, yet God or the Creative Force is, as you see, love and/or passion. [*Or*]

Sorrow and Joy

Sorrow is for a night but joy cometh in the morning.

Joy must be innate in energy itself. It cannot be elsewhere. The response of man, animal, bird, flower, tree to sunlight, dawn, the new day—not only with song as in the case of the birds or squeaks and grunts or other sounds of satisfaction, as in the case of many animals (monkeys, zebras, deer, sheep)—demonstrates that. One need only consider human childhood before there is reason or "conscious" registration of stimuli (thought). The three months old baby gurgling and wiggling and smiling. The two weeks old puppy wiggling its tail, running, playing, expressing delight. The kitten, the frisking foal or calf.

In fact, joy is essentially implied if not actually contained in all the natural forms from spheres to grains, from tree to flower and root to twig, from amoeba to man; and form, as all know, is either a willed or a compelled expression of matter-energy in space-time, without the presence and unity of which they could not be. Look out of your window; look at the overarching sky, note a leaf, a waving branch, a running or still animal. Feel the moving winds—its movement, *form* in motion. Listen to music—rhythmically arranged energy—and note that pleasure. Joy—frequently exquisite joy—is an unescapable accompaniment of their sensory registration by yourself, a registration which you are constructed to register and without which you could not only *not* know joy or its contrast, sorrow, but life itself. For life is an unescapable and unbroken experience of these from birth to death. [*Or*]

Outline for Chapter on Emotions

Feelings, emotions, are to each one of us the most important things in our lives. On our emotions depend our relations to everything outside of us and, ultimately, our happiness or unhappiness. Fear, envy, hatred, love, affection, desire, depression, sadness, terror, sorrow, self-confidence, elation, peace—all these and more, and in combinations of unfathomable complexity, are the realities of our life, more real to us than either the interior fundamental instincts of self-preservation and sex or the exterior objects toward which our emotions are directed. Thus we can see that each lives in a little world of his own, having in common with others only the basic urges of the body and an exterior world which satisfies or frustrates them. But, modifying that, it is obvious that all of us do not have the basic urges of life in the same proportion, or the same exterior world, or the same interior equipment with regard to sensory ability or learning or memory or intensities of reaction. And there is not a single moment of our life when we can cease to know the reality of emotion. *Not a single perception of any kind is made un-accompanied by some sort of feeling.* Why should this be so? Emotion is the great variable between the fundamental necessities of existence. The outside world is something which does not supply these necessities without action on the part of the individual. Nor once satisfied do the necessities permanently cease to exist. Nor does the outside world lend itself to manipulation always in the same way, nor is it always the same. It is constantly changing too. Emotion is the great equality sign between the individual and his surroundings. Thus, emotions are a necessity for action and, because of our ability to remember and associate, also effects. Emotions are the "how" of life, *the* means of living, *the voice of those internal urges in constant conversation with what is outside of us, praising it when it satisfies our need, complaining when it does not, fearing it when it threatens.* Without association and memory, our emotions would be very simple. But the evolutive force acting for the individual and the race depends on that. And *it is this very quality of emotions that enables them to be creative as well as destructive.* And it is also this very quality which enables us to define emotions at all, as we do, by the actions which they precipitate. For instance, a man will kill himself. Why? This seems to be the very antithesis of self-preservation. But it is intrinsically not so. What has happened is that he has associated within himself certain things so closely with self-preservation that he cannot separate them. The details of his associations do not matter to him. What matters is his feeling, perhaps despair, sickness, or disgust. The struggle for new associations with his fundamental urge is too much for him. He cannot cut out what has seemed too much for him. When he kills himself, he is really preserving himself—or so at least his emotions reason. It is a lesson learned too well. All emotions of great intensity are learned too well. But when they create, they make all the pleasure and beauty of life. And when they destroy, all the pain and ugliness. With intensity comes a frozenness, a fragility, a sensitivity, a localization of environment where they can thrive. A person who is envious is never intensely envious until the emotion is directed at some particular thing or things. The same can be said of the man committing suicide: his emotion is localized, fragile, and sensitive. Love the same. Frustration the same. Self-confidence the same. This should be obvious since we can almost measure emotion by the acts it perpetrates, the feelings associated with the acts of our lives. That is not to say that emotions are ever single or undivided. They seem to evoke each other. It is as if the drives of our being said to their slaves: you must sustain us, how you do it is not our concern; we cannot make any allowances for the fact that you are of different strengths or that one has more experience than the other; fight it out between you as to which will be dominant; satisfy us, and that is what we ask. And they are all there, with what they have learned and their different strengths. And they come and go, as the outside environment changes and the basic urges ceaselessly push them. And the reality of our life is being pushed away from the painful set and pulled toward the pleasurable one.

But, intangible as our emotions seem—for after all, in perception, we only understand acts, deeds, sounds, colors, and so on and only associate our feelings with those of others through similarity of perceptions—they are at base the evocations of chemicals, fluids, gases, substances, elements, in different combinations. If this were not so then nothing that we ate or drank, no medicine or surgery, no fresh air, no injections or whatever could change our state of mind, our mood, or emotion. Look for example what two or three drinks can do toward changing a person's attitude toward life. Or what a drug like opium can do. Or cantharides. Or an injection of insulin. Or an operation on the thyroid gland. Or the removal of the sex cells. Or a tuberculosis cure. And recently some scientist has discovered that it is manganese that is responsible for the emotion of mother-love. It seems that no matter how pervasive whatever elements are that are responsible for our emotions, they can be called into action, checked, influenced by two methods, and, what is more, that these two methods are constantly working together—one method is the obviously physical and chemical one, as in drugs and surgery. And the other is through perception. *Over perception we have no control at all.* Experiences balance perceptions, often neutralize them. But over the chemical and physical one we have. Think what possibilities this last method suggests. Not only curative, but eunuchizing. The thought of such a thing makes one reflect at once how much one loves one's emotions—even when they are frightful. They seem to justify life. *To get all the destructive ones banished, even suicidal and hateful ones, would leave us with the sense that self-preservation, living, and so on was purely a commonplace thing. We would never have a sense of triumph, any exaltation which follows on the triumph of one emotion over the other.* There could be no super-men in the Nietzschean sense, for all would immediately be able to adjust themselves to whatever situation. A feeling of despair and frustration, instead of evoking great acts in the great man, could be quelled by an operation. If we lose the possibility of suicide, we lose also the possibility of sublimation, which in the main has been responsible for most great achievements. We would lose at the same time the cathartic and exalting pleasure of great art. *If a man who had been drugged against sorrow were to witness a performance of Hamlet, his reaction would be the same as that of a eunuch in a whore-house.*

The So-called
Progress of Mind

The Mechanism Called Man—His Future

Isn't it entirely possible that we, the man species, will develop senses just as recently we have developed capacities which we did not previously possess. If man is a result of purely mechanistic processes, what is to stop their extension through him and so his development?

‡ ‡ ‡

Necessity is the mother of progress. In connection with all thinking, it should be noted that it arises mainly from stimuli or pressure from the outside. Sometimes, as a secondary compulsion from stimuli or compulsion originating from within the body—as heart pain, indigestion, compulsion to evacuate, urinate, in sum, internal pain or irritation of any kind. But since the body has been evolved by nature, *all* creative stimulus is originally from the outside.

Necessity is the mother of invention. It is a compulsion. [*Or*]

‡ ‡ ‡

In the short time that a man or woman has in which to achieve a working knowledge of life, let alone to solve the mystery of it, they are met first with the necessity of grasping the merest outlines of its forms, procedures, rules as well as avoiding collisions with others, after which comes the necessity of self-maintenance, the driving love or sex madness (compulsion)—the same wholly befogging and betraying to the hereditary instinct, if any, to acquire knowledge, plus the urge to precedence in the matter of place and fame, wealth, applause, and what not.

The conduct enforced by such compulsions, coupled, as all too often it is, with physical defects, social illusions, limitations, and what not, [often results in the fact] that the major part of life has slipped away and old age is at hand before anything even of personal value is achieved. Such protection or advantaging, instincts or reactions as might have aided many have never existed in their particular organisms: so that age after age goes by in which nothing other than a struggle for the meagerest and briefest form of existence has conditioned and destroyed billions upon billions, leaving but a fraction of the total sensitivity of the organism throughout—this time in space-time—for the accretion or accumulation of those favorable or constructive reactions which have permitted or brought about the organized relations which we call society, the state, knowledge, and so forth. And at that, the durability as well as the direction of this so-called progress, insofar as the immensity of the future and the universe is concerned, may well be questioned. [Or]

‡   ‡   ‡

Science is neither a doctrine nor yet a mental solution of the mystery of the Universe. It is a body of verified data seemingly increasingly useful to the sensory and so mental extension of man, and so the forces which are about the business of evolving if not directing him (or themselves). But whether ultimately so remains to be seen. Great and amazingly contrived creatures, long before man, have appeared on this planet. And for immense periods of time, because fairly carefully adapted to their environment, have continued to exist. But changes in their environment having arrived permitting something newer and more closely accommodated types to appear, the older ones, however seemingly grand the concepts of them, have disappeared. Consider Behemoth. Consider the Dinosaur, the Plesiosaur, the three-horned rhinoceros, the sabre-toothed tiger, the giant sloth, and also their fate. How sure is it, for all of his achievements thus far, that man has come to stay? And as for his rumored objectives—eternal life, complete understanding of life, control of life? Well, consider the position of the earth in space or our solar system in space and the cosmos. Then consider what we know of the cosmos and its laws and our subjectivity to the same. And then say if man has any such conscious objectives (I mean man as a whole—not a few thinkers scattered like infinitesimal particles among the endless billions of so-called entities or men), and if so, what possibility of their realization can be logically asserted. And even assuming that at some far off time some remnant of the human race, mentally and physically or psychically developed to achieve such ends, should so achieve them, what in common, if anything, would they have with the race that we know? And what satisfaction, if any, could it afford Sinocanthropus or Pithecanthropus or the Piltdown man or the Neanderthal man, to say nothing of their ancestors—the protozoa, fishes, reptiles, mammals, or their decendants—all of quadrillions, sexillions, octillions, who have intervened between them and us, let alone all of the sidereal numbers of changing men who are likely to intervene between us and the ultimate group who succeed to eternal life and cosmic understanding if not control. Does the thought clarify anything or not? Does it spell absurdity or not? [Or]

‡   ‡   ‡

More and more, man tends to mechanize himself outwardly, that is, in all his relations with his environment, which in great part is his life. Consider first his early, old time mechanical devices—the wheel, windmill, arrow, horse, sail, waterwheel—and then, today his later and latest ones; and how, now, these last appear to almost turn on him and as completely mechanize him in all of his actions and even thoughts, as beforehand his reactions to a mechanical world compelled him to seize upon and use his earliest mechanical aids. The wheel originally might have been a rounded stone that he could roll rather than carry to where he wanted to place it. And the rolling stone might have suggested an imitation of it—a stone with all the sharp corners knocked off. Lastly the wheel of stone and then later of wood. Today the notched wheel, the cam, and the balloon-tired wheel. [*Or*]

T.D.

‡ ‡ ‡

Most of us still think of ourselves as the final triumph of biological evolution; we are convinced we have come to stay as rulers of the earth. I wonder why. A being watching us from another planet might see things very differently. Gigantic reptiles, dinosaurs, ruled the earth for millions of years, but failed to retain their supremacy. Then huge mammals terrible in their weight and strength, but almost brainless, governed for many million years more. Man has ruled only for a fraction of one million years. Why should he suppose that he has come to stay? Rather it seems to me he must still establish his claim to be the permanent governor of the earth. His own acts will decide whether he is fit to rule in perpetuity or not. We must maintain our position by fighting for it.——Jeans

Most likely a decision on the part of the forces expressing themselves through him to alter or abandon the man mechanism for something more effective or more suitable to changing conditions, may dispose of him entirely. Certainly as evolutionary data indicate, the frame and organization of man is still changing, whether for better or worse man himself can not learn. [*Or*]

‡ ‡ ‡

If, as the mechanists hold, man and other life forms are no more than chemical or electro-physical emanations of nature or the cosmos, and as such emanations, strictly or mechanistically limited, it follows that the possibilities of growth, change, development, expressions of seeming consciousness and even consciousness and wisdom—in so far as nature's laws (or natural law) may be said to be conscious and wise—are in and through these same forms or mediums illimitable. That is, there is no telling how much of its supreme wisdom—*if it is Supreme wisdom*—is ultimately by nature to be allocated to these forms—or how little abandoned. Is there any reason to suppose that illimitable nature already expressing itself in illimitable ways should really abandon the same in favor of man—or out of all forms of expression to make him the supreme force, and if so—how greatly would she have to change him? And what relationship to that changed form would our present man-form bear? [*Or*]

‡ ‡ ‡

Man contemplates the race and makes certain deductions. But with the knowledge any one man has so far—or by the contemplation of the so-called accumulated or stored knowledge of the race thus far—can any one thinker be said to have contemplated let alone understood the race and its underlying chemisms and compulsions let alone its environment—earthly or cosmically and the influence of the same on the chemisms which are involved in the formula called man? Obviously not. For there is no thinker who asserts any such equipment or let alone the mentality wherewith to deduct accurate and wholly interpretive data in regard to man and the proper line or path of his progress. On the contrary, assertions and contradictory assertions are made by each and everyone. Let us begin with a man like Einstein. He will begin by asserting that Free Will is a myth, and in the very same breath assert that man should abolish war. But without Free Will—how?

‡   ‡   ‡

The later Darwinians preached the doctrine of human perfectability, a doctrine in which the modern world has believed and still professes to believe. Granting that there is a benign and omnipotent creator of the world, who watches over the fate of man, the believer's sincere conviction must be and is that such a being thinks according to certain fixed laws which we call physical and chemical, and that not only may these laws be discovered, but should one's life be, in so far as possible, aligned with and hence guided by the same, this must certainly lead one to perfection or an approach toward the same. [Or]

Mechanism
Called Memory

THE SUN SHINING ON A DECAYED LOG ALL DAY WILL FREQUENTLY store itself in the dessicated wood, leaving an after-glow visible throughout the greater part of the night. This is a physical process not unakin to the mechanism called memory in man. The glow left by the heat is the log's memory of the sun.

T.D.

‡　‡　‡

Unless a thing is written down or carved in stone or formed in metal it is forgotten. Mountains are remembered because they stick around. Ditto rivers, lakes, plains, jungles. Ditto the sea and the stars and the sun. Remove them completely and all records of them and the death of people with memories will end all so-called memory of them.

T.D.

‡　‡　‡

When the physical evidences of anything are lost—decay, disappear, the knowledge of that thing in the "minds"—that is registrative faculties of men—disappears also. If there is no physical presence or physical registration of past presence in books, tablets, monuments or markings of some kind—there is no "memory" of that thing—and so no knowledge of it anywhere.[Or]

‡　‡　‡

All of us think we remember a great many things that we don't remember at all. Most of our memories of the distant or even immediate past are composite memories. Our minds working sub-consciously take bits of registrations of events that happened days, weeks, or years apart and superimpose or piece them together into what appears to be a whole or complete memory or representation of what we actually saw at a given moment or period but it can be very erroneous as has often been demonstrated by tests in psychological courses.[Or]

T.D.

‡　‡　‡

Consider all the dictionaries, filing cases, address lists, books that set down and make readily attainable to our so-called minds specialized information regarding a thousand or hundred thousand fields of fact, developed recently or in the past by human research: geology, physiology, astronomy, aeronautics, war, seamanship, history, geography, medicine, surgery, painting, architecture, agronomy, engineering, government, finance. And although Webster's unabridged dictionary contains more than 500,000 words and an ordinary desk dictionary 80 to 90 thousand words, the average adult's writing vocabulary consists of approximately 2500 words and the speaking vocabulary of the average adult ranges from 2000 to as low as 500 or less. And man, the individual is assumed to have somewhere in his brain an immense storehouse of facts which automatically spring to his tongue regardless of whether the facts are present in flesh or matter-energy—or some symbol of them stored somewhere—in a dictionary, a filing case, a library, public or private, or in an assistant's mind.[Or]

T.D.

‡ ‡ ‡

The evolution of man—his death full of experience and wisdom (which he himself forgets as he ages) added to the birth of the infant that has to learn all that the aging man forgets is proof positive that nature does not intend memory as anything beyond a temporary life device here—not probably—elsewhere. [Or]

‡ ‡ ‡

A fossil wasp nest, eighty million years old, has been found in a rock formation of Utah, by Dr. J. B. Reeside' and Dr. C. E. Dobbin of the U. S. Geological Survey, and has been presented to the Smithsonian Institute, Washington, D. C. The significance of the discovery is that an insect, so long ago that it seems like an eternity, had already achieved man's two latest steps in alleged progress, totalitarianism and command of the air—also at the same cost, loss of individual freedom. In all the 80,000,000 years since that nest fell into what was then a puddle of mud, the wasp never developed any further. If the stinging insect has any message for man, it is the suggestion that perhaps he too has reached the same evolutionary deadend street and must stop, detour or die.

It appears not to have registered and remembered anything new in 80,000,000 years! [W]

‡ ‡ ‡

Memory should be brief—must be, else there could be no room in any organism for the endlessly accumulating data of each day—to say nothing of that of the months, years, centuries, ages. Think, for instance, of trying to memorize or remember the life and time experience of each particular animal, insect, tree, flower, grass blade, to say nothing of that of each man or woman, tribe, nation, race, or of the life histories which the number is endless. Limitation and so at least partial recognition of each limited life period of each particular type of being (any of the above) has seemingly been arranged for by nature. Death is her method of arranging this; death by contest or conflict, by accident and decay. The time limit for things appears to be adjusted to the nature of the service to be rendered by each particular mechanism—no longer and no shorter and by the same token, the memories of that time limit are quite obviously and necessarily confined to the matters and materials and aids and actions of the particular environment of a given mechanism functioning in a limited portion of a given period. Also, for one thing the limitation by death process automatically evokes in the matter-energy registering mechanism the illusion of the unlimited duration or extension of its memories and via these memories, if enduringly recorded (which they are not) of the endless memory duration of itself. [*Or*]

‡   ‡   ‡

Now intelligence is as much memory as perception; and for it there is always in the transformations it is watching something familiar which carries it back to what it has already witnessed, and forwards, expectantly, to something it may be going to witness. Hence to Intelligence there is never mere repetition, just as there is never utter novelty. And its frequent doubts are always conditioned by its habitual beliefs. That explains why Intelligence is so chock-full of prejudices, as all those are aware who have ever asked it to accept miracles and ghosts on their testimony or on someone else's authority. Such people exclaim at the sceptic's blindness to evidence, because they do not know that doubting and even denying are part of Intelligence's active rhythm of grasping and acquiescing; a Protean Shifting, a process of assimilation and elimination in which the already experienced and accepted selects that which shall be accepted or rejected.

‡   ‡   ‡

The prime necessity of life and of the Universe, for that matter, is ability to forget or rather the inability to remember—It is that, along with death, that provides the sense of change, freshness, newness. The old is only old to the old. To the very young, it is new. [*Or*]

‡   ‡   ‡

We know that all forms of energy, sunlight, heat, magnetism, the cosmic ray, and their reflections, registering organs of as well as forms created by them—trees, flowers, animals, man—are constantly impinging as stimuli on the nervous system. With the brain, and the endless filaments of nerve leading to it, crowded as they are with incoming registrations, as an implement of registering and reflecting? You have seen electricity stripping the particles of silver from a plated knife in a chemical bath, and with order and clarity, gathering them on the other pole of the magnet. If, as Crile painstakingly demonstrates, the white portion of the brain (cortex) is the storehouse or registering place of stimuli which enter via original or previously created paths, and if the newest stimuli are transferred or referred to collected or related material of the same kind with the speed of electrical energy, or as frequently must happen, cut new paths of their own, how reasonable then to assume that not only such new associations, but the natural reactions such new associations might evoke, would give rise to altered reactions, which would be stored as newer deductions at the same time that they evoked exterior actions or interior emotions or resolutions or both.

Thus a new kind of danger would be instantly referred to as well as associated with older and so known forms of danger, already registered. As we know by actual experience, these new stimuli bring about recombinations of data or of action or impression, just as a new color of paint added to another color brings about a modification or change of color. The older registrations of danger and of what was done or might have been done at some previous time evoke, or effect, or suggest, let us say, some modification of method of defense or escape or what not. And more, not only would these stimuli be registered as so-called thought, but they would or could be registered as action of a new, that is, different kind. And they would be compulsory (that is reactions to stimuli) and not anything springing from that mythical central thinking and controlling and directing authority known as the ego, with the mythical power so constantly referred to as free will.

‡ ‡ ‡

How does it come that a drowsy or dreaming mind can register scores of earthly scenes not there or then in eye-view, or temperaments not then and there present—often long out of conscious thought.

Also, on occasion (as has happened to myself, for instance) hear voiced arguments, often erudite and clarifying on topics which, up to the time of their presentation in a dream are totally unfamiliar to the dreamer. (I have, in dreams, listened to profound legal discussions, involving data totally unfamiliar to me.)

Somewhere in the so-called mind is supposed to be a storehouse of memories—previously registered impressions. But how about synthesis of these being contrived in the blood, or actually the previously registered scenes re-registering themselves from without (afresh, that is, anew) via radiations from them, wherever they are? Human chemistry, its blending processes and their effects are little known. Why a "mental store-house" at all? [Or]

T.D.

Myth of Individuality

WE ARE NOT OURSELVES ONLY—NOT MERE PROJECTIONS OF AN IM-mediate unconscious. We are also a part of past human experience and thought, and part of present human experience and thought—and of our immediate—yet always changing human environment.

‡ ‡ ‡

Every living creature, unless perhaps it is the oyster, represents but one half of a sex or reproductive mechanism, which, without the other half is nothing. And that means you and me. It follows that your so-called thoughts and moods and actions are automatically concerned with and affected by the other half. Such being the case your so-called individuality rests where?—in yourself or in your self *and* your other sex half?

‡ ‡ ‡

In the Upanishads we read: "In the beginning . . . was self alone, in the shape of a person. . . . But he felt no delight. Therefore a man who is lonely feels no delight. He wishes for a second."

Man is not a complete thing. He is but one-half of a sex mechanism—each one incomplete and worse, meaningless, without the other. His loneliness is not unlike the pain that follows an amputation. [*Or*]

Society

The biologist, if called upon to add his contributions to the subject of human society, would start with the assumption that our society, however unique some of its features, must be the product of evolution. It had to have origins, somewhere among man's simian connections; those origins in turn had others. And in general he would suspect that our peculiar way of living together which we call "society" (or "civilization", when we dwell together in great numbers and have to set up a complicated machinery for mutual adjustment) will probably be found inherent in Nature from the time that one-celled animals conglomerated into loose colonies.

But *individuality* does not exclude the social tendency; doubtless it greatly contributes to it.

‡ ‡ ‡

A German father, looking at the drawings of a ten year old son will mark only the individual qualities and will not readily perceive the influence of a general European type of drawing and painting. But if he looks at the drawing of a young Japanese boy he will readily recognize the influence of the Japanese style as a whole. In each case the naive attempt of the boy is controlled, halted even in its special and general details by the artistic traditions amid which he lives.——Schrodinger

His German style is not an individual possession. [*Or*]

T.D.

‡ ‡ ‡

We can only know ourselves by being ourselves and even that we cannot know truly, since whatever we do or *think* we *think* is nothing more than a reaction or reactions to stimuli—sensed or not sensed by our so-called mind, (reaction apparatus) but nevertheless composing and directing our physical and mental processes. We have no specific individual reality—none. And if other people think they know us, they know only an *appearance* and a very changeful one at that which they call you or me—John Smith or William Jones—never the forces which are making and operating or driving us and which same we do not even know ourselves, for we do not know from day to day what they are going to make us do or how they are going to make us feel—whether strong or weak, grave or gay, baleful or generous and kind. And it is the same when we imagine we know others. What we know of others is only that which we register concerning them at special times and in special ways—never the sum of mysteries that are bringing them into being and shunting them onward from infancy to age; into and through so-called *"Life"* which is too limited to be worth talking about and thence into so-called *death*—which is obviously more of *life* or energy, than this minute pinhead of a world or planet could ever know. [*Or*]

T.D.

Absolute Law

Matter and light appear sometimes as waves, sometimes as particles. Relativity establishes the universe as a uniform and related whole or energy—(matter-energy). In connection with these facts one person (Dr. Gustav Stromberg of Mt. Wilson Observatory) advances with the thought that the development and growth of each individual are directed and controlled by very complicated living waves of energy, some of which originate in germ cells, while others, like seeds ready to be planted, and which, like seeds, are instrumental in organizing a new individual body, dart about in space at the speed of light. Each such wave or seed or organization is referred to by him as a "genie", because of its relation to the genes or heredity carriers of all animals, insects and vegetable forms. Also, according to Dr. Stromberg or his theory a genie having effected or synchronized, perhaps enzymically or catalytically, the development of a human organism, *in utero,* it can, the organism wearing out and ending, contract its wave system—(the wave system that has produced the above energy result) leaving itself as it was at first, the original *genie* or energy seed and still capable of darting about in space at the speed of light, and, as theorized, indestructable.

To do all this, however, according to Dr. Stromberg, it is something more than an immaterial pattern of vibration—something that might be set over against the historically imagined "soul" of the religionists and the philosophers. For, the only way to account, scientifically, for the genie's purposeful ability to organize molecules and so life types or forms is to conclude some connection with a vast, immaterial intelligence, or God.

But here we come upon the problem of energy which plainly in its earth and evolutionary form, as well as in its universal or stellar form, is electric. But is electricity mental? Does it, as the emanation or representative of the over-energy—"think"—"decide"? Or, what is not quite the same thing, act and react, according to chemo-physical laws *willed by* or possibly *conditioned* in (and so, never to be changed or escaped from,) the very substance that is above all energy—and out of which it takes its rise?

Assuming this last, we have what the scientists of today and the thinkers of the past accept as the unchangeable laws of life—the laws of its chemistry and physics as these are today expressed in space and time. And if so we (men) as well as all the involved forms of nature, elemental as well as protoplasmic, and whether they are sufficiently organized sensorially or not to express it as man can and does, are confronted by the fact that life as a whole is a mechanistic or energy directed process. And unless the energy which erects, controls, and directs man is the direct and orderly emanation of a super mind, or is, in its entirety, that mind itself, life has no meaning beyond the sensitivities and compulsions which each ultimate wave particle of matter or energy as described above is automatically capable of bringing about here, i.e., such a life as we see here from protoplasmic germ to suns and flowers and rats and kings plus the orderly and yet mysterious forces within ourselves which make *us,*—and yet only such *us* as serve to function mechanistically with all else and make us as well as all else *go.*

Only that—as all who have been sufficiently well organized chemo-electrically are now able to sense—is no real individuality. These energy seeds of Dr. Stromberg's, springing as he may well feel from boiling suns and traveling at the speed of light—or from some other energy process in space, may well be what he pictures—seeds instrumental in organizing life forms of whatsoever type. But in themselves, without the universe constituted as it is, without the various galaxies from which they might spring and to which they may travel—the new nebulae freshly brought into being by exploded suns, the endlessly scattered solar systems with their attendant planets and the satellites of these, the interstellar clouds of cosmic dust of a varying matter-energy nature, and with which they may and do combine, what opportunity would they have for organizing a new individual body of any kind? And from whence other than energy-mind or cosmic law could they have secured the pattern? At best they could only function as intelligent energy seeds or catalyzers and tending, subject to the chemical and physical limitations of any particular galaxy or solar system, to bring about the construction and possibly, life-term direction of some type of organism already conditioned and limited by that particular system or planet.

And in that connection how much true individuality would it have? How much of a soul of anything could it really be?

[Differing theories exist today, relating life processes to the DNA molecule, which we will not try to explain here. However, this colorful *Note* may stand, if *taken with a grain of salt! Editor's Note*]

Myth
of Individual
Thinking

Individual Thinking

ANYONE WHO IS CERTAIN THAT THE HUMAN MIND DOES ITS OWN thinking—has individual creative thought power—will have to explain the wondrous dreams and illusions brought on by any of a number of drugs injected into the veins or taken by mouth—willingly or per force. Among these are Peloti, Shanchi, used by the Jivaro Indians of Equador,—Hasheesh, opium, morphine, cocaine, heroin, chang. Also he will have to explain dreams and the fears induced by various forms of illness. [Or]

‡ ‡ ‡

By most proximate causes and proximate results, proximate results alone are contemplated. Man is rarely equipped sensorially to do better, let alone much better. By nature even genius is foiled. In nearly all men there is scarcely any consciousness that the original causes are often numerous and widely different from the apparent cause; and that beyond each result there will be multitudinous remote results, most of them quite incalculable. [Or]

‡ ‡ ‡

Custom and usage relieves so many from any direct or clear contemplation of the cruelty or folly or meaninglessness, even, of the things that they do. [Or]

The Custom of the Country

As long as thousands of men kill defenseless deer every year, "just for the fun of it", will they feel very deeply about the bombing of civilians—?
Custom takes the place of thought.—So does imitation. [Or]

‡ ‡ ‡

Why do you pick up a fork? Because you will to eat with it? Not at all. If you were a Chinaman you would "will" to pick up chop sticks. But why chop sticks? Because you never heard of a fork? And because you did hear of chop sticks—and before *hearing of them* saw them, and more, were not only compelled but trained to use them—the custom or training or knowledge or age-old eating equipment of the country being chop sticks. So there was no free will, nor *individual thinking* nor individual knowledge connected with it. [*Or*]

‡ ‡ ‡

A habit is not special and individual thinking. It is a response to a desire which when gratified brings pleasure. But the desire in the first place is never a self-willed thought, that is, a mental willing on the part of the desirer to desire something, say food, or warmth, or more air, or a new suit of clothes, or to get rid of a ragged coat or a chill, or fever or pain or a harassing debtor. It is a compelled chemical or nervous reaction to a troubling irritation of some kind. That nervous organism, the body, must respond in some way. If I touch you with a hot poker you do not will to withdraw. You automatically withdraw. And when next you see a hot poker you do not will to stay away from it. The hot poker it is that evokes awareness in you first of its presence, next of the pain it can and will cause and next consciousness (no willing in that) of any self-preservative or escape mechanisms that you may be possessed of—your legs, the additional space about you into which you can move in case the poker approaches—your voice—as that permits you to cry out in warning, et cetera, et cetera. But that is not thinking. It is reacting. It is automatic. It has nothing to do with free will or any willing of any kind. You are compelled—not urged or persuaded to do as you do. [*Or*]

‡ ‡ ‡

Even in factories machines grow by reason of use. The operator fecundates the machine or the machine fecundates the operator—or both. Here a process is delayed because of some associated process that interferes with it and the mind of some extra-sensitive operator is willy-nilly (given time enough) constrained to note it. It becomes, let us say, an irritation. What will end the irritation? Why, if this spool is moved up here a little, and that one, now directly opposite, down below. Presto—an invention! The machine has grown. The operator has grown. But there are fifty machines all alike, or one hundred. And as many operators. In ten years, this one has noted this. Another one, that. The machine performing badly here, fouling a little there, has suggested to one or another out of a hundred enough to evoke the thought or reaction, that such and such a change would be valuable—quicker, less noisy, more comfortable. So machines have grown; do grow to this hour and day. But it is never the operator alone, but the two of them in union, like a man and a woman that produce the change, the new thing. [*Or*]

T.D.

‡ ‡ ‡

You think about a girl or man. You give way as some would express it to "thoughts" of love, desire, union, marriage, children, a home, the complex and varied social pleasures which, idealistically, are looked upon as the results of such a union. But if it were not for the existence of the two sexes—yours and the other, where would be the possibility of such "thoughts" or rather reactions as the above.

How would you think of a male or a female if never had there been one? Your "thoughts," as you see spring from or, are reactions to the other half of a sex mechanism which is so devised physically and chemically, as to evoke—assuming it to be joined with yours—each half, in the other—all of the above "thoughts" or reactions, but not otherwise.

And they are not "thoughts" originating independently in your own brain—of the brains or chemical and physical presence of any other related organisms. On the contrary all that you personally are supposed to feel independently of any other are but reactions to those other chemical and physical presences which are biologically part and parcel of yours and without them and the joint arrangement of interacting processes between the two could never be. [*Or*]

T.D.

‡ ‡ ‡

Consider how wave motion, wind motion, cloud motion, the motions of energy in any form evokes or supplies the sensation of form, color, sound, and so the alleged individual "thoughts" concerning these things. [*Or*]

‡ ‡ ‡

Our reactions to things are conditioned by the things themselves, in other words our primary perception of it, and later by memory, that is all our past experience which can be brought to bear on the instance. There is always, in the transformations we are watching, something familiar which carries memory back to what it has already witnessed, and forward, expectantly, to something it may be going to witness. Hence, in our reactions, we never have repetition, and conversely, never utter novelty. Our frequent doubts are always conditioned by our habitual beliefs; it is our past experience from which we have drawn certain rules that makes us so full of prejudices, that makes us unwilling to accept miracles and ghosts, either by actual experience or, still less, on someone else's authority.

However, each experience which is in opposition to the rules we have formulated from past experiences alters the rules to some extent, though not completely—rather merely through effecting a new synthesis. [*W*]

THEODORE DREISER

‡ ‡ ‡

A man will look at a barometer and see a perfectly clear liquid cloud up most delicately and slowly before his eyes and think of it as purely mechanistic and unintelligent. But if in a fellow man or woman he sees as the result of some exterior word or appearance or action on the part of another, or many others, an eye darken, a pallor or flush overspread a cheek, a muscle—as for instance one of those of the mouth, nose, arm or eyelids, contract or twitch a smile or a tear appear, or as also may be the case, a cry issue, he will not think of it, as he does of the barometer's action, as a mechanistic and so unwilled response on the part of the organism to exterior stimuli—but rather as some *mental* response which he will attribute to thought and even *will*, rather than to any of those many and complicated chemisms of which he is a compound and to changes in which, effected by the stimuli above enumerated, he owes the changes he expresses.

It is not mind or thought in the sense that we imagine these things to be that causes him to leap out of the path of the approaching express once he sees or hears it, or both. Nor is it mind or thought that causes him to get up and leave a too hot room or seek any shade when afflicted by a hot exterior glare. Neither does thought or his own so-called *will* compel him to take a drink of water when he is thirsty or seek food when he is hungry—or become desirous or exalted when he sees a lovely girl. The sensations and changes which accompany all of these encounterings of stimuli are chemical and not *mental*—barometric and not *willed*.   *182728*

Try not feeling comfortable when you come out of a biting cold into a warm room, or compelling your stomach not to feel painfully empty when it is empty and the odor of your favorite foods assail your nostrils, or *willing* not to be affected chemically and favorably when some agreeable perfume greets your nostrils. Try. [*Or*]

T.D.

‡ ‡ ‡

Anyone can see how astronomy would begin—Night, either with or without stars, the moon, possibly storm-swept, wild animals abroad, May—and then with the lapse of time, dawn, birds calling, animals stirring, the sun in splendor rising—at least, its light filtered through clouds and primitive man noting it, over and over—its return and its going again, its warmth and the fading of the same in winter. The sun, the moon, the stars would slowly but surely impress themselves—register themselves as entities to be wondered over, admired, feared, worshipped as the fearful and wonderful are worshipped to this day. In the slow course of time, sun, moon, stars, their relationship to the earth and its to them would be impressed upon the organisms of that day—in so far as the organisms of that time were capable of registering such impressions—no more and no less. Language may not have existed. Thought—the illusion of individual thought as it exists now would not have been. But the impressions would be what they are today, registrations of stimuli from without. And though the animal might have responded with grunts, it would be "thinking" as a photograph film thinks when it registers a picture. [*Or*]

T.D.

Problem of Mind

We so called "individuals" say we can't get our mind on something—some particular problem that is disturbing or distressing us and that requires "our" attention and "our" concentration. And usually we add that this is due to the fact of our being disturbed by this, that or the other thing—noise, heat, cold, a pain (ear-ache, tooth-ache, head-ache) or the ill thoughts or bad conduct of some one other than ourself. But all of these things as you will note are inpouring stimuli from within or without the body to that amazing telephone switchboard, the brain, wherein automatically and electrically, of course, being transferred to its various mental association centers, messages or calls as are best taken care of in such centers. For instance, impressions from without which require nothing more than to be registered or filed along with registration of a related character—additional impressions of trees, flowers, houses, dogs, clouds, automobiles, and the like—if filed at all. It may be they do no more than refresh some general impression as more water refreshes grass—strengthen it structurally.

However, the painful registration of a flea or fly or mosquito bite or sting would not be referred to a registration center dealing with clouds or still trees in pleasant sunlight. On the contrary and most obviously it would be referred to (if being intelligent energy, it did not go of its own accord)—to that particular motor center of the brain dealing with physical reactions against injuries of any kind, but more particularly with the muscles of the arm or leg or eyelid or whatever having to do with the mechanical protection of the body at any point—as for instance the right or left arm or hand motivated to strike at the mosquito or fly or to rub the injured knee or chin or ear. For lesions or injuries to or attacks upon tissues, muscles, cells, arteries, veins, or organs of any kind inside the body—internal processes such as hormones increasing or decreasing flows of blood, or muscular pressures or powerful discharges of energy as well as digestive acids of one kind or another, are available and mechanistically—that is after the fashion of a telephone switchboard or police or fire alarm system are released and set in motion.

In times past this has been thought to be the result of conscious willing processes of the mind; later after Freud appeared, the unconscious or below conscious thinking and willing. And this may be true, or at least have some relation to the truth. For all special forms or phases of energy—such as those named—nervous, electric, magnetic, gravitational, radio active, telepathic or whatever may be either limited or fully powered phases of universal energy and as such—(a theory this, not a substantiated fact) may possess sensation, emotion, wisdom, will, selectivity, predilections, antipathies as well as any or other qualities as have given rise on this planet to man and animals, all flora and fauna, their especial disorders—as well as light, heat, sound, color, humor—in sum all of the things which the assumed human mind is called to deal with.

In other words universal energy may be universal mind. If not, universal control—the avoidance of disorder as opposed to order in chemical and physical functioning anywhere. [*Or*]

T.D.

‡ ‡ ‡

When you are tempted to emphasize the actuality of individual knowledge, consider for one thing, the growth of technology, and the fact that one of its most distinguishing characteristics is the steady intensification of the division of labor—that is, more and more specialization, more and more breaking up of operations into smaller and smaller activities—each involving repetition of one simple operation, rather than a varied, complex operation, requiring judgment or quickness of reaction to a variety of stimuli, all streaming in at once. This last might be called a larger variety of skill, or knowledge, if acquired skill is knowledge, or if not, then merely the automatic repetition of the previous knowledge provided by others, which in the past has been called initiative. And has not this, throughout all time constituted the sum of the "knowledge" of most men?

Consider for instance the "knowledge" possessed by the average doctor anywhere. You know quite well, of course, that a doctor in any country before he can practice the medical art, must be taught or shown (made familiar of by demonstration plus repetition) various slowly acquired facts which are by no means in his so-called mind at the time he begins the study of medicine. On the contrary, beyond a mere collection of passing observations of the effects of medicine and diet, he may know nothing. And in America, as elsewhere, seven years are required to familiarize himself with the practices as well as the theories of the work he is to do. But once seven years of study and directed experiment have been indulged in, and via observation and memory as well as practice, it is asserted by the degree given him that he does *know* the art of medicine or surgery or both, and is therefore fitted to practice either or both.

But can it be said that this ability to practice is *individual* knowledge? His own personal knowledge, as opposed to the endless replicas of it to be found stamped upon the registering faculties of all the medical graduates and practicing physicians and surgeons of his day, throughout the world? To say nothing of all the dead and gone physicians and surgeons of many by-gone centuries? The sense or feeling of *individuality* which this conveys to some, almost all, is admitted, but that it is in effect *individual* knowledge is obviously nonsense. It is not even applied individually, the appropriate medication being almost invariably suggested by and patterned after previously or currently acknowledged results. A doctor who did differently would not long be a doctor.

But this, as you can see, is mere mechanism—not willed action. Also it is equally true of the lawyer, the jurist, the architect, the technician, the soldier, the priest, the sailor, the newspapermen, the editor, the publisher, the painter, the novelist, the poet, the merchant, the thief. Could anything be more mechanistically patterned after previous models than the thoughts and actions of each and everyone of these?

Consider the mechanistic procedure of the priest, the *clergyman*, the soldier, fresh from his military academy—and the thief! Does nature really individualize them? Or is not its object (results being accepted as evidence) to do just the opposite? For once in the evolution of processes and workable forms, a form or mechanism suited to a given environment is achieved, the mechanistic method appears to be concentrated on a mass production of the same—that is, to produce not one individual, but a species capable—like the race or nation or tribe, of utilizing the resources of a given area or technique. Or, if that is not the right picture of the process, perhaps it is that once a form is evolved, its only chance of subsistence lies in a multitude of the same—the flock, or herd, or tribe, being better self-perpetrating mechanisms than any simple individual could possibly be.

But where in all this startling and often brilliantly successful procedure is there any trace of individual knowledge? The form and technique of each particular species as you can for yourself see, having been most slowly evolved year by year, century by century, age by age, from protoplasm upward, it follows that the creative thought or compulsion must have centered there, or if not there, then in the force or forces that generated protoplasm. But alas, here we pass to either the accidental or ordained just position of various elements, under particular conditions of light or heat, plus gravitational compulsions and macerations, which brings you into the realms of cosmic law as it effects the structure of atoms, and the various elements compounded of them. And you are then compelled to ask, is there any thought in this?

The answer of the physicist today at least, is, of course, *no*. And if no thought, then no conscious knowledge. Only a process which is not willed, but *is*. The ones that come nearest to even a suggestion of willed power in all this is that force in the nucleus of the atom which is greater than the repelling force between the protons of the atom which circle around its nucleus and which causes them to fly apart, and of itself is capable of holding them together, and is therefore responsible for holding the universe together. But is this a force with wisdom, or merely a conditioned force incapable of doing other than it does? If this latter, then there is no such thing as individual knowledge anywhere—not in any earthly creature or species, or element, or in any combination of elements and therefore not in the universe itself. At least it is not in the individual and that is what this particular argument set out to prove. [*Or*]

T.D.

Myth of Free Will

Suppose that a man builds a battery; he makes a solution of sulphuric acid; he puts in a copper plate and a zinc plate. Then he attaches wires to a bell; and when he closes the connection between the battery and the bell—the bell rings. But assume then that the battery, finding itself to be a battery, (although, as in the case of man, not knowing just how or why), exclaims to itself—By God! I made that bell ring! I am a battery! I am supplying this current, my own energy into that bell! Yet man says to himself—See, I am a man. I am making my way in life. I am master of my fate. Why, I build and invent things. See! I have built a house; or, I have become a father! or, I sing, I talk, I write. And all these things I do with my own energy, and through my own will!

‡   ‡   ‡

A dog will arise and move out of a hot spot into a cool one. A man will do the same thing. A dog is assumed to be doing this not intelligently or consciously—that is, he is not *thinking*. A man, when he does, is assumed to be *conscious* of the heat, or "thinking" of its irritating character, and also of moving to a shady place where the heat cannot disturb him. But a bird, a rabbit, horse, cow, pig will do as the dog and the man do. Are none but the man *thinking*? Or is the man, like the others, merely reacting?

‡   ‡   ‡

You think you can write an even, legible hand; that perhaps it is because you will to do it. But, let something frighten you—or let yourself get sick or extremely tired and then see if you can write evenly and legibly;—whether by *willing*—your own free willing you can achieve it. [*Or*]

‡   ‡   ‡

You can "look" as you think you do of your own "free will" but what if there was nothing to see—but what if there were nothing outside your eye to see? Eyeless fishes suggest that with only darkness there is no need for any eye and it ceases. But suppose also that in spite of your possession of *feeling* there were nothing to touch or feel. What would become of feeling? So too with hearing, tasting, smelling. Do they not all suggest that each was prepared for service in connection with something else—and that without that something else they would be meaningless? Like male without female; strength without weakness, or something to lift; heat without cold; light without dark; sorrow without joy; wisdom without ignorance and so throughout the entire duality called life.

‡ ‡ ‡

When the sun goes down a great upward migration takes place in the reaches of the sea. During the darkness of night, within a hundred yards of the surface (300 feet) this hungry host can be found fighting and feasting amid the plenty (plenitude) that populates the top. With the breaking of day, however, the mighty hordes return to the reaches whence they came; for they are afraid to face the sun (Tropisms). In their battle with the abyss they long ago lost the power—the internal chemical adjustment—that would have permitted them to endure the light. [*Or*]

‡ ‡ ‡

If a person is not motivated from without why will he proceed in each and every instance of inquiry, self or other, to enumerate in so far as possible the things which motivate him [or once did,] and nearly always from without; bills, enmities, duties, compulsions, opportunities, other people, who favor, dislike, oppress, ignore, or otherwise and in every conceivable way affect him by their thoughts, moods, depressions, elations, (unspoken more often than spoken), and more; in the case of internal ills, how he earnestly assures you that he came by them from without.

As a child he lacked schooling, was poor; his parents were cruel, he lacked this or that, or could not go here, there, elsewhere to see this or that, be benefited by this or that which was ever on the outside, not in. Say it was the mountains, or a school, or the sea, or a relative, or a great play, or a different and more favorable and more beautiful climate—but on the outside, not in. He has not had the benefit of such and such advice, companionship, social aid; again, it is the weather or the state, or the nation he lives in, or the loss of something outside himself—his wife, child, income, possessions— really an innumerable list.

The Cow Birds

Birds fly up in the air in flocks and quite often wheel here or turn there or split, some part of the group going this way, the other that. But according to which particular bird's idea if any—or according to the ideas or moods of what particular birds? For in some cases it is quite obvious that a flock will be split by reason of the super speed of some birds, the slowness or lesser flying strength of others. Sometimes the force of a gust of wind or the appearance of an impeding object will cause one part of a flock to turn this way while the lack of vision of the object at precisely the same time will cause another part of the flock to go in another direction. But this is neither thinking nor willing in the ordinary sense of those words. It is nothing more than reaction to exterior stimuli on the part of some—absence of any disturbing stimuli on the part of others.

But now see how closely this can be duplicated by the action of inanimate objects when controlled or directed or both by so called inanimate forces—or a force. For instance, take a mass of newly fallen leaves suddenly acted upon by a November wind. Hundreds—even thousands of leaves may be swept up and driven in a given direction, quite often resembling a flock of birds. But now, as in the case of the birds, may come from a contrary direction another gust of wind. Or in their path, hurried as they are by the first wind, may appear a tree, a rock, a house, a chimney. Instantly there will be division—a part of the leaves flying in one direction another part in another—some up, some down, some right, some left. But all, like the birds responding to obstruction or exterior stimuli—no problem of thought or will being involved. [Or]

T.D.

‡ ‡ ‡

Man's nature, complex and turbulent, is not due to himself anymore than is that of a spider, a bull, a lion or a sheep. Nevertheless, by reason of it and the compulsions by which he is motivated, the varying societies of which he is a part and has been through long periods past have come into being. Of himself individually he did not will them or "think" them out by slow degrees, one generation forgetting another and its ways, but finding always a generation in possession and action and nearing its next generation to follow. The next generation to follow chemically motivated by nature and having before it the example as well as the equipment of the generation in charge to observe and react to, as well as all the material equipment or paraphernalia which that generation had inherited from others preceding it. It is obvious that it could only model itself on or after what was, that is, its clothing was handed to it by its parents, likewise its foods, likewise its methods of obtaining and cooking and serving the same; like whatever methods it had of protecting itself from nature and its extremes—the heat and cold, the rain and drought, the weapons and tricks of its enemies etc. If there were any traditions, arts, useful forms of knowledge, games for entertainment, etc. all these would be impressed upon the rising generation by the passing generation. And hence the character, habits, knowledge, customs, costumes, food and drink, weapons and resources of any given people—the Chinese, the Hindus, the Greeks, the Romans, the Bushmen, Indians, etc. would be accepted or passed on. These could not be apart from the existing examples, customs, models, etc., any apriori method of originating anything out of thin air—or that intangible thing called the mind. What could be and was—was the unescapable compulsion of reacting to what already was plus, in addition any accidental variation favorable or unfavorable of what was. If favorable, the variation was likely to register itself as such and become embodied with the other favorable or self-preservative registrations pouring in from everywhere. If unfavorable, it was most likely to be avoided or at any rate eventually to be discarded. Original creative thinking as such never was and never will be. Growth and change or so-called thought spring from the constant reregistration of what is, plus all types of favorable variations from what *is*. [*Or*]

T.D.

‡ ‡ ‡

Anyone who has given the slightest attention to physiology knows how much of a formula he is. For one thing he knows that he did not create his body—it was created for him in the womb of his mother—and without her having any conscious knowledge of how to do it. He did not create the first cell or egg out of which he grew, nor any of its endless successors which grew out of the first and joined in various forms to make his body, his skeleton, his nerves, his arteries, and the various organs of his body—brain, spinal cord, heart, lungs, liver, kidneys, stomach, reproductive organs and his various and mysterious glands. And not only that but:

Neither the conscious nor the unconscious processes of the body are under your direction. The conscious processes seem so—as when you decide to take a train or shake hands or write, or fight. The unconscious processes are plainly not under your conscious control. Your heart beats but you do not will it to do so. Your blood circulates, your nerves register, your stomach, liver, kidneys, lungs, and all your various glands that constitute and effect that astounding chemical synthesis which permits you to live, all work without your willing and without your knowledge. The only knowledge concerning the fact that there are various processes at work in you through various organs which in all likelihood you cannot name comes to you in the form of a pain, an ache, a sense of nausea, a sense of discomfort or the sudden cessation of some power that you have always had, the power to taste, smell, chew, walk, hear, see, feel, or think clearly. Today of course if you have the money you can go to a specialist and ask him what is the matter, and according to the sum of his understanding he will tell you or guess. If you have no money and not too much intelligence of your own you will do as primitive man did when anything went wrong—suffer. And if the unconscious processes or rather the to you unknown intelligence at work operating and regulating your interior mechanism cannot fix it, you die. And yet you think of yourself as a free agent. As having free will—or a non-dependent power to go, do, be.

‡ ‡ ‡

You are stirred pleasantly or unpleasantly, nervously or emotionally, by many, by no means all, of the endless things that environ you. For sensorially you are not consciously affected by the speeding planets of our solar system; by the weight of the air above you, which is no less than 14.7 pounds to the square foot and which your body sustains without your knowledge; by the convulsions of the liquid fiery elements that are forever arranging and rearranging themselves below you in the earth; by the endless radio and telegraphic waves that are speeding past or through you—waves of song, of humor, of wisdom, of folly, of sorrow or joy. Yet you sense them not at all.

So, too, with your internal economy. Consider all the labors of your digestive system, your circulatory system, your glandular organs—the digestive and distributive process so carefully and correctly and meticulously carried on in and through you—yet as a rule without a trace of a nervous or painful disturbance in you—through you—unless some functional disturbance or break in the constructive or distributing or maintaining processes has occurred. Then, and then only, when some general danger as opposed to some local and mendable ill is at hand, is the central nervous system used to convey news of the ill. You become nauseated. Or a pain, somewhere, indicates the locality of the trouble. A nervous or emotional excitement or depression due to the reception of the news by all of the cells, to say nothing of the molecules, the electrons and protons of the atoms—sets in. All are aware. Not the brain alone—that giant switch-board of the human body, but all of the body—each blood corpuscle, and likewise every germ and individualized unit of virus that is or is not directly reached by it, is fully aware.

You feel bad or you feel good. You feel very bad or very good—great. You lie down in misery or depression, or you jump, dance, leap and sing or shout. In serious or important instances of either delight or sorrow all of you participates, and what is more, all of you communicates to your environing world something of what it is that has occurred. You cannot conceal it, for from it go waves as from a radio or telegraph station. Those nearest you sense it telepathically, or you speak. Others at a distance, like homing pigeons, that, a thousand miles away from the cote,—sense, from the cote itself, its radio emanations—where it is, in what direction—also sense not always where you are but something of the misery or joy that in telepathic waves is speeding outward from you. But the important point to note is that the telepathic waves that leave you to travel great distances are energy waves—not as in the case of some odors of the body or blood molecular particles. And these last, being as small as they are, can only be outgivings in wave form, of the atoms or their electrons, or mayhap, fragments of electrons, if such things be—photons or quantums. So that the moods and fears and even the physical pains, which you still do not look on as mental, are none the less mental—the telepathic waves that carry the news to others. They are your actual joy or grief—hate or love; desire or disappointment, courage or fear in infinitely minute energy-particle form rushing from you—each separate minutest energy-particle of you—through all earth bound space, if not further, and therein setting up new relations with all other related minuteness of energy—so that, at last, what disturbs or elates or tortures you, disturbs or elates to the same degree that such minuteness can convey to other equivalent minutiae of energy—(all else, that is, of the immense relativity called life) the state or condition of the infinitesimally divided energy that is, for the time being, assembled in you.

And these are your "mind". And it is the disturbance of these—either within or without you, by the entering or departing and arranging or rearranging these same energy-particles, that are for the time being inhabiting and so constituting the cosmos called you that present themselves and their reactions to each other, and to all else that is within or about or around you—as *yourself*—your mind, your emotions, your memory, your strength, your weaknesses, your "ideas" or your lack of them. And so long as they are magnetically attracted each to the other—*you are.* And when that attraction ceases you are not. For they are, by other attractions more forceful than yours, magnetically released. And go to join others, that are parts of assembling of "growing" yous—like any sun that grows by magnetic attraction, and ceases by magnetic dissipation.

And this energy that in this astoundingly minute form inhabits and energizes all space—and that by turns, via *will-less* mechanism or some *will-full* self compulsion (and by turns) assembles and dissipates all of these things. What is that? Matter-energy? The universe? The Creator?

Do you name it as you choose. But by man, or by this something that creates him and that therefore through him, as a toy or a pleasure device, expresses it, it has been called God—or the Lord of All. But if so, it is thus that through these, his toys or pleasure devices, he chooses thus to be denominated. For without this natural power there is no power—not any assemblage or action, whether of atom, or man of sun or sidereal system. Nor any mind, save the all-mind—thus variously—and so vicariously expressed.[*Or*]

T.D.

Myth of Individual Creative Power

ALL THAT MAN HAS "DISCOVERED" OR "INVENTED", IN CONNEC-
tion with anything, architecture, art, economics, engineering, science, government, trade, war, was worked out ages before man arrived, and this in connection
with animals, insects, primitive sea and land forms—their internal structures
and economics to say nothing of their external and their (by nature) mechanistically constructed and regulated environment. The greatest mind is nothing
more than a mechanistically directed implement—its "vanity", if anything,
a chemical energizer, intended to make it go or work. [W]

‡ ‡ ‡

Evolution is a record of the mentality of nature. So is astronomy. So is
biology. So is physics. So is chemistry. So is geology. So is botany. So is
human history. Some prefer to call them records of the *Natural* Forces of
Life or of the Cosmos. Some like to look on these timeless movements and
formations of matter-energy or energy-matter as mechanical. The Religionists
lump them, extract all possibility of evil or error and call them God. But
if [we] honor the few things human beings via these same natural forces
working through them—achieve in the way of discovery or *invention* (so-called)
with the name of *mind* and *thought*, why deny the same to these larger
and so much more wondrous forces and their activities—and particularly
because we cannot understand them? The stupidity! The colossal vanity!
[W]

‡ ‡ ‡

The greatest imaginable genius is manifested in the construction let alone
the maintenance of the human body. But as yet, how much of that genius
does the average man or insect or animal or tree or flower, sense, let alone
comprehend. Science does not. It is continuously uncovering new marvels
the procedures of which, when it understands them, it occasionally follows,
particularly in its searchings for information elsewhere. But the ability to
originate the same or their equivalents!—not even a suggestion of that yet.

‡ ‡ ‡

Conventions and traditions, prejudices and ideals and religious beliefs, systems
of morals (like the ten commandments) and codes of good manners—varying
according to geographical and historical circumstances, mould into different
forms the slowly if not entirely unchanging material of human instinct, passion
and desire. Thus the Indians preferred to represent their dancing Krishna
as standing on one leg and waving two or three pairs of arms over his head.
They had bronze to work with and so could do that. The early Egyptians
had granite, a stiff and intractable material, not to be poured like bronze.
With the best will in the world they could not have imposed such a form
upon granite. It could not be done. They had to work with what they had.

‡ ‡ ‡

The word creation applied to art is wrong. Art is not *created* by an artist.
He is not an original source but a contact instrument with and through
which life in many forms expresses itself. And life provides not only the
beauty but the artist, admirer and slave of beauty, and the *hunger* of the
artist which causes him to react to or seek and then to express the beauty
and the drama or arrangement which have, for the above reasons, assailed
his internalized sensory equipment and caused that to react—that is to register
the beauty or drama or both that is affecting him stimuli-wise. Not only
that but he depends upon a relatively sensitive public to verify the accuracy
of his reactions. In other words, they too, in a lesser measure maybe, react
to the same stimuli that he does, and so automatically verify his.

Again, a writer thinks that he has a sense of style, or that he disciplines
himself in such a way as to be able to register brilliantly that which he
feels or sees. But when one says *feels* or *sees*, one gives away the whole
secret of "understanding" and "expression"—or fine writing. For seeing clearly,
feeling and understanding and desiring to write what one sees, feels, thinks
or registers are not things which can be willed by anyone. They are environmentally compelled reactions in yourself. You see of course, but unless you
close your eyes or blind yourself, you cannot stop seeing. And neither can
you make yourself feel or stop feeling. If you are so constructed as to *feel*,
you will feel. If not, you won't. And no one can help you to feel more
concerning anything unless that extra sensory capacity is there, built in you
by nature. All that can be done for you is to call your attention to facts,
or phases of life and so forth, which you do not see and which once they
are brought to your attention, you may respond to. But as you see that
is an outside force working on you, driving you; and without it you would
not see. More, without the natural capacity, no living person can give [it
to] you.

And as for thinking (that is synthesizing and arranging within your so-called
mind what you see, hear, feel, taste, smell), try and do that if you have
not the mechanism or chemism or both that automatically do these things.
Try and respond to the beauty of life sufficiently to write a poem as sensitive
and delicate and beauty-full as Shelley's "Ode to the West Wind," or

"To a Skylark"—try and do that. If you can do it, you can, and that is all. To be sure, you will have been provided by nature with the requisite sensitive temperament, likely to be set emotionally on fire at some point—spontaneous combustion as it were. Also the environment, the evolved civilization in which such a thing could occur; in other words, you were made or evolved by nature (not, except as an implement or device of nature, by man) to do it.

If you doubt this, go to some poet or some professor of poetry, and ask him to show you how to write such a poem or a better one. Read not only poetry but books on how to write poetry, and then try. Poets are born and grow, they are not made by man or schools or instruction. They are made by life in the womb, or perhaps the world of one's ancestors, and arrived with and through the womb, but not otherwise, and only react to the life around them as above.

T.D.

‡ ‡ ‡

What we see before us as we look at the multitudes of people and the various things of civilization is a vast panorama of effects. We do not see the causes of those effects because the causes reach back in time as all know—and the causes of today, which are to have their effects in the far future, are working in invisible (to man) places. And they are discovered and understood if at all, in so far as man is concerned, by geniuses or seers or prophets, so-called, but never instanter by any one single genius or seer. Individual creative power is a myth. Life slowly evolving this and that thing permits of its perception and mental synthesis by individuals of succeeding generations evolved and prepared *as they are* by the successive appearance of these various things in the past as well as here and now.

Thus Newton did not discover gravitation alone. He was preceded by Galileo and others: but each of these others with lesser knowledge than he had. Thus, also, John Sebastian Bach was the crowning genius of the polyphonic school of music, which in its turn was the supreme effect of the life work of Huebaldus, the Benedictine monk of a French monastery who lived in the tenth century and may have been the inventor of polyphony—the cause, although the world has never known of him.

Thus the cause, which is always serial and not particular and individual, is like the root of a plant. It is not visible. The effect or invention or discovery is like the flower which is so much considered that the plant is forgotten and the root not even thought of. We think of Watt as the inventor of the steam-engine—rarely if ever of the invention of the tea kettle with a lid—or the invention or use of a lid for a pot as the real cause of the eventual invention of the steam engine. In sum, the wisdom of life and the universe is gained from the perception, if not the understanding of causes—since causes are only relatively, never wholly understood, and never from a comparative study of effects. [*Or*]

‡ ‡ ‡

Man began his exchange operations and so his knowledge of mathematics by counting his fingers or laying the things he wished to exchange for something else in a row on the ground and opposite each having the possessor of what he wished to secure put the things he was willing to release for the same. But nature's ancient knowledge of mathematics or numbers and the weights and measures these serve to identify is attested by every creature, animal, vegetable or mineral.

Water, for instance, a compound, that runs as streams or falls or rain drops—or floats as minute measures of fog—either flowing as mist or floating as a cloud—now vanishing completely or reappearing as cloud forms according to the degree of heat or cold applied to the moisture, or as snow crystals—among the most beautiful geometric forms in nature, was known to Nature as one of her arithmetical and geometric playthings since ever time was, perhaps Man, of his own devising or designing, could not design, let alone create these masterpieces. He can only copy what he sees.

When it comes to so-called living creatures—men, insects, birds, fishes, the endless species of animals—only note how carefully and accurately mathematical nature is. The two horns placed on the two horned rhinoceros of ancient times. The two carefully curved tusks of the ancient hairy mammoth as well as the modern elephant. The three toes of the extinct horse. The five fingers and five toes of endless animals including man, to say nothing of two eyes, two ears, a single tongue, two to ten teats of the females of so many species, a given number of ribs to a chest, an exact number of bones to an entire skeleton, regardless of the nature of the skeleton or its spine of which it is a member.

Two wings to a bird, an exact number of feathers to a tail. Five claws to so many species of birds—all so carefully devised as to length and strength! And man imagines he invented the science of mathematics.

T.D.

Myth of the Creative Mind

What am I myself? What have I done? All that I have seen, heard, noted I have collected and used. My works are reverenced by a thousand different individuals. . . . Often I have reaped the harvest that others have sown. My work is that of a collective being and it bears Goethe's name.——Goethe.

The direct adequate *dynamic causation* of every event, however minute, remains the only possible working hypothesis for the scientific worker. There is no more reason to abandon it than to abandon counting and weighing because no two things are exactly alike.——H. G. Wells.

The human mind is as much a product of the struggle for survival as the snout of a pig and perhaps as little equipped for the unearthing of fundamental truth.——Arthur James Balfour.

The theory of invention or creation as a part of the mental equipment of man is a superstition born of ignorance of all that has gone to the making of any so-called discovery or invention or creation; a superstition fostered to a degree by the *great-man* theory and the propaganda relating to the same. In historic times, and no doubt before, almost always rumor attributed all to a leader or creator or so-called independent thinker, little or nothing to circumstances (opportunities plus necessities) or compulsions conditioning him. Yet these same, plus some touch of curiosity in a given direction or some ill or frustration backed by a reasonable supply of energy and sensory response (nothing invented or created by the individual himself) have tended to elevate him above his fellows. And yet, by the uninformed, sole responsibility for his work or success has too often been attributed to him in quite all fields. Fortunately the immense work of the evolutionists and their successors the biologists, physicists, chemists and then historians and philosophers, have quite adequately demonstrated and tended to dispel this illusion. True the product of many evolved products of circumstances and ills and seemingly personal achievements linger on as the individual creation or achievements of many single men, Cyrus, Darius, Xerxes, Alexander, Hannibal, Caesar, Augustus, Attila, Charlemagne, Napoleon, Washington, Lincoln, to speak only of the Generals or Statesmen or Rulers; but with the fables connected with most of them reduced.—For now it has to be much more clearly seen that,—no condition requiring a solution—no public demand. No requirement of a leader—no leader. In short, in dull times most however capable, inventive or great die for want of opportunity, to demonstrate their especial gifts.

And the same is true of Philosophers, Scientists, even the great figures of religion. One may go back beyond Jesus to the prophets whose vague utterances were construed as predictions of His coming. But not back of the Upanishads and the Vedas—the speculations of no single man, but of a race whose Khandas and Sutras and sayings present, and often with greater clarity and force, all that is essential in Christ's or any other's insistence on his union with God or nature. *"Brahman is in all that is. He is also without."* So say the Sutras. Even in the sayings of Akhnaton, the Egyptian King, B.C. 3000, are to be found the seed and the substance of Christ's teaching. As for the others—if one considers Buddha, Lao-Tze, Mohammed— one sees, and swiftly, not only how they owed all to tradition, but how also the "great" religions which are ascribed to them were made "great", not by any particular founder, but by the reclassification and re-emphasis under favoring circumstances, of much that had been thought and said before, thus the progressive tinkerings of their priests and apostles and those who could most profit by them.

While this is not as precisely true of the poet or seer who does not create, but, because of a keener sensory response labeled "intuitiveness" to life, the world, the dynamics and physics of the same, reflects and so is capable of master-generalizations which he proceeds to write down, not primarily and exclusively "out of his head" but from what his "head", if you choose to put it that way, responds to or observes; it is still relatively the same.

For here is but another illustration of those same chemic or dynamic compulsions of which the seer or poet is by no means the creator, but to which he is subject and which operating in or through him bring about and enforce his master-generalization. For before the poet was, was the world about which he poetized and which created him and his poetry. And before his thought was the chemic-dynamic compulsion to thought in him and to which he responded, as a machine—not a separate or individual creative force.

One only needs to think of Newton, full of all the mathematical and physical lore of his day and of an inquiring and speculative turn—anxious to know more of the mysterious world about him, but nevertheless having to wait to see the apple of the tree under which he sat fall to the ground before his eyes, before he could awaken to the wonder of its falling instead of rising and so sense the law of gravitation. But if not he, then in the long, easy flow of time, some other man or mind would have come to it—one sufficiently responsive sensorially to such dynamic procedures in nature—as to note and ponder the same and thereafter, not before, acclaim the law of *gravitation.* Or let us think of the aeroplane and then the Wright brothers—but before them the long time of flight dreamers and experiments back to none other than Leonardo looking at the wings of birds in flight and so hitting upon the idea of the aeroplane—engineer and technician that he was. But there was Watt, a physicist by nature, watching the tea kettle lid bob up and down responsive to the expanding steam within and thinking of the steam engine. Or Roentgen, the Dutch physicist, a paper screen covered with Carium Platinocyanide lying near his highly exhausted vacuum tube in a black cardboard box—with which he was trying to learn more concerning the conduction of electricity through gases, when suddenly the paper fluorescing, he accidentally discovered the X-ray. Or Michelson with his set of mirrors and his big stone afloat in a vat of mercury retesting the truth of what was then generally believed, that when two speeds are added together they produce the sum of the speeds, but finding that in the case of light and the motion of the earth it was not true. And so giving rise to relativity. Or Francis Bacon, impelled because of his scientific bent to stuff a newly killed chicken with snow in order to see whether cold would act as a preservative—and so discovering the science of refrigeration.

One could go on from wireless and the aeroplane backward or forward and show that all inventions and discoveries and even life—changing thoughts attributed to the creative power of the mind are mere extensions of the accretions of experience, each usually suggested by something else that had gone before—excluding of course the master-generalizations of poets and seers previously referred to. Today, invention (the creation of earlier days) has actually become a business. It has been taken out of the hands or minds of the lone thinker or observer—the curious mind, either puzzled or frustrated by some lack of something, or the aberrant action of something that should go thus—and has been placed in the hands of the technicians of our great manufacturing industries so that now inventions stream out as boxes and bales—the electric eye, television, the electric range finder, the artificial *horizon*, etc. More, all that has been found since the days of Greece and Rome—every great achievement of modern science can be taken step by step back to Galileo and Copernicus and from them to Aristotle—called the founder of science only because there are gaps in our history which do not take us back farther than Archimedes and so leave us wholly in the dark as to the secret of the anonymous discoverer of the wheel.

Strictly speaking, man does not invent or create anything and never has. It would seem unnecessary to call attention to the fact that long before any so-called "inventions" or "creations" by man began, he himself and all of the world that went with him was not so much created or invented, as evolved, as we all know, or think we do. And regardless of his thoughts in the matter, the process of evolution for everything, sometimes successfully, sometimes unsuccessfully, has never ceased. Merely to walk through any Natural History display anywhere in the world is to be persuaded to dismiss the thought of direct or individual creation or invention, and at the same time to come away with an almost stupefying impression of the endless and ceaseless labor of changing and adapting which the universal forces are about. To see the horse through incomprehensible periods of time evolved from a little plaything no bigger than a cat, to the strong, swift, thing of today, is to grasp this amazing, if not always wholly beautiful and constructive process. To see the beauty of shells and ferns and corals and birds and precious stones, is to recognize the true source of beauty—the real master-artist.

Completed, if he really is, the horse is a masterpiece. If man had made, or, as he would put it "invented" him, he would consider the creature one of the rarest products of his genius. And yet today, if man were even partially aware not only of the astounding number of forms—animal, vegetable, and mineral—"invented" in the same way, and the other countless forms evolved and later discarded by this creative process, possibly in favor of other things better calculated to survive in the medium for which they were built, he would from then on have no thought of anything personal or strictly individual in the things he finds himself devising or hoping to devise. At best he would see himself not an heir, but in the main a nervous and troubled participant in a vast scene crowded with astounding forms and mechanisms, all "evolved" but rarely through him, or his race even, as instruments almost entirely without let or hindrance from him other than by way of self-defense. And none of these existing for the exclusive use of man, either individually or collectively, but rather for all nature. Yet man once dubbing himself "Lord of Creation."

Of course we have seen, and recently and swiftly, the machine enter the spectacle of created things. But not so swiftly that it was not preceded by an unbroken chain of evolved implements of all kinds, and all essential to the ultimate appearance of these others. For where would be the machine of today without the wheel of ages since? Or the more recent "eccentric cam"—the tone key to all intricate machinery? Or the Lever? or the rule? or the Scale?—one weight set over against the other? The ancestors of our machines are thousands in number. And the "discovery" of so simple a thing as the wheel, although lost in antique darkness, could still have been no instant discovery or invention, but must have had its beginning not only in earlier evolutionary forms, but in the still earlier necessity of man to move something, perhaps no more than a stone, which, when he found that he could not carry it, he may have rolled. Yet but for the wheel, no wagon, no automobile, no train, no steamer, no aeroplane, no possibility of social distribution such as we see today. And but for the bird with his outspread wings, no aeroplanes, even though the wheel is a necessary part of the same.

So recent a thing as the armored battleship when it first appeared in America as the invention of some military genius of our American Civil War was no more than a variation of one of the oldest concepts employed by the creative evolutionary force. For in the animal world, and apparently before man ever appeared, behold the two-horned almost solidly plated rhinocerous, the bony turtle safe within its box-like fort or casing, and the armored armadillo, all examples, randomly selected out of thousands, and all illustrations of a thought or special concept which appears or runs consistently through the story of evolution. Related devices among men are, first, the early fort, or any obstructive or sheltering casing, and later, for the individual, the armor of the early Egyptian, Persian and Greek warriors, battle-plated all of them. Still later, in the middle ages, one sees the same thought, or necessity, culminating in the completely metal-plated man and horse.

In short, considering all such developments or evolutions, from the early tree root used as a plow to the modern steam shovel, from the turtle to the battleship, from the thrown stone, or slung shot, or arrow, to the howitzer and the machine-gun and the bomb, there is no evidence of any lone mental concept or creation on the part of anyone or anything which could be pointed to as an instant and individual invention or creation. In the main, in so far as the things man has done, or invented, they are no more than adaptive and improving bits of handicraft, all suggested, not only by the things already done or methods already involved and in use in nature or by earlier man, but also by what at the immediate moment, and because of constantly changing conditions, required, and that obviously, to be done.

Yet in proof of his "individuality" and his right to persistence as an "individual", man continues to call attention to his creative powers here on earth. Witness, he can make tools, machines, buildings, books, pictures, all extensions of the creative force that is in him, but which in the main he believes are personal to himself. This done, and as a presentation of that kind, he conceives of himself as thinking instead of reacting, inventing instead of improving, designing instead of copying—in short, creating a race as well as a social order, all of his own devising. He has written his history, filled libraries with stories of *his* inventions, and the world with clamor as to *his* creative powers.

Even more astounding, he struts and plumes himself (probably by some play-master's permission, or, and better, some imperious compulsion which supplies him with this quite mystical cheer) whenever he achieves some one little advance which he looks upon as his own—consider the crowing rooster. The ancient, and for the most part forgotten, processes by which mysterious and evasive elements and energies have formed themselves, he does not know.

But in this connection, let us consider the tree. Here it is. And there is its evolutionary history. And here are its present varied forms, or family connections. And here its present particular process of manifesting, maintaining, and replenishing itself. It too, if it possessed such a thing as a voice, might claim not only individuality, but even a degree of mind and inventiveness since trees vary so in size and physical arrangement and result or product; and not only that but actually succeed in varying themselves one from another in texture, flavor of fruit, color of blossom, bark and the like. The whole process of natural selection is no more than that, and the how of it is even now being clarified by the biologists working in the field of the chromosomes.

Considering all this, might not the tree if it could speak well ask of man, "Can you make a nut? Can you make it grow? Can you line a central pocket of a nut with velvet and fill it with a kernel that, given similar or even relatively similar conditions such as environed the parent tree, will make another tree, another nut, or hundreds of them, each capable of reproducing trees?"

But having asked that of man, man might in turn inquire, "You—you—can you make a spectroscope, a telescope, a microscope, a dynamo, an aeroplane, a radio?" After this exchange however, would not both be compelled to acknowledge a creative power outside of themselves which dwarfed all that either could do or dream of? For both are faced not only by the mystery of their own organic appearance here, but by the endless billions of mysteries and wonders which neither of them could invent or create, but which in turn, and like themselves, have been or are "invented" or evolved under the mystic direction of the forces which surround and include them, and make their world.

For if each in its turn does not derive from some mystic source or force—its form as well as its energy—if they are not blossoms on some energy vine that was before they came and lasts long after they are gone—then what are they? from whence could they have come? The blood stream is man's vine running back through all generations to the beginning of man. And both might, in sum would, be compelled to conclude, and in unison: We seem to be rooted in some seemingly endless, deathless evolutionary force or power out of which we have come. And if so, is that force mind—or what?

Indeed the organizing principle as demonstrated by man copies very closely and yet not as artistically the organizing ability of nature. The first is called a mental process, the second a mechanical or natural process. It is ordinarily thought to be best illustrated by the process of evolution or natural selection or the mechanical situation as in the case of Mountains—their appearance and disappearance. Let me illustrate: A man will sometimes set out trees by thousands in imitation of a forest, but before him, after all, is the model—the forest. Where nature has had time enough to perfect a true forest you will find that it is beautifully arranged, really more carefully and gracefully, than the forest which the man makes. You need only wander through a beech forest in such parts of the world as they flourish, or among the giant Redwoods of California, or the Georgian Pine Groves to see how perfectly and gracefully they space themselves. The forest-organizing ability of man could not possibly do better. The one is a natural process; the other is supposed to be the mental achievement of a human mind.

A more complicated picture of the two methods is presented for instance by a marching army or a parade of any kind, and then a horde of driver ants that approach in an evenly-measured belt six to eight inches wide and hundreds of feet long. As is well known, the belt travels fast and destroys all that it encounters from animals and men to trees, if the tree is by any chance a part of its food supply. The army or parade is a so-called mental achievement of man; the glistening black belt of the drivers is held to be an instinct of nature's—not mind. A still more complicated picture is presented by a great railway system organized by man. Here are the thousands of miles of tracks, the thousands of cars of different descriptions, different service uses; the signal system which completely protects a 3,000 mile line and all its branches; the dispatcher's office with its accurate knowledge of the movement of all trains at all times; the engine service with its divisions, its roundhouses, its cleaning service; the passenger stations with the ticket service; the freight service with its complicated commercial arrangements for the receipt, transport, and billing of goods and the like. The Pennsylvania employs as many as 60,000 men. The New York Central relatively the same number, and all of this is set forth as the result of the mental processes of man over a period of time.

The individual newly come to life and at the age of fourteen or fifteen seeing these things assumes the achievement before him to be of recent origin. More he is inclined to look upon it as the work of a relatively few minds of his day. Of course those who know of the evolutionary process know better, but contrast with this:—a mental achievement of men with a natural achievement of nature's which preceded the railway system by ages and by reason of which the railway has come into existence. I refer to the home life and the communal life of men which is no achievement of the thought of any living men but a race thought and a race evolution which is hundreds of thousands of years old. You have only to think of the houses or cottages that dot the entire world, their fires for warmth and cooking, their utensils and tables and chairs and wells or their water systems, their barns with their horses, cattle, sheep, and their fields carefully arranged to provide food and clothing by which they live. Here is something which man did not invent; which he did not think out, but into which he was guided by instinct as well as by necessity. Every household, although far more complicated than any such unit as a box car, a baggage car, a passenger car or station, works efficiently and often beautifully—the children, the school, the church, the factory, the entire service which has gathered around the home as a center and which is actually operated from it in all of its ramifications, one of which would be the railroad itself. It is not managed by any *one* individual or any group of individuals. One might say of it that through the instincts provided by nature and by reason of the difficulties which those instincts encounter and which they seek to overcome, the survival instinct, the love instinct, the play instinct, all of these millions of homes wherever,—with their furniture, their lamps, their books, their utensils, their clothing, all that makes them possible, are not a product of human reason and are not operated by human reason, but rather to this hour are operated by the instincts with which these natural mechanisms—men—are provided. Yet the railroad is looked upon as the result of the mental cogitations of man. But the homes of men cannot be looked upon as the result of the cogitations of men because obviously they are not. Love is not the result of a mental cogitation; neither is hunger; neither is the desire for survival; neither is the desire for pleasure. But having so said, which of the two is the greater mental achievement— nature's or man's? [W]

Theodore Dreiser

Myth of
Individual Possession

THE FIRST THING TO CONSIDER IN CONNECTION WITH THE THOUGHT of possessions is that the value of anything has no mathematical equivalent. You can say of a measure of land that it contains, or is in extent, twenty acres, and that assertion will remain true. Twenty acres will not shrink to five or expand to thirty over any period of time. A quart of anything remains a quart, a pound a pound. A mile is 5,280 feet. A building a hundred or a thousand feet high, and so on. But the value of any given thing cannot be known in the same way. It has no stable mathematical equivalent. A discovered diamond may weigh an ounce or twenty carats and be of a certain clarity and radiance. But its value is something else. That cannot be accurately fixed for any period of time or place. Similarly with a ton of coal, a bushel of wheat, a pound of coffee. You can say that at some given time and place and under certain conditions a ton of coal, a bushel of wheat, or a pound of coffee is worth so and so much. But no more. For values in these or any other matters are constantly changing. They depend on time and place, supply and demand, custom or taboo, mood or taste, or the lack of either or both. There are no fixed values or value measures. Yet value, however unstable mathematically or in any definite fixed terms still remains the essence of any possessions, and this essence relates to quality, or charm, or comfort, or design, color, size, taste, weight, radiance, and the like, the while the mathematical, whether in money or exchange of any kind, varies constantly.

THEODORE DREISER

‡ ‡ ‡

When one thinks of it there is so little of anything that one can personally possess. "Health" is like the weather, for instance, that barometric and almost mythical thing that dogmatically at least is presumed to include physical if not mental strength, energy, appetite, nervous and so mental ease, the full and pleasant use of all the five senses in perfect working order (if not precisely [possessing] any definite material or mental means wherewith to excite and enjoy them), is none the less as evasive as the secret of life. One deals with [health] not as a stable quantity or quality but as something which like the weather or the movement of the planetary bodies changes from not hour to hour but minute to minute. The psychic or mental yield of its possession is supposed to include not only mental and physical ease and content, but subject to the *"wish"* and *"will"* of the possessor—enjoyment of life in almost any of its manifold forms. But—on examination—how elusive and even fabulous that proves. For with health—at times even without it—most often excessively so without it—is bound up desire, the exact source, to say nothing of the quantity, quality and direction of which in nature no one at least as yet can determine. For the physical or mental *"desires"* of the so-called *"individual"* are as variable and as complex as the exterior excitements or impacts which play upon him and which are as extensive and variable as (maybe) the Universe itself. And also these are not *wished* or *willed* by him. They are not only evoked but provoked in him through his various sensory channels and responses. Yet only to the extent that these, at the period or moment of impact from without, are capable of registering the same. And such registrations vary enormously, not only because of the interior condition and equipment of a given human organism, but the external environment of the same—two sets of conditions which are likely to make for an unstable rather than a stable harmony.

We will say that you are mentally or sensorially or emotionally equipped to enjoy a beautiful landscape, but that you are nearsighted. Or that you have, let's say, mental and more emotional knowledge of the exquisite odor of flowers, and more, a desire to enjoy them, but that your own sense of smell is defective. Or that as to music, concerning which you hear thousands rave, you are tone blind. Or that as to travel and the pleasures of it which you can well sense, you find yourself physically or financially unable to either endure, or, worse, pay for. In the realms of love, food, drink—in short, the various physical or sensory pleasures of life—these frustrations or disharmonies, due to lack of balance between external and internal conditions or equipments, are endless. [W]

THEODORE DREISER

‡ ‡ ‡

In connection with possessions one should consider *beauty* which cannot be possessed, although there is an entire world of it. A free bird is more beautiful than a caged one—bird in flight. But a flying bird cannot be possessed. Color or beauty in any free form—a rainbow, a blue sky, a blue lake or sunset, is not anything you can deposit in a bank, only in your temperament. The value and majesty of wildness cannot be enclosed by a fence or the walls of a room. Yet, unpossessed as property, these things can still obsess you, *possess* you, and do. For illustration—Shelley, Keats, Poe, Omar, Turner, Van Gogh—in sum, all the great artists and poets of the world, who, owing nothing, possessed via reaction to unpossessed beauty all the beauty there was or is.

Beauty can sometimes be transmitted to sound and so be captured, in a sense, possessed. [Added by T.D.]

‡ ‡ ‡

One of the prize possessions of quite everyone, I presume, is their "personality" or "individuality" and its co-efficient, their point of view. Most inhabitants of the world capable of thinking about the matter would insist that they have a point of view in regard at least to what they thought about. What that might be is usually a matter of arbitrary selection on the part of the individual—religion, morality, peace, war, kindness or cruelty, wealth or poverty, and related subjects.

In a vast number of cases, thinking definitely on any subject in which they are vitally interested, they would go so far as to associate their honor and integrity with their view point. They believe and believe firmly, and their belief like their assumed individuality is a distinct possession, yet mark how insubstantial and evanescent quite all such possessions are.

An individual at a certain age, particularly when young, will believe in one thing, whatever it may be, usually something current applying to the social economic state in which he finds himself. At another period, and resulting with the exception to things exterior to his definite point of view, that same will change. A believer in Christianity, or Mohammedism, or Buddhism will [sometimes] slowly and almost unconsciously relinquish his very definite view which he holds at the time as an almost priceless possession for something entirely different and then may hold to the second thing with the same figure of possession. A tory will become a liberal, a liberal will become a communist, or an anarchist, one who is at one time of his life and usually and invariably by reason of economic feel, a firm believer in the value not only of individual power but of individual material possessions, will relinquish that view point for one which dismisses these values completely and substitutes for them the value of mind and the freedom from the burden of possessions and of power.

The love and tragedy of eighteen and twenty is the butt and the jest of the sophistication of forty; looking back on the first state as an illusion and an utter folly and the second as the equivalent of peace and a reasonable amount of mental and physical comfort.

The Myth of Possessions
In a castle of prosperity
A thousand servants
In a castle or close of prosperity
Possessions—
Flowers
Walks
Trees

The company of those who delight in thinking
On possessions,
Yet contemplate only
That which cannot and will not be possessed
That fades and flies
Even as they who stand and gaze
Or dream
Of that
Which will not fade
Or fly

One of the sayings of Ganaka, King of Mithila, an ancient country of India, has remained famous in Indian literature and deserves to remain so. When his capital, Mithila, was being destroyed by a conflagration, he turned round and said, "While Mithila is burning, nothing that is mine is burnt."

If you will consult the Dictionary (Websters International, 1929) you will find the word *possession* set forth as "fact or condition of a person having such control of property that he may legally enjoy it to the exclusion of all others, having no better right than himself. *But what constitutes such a possession depends upon the subject matter and the legal system involved.* In general, all legal systems recognize as having "possession, him who (like a thief,) has achieved physical control of a thing and is holding it for himself."

To be sure, law discriminates between legal and illegal possession by any means. But at that, it only engages at all times of stable government, but not otherwise, to assure the legal possessor that in so far as it is able it will *seek* to protect him in his possessions. And where it fails, it will endeavor to apprehend and punish whomsoever has dispossessed him. But never agreeing to make return. It feels that it cannot engage to do that. Oftenest you personally must suffer loss whereas the robber may suffer no punishment. But that, as you see, spells only quasi-possession. You hold a thing not wholly as an inalienable possession but subject to theft or loss; also to taxes for protection of you in your use of the same, which constitutes a partial loss. Also subject to eminent domain, which means that if either City, County, State, or Nation desires possession of your property, or possessions, it can take them, rendering in return therefore not the possessions themselves but an equivalent either in money or goods of a like character. But none-the-less, as you see, your personal possessions become impersonal—worth more or less according to a given opinion or condition at a given time. Also the character of the thing given you in place of the thing you had will not be that thing—likely something decidedly different. At best, upon demand of the State, or accident, they become something of a like character only—not your primary possessions.

But more than that, there are connected with these same "possessions" other qualifications and modifications which greatly depreciate the so-called fact of possession, since in addition to all that has been said already, they are, as our American law reads, subject to *"Acts of God"*. That is, they are subject to storms, tornadoes, lightning, floods, fire, explosion, earthquakes and tidal waves, for which neither the State nor any insurance company assumes, unless heavily paid, responsibility. To these again are added deterioration and disintegration from so-called natural causes—the actions of time, heat, cold, damp, insects, and the ordinary wear and tear of use which must be met with repairs, always expensive, and finally and regardless of repairs, with total loss. Your possessions of say twenty years ago. Where are they? Your possessions of so little as ten or even five years ago? Your car of today. Is it in your garage? Have you called up to learn? Your House. Is it standing at this moment? So you see how dubious your own sense of possession is. Forefend as you will and as you know, your so-called possessions are highly unreal. Despite anything you can do they ultimately decay and disappear.

But there are still other qualifications and modifications of possession which come in the form of changes of style, taste, and personal mood in regard to them. As regards this last, consider the *enforced* "possessions" of so many who do not want what they have or "possess", and in many instances, and willy nilly, must use; who object, that is, to the form and character of the things about them—their color, shape, age—also to what they must wear and at times to what they must eat. The drab furniture of a person who has little or nothing, or, who having something or much, has yet seen something better, something more beautiful in form, which because of that, and at once, has made the other meaningless! Neither in either case desires what he has. It has become not a valued "possession" but an irritation and a weariness. He no longer wants it, and if possible, will not have it, his one dream being to escape its reducing presence.

Hence these, while counted as "possessions" are none-the-less afflictions which one does not willingly "possess", but by which one is almost evilly "possessed"—something that produces discomfort, unhappiness, even pain and rage. They are not representative of anything that conforms to the idea of value which is what the word "possession" is supposed to convey; nothing of its gratification, delight, comfort. On the other hand, all that such "possessions" sensorially convey are moods of deprivation, degradation, discomfort, and dispossession, even to the point of social destruction. So much so, and at times, that is, in given instances, the so-called "possessor" in the hope of avoiding such "possession" will abandon all of them—flee or even kill himself. He will not endure that which others, looking upon the same, count as his "possessions".

Nonetheless, in these and all other instances of possession, loss or change, rent or taxes, or repairs, and whether the possessions are desired or not, or are destructive or not, or hateful or not, are still legally and socially looked upon as possessions, or property that must be accounted for as such to the state, or abandoned, which abandonment quite frequently follows.

What you have enjoyed, if at all, is an evanescent comfort or charm—yet never wholly, for you alone,—not even your bed—, and worse, one that you have constantly paid for. Never was a single thing a true possession, that is, personal to you alone. Rather it has been a rented or taxed comfort or discomfort, which for a period only you were permitted to use, or were compelled to endure, or did endure, and which perforce, and in due course, you were compelled to surrender, or which vanished before your eyes as by fire, decay, break, or loss through theft, or other causes. And yet you have continued to think of them as "possessions", purely personal and entirely yours.

Another phase of this idea of "possessions" involves the fact that rarely, if ever, is it that a person secures singular and so complete possession of anything even though he seek so to possess a thing or person—as a slave. In fact, so-called possessions are rarely, if ever capable of being held to purely individual use. You think of your watch, for instance, as a highly personal possession. But is it? Primarily the reason for a watch is its use in synchronizing your affairs, obligations, movements, with those of other people who possess or share, or are supposed to, watches or clocks, public or private. And because of that, their use of watches with which you synchronize yours—not your personal use of it as a time-marking instrument—is what makes it of value to you—but never as a singular personal possession as you can see. For it is a race watch, not a personal watch that you are using, just as it is a race radio, not a personal radio that you "listen in on". For except for other radios, just as except for other watches in use by others—and no one of them devised by you—your watch would have no meaning; you could not use it; you would have nothing to use it for.

If this statement seems dubious, consider yourself entirely alone on an island and in possession of a watch. In that situation, its only possible value to you would be as a measure of your past or present *mental* relation to the periods and forms of activities characteristic of an outer world full of, or at least inhabited by, other individuals in possession and use of watches or clocks, users or time-measurers like yourself. In the past, you see, you were associated with these others who made your life for you—your sense of it. Hence it is with their present goings, comings, and doings—or those of others like them—the race—always synchronized by watches and clocks, that causes you to be still mentally concerned as to time. Indeed, their continued existence somewhere always marked by the use of watches and clocks or some form of time-measurement holds for you the only meaning of your watch or your own continued existence. For through these other people—your nation, your race, the peoples and conditions of past times—you either live or are not alive, and because of that and their relation to time-measurement, you have become time-conscious and so watch-conscious. But without them to think of, to wonder over, to measure all your life and character by, how long do you suppose you would remain time conscious? How soon would life and time become a myth? You would be like a man in a fog or the dark. There would be nothing to indicate the meaning of your existence.

You are not an individual but a race unit—identical with all other race units and your watch a race watch as I have said, and that is ideationally synchronized by you with all other watches the world over—all time everywhere, which in itself, if you chance to know (relativity having explained all this) is quite an astounding illusion under which you labor. For the same time is not everywhere. In sum, a figment of evolution, such as you yourself are—an evolutionary myth.

But to return to seemingly more real and stable things. An individual secures a house, buys furniture, fills the house with his or her so-called "possessions". But for what reason? Immediate and continuous personal use without use by any other? That would certainly be a fair illustration of exclusive possession—which is what possession means. But the thought is obviously nonsensical. Even if you were entirely alone with your possessions as you were with your watch on an island, and alone used them, it would still be a fact that you could not and would not (the race of which you are an integral and indivisible part, being what it is—an organic whole evolved by forces outside itself)—you could not consider such singularly race-things as personal and private possessions. For the very idea of a chair or table or home or any other implement or thing does not even suggest to your consciousness lone and exclusive use by you. Whatever it is you are thinking of be sure it is a social idea or implement. And any use that might be implied by it to you would be a social use—by no means singular. For you yourself cannot contemplate yourself as entirely alone, that is, without relatives, people, a countryside, a town, a world around you. Such a condition—the entire absence of humanity that is—would spell death to you and would be death, since to yourself alone you could not exist—ideationally or practically. In a twinkling your thought of an individual possession would depart—for from whom, what other individual, would you be withholding it? And without the thought of someone to withhold something—anything—from, what becomes of possession? No thing can exist in your mind as a personal possession without these others.

In connection with this, consider your moods or emotions in regard to what other people think or say in regard to what you do, wear, see, think, where and how you live, go, or act—and then study the effect of these moods or fears or emotions on your personal possessions. For you are not to forget that all psychiatry is concerned with that, and that our asylums, hospitals, jails, and graves are full of the victims of race compulsions as these have affected so-called individuals or units. In short, how much are you governed by others in all that you seek for yourself—how little by yourself, your personal choice, if you can conceive of having a personal choice? For you are not to forget that your choice of anything—house, girl, dog, boat, resort, profession, party, religion, quite anything and everything—is racial, and not individual. For instance, *your* idea of a house to live in, a suit of clothes to wear, a profession to follow, the kind of food you eat and what you feel is good for you—how did you come by such ideas, notions, conclusions? Did you make the profession or was it made for you—already in existence when you came? And if you were born in Africa on the Congo, would you build a Kraal or an American cottage? And if you were born in India would you naturally wear the native or a foreign costume? For you are not to forget that food, clothing, customs, notions, religions, physical appearance and even degrees of durability vary with races, climates, nations—so that in China a so-called "Individual" is still a Chinese individual, and in the Arctic an Esquimaux individual or type, and so on and so on. So that his so-called individual possessions curiously enough in different countries and different races take on different national, race and climate characteristics, and this in spite of his imagined desire for individuality in his possessions. He cannot even achieve possessions that are individual and so personal—try as he may.

But granting for the most part you experience, or think you do, a sense of personal possession—purely personal like your possession of your tie, handkerchief, shirt, socks—still even these,—and because of your need of your fellowmen to compel their use or to admire them—are not personal but are used by you because of group or race usage or heat or cold, according to climate, but not otherwise. You wear a tie, shoes, socks, such as you do because other people in your country, your city, your continent, your climate, your circle wear ties, shoes, socks exactly like them. And when you do, you do it in order to be or feel in style; hats the same, shirts, overcoats, mufflers, etc., the same. But if you were in China, India, Arabia, you would dress differently, according to how the natives dressed or the climate demanded. As for your other and less intimate things, you will find, if you will but pause to consider, that they are as much, if not more, for the use and comfort and inspiration of a family, friends, relatives, neighbors, and if not these, then for the eye, the admiration, and the attraction of the many, who, for one reason or another—social, commercial, political, artistic,—each "possessor" of anything would like to impress. In sum, your possessions whatever they are, have much more than a quasi communal as well as ceremonial character, because you yourself are communal, ceremonial, and not in any way individual or personal. It is the Race's, Nation's, or community's instincts expressed through you—the so-called individual—that makes any so-called private possession *seem* real. For these instincts are never individual or purely personal reactions or effects. Hence this thought of exclusiveness in connection with these or any other so-called personal possessions is utterly illusory.

But there is still another way of coming at a clearer conception of this illusion of possessions and proving them to be illusions. You use, let us say, a railroad to travel on. But is that a personal "possession" of yours, or rather a social or general, or racial possession? You use a public library, an art gallery, a theater, a hotel, a market, a storage warehouse, a church, a ship or aeroplane, a public highway or "private" street, a bridge, also electric light, gas, the telephone, the telegraph, as a matter of fact, anything and everything that makes your personal "possessive" life possible. But what of these are personal or yours? And where would your so-called personal possessive life be without them?

As you can see for yourself, there is nothing either personal or private to you about any of these things, any more than there is about the government under which you live, its legislative, executive, judicial, and diplomatic branches. And more, it is only in an exceedingly minute way that you have the benefit of all of these things which are none-the-less a major portion of your sense of life and possession. But you did not and could not personally create, or duplicate, or operate, any of these things. If you live in a City, think of the absence of a police department, a fire department, a street cleaning department, a mail service, a telephone service, and so on, without which even your more intimate city "possessions" would rapidly diminish, and not only that, but swiftly becomes meaningless. And not only these, but your very life. For the life of which they are a part and of which you are a part would have vastly diminished or vanished. Therefore, as you can see, your true "possessions" and values are more social and racial than personal—by no means purely personal.

Perhaps, however, the chief source of illusion in connection with material possessions springs from the average mind confusing minor seeming material "possessions" with major ones. Also because of the fact that the average man cannot grasp the truth that *value* has no mathematical equivalent. That is, he feels that with whatever romantic, sentimental, aesthetic, or practical quality or value he ideationally chooses or is moved to endow on a thing, that that endowment by him gives it a distinct and even tangible *value* and that that value can be expressed in terms of money, or, if not money, then something that is the equivalent of money, and which equivalent he then chooses to think represents the value of his possession—is, in short, the equivalent of it.

But of course this is not true. No personal, private or public value has an exact equivalent anywhere. None-the-less, because most people are in immediate contact with a chair, bedroom suite, a piano, or an automobile, anything that seems purely personal and of immediate use, they proceed to confuse these with the much larger holdings of not only themselves but of others. That is, they attribute to these larger matters the same substantial personal and intimate reality and *"value"* that they attribute to these lesser things and so proceed to confuse the larger things—corporate shares in railroads, steamships, water power plants, coal mines, government, and what not else, with the watch in their pocket and the coat on their back. In short, because of the chair, the piano and the automobile, these others take on a seeming of reality and even personality or substance intimate and personal to them, which is entirely erroneous and illusory. For with the piano, the chair and the automobile, they are at least sufficiently intimate to *suggest* personal possession, whereas as to these others—railroads, electric light companies, gas companies, giant stores, office buildings, warehouses, ships, and their symbolic equivalents in the form of money, stocks, bonds, insurance, investments and so forth—no such individual and possessive contact exists or can exist. It has never existed for anyone.

You can understand this best, I think if you will think of the dime or the dollar in your pocket, and then try to think of, and more, mentally realize, not so much as a billion or two or five or seven billions of dollars, of which today some men or their Corporations are in "possession" but rather of so little as a million or two or three millions of dollars. How conscious of these, their absolute or even for the most part their relative values, do you suppose either you or that average man we all talk about, or the millionaire, or the billionaire who has them really is? Exactly conscious? Even approximately conscious? At all conscious? The answer is, no. And the reason for that is, as I have said before, that value has no mathematical equivalent. It is a matter of opinion, sometimes of law, which is congealed opinion, but no more than that. So recently as January, 1935, in a public discussion of our great financial or "possessions" problem, it was asked of the Supreme Court of the United States whether congress by law could make a dime into a dollar, and it was asserted by the Attorney General for the Government that it could. Which proves of course that the rumored exact value of anything is a myth. It is all relative. You cannot truly estimate a correct value of anything because mentally or materially or from the point of view of beauty, it cannot be grasped. It is the same as attempting to realize sidereal distances, which, as you know, ever remain mental abstractions—not realities.

Suppose you write $100,000 or $100,000,000 on a piece of paper and then proceed to think about them. After five or ten minutes or a week, I will ask of you, what if anything you realize in connection with them other than that they are a row of figures or symbols. If not just those, then what? A house? A railroad? A bundle of bonds? A large company?—its plant or equipment? But how exact or real is that? And is not that all that you can realize in connection with your attempts at realizing a hundred or more millions of dollars?

To be sure, your attempts at realization may be and can be seemingly, not actually, aided by some piles of printed paper labelled money, or stocks, or bonds, or shares, or actual piles of bullion—gold or silver. But these, if you attempt to translate them into more substantial or understandable and at the same time usable things, become what? Well, let us see—yachts, lands, cattle, trips, food, clothes, buses, cars, railroads, public buildings, and the like, on which from time to time certain prices, ever varying but still prices, have been put, and which you either in part—never wholly—use, or draw interest on, or sell; or you read of if not see them and perhaps think of as equivalent of these same buildings, etc.

But are they? You know what your answer must be. "I don't know." To be sure, in some cases you can take $100,000 or $1,000,000 and buy a building with it, or draw so much interest—3 to 7 per cent on it, or exchange it for something. But then what? Have you a million dollars' worth, or an exact exchange? Your answer is, "Maybe", or, "I don't know", or "It's worth more I think", "Or less". Even the fact that at a sale or trade you might get your million dollars back or even more than a million would not prove that you had gotten its exact value or that what you bought was still worth a million, if it ever was. You might be fooling yourself or he might be fooling you. Let us hope it is the first way. But as to any exact value, no. It could not be determined. And let us illustrate further as to that.

You pay, let us say, a dollar for a dinner. But is it worth a dollar? And how would you go about proving that? It may well be, and no doubt is, a belief, your belief, that it is or was worth a dollar, but what of that? Would it be worth a dollar to another? Try and think that out? Again, you can look at a house, a dog, a bird, a building or picture, a suit of clothing, or contemplate a trip of some kind and say it is worth so much. But is it? And how do you prove it? By the happiness you get? or the disappointment you experience? These are the best ways, but as you see, they are not exact. What you can do is to put one thing beside or opposite another and say, "I will give you this for that." Which proves what? Exact value?

Something that anyone else anywhere would agree with? You know that is not so. And yet, that is all you can do; no more. Only the theory of relativity works here. That is, you can put lands, mines, ships, buildings, over against gold or printed paper or other mines or ships, but you still have nothing wherewith you can accurately and intimately measure them. It cannot be done and never has been done.

To be sure, you can look at a house as you do at the symbols or numbers supposed to indicate sidereal distances, and say it is worth so much to you. But as to the actual cost or the actual value of the thing—the labor put in or on it, the value of the labor, item by item, and detail by detail, for which the thousand, the million or billion dollars is said to have been paid or was paid, what of that? There is, as you must know if you stop to think, no way by which the mind can settle that. It can put a dollar on a table and a bushel of wheat opposite and say that the dollar is the equal of the wheat, or the wheat is worth a dollar. But the dollar can buy less or more wheat, according to demand. And how real or stable is demand? At once, as you see, you are in the realm of the Mythical, wherein you have always been and where you will remain.

However, in regard to both public and private "possessions," there is yet another aspect or condition which remarkably modifies the validity of both and leaves one wondering as to how and why thoughts relative to both individuality and possession can really maintain themselves. It is this:

We will go back to our piano, lamp, painting, carpet, and other things of the same kind. And you are, we will say, still, as you think, in full "possession" of these. But you are to remember along with all else that has been said, that constant association in connection with them causes their reality as personal possessions to fluctuate as does the chemical in a barometer. For these—their values to the possessor—depend on the temperaments and moods of those who hold them as real and valuable. And how stable are these? The real value of anything is, as I have said before, no more substantial than the mood or desire of the so-called possessor. If the desire for, or delight in the possession is exceedingly keen, the possession has the value of that desire and delight—but no more. And that is not mathematically measurable. Not only that, but familiarity, long association with the possession, sometimes increases, sometimes decreases the sentimental value attached to the same; and bear in mind that is as real as any other value—maybe even more real. Next, pain or irritation of any kind can, and frequently does, sometimes instantly, change and most frequently (not always) diminishes, and not infrequently destroys completely the value of the thing "possessed" to the possessor. It can become, as you well know, hateful, and so valueless, not necessarily to others but to you, and not only as a chair or table, but as a "possession" which is something else again. And not only is this true of a chair or a table; it can be equally true of a house, of clothing, of a horse, a dog, cattle, your wife or husband or child. In short, any seemingly stable material or mental thing. Also of things which are by no means so real or stable, such as love, friendship, good will. Even a city, a country, a nation, a race, a continent, life itself can lose value after this fashion. If you doubt this, consider any city, region, resort, or country by which at some time or other you have been fascinated and contrast your older valuation with your present one. For such things as you now know can increase or decrease in value by reason of no more than a rumor of beauty, or gaiety, or profit, or pleasure connected with them—and whether the same were even approximately true or not.

In that connection, consider the recent value changes in cities like Leningrad, Constantinople, Vienna. Many are still alive who saw them glow with color, romance, power, plus all the "material" values which invariably accompany these first—the values for instance, of their houses, lands, paintings and the like. Many have lived to see these diminish almost to the point of desolation by the evanishing of those same most insubstantial of all insubstantial things— *gaiety, color,* and the rumor of *power* that went with them.

Hence, not in the real estate and the buildings, nor yet in the equipment, location, nor the population or wealth of cities or countries lies their surety of endurance, or their seeming or worth as possessions, but in the *thoughts, moods, beliefs* of people everywhere *in* the reality and durability of that alleged power and gaiety—no more. When that vanishes, as such insubstantial things so easily do vanish, the seeming reality also ends. In the case of the Cities mentioned, it was no more real than a mass mood which in its turn may have been, and no doubt was, based on an illusion. You saw the illusion of the wealth and prosperity of America disappear almost overnight. It was in the Fall of 1929. And a matter of more than a few days!

Lastly I should like to point out and emphasize that there is always a seeming of matter and of value as well as of energy or power in connection with anything. But these values are variable, relative, and never definite or real according to any fixed standard; because there is no fixed standard. That is a myth. And so these things which you are contemplating involve a seeming, and a seeming only. What you do is to accept a current and always changing and passing notion of values. In that connection, and merely to cite one instance, consider the enormous value put upon Christian relics in the middle ages and their value today; or your gold certificates of 1929 and their value now, or gold itself, which is said, or is supposed, to be the equivalent of this or that of which you are thinking—comfort for one thing, happiness another. But what is that? Mere thought, or what?

Grandiose moods or notions frequently pass current in your mind for substances or deeds or actions of seemingly measurable worth to you, but which are rarely, if ever, so; rarely in all time have they ever been so. You are but dreaming of things. You do not know your true wealth, your "possessions", their "values". These are figments of the mind. There never was, regardless of whether there ever will be, any true way of fully sensing and so fully knowing what it is that you possess or what its value is to you or others. You merely think you know. And at that, as I have shown, you do not even "possess" it. It, as much, and more at times, possesses you! And to your destruction!

Myth of Individual Responsibility

THE MYTH OF RESPONSIBILITY FOR ANY ACTIONS OR DEEDS OTHER than those we have been trained or conditioned to perform is obvious. Consider the education or training of animals. Do we, in their relations with us consider them responsible for anything other than that we have trained or taught or conditioned them to do? Of course not, for we know that by a proper application of rewards and punishments they may be taught any course of action within their powers—even those most contrary to their natural instincts and propensities. They can be taught to sit, stand, box, jump through a loop, retrieve, guard a house or car, etc. But it is direction from without accompanied by the forces of pleasure or pain that finally make him responsible to you and to himself for the correct performance of what you have taught him to do.

And in so far as man's evolution is concerned, nature has employed no other method. Obstacles, obstacles, obstacles, and compulsion, compulsion, compulsion—to overcome them or die. But compulsion is not free will and without free will there is no responsibility—only compulsion. For is it new experience that has made both dog and man apprehensive of pain? You menace the dog with a stick or hunger and reward or pleasure him with food. So has nature done—and still does with you. Its evolutionary instruments—the state, the tribe, the social group—threaten you with law, ostracism, poverty, hate, pain, and reward you with salary, respect, applause, social favor and what not. And like the dog you respond. But only for reasons of these. And with these removed neither you nor the dog would have the faintest trace of responsibility. [*Or*]

‡   ‡   ‡

There is no intended evil.

Birth control has no place in the economy of the oppossum and a score of young may be born at one time: But this means tragedy, for there is usually room for only a dozen at the 'milk bar', and only first comers are served. One's pity is stirred deeply at the thought of the diminutive blind little being, thirteenth or fourteenth in the bread line, fighting its way up hill and into an unknown cavern, only to find no unoccupied fount. For a time it creeps about, futilely pushing its more fortunate brothers and sisters, but finally succumbing to the pangs of hunger, it tumbles out of the pouch to the ground.——William Beebe, Director of Tropical Research, N. Y. Zoological Society.

What responsibility has this little mother—a mere machine! Yet what great emotional labors and pains she is at to feed and protect the others, the while not knowing of this structural cruelty. In India they worship the Elephant God, who sometimes nods or sleeps and has to be awakened to the errors or frailties of other (lesser) gods, which is the same as to suspect nature of nodding or sleeping. And (in the Old Testament) Amos asked concerning the congenitally crippled or fluid or weak—"What then, did the hand of the Potter shake". [*Or*]

T.D.

[Another typical *Note,* here, a quotation filed under many headings, with Dreiser's comments above and below. *Editor's Note*]

‡ ‡ ‡

Responsibility in man if not [in] animals or the sense of it springs from training and nothing more. Nature or matter-energy or physical and chemical responses conditions you (as it did your ancestors via evolution) to respond to heat, cold, light, darkness, sound, pressure, etc. What you could get to eat and live by has conditioned you to respond to what you eat—perhaps even to *like* what you eat. In America you are conditioned by the political system there holding; Your parents, leaders, etc., to like the American flag, the American school system, American customs and rules. If you had been born in Russia, Japan, the Arctic, or the Congo you would have been differently conditioned—perhaps to like ice floes, snow, the dark—or heat, flies, snakes, lions, Kraals or thatched huts—anyhow to endure and expect them. In Japan the Emperor would be your ideal; in Russia Lenin—and more, you would be held responsible for any troublesome variation from these conditioned responses. [*Or*]

T.D.

‡ ‡ ‡

In America alone the coddling moth annually ravages the 2,000,000 acres of the national apple industry. This loss plus the urge to stop it, plus *ignorance* as to its cause, brought about the discovery and elimination of the cause. So great was the loss in some instances to particular individuals that small growers failed—had mortgages foreclosed. In several cases these losses brought to their owners nervous depressions, illness, and death.

So break down, death of individuals, sufferings of various kinds—disorder as against order was brought about by the necessity of the coddling moth to eat or die. *It is blameless.*

‡ ‡ ‡

Both subordination and insubordination are guaranteed by the contrasts which nature presents and without which it could not present itself as it does. Big and little; heavy and light; short and long distances; strong and weak; hot and cold; condensation as opposed to diffusion; tenseness as opposed to relaxation; speed as opposed to slowness; dark as opposed to light, etc., etc. Not only that, but each thing being itself, in the main, an assemblage of many elements or minute portions of them—each and every one of these having its opposites as well as its affinities to deal with—it follows that there is required an enormously complicated series of adjustments between each unit or group of units, however small or large so that no so-called mind, as yet developed, nor any group of researching "minds" has been able to more than partially trace, let alone map, the order and certain consequences of these various adjustments and readjustments in the endless fields in which they occur.

On the contrary, and at long last, all adjustments of whatsoever forms or combinations of matter-energy—whether these same relate to island universes or the all but insoluble activities of the electrons, atoms, molecules, the attractions and repulsions which characterize the same remain, in so far as man is concerned, unknown not only as to their operations but the source of the same. All man knows is that *they are*. They function in seemingly accurate ways to effect many seemingly accurate results—the same to be registered, in the case of man, by a number of accurately devised sensory organs—but whether for the sole pleasure or pain of man or any of the other sense equipped and so sense registering creatures is not clear.

One thing, however, is clear, and that is that a seemingly universal law of limitation governs all evolved or created things, be they what they may. And these limitations, specifically governing each given thing, may not be transgressed. Water of a limited volume may not successfully dispose of or put to naught fire or heat of a great volume. The first is dissipated by the second and under these circumstances the second remains modified but superior. So too with a lesser and greater solid of the same atomic texture. The lesser cannot outweigh the greater. A little strength cannot dispose of a great strength.

None-the-less, in connection with the evolved species of the evolutionary chain, there are affinities and oppositions and so limitations which appear to take their rise from chemical-energy sources which appear to be associated with protoplasm and its derivatives only,—and which are by no means as direct and instantaneous as are those which show and operate in non-protoplasmic matter-energy. The former are usually described as sensory and more definitely still, as emotional sensations or reactions. And they bring about limitations as well as liberations,—compulsions to act as well as inhibitions against acting,—affinities as well as oppositions, which are as different to inorganic matter-energy reactions as is organic matter itself. Here the words "mind," "personality," "individuality," "temperament" and what not else have been introduced to explain these affinities as well as oppositions between the endless creatures of the protoplasmic or evolutionary chain.

Yet basically they explain nothing, unless it is that all energy—which is basic in every organic and inorganic thing, is sensitive as well as emotional, and for those reasons, and no others, responds to whatever matter-energy conditions immediately as well as remotely are in a position to affect it,—the more immediate the most, the less immediate the less. It would follow that energy itself, or if not that then an immaterial something which produces, directs and controls energy, is responsible for all this—in other words all that is.

Myth of Individual and Race Memory

[This note under large picture entitled *"Ancient Gods*—Faces in tower of Bayan depict gods of a forgotten civilization of masterbuilders, the Khmers, whose most famous temple is the Angkor Vat in the jungles of Indo-China." *Editor's Note*]

They carve things on stone in order to have themselves or others remembered. The Pyramids were built for memorial purposes—but it preserves not the names of the builders. Memorial (the word) almost suggests today, the absence of memory. . . . [*Or*]

‡   ‡   ‡

[Another picture shows an outline sketch: *"The Honey Gatherer*—Oldest picture in the world—Spider Cave, Valentia, Spain. 15,000 years old." Under it, the following note. *Editor's Note*]

Only chance causes anything to endure in thought. Think of all the civilizations and archeologic wonders in North and South America brought to light or into the registrative sensitivity of mind by the growth of the notion that the world was round and Columbus's determination to test the truth of it. [*Or*]

‡   ‡   ‡

[Third picture, *"The Ruins of Mitla*—These Aztec buildings discovered in 1533 by the Spanish cleric, Fray Martin de Valencia, still stand as monuments to culture of that civilization. They are located in the State of Oaxaca, Mexico." *Editor's Note*]

When the physical evidences of anything are lost, decay, disappear, the knowledge of that thing in the "minds"—that is the registrative faculties of men disappears also. No physical presence or physical registration of past presence in books, tablets, monuments or markings of some kind, no "memory" of that thing. And so no knowledge of it anywhere. [*Or*]

‡   ‡   ‡

Every fly has a history, every ant, gnat, midge, electron, every vegetable, tree, flower, weed. The Universe, the solar system, the earth and all the races and tribes thereof, each has its history. But wherein, if anywhere, lies the history of all this, and to what advantage, even to the creator of the same, assuming there were one. History, recorded history, such as men know, is of so brief a length, that twenty thousand years back from today it crumbles into shards, bits of pottery, bone, teeth, scratching on stone—no more. And it is to be remembered that it is not the memory of man that extends to that length—but the thoughts and inquiry of a very few men—archeologists, geologists, botanists, paleontologists, and most of these of recent origin as many know, who became stirred by the almost totally indecipherable scraps of earlier lives, to attempt to realize and so bring into memory a little of the data of what has been.

But this is not memory, neither man memory, nor race memory—For the men and the races of them following these earlier tribes and people had already forgotten all that these recent explorers seek to bring into knowledge. [W]

Impermanence of Knowledge

Consider all the data and law that goes today with railroading, hunting, individual farming, individual salesmanship; and then contrast these with the knowledge that went with archery, falconry, the manufacture of suits of mail, embalming as the Egyptians knew it, actually written knowledge in regard to Egyptian mythology, Greek mythology, Chinese, Japanese, and Hindu mythology, and all the rites and ceremonies associated therewith. Of these ancient accumulations of knowledge, what actually endures in the mind or memories of man today? To be sure, in fragmentary ways these remain in archeological accumulations, frozen in book or monument form, and like all the knowledge that was a part of prehistoric man, certain to be forgotten entirely. Yet in its day it was knowledge as important in its forms and usefulness as is the knowledge of hunting, fishing, road-building, rail-road management, and salesmanship today.

But consider also that railroading knowledge is likely to give way to knowledge of transportation by bus, by airplane, by wireless telegraphy, or by forms and methods at this time unknown. Already it is predicted that the entire business and hence knowledge of printing, book-binding, distribution as in stores and libraries, is not only likely but certain to give way to the film as, in the first place, recorded by photography, and in the second place, transported by television, and recorded and presented, as well as stored in film reel form. Here you have a world of what would be called current practical knowledge, displaced and in time certain to be forgotten because of the arrival of other forms of knowledge, other methods of recording and distributing human reactions to stimuli.

Where, then, the remains of so much that is knowledge now? For as you can see for yourself, vast stores of new knowledge—Niagaras of it—relating to war, to the achievement of peace, to the manufacturing of textiles, chemicals, food, is rushing in, and the old is disappearing and by degrees being forgotten. At best you have, insofar as knowledge is concerned, an endless becoming as well as an endless concluding and disappearing. It has no permanence, and can have none any more than has memory, which is a thing that has to be refreshed—that is, all of its fads or registrations must be re-impressed and re-re-impressed, or the so-called "memory" (impress) of them vanishes completely. Hence neither knowledge nor the "memory" of the same endures. In reality it consists in its temporary serviceability to the endless push of creative energy which has no fixed place of abode unless in the eternal changing of form and knowledge. [W]

‡ ‡ ‡

The so-called thought of a race, a nation, or a tribe, or an "individual" is not to be found in these organisms bearing these names, but rather these organisms are registering implements of varying degrees of complexity, which register as does a radio what their environment has to offer. If you wish to see where all the thought of the world is, look out of yourself, gaze upon it, for it is outside. See the lamp posts, the buildings, the side walks, the water plugs, the other people, animals, birds, trees, fishes, the automobiles, churches, schools, banks, railways, ships, telephone and telegraph wires, airplanes; indeed, each and every evolved or man-made thing, whether in use or disuse, stored in shops and factories, art galleries, and libraries, jewelry windows, and what not. They are part and parcel of *your* so-called thought. In short, your so-called thought is nothing more than the enforced registrations of these things by the mechanism *you*, and the other mechanisms like you which still *think* of themselves as "conscious" individuals. For there is not a thing made by the hand of man, or evolved by the hands of many men, throughout countless periods of time, and which you see or can see, before you, that is not merely a form of endless condensed registrations of universal energy or "thought" which parades, and has paraded, as life and "thought" and emotion, but which is only temporarily "real" or congealed in these or any other forms, since it is always in process of change and is never quite the same thing or things from moment to moment.

That electric light post that you see across the street—you think of it (that is, that sensory registration mechanism, or switchboard, your brain, joins it up with other past registrations of other lamp posts, electric lights, etc.), and since you know nothing, let us say, of the physics or chemistry of their origin, or of the evolution of light posts in general—you think of it as an original, and man-made thing—maybe something made by one man or at most, a lamp post manufacturing company. And you take these various sensory registrations of this seemingly solid thing to be what is called "thought" and that you alone may be seeing this lamp post, and thinking about it in just this way, at this time; more, if some one said to you that that lamp post and the form of light it carries, and the street in which it stands and the wire underground or overhead that brings the electricity are—all of them—nothing more than stratified registrations of energy stimuli, operating upon and through the man mechanism, during incalculable periods of time, you might not understand. And you might reasonably enough doubt it. But the lamp post itself is a very old, and now solidly materialized thought, or series of mechanical reactions, modified and remodified and added to by others—thousands, and perhaps millions, even billions of people, over thousands and thousands of years.

Once, no doubt, it was not more than a brush fire in the camps of early savages, a flaming piece of wood; later, a tarred stick carried aloft in the hand. Later, perhaps it was a fixed wooden post or stake, carrying a shell or pot of oil, or a pot with a floating wick in it. Later it was the Greek oil urn with its wick, placed on a stand. Then the ancient lanthorn or the mariners and the street guides. Then the post carrying an oil lamp; then the gas post of so recent date. And now this electric thing, plus the fire sign.

But see this was never any one fixed thing. It has been a necessity (that is a registered need or compulsion like hunger of the stomach) which has grown (that is, which has been added to) until it has become the fixed metal and wired thing that we see. In all of its changes—those effected through and perpetuated by man, it has never been anything other than a necessity or compulsion comparable to the hunger of the stomach, which has slowly become fixed in wood, stone, iron, supporting (and that perhaps derived from volcanic fire) wood fire, fat fire, candles, kerosene, gas, and at last electricity. But each and every one of them a materialization of an idea or (as we now know ideas to be) compulsions from without on an internalized mechanism—the sensory apparatus of man—which again reflects [them] into the external world [from which they came].

But all this concerns but one form of fixed or frozen thought—the electric light post. Consider the paved street you are walking on as another evolution of the same kind. After that, the store, apartment house, hotel, street car, bus, automobile, railway engine, ship—anything and everything presumed to have been invented or created by man—often by a single man—or a group of men together. If you wish, see the processes by which they have been internalized as so-called ideas and then in turn externalized as frozen thought—such as a book, printed music, paintings, furniture, clothing, weights and measures, pots and pans, turn to the chapters entitled the Myth of Individual Creative Power, the Myth of Individual Possession, or the Mechanism Called Memory. These three will trace out for you a few more of these processes and you will see that you are really moving in a world of relatively fixed or solidified thought—and more, that your so-called individual thought is nothing more than a series of very rapid sensory registrations which, by the mechanism called your brain, are automatically (not consciously) assorted and transferred to this or that other group of past registrations most closely associated with these new ones. . . .

The point of it all is that quite all of what we human mechanisms consider new thought, and more, new thought of our own, and not only that, but new action evoked by our new thought, is nothing more than the mechanical and not consciously planned or executed, and what is more, compulsory, (that is, unescapable) registrations and re-registrations of a world of old and frozen, or solidified, or fixed thoughts out of many times and lands—plus, in the inrushing of light and energy, of the sun and the universe upon all of these and ourselves, timeless energy operating insofar as we are concerned after the manner and via the methods or compulsions of evolution, plus some slight rearrangements of the same—due to the compulsory association of these newer registrations and reflections with old ones that chance to be internalized in you—but no least wavelengths of it all having anything to do with "mind" as we speak of it—or conscious re-registration, or free will, or individually planned memory, or selection, or taste, or smell, or hearing, or feeling.

In short you are exactly what the evolutionary theory has this long while posited you as being—a slowly evolved mechanism in a slowly evolved world of other mechanisms, each and everyone necessary to the registrations and activities of the other—and as such forming a whole however a rough, cloudy, time-space-scattered unity. This none-the-less cannot exist except as this same space-time scattered and energy united multiplicity—our so-called universe in all its varied forms continues to function. Only how, we do not know. But this thing is sure—you are moving amidst a universe of solidified or partly solidified matter-energy forms. And they are the result of primal energy materialized. When we register these materializations as we constantly do we call the process *thinking*. [*Or*]

The Force
Called Illusion

IN GENERAL, MEN EXPERIENCE THE PRESENT, OR LIFE, WITHOUT any *sense measure* of its totality and without the ability to estimate or gauge its content, true worth or the significance of the same. And when it has become the past it is even less understood—none other than a myth. [*Or*]

‡ ‡ ‡

The magic of cities—How definite and compelling in youth—particularly isolated youth, yet how indefinable—almost in many instances, unrealizable. For in reality neither cities nor towns are magical. Their inhabitants are largely—almost exactly, like the people in other cities. The attainment is really a matter of train or ship or aero-plane or bus or automobile or truck; by paying one's fare or hitch-hiking or stealing a ride or working one's way. And the sight or examination of one city detracts from the fresh, uninformed and unrestrained enthusiasm for another. In fact the examination of ten cities makes possible the selection of one or more, as better, sometimes one as best. At the same time it makes impossible the sense of magic which comes with the fresh and inexperienced contact of one large city—one's *first* large city. [*Or*]

‡ ‡ ‡

Take the replica of yourself that walks abroad in dreams—doing this and that; saying thus and so—laughing, fearing, raging, crying, repeating the aspirations, fears, desires, hates of the living body—What of that? It has no real body. If anything it is an emotion of a prone, unconscious organism. Yet what is that that walks or speeds or flies abroad—it is here or there instantly, in the world of space it knows by day, but not otherwise—No other world anywhere else. [*Or*]

‡ ‡ ‡

You think of metals as heavy, and more, as falling hard, crashing through things, sinking rapidly to the bottom in water. But you are to remember that you are thinking in a very vague—decidedly not an exact way, probably about iron, lead, copper, gold, silver, zinc, tin, which at some time or other you have seen in blocks or bars and each of which contained enough of whatever metal it was to weigh a great deal. As to a very little of it which might and can weigh almost nothing you rarely think—for instance of copper or lead or gold shot or flakes, so minute that they will float on water or air—blow away and remain aloft for long periods as dust or smoke. (Don't forget smoke in large and condensed quantities—carbon—can be very heavy and sink or kill as quickly as any metal).

But the point in connection with all this is this: that in thinking of gold, silver, iron or any other thing on earth or in space or time you are not thinking of all that is either a material part or an attribute or characteristic of it—far from it. On the contrary, as a rule, you are not thinking of its total reality or import, let alone as a color, or a flame or a poison or a medicine or a food or a thought or an emotion—each and all of which in some form or other it may well be—even a note in a song. You are not thinking of any of these things, mayhap for a very good reason you are ignorant of them—and likely to remain so—as do many, many people, from birth to death. For man to this hour does not know the total of the attributes and their ramifications of anything. Which rather clearly indicates that your seeming *consciousness* of any one thing is so minute a fraction of its true reality that it actually borders on—if it truly is not *no thing*. [*Or*]

‡   ‡   ‡

You think of a noise as a thing in itself. And silence the same. But without silence there can be no noise. And without noise there can be no silence. The one is absolutely indispensable to the other. But noise, taken as a part of silence has something more to be said for or concerning it. For noise, to be noise, must consist of matter in its energy form plus space in which it can travel or move, plus time in which it can endure, plus resistance or the contact of energy with an opposing force, plus sensation in one or many forms—ears, antennae, papillae, plus silence or, at least the absence of a greater noise environing it. So exactly how much reality as a thing in itself has noise? [*Or*]

T.D.

‡   ‡   ‡

Life is literally a tissue of illusions. Consider the old plea for extravagant expenditure, that "it is good for trade." Also that other still continually waged, that whatever gives employment or work is beneficial to man and society. But look at these things more closely as did Herbert Spencer in 1870—or earlier. As he pointed out, they disregard the nature of the labor. If a thief hires another thief to assist him, he is giving employment. But to what end? Is it good for man or society? Crooks, political and financial, employ lawyers to assist them. Perhaps this is good for trade in one sense. It expends and distributes money. But is it beneficial to the social organism which insists on emphasizing law, order, honesty, as well as prosperity? And so those who say these things contemplate these dishonest ramifications? Can most of them think so far? The truth is, they do not and cannot. And the chemic and physical direction of life or man—by powers outside man, may not require that he should understand. In other words; life may be a formula which requires dishonesty as well as honesty to make it the interesting, dangerous, and dramatic as well as the comfortable thing that it sometimes is. To keep it going, perhaps it is required that danger should always track security and peace; that poverty should always endanger wealth; that theft should endanger honest saving, and per contra, honest saving endanger theft. For singly, danger, poverty, theft could only result in chaos and death—but together, they present phases of the vivid thing called life and keep it vivid. [*Or*]

‡ ‡ ‡

Life sets up a series of illusions which cause people—all creatures very likely—to struggle to live, reproduce and so perpetuate the seeming reality of things that for most prove unreal: the illusion of enduring love that drives youth into marriage, begetting of children, the support of a home. It also, via a variety of disasters to come, sets up the fear of a workless, lonely old age which most of those so fearing will never live to see. And nature, not man, is the guilty inventor of this. [*Or*]

‡ ‡ ‡

Is an ideal any the worse—any less forceful, for being unrealizable,—impossible? All too often, and in a bad sense, it is more forceful, and leads to retroactive-regressive results. . . . Hang a carrot just out of a donkey's reach and he will start to run, and he will go on running. That is the basis of all the savings banks and beehives and successful dogmatic religions or stock markets as well as race tracks, gambling houses, and oil stocks.

For instance, heaven is the unattainable carrot held out before the Christian—as escape from hell or purgatory is the carrot placed just beyond the finger reaches of Catholics. If they could be assured of escape—wholly assured—they might stop leaving their fortunes to the church or paying for cathedrals or stained glass windows. But they cannot be sure and so they go on toiling for the church. Ditto the individual who puts aside his money in a savings bank on the theory that he is providing for a happy old age for himself, whereas, more often than not it is the happy old age of the bank he is arranging for. For ad interim he, himself may die, or by the time he has accumulated enough to make himself truly comfortable, he is too old to truly enjoy the comforts he has arranged for. His ad interim discomforts have seen to that nicely.

Worse, he has probably added to the discomforts of others—his wife and children. For it is not the saving of savings, but the profitable and constant use of them that makes them worth having, as the growth and prosperity of all savings banks demonstrates. It is the donkey-carrot illusion that is put forward by the bank for its benefit—never for that of the petty saver as you may well guess. [*Or*]

Force of Illusion

Home is not a place. It is sometimes a synchronization of a multitude of subtle and constantly changing substances and rhythms and values and reactions on the part of a number of people together as a family; or of two people—male and female—the sex unit where mutual attraction has developed. Its character as a home may be qualified—added to or detracted from by its geographic position as in the country, a city, a town or a village. Also by the presence or absence of trees, flowers, grass, birds, a view, a cat, a dog, more than one cat or dog, a horse, a cow, an automobile, young children or no children. Again it may be qualified beneficially or the reverse by harmony or disharmony in the matter of religion, politics, morals, economics as these relate to income and expenditures—waste or thrift. Also by taste or a sense of beauty, present or absent. In sum, a home, although customarily thought of as a definite and so easily definable thing, is on the contrary an indefinite and almost indefinable thing—and in varying ways may evoke love or hate, peace or turmoil, health or disease, sanity or insanity. Extended life or violent death. Home sweet home is, as a definite thing, a myth. [Or]

T.D.

Magic

If you go into a psychological laboratory you may see a number of black cubes varying in size from two inches to six inches. If you pick them up you will find that the largest seems to be distinctly lighter than the smallest. Actually they are all equal in weight. So accustomed are we to finding a direct relationship between size and weight that the biggest cube looks the heaviest; and, accordingly, we get ready to exert a lot of energy to lift it. When it comes up quite easily, we get the impression that it is lighter than it actually is. On the other hand, we expect to be able to lift the smallest one with much less effort, and, when it offers unexpected resistence, we judge it is heavier than it is. [Or]

THEODORE DREISER

‡ ‡ ‡

This [is] true of [the] laboratory of life, filled as it is with varying sizes and weights of people. How surprised we are when we encounter some seeming giant who has no strength at all and again some seeming minute nobody who proves to be a great force. The tortoise who wins over the hare. The strong spirit in the handicapped body that directs and aids or uses the weak mind in the perfect body. And yet these contrasts are indispensable if life is to be as interesting and entertaining and picturesque as we wish it to be—and as it is. [Or]

T.D.

The Myth of Reality

I dreamed I was born and grew up and was a Pilot on the Mississippi and a miner, and a journalist in Nevada, and a pilgrim in the Quaker City, and had a wife and children and went to live in a Villa at Florence—and this dream goes on and on, and sometimes seems so real that I almost believe it is real. I wonder if it is? But there is no way to tell. For if one applies tests they would be a part of the dream, too, and so would simply add to the doubt. I wish I knew whether it is a dream or real.——Mark Twain in a letter (1893) to his sister, Mrs. Theodore Crane.

In the face of the fact that I am sitting at a very long and sturdy, as well as graceful, African snake wood table that has been in existence since 1930, and, barring the accident of fire or rough usage, would naturally endure for hundreds of years, it seems to me a bit odd that I should be writing on the subject of the Myth of Reality, and that in the face of all else that I see, hear, feel, taste, smell the endless varieties of forms, living and active, or still and stationary, and so seemingly, if not actually, inert or lifeless, which, of course, as all know, they are not. For, as to my table, for instance, I can take a torch and set fire to it, and then what becomes of it—its reality? It becomes, as you know, heat and smoke for a little while—not for long—for these, in their turn, mingling with the cooler air about them, again change my table's heat into the faintly warmed atoms of the fifteen or sixteen differing elements of which the air is composed—my table's black smoke temporarily darkening the various atoms of the same—no more. And so causing me to ask wherein consists the reality of my beautiful table? For it had form as well as substance—a truly beautiful design, and yet with heat applied, behold, even its lovely design has no duration and so no permanent reality. It can be obliterated by heat.

For, in order for it to be real to me again—that is to be solid and endure—some force of some kind would have to be able to reassemble the heat and smoke into which we saw it change. And not only that but to give the reassembled heat and smoke the actual form they possessed at the time they constituted the lovely table—a proceeding which we know would require not only extraneous energy on the part of something or someone—naturally we think of a human being, or at least an intelligent force which same knew the table as it was—its exact design—a prerequisite not so easy to conceive under such circumstances.

And yet the table, undisturbed by various disintegrating elements or forces—heat, cold, damp, motion—as in transfer and the like—might have endured for thousands of years and so have possibly enjoyed a none-the-less perpetually uncertain duration, which, to me, by no stretch of the imagination, can be looked upon as anything other than a temporary illusion of being, and that ever at the edge of change and final disappearance!

In sum, to me nothing is more illusory than the idea of an individual life complete or even partially so—that is, to itself alone. Rather human life—the totality of all of its forms and their ramifications—is no more than a fragment or special and yet minute extension of a much greater life—the Supreme directive force of the Universe—no less—which creates, regulates and qualifies all that by man is called human life, or animal or vegetable life. For not only are these integers or seemingly individual units comprising human, as well as all animal and vegetable life, not individual in the sense that they are unlike or different to all the members of their particular groups, nationalities or species, but rather in quite all ways they are alike, and more, and on occasion do not respond as individual units but rather as masses to whatever it is that contributes most to their likenesses and not their differences. Be they gulls, fishes, ants or men, the forces which contribute most to their well being—nourishment, safety, ease or entertainment—are pursued by most or all—in fact to such an extent that it becomes a question of whether there is any faintest conception, let alone realization, in the lower orders or species, if not of men, of such a thing as individuality even as the fact that might apply to themselves.

But this problem is far more subtle and curious than appears in the above long table discussion. In sum, from either the most casual or the most searching examination of any given material object, animate or inanimate, one is compelled to conclude that this so-called reality is almost invariably a compromise between various elements or seeming substances which are not always friendly to each other by any means. In fact there are molecules which by nature have only to look at each other to suspect the worst. For frequently when apart they can spend centuries leering at one another. Yet, arbitrarily joined together, as they frequently are, by the injection or accidental invasion of a third element, such as hydrogen say, they procede, like many previously antagonistic humans, to most peacefully co-operate and are occasionally looked upon by man as a new or distinct element which, none-the-less, can be broken down and the old hate between the two original enemies restored! In fact the biologist will tell you of innumerable species of lower animals of which two come together and coalesce into one. Also where one will break up into two or many; and again of "individuals" that branch off of others but never separate and so become what are called colonies—a sort of super individual. And yet is it? Or what is it—a colony or an individual?

But this is but a mere hint as to the amazing ramifications of this problem of *reality*. In fact evolution as presented to the world by Darwin, and others after him, is nothing if not the story of transmutation of so called *personalities*, which latter are nothing more than chemo-physical organisms compounded of the various elements of the universe—all of them—but in varying proportions. And thereafter these same compounds, operated upon by varying earthly as well as inter-stellar environments, provided, of course, by the ultimate super-consciousness or creative force, which is at once All and so over all, continue to change not only themselves but those with which occasionally, they blend for a period of time anyhow.

But to see that no permanently enduring or changeless *individuality* or *reality* is intended one need only contemplate the endless, as well as endlessly, varied procession of forms or species here on earth, if not elsewhere, which come, endure for a brief period and then die, giving place, by degrees, to new and yet equally varied forms which, even here, in the brief span allotted them, are still changing—oneself included. For from inception to death there is nothing if not change—physical as well as mental. And accompanying that, and making the stay of these purely seeming individualities all the more confusing and unreal, is the endless variety of illusions which, perforce, they are compelled to contemplate, and for want of individual illumination, to accept as real.

For instance, let us begin with the 93 elements of which the universe is or was, for a time at least, assumed to be composed. To such as ever heard of them—and there have been and still are many who have not—each and all were assumed to be unchanging, separate and distinct phases of matter—not matter-energy—and so not to be broken down as most of them since have been into two or more elements—and so proving them to be non-enduring and so merely temporary appearances like so many other things with which man found himself in contact. Thus the water he drank, and which today all know to be, or should, a combination of oxygen and hydrogen— two units of hydrogen to one of oxygen—was to him a single given substance which he found necessary to the continuation of his own life, as well as that of all the other living creatures, animal and vegetable, if not mineral. And as for the air he breathed—that also was another wholly individual substance insuring his existence so long as he could inhale it, but not—certainly not—a combination of fifteen or more elements (see your dictionary), yet creating the illusion of one-ness or individuality.

And again there is his placid blue sky above him by day which same he thinks of, or has in the past, as a separate and distinct and very favoring color—one that pleases and soothes him, and in general makes life here on earth more livable than otherwise it would be. Actually, however, it is nothing more than a modification or dilution of the violet rays in the spectrum of the sun which, if they were not so diluted, would destroy life on this earth. In fact real sunlight, or that white light which comes from the surface of the sun and includes all colors, would, unless modified by the dust particles in our atmosphere, make life here as we know it impossible. For they scatter and so make less violent more of the short blue and deadly violet rays than they do of the longer red and yellow waves which you see best of a morning and at evening. For then the sunlight as a whole—the various rays—must pass through more of the dust laden atmosphere, whereas at high noon, in scattering the blue light, the dust and gas in the upper atmosphere paint the sky a mild blue and so save the man race from what would be, for it at least, an untimely end. . . .

But this fact of illusion relates to so many things—interferes in so many ways with a correct comprehension of what is about us and to what, and in what manner, we are reacting—that it will be interesting to set down here a few seemingly minor and yet really startling discrepancies between what we think we know and what in truth we ordinarily do not know. Thus people will tell you that a shop is on the right side of the street. Yet in order for that to have meaning to you you must know where that street is in relation to other streets, also which way it runs—east, west, north or south, and which way you will be standing or walking in regard to those directions once you arrive there—and unless signs or some individual or other is in a position to inform you you are lost and your time will be wasted and very likely your temper tried. Whereas, if someone told you that someone else—an acquaintance—was sitting on the right or left bank of a certain local river, that would have some meaning, although even there it would be relative to the direction in which the river was flowing, and that you knew that—not otherwise. Yet again when it comes to the nautical phrase "fore and aft", that has meaning with regard to a ship or even a train or bus, but assuming that the ship might be turning around it could provide no absolute direction and might, by degrees, correspond to all points of the compass.

And so too with such presumative directions as East and West, up and down, near and far, high and low, strong and weak, heavy and light, dear and cheap, fast and slow, large and small. We say a planet is large and an atom is small or a man is strong and another weak, but what do we mean by any of these things? For instance, what is our standard of size or weight, or strength, or speed or what? Have we any standards for any of these things—cold or hot? new or old? now and then? Here or there?

I think of a suit of clothes I have as new and another as old—but the first as new because I recently bought it and the other as old because I have had it for a year, and even though it is still as good as new. But actually all of these things and many others are so relative to what others have or have not, what they think as to this or that, that it becomes absolutely impossible for anyone to say anything definite or precise about any of these things. So much so is this true that in this matter of mentally trying to achieve anything in the way of precision or definiteness in connection with any of these matters one becomes not only mentally weary but confused, as though one were facing an immense unreality in which float only a seeming of things. In sum, the more one seeks to approach and approximate them the more swiftly they fade and vanish, yet only, after a little time, to return and parade themselves for what they are not—real or reality. For as Shakespeare truly says—"there is nothing good nor ill but thinking makes it so." Only whose thinking? Man's? Or that of the Creative force that wills and so compels him to seem to think? Or that of the glorious William who seems to have realized that he was not really real at that?

However, interesting or not, let us take, for a change, the water we drink which, as we all know, presents itself to our senses as a single undivided element, yet which same, which many of us do not know, is a combination of two very separate and distinct elements—(1) oxygen—a colorless, odorless, gaseous element, and (2) hydrogen—similarly a colorless, tasteless, odorless, gaseous element—the lightest substance known and a constituent of all acids, as well as water and most organic compounds. Yet two volumes of hydrogen and one of oxygen when combined make the clear limpid substance which falls from the heavens as rain or snow, freezes as ice, floats as clouds in the sky, and when heated, turns to steam, which last, when sufficiently heated will change again into a gas which will burn you quite as badly, or nearly so, as fire. Also, as you know, when cooled it will assemble as a lake, bubble as a spring, flow as a river and, when combined with sufficient salt and many other elements, will make an ocean or many oceans, occupying as they now do, three fourths of the surface of the globe. Again, as a fog, it will conceal from your eyes your land or your sea, and, as a mist shone upon by the sun, or moon even, will glow as a rainbow in the sky. Also, when shone upon by the moon, particularly when the mating season is upon you and you have your man or your girl with you, it is likely to result in love and marriage. In sum, a very powerful as well as changeful element or illusion, without which neither you nor I nor any animal or vegetable, to say nothing of poet, musician, painter or writer, could endure for more than a brief period—all being earthly, physical, as well as mental, and so being so utterly dependent upon it for life, as well as beauty, etc. etc.

Only once more—and again—there is the air we breathe, and which once —before the days of chemistry and physics—was thought of as a single independent element on which, for some mysterious reason, our minute to minute existence depended, and on which same it does still depend. But as a single independent element? No. Rather it turned out to be a combination of some fourteen or more elements—thus: nitrogen and oxygen nearly in the ratio of 4 volumes of nitrogen to 1 of oxygen plus 0.9 percent by volume of argon, 0.3 percent of vapor and minute quantities of helium, krypton, neon and xenon. It also contains very small amounts of amonia, nitric acids, sulphurous and sulphuric acids, as well as suspended particles of dust, bacteria, yeast spores, etc. Of the principle constituents it is to be said that the oxygen supports combustion and renders the air respirable for animals, while the carbon dioxide in the air is the source of carbon for growing plants, while the nitrogen and argon are inert diluents. One liter of air at $0°C$ and 760 mm. pressure weighs 1.293 grams, or 1/773 of the weight of an equal body of water. Like other gases, it is compressible and elastic; it transmits sound and is used, as compressed air, to transmit mechanical power. Also it is liquefiable. And it extends perhaps a hundred miles above the earth, but with rapidly decreasing density; half its mass being within four miles of the earth's surface. As to its weight or pressure at sea level, as well as on you on the ground, that is about 14.7 pounds to the square inch. Yet, unless you are told you are not aware of that either—your obvious feeling being that you are not carrying any such weight, which same constitutes another one of your illusions.

But, in connection with that, let us step into your kitchen and see what happens to so called *reality* there. For one thing, as you will notice, a crystal of salt dissolves before your eyes in water. Sugar the same. The tomatoes you squeeze become as fluid; the potatoes you mash, a mush. Again, what were a variety of meats and vegetables becomes, with pans and crockery and fire, a dinner on the table, having in and of itself a specific individuality. Ice becomes water. Cold water becomes hot. Wood in the stove becomes smoke, visible fire, invisible heat waves, that vanish. Milk separates into two things—skimmed milk and cream. An invisible electric current becomes light and heat in your bulb. Gas becomes a visible light and heat—then invisible heat in water, metal, iron, the air of the room. In sum, transmutation of personality or so called individuality is nothing more than the law of transmutation of energy operating in everything about you and inside of you.

For if you will trouble to invade your own interior with the light of the biologist as your guide you will discover that however much you may think of yourself as a complete and very separate individual, none-the-less in your veins, arteries, and organs generally you will discover minute beings which are extraordinarily like some of the smallest and lowest of the microscopic animalculae of nature which yet lead independent and seemingly highly intelligent and certainly useful lives. For these go about in your body as citizens go about in the streets and houses of our cities. Known as corpuscles, white or red, they have minute individualities, as well as labors or trades which they follow with the greatest skill and thus evidently earn their right to be. For among other things some of them act as soldiers or warriors, brave and very frequently death defying. For when disease germs attack your body from without, it is they who respond to your call and attack and destroy until either the enemy is eliminated or they themselves are slain and the fight for the life of your body is lost. And this makes them not only courageous, as you will note, but patriotic, because they give their lives for the life of their State as a whole, which is you. And more, if the skin of your body is cut or broken it is they who do the repair work, even to the extent of building themselves into new tissue with which the cut is healed. Other of these little beings carry food and air about to repair muscles and bone structure, build hair and nails and what not—a multitude of services which make possible the life, as well as the super individuality, of the remarkable world in which they find themselves—a problem within a problem. For which has more individuality—the corpuscle or the man?

But the number of illusions or mysteries to which, as I said before, man is subjected by his environment, is legion. Thus a seemingly clear drop or glass of water which you drink with the greatest assurance as to its purity can, via the aid of a magnifying glass, of course, be seen to hold or contain a quite amazing menagerie of strange shaped animals all moving about eating, reproducing, sometimes eating each other. Yet a moderate degree of heat applied ends their appetites and activities forever. But meanwhile the average water drinker assumes that he is drinking clear water.

Again, human beings, for want of greater knowledge, long ago concluded that their particular male and female personalities, such as they showed to be at birth and later—as they changed from youth to old age and death—followed a definite plan, of course, laid out or down by the over ruling or Creative process and this pattern was thereafter not much altered or affected either by the society where it chanced to find itself. However, due to the researches of science and the growth of knowledge, it has become clear that the human organism, as well as its mental and or temperamental character, has ever been and still is almost unbelievably malleable, responding, as it does, accurately and contrastingly to the contrasting practical, as well as cultural conditions by which it found itself surrounded, so that only to the impact of the whole of that integrated culture and its natural environment can we lay the formation of the various contrasting types of beings which we find today—French, German, Italian, English, Russian, American, Hindu, Chinese, Japanese, African, Negro, Esquimau, or American Indian. In fact, subsequent to the year 1937, when it became known that new types of fruit-flies were being produced at the California Institute of Technology by bombarding their eggs with X-rays, it was asserted by one of its biologists—Calvin Bridges no less—that "were it not for social barriers, at present admittedly insurmountable and also because of the long lapse of time between human generations, human characteristics could certainly be altered in the same way"—in other words new types of humans brought into being!—the world changed by man who himself is thus constantly being changed!

THEODORE DREISER

Varieties
of Force

Environment IS ONE OF THE GREATEST—PROBABLY THE GREATEST force—because it is a collective force. You have an excellent illustration of it in the Parable of the Sower and the grain he sowed. Some seeds fell by the wayside and the fowls came and devoured them up. Some fell on stony places where they had not much earth and forthwith they sprung up because they had no deepness of earth; when the sun was up, they were scorched and because they had no root they withered away. Some fell among thorns; and the thorns sprung up and choked them. But others fell on good ground and brought forth fruit—some an hundred fold, some sixty fold, some thirty fold. [*Or*]

‡ ‡ ‡

The force of *environment* is demonstrated by all trained animals. Environed by the jungle they are savage. Environed and regulated by civilized (so-called) man, they become tame, friendly, perform tricks and often care for their trainer. But there is no willing in it. Their appetites are appealed to in different ways. They are petted, shown, compelled. Finally they act as though they possessed free will—were self-motivated. All environment is educational. All education is environmental.

Environment

Fishes from great depths are usually brought to the surface dead or in a dying condition. At the depth at which they have come into being and in which they often must live—to stray from the same meaning death—the gravity pressure on every part of them is enormous—thousands of pounds to the square inch. And to release them from this by bringing them to the surface is to release the higher concentration of gas in their tissues as fine bubbles into their blood streams, which means death. Even the groupers which are to be found at no greater depth than 35 fathoms, which is not much sea depth, when hooked and drawn upward offer a peculiar phenomenon.

As they take in their line, against the dead weight of a grouper, the line suddenly becomes slack. However in a few minutes the fish with the line in its mouth bobs up to the surface in an inverted position, its abdomen greatly distended. The effect is not dissimilar to an extreme case of *the bends,* that disorder to which men working under compressed air are subject when they emerge too rapidly. The higher concentration of gas in the tissue under high pressure escapes as fine bubbles into the blood stream. Unless the distention is relieved in some way not fatal to the fish it dies.

Judge from this the weight of environment on you. In the Congo is one type of environment. In China another. In the Arctic a third. In India a fourth. In Germany a fifth. In England a sixth. In America a seventh, and so on. There are religious environments, slum environments, wealth environments, crime environments. When those so environed and affected by it emerge into another it may mean freedom or defeat or suffering or great gain. [*Or*]

THEODORE DREISER

‡ ‡ ‡

Many surface fishes have peculiarities that make their handling difficult or impossible. *Fishes of the open sea, that normally never approach coasts at all, display a peculiar bit of behavior.* Living in a uniform medium, with no obstacles to avoid, many seem to be totally lacking in the ability to evade barriers such as aquarium walls or similar blocks to their path. Either they cannot or will not turn aside, but go on to crash their heads into some obstruction. Obviously there are but two alternatives: eventual death from contusions, or the learning of a new habit. The latter seems never to occur. Among these creatures of such habit are the mackerel, Spanish mackerel, hammerhead and several other species of sharks, and the sea herring. The great leather-backed turtle behaves the same way. This may seem difficult to understand, since these turtles periodically reach sandy shores for purposes of egg laying. However, at these times they approach a sandy shore and become grounded gently. [*Or*]

[Dr. Muhlfeld has told us that the fish from great depths which Dreiser describes are now considered fish from middle depths; oceanographers can now reach down more than a mile where fish are found that are constructed with some internal adjustment to withstand enormous pressures. By the same mechanism they can also live at the surface.

It is now known that whales and large fish emit a tone—such as the so-called *whale song*—which warns them of approaching objects. When too close to an obstruction, however, the sound wave returns before it can be "listened to." Thus cannot be "re-learned" as a physical constraint is involved. This is analoguous to the sonar systems of submarines. *Editor's Note*]

Instincts

There are many things in animal life, such as the precise concert of action among flocks of birds and fishes and insects, and, at times, the unity of impulse among land animals, that lend support to the notion that wild creatures in some way come to share one another's mental or emotional states to a degree and in a way that we know little or nothing of. It seems important to their well-being that they should have such a gift, something to make good to them the want of language and mental concepts (if it is true that they lack mental concepts) and so insure unity of action in the tribe, flock, herd, swarm, school. Their seasonal migrations from one part of the country to another are no doubt the promptings of an inborn instinct called into action in all by the recurrence of the same outward conditions, cold, heat, the presence of food or the passing of it and the like.

But the movements of the flock, herd, swarm, school seem to imply a common impulse, awakened on the instant in each member. Whether or not they are conscious of the process, have systems or methods as we think we have systems or methods, is not known. But like conditions in them as in us appear to awaken like impulses. In our case, we talk, write, telegraph, assemble and in case of danger, arm. Unity of action in that case appears to be reached, except the instances of the chattering of birds, without outward communication. Yet there is the eye and what it sees, the sense of smell and what that may register of excited blood states plus the intense sense of hearing and what that brings in the way of physical intensities and movements in connection with the others. [*Or*]

T.D.

Energy

What does energy want to do?
Sing a song? Dance a jig?
Build a giant Redwood?
Form a colony on a duck-weed?
Be a beggar? Be an Alexander the Great?
And always quit but only to begin
again or die?

T.D.

If "thought" is not some form of energy how comes it that noise, whines, howls, shouts, shrieks, screams instantly displace thought—make it impossible? One force displacing another.

Matter-Energy

Can there be matter apart from energy? No.

Can there be matter apart from mind—or mind apart from matter? If not where do the combinations of matter and energy—or matter and the physical actions and rhythm and emotions supposed to be mental—the nations, convictions, dreams, taboos—go to when the individual dies—or the material disintegrates into (humanly) invisible energy? If matter cannot express itself without what we call *mind*—or *mind* without matter—which is which? [*Or*]

Definition of Energy

Energy—1. strength, power, or spirit shown in words or action; 2. strength or power whether exercised or not; ability to act; mental vigor; 3. the effect or result of activity: Phys., the capacity for doing mechanical work, the principal types being those due to motion and position. Synonym; power, force, vigor, strength, might.

Power is that principle which in all things moves, governs, changes, effects, accomplishes. The power of the mind to think, the power of a nation to enforce its laws, the power of an animal to move—these examples show how general is the application of the word. Power may be exerted or latent. Energy, force, vigor, and strength are particular forms of power.

Energy has its root in the mind and is the power of producing an effect, whether exerted or not. A speech which galvanizes a sleepy audience into life is an example of energy actively at work. To predict that a man will act in a certain way under given conditions because of the energy of his character is to bank on a latent ability for efficient action.

Force can mean power exerted on an object, it can mean mental and moral strength, or it can indicate constraint or coercion; as, the force of a collision; the force of a stream of water or current of electricity; force of character; the force of an upright or unyielding attitude of mind; a promise obtained by force.

Strength of mind connotes resolution; strength of soul, the power to endure or persevere in the face of temptation or heartache; strength of body implies a frame, a muscular system, and a constitution capable of standing up under severe physical strain. Vigor is that fresh quality of mind and body that has its roots in health. Antonym; lifelessness, languor, lassitude.

Energy

There is an authority about free energy as opposed to or set over against stabilized or solidified energy (matter) which this has not,—at least not to the same degree. Energy generates the steam that boils water, lifts the tea kettle lid or runs the engine that pulls a freight train or drives a steam ship. Free energy it is that blows the heads off of mountains; that explodes a giant star or shatters a building, or quakes the face of the earth,—all these latter, as you know, being stabilized forms of energy.

Consider a lightning bolt and the rock it shatters; a marching army and the relatively inactive city it is moving to destroy; the wire (stabilized energy) over which a current of energy travels, and the relative freedom of the current; the nerve plasm along or through which the nerve energy speeds—the one fixed, the other relatively free.

Whether it is free energy that compels stabilized or solidified energy to be so, or a rhythm that belongs not to energy free or solid but to some immaterial something which governs and frees or stabilizes energy is yet to be determined—if ever?

However, it may be that that something that governs matter-energy has so arranged this universal process so that no phase of matter or energy may eternally be compelled to maintain or endure any given state. Change may, in the long run, be that which eases and gratifies all. Certainly it provides the contrast without which life (as we know it) could not be. [*Or*]

Explosions

Note explosions in the universe, in earthly wars. In contacts between chemicals. In contacts between men. In the human emotions. Human germs are today blasted inside the human body by explosive chemicals. For instance: Disordered nerve filaments—(nerve ends) that have ended in insanity, straightened (put in order) and insanity (disorder) ended by an explosion of insulin. Tuberculosis germs can and are being blasted inside the human body by two drugs—Dinitro-Phenal and sulfanilamide. Dinitro-Phenal—a carbolic acid or phenal compound—a war explosive—can penetrate the tubercule germ easily. It makes the germ's body more vulnerable to an attack by another drug—sulfanilamide. Truly this is war—standard war—on germs. It is explosive energy blowing up another form of energy. [*Or*]

‡ ‡ ‡

Liquid-oxygen explosives are so sensitive that they cannot safely be transported from place to place. They are conveniently used by transporting the non-explosive combustible material (absorbent combustible paper cylinders filled with wood pulp of powdered cork or spongy aluminum) to the spot or place where it is to be used and then pouring on it or dipping it into liquid air until it has absorbed all that it can. The resulting mass is a powerful and sensitive high explosive. The paper cylinder becomes a cartridge of dynamite—as easily exploded by accidental shock as by a blasting cap. So true is this that the explosive is usually manufactured in this manner at or in the very *place* where it is to be exploded.

Here is something so little a definite reality in one form that it is constantly on the border line of becoming something else—fire—heat—sound waves. [*Or*]

THEODORE DREISER

Electricity

The eminent French physiologist, Claude Bernard, had the idea that the impulses which pass along nerve fibres set up chemical changes which produce heat. About 1850 he measured the temperature of a rabbit's ear and then severed the nerve which delivers impulses to that structure, expecting, of course, according to a theory of his, that the ear, deprived of nerve impulses, would be cooler than its mate on the other side. To his great surprise it was considerably warmer! For the truth was, although he did not know it, that the nerve impulses instead of keeping the ear warm served to keep the blood vessels of the ear moderately contracted, and in severing the nerve he permitted the blood vessels to enlarge so that the warm blood from the internal organs flowed through in greater quantity and faster, making the ear warmer. However, because of this mistake of his, which he recorded, it became possible for others to see, later, that he had made the great discovery—previously unknown—that the passage of blood in the different parts of the body is under nervous government—the most significant advance in our knowledge of the circulation of the blood since Harvey's proof, more than 300 years ago, (dating from April, 1940) that the blood circulated in the body.

All the blood streams of all earthly creatures are similarly under nervous control—electric control. Weariness, caused by external pressures and shocks will slow down the flow of the blood; excitement, stimulation from without, will cause it to flow faster—the heart to beat faster. But these are not directions from the mind, they are energy stimuli from without. So it would look as though the flow of the blood is not under the control of any "Mind"—nor even under those of all the other so called "minds" that live in the world. They are under the control of something else—universal energy.

‡ ‡ ‡

Your entire body is (basically) electrical and receives none other (basically) than electrical stimuli.

In extreme cases of delight you experience a collective sensation which includes, seemingly and probably measurably, every cell—and if so very likely every molecule and atom of the body. If this last is true it is a complete physical and/or protein so complete electrical experience and which therefore is not confined and so individual to any given brain center—(which is no more than a transfer or switchboard center) but is simultaneous and identical to all units of the body—cells, and all electrically controlled and directed molecules, atoms. Hence here is not "thought" but sensation—the mechanistic registration—exterior as well as interior—of inpouring stimuli.

The Trinity

The forces of the Universe, binding, repelling and stabilizing appear to be three—Triune (Father, Son, and Holy Ghost of Christianity). They are the positive proton in the atom, the neutron, and then a sub-atomic binding force (no name) which holds the protons together, keeps them—since both are positively charged and as such repel each other—from blowing up. It might be called the stabilizer or Holy Ghost.

T.D.

[Other *Notes* on electricity as a life force are outdated by the recent theories concerning the DNA, or life-molecule. Telepathy, however, still a mystery, is now being taken seriously. Experiments were even made by one of our astronauts from the moon! *Editor's Note*]

Telepathy

In universal mind there can be no progress—In human, sensory reaction there may be—appears to be. Is man getting or recovering telepathy?

Telepathy or extra-sensory perception (E S P as it is now called) is like sharp-shooting. Average men and women are no more capable of calling cards which they cannot see *correctly* than they are of making bulls-eyes with their rifles time and time again. If extra-sensory perception or telepathy is to be studied it must be with the aid of those who seem to have it.

Professor J. B. Rhine, who is trying to demonstrate the reality of telepathy, follows the method used in the physical sciences.

To account for the perturbations in the Orbit of Uranus the existence of an unknown outer planet was assumed. Later Neptune was discovered and the assumption confirmed. Then it was found necessary to assume that there must be a trans-Neptunian body. Again pre-supposition was justified, this time by the discovery of Pluto. So in atomic physics, where such particles as electrons, protons, neutrons were assumed to exist long before their tracks were photographed.

It is impossible to advance in science without making these preliminary assumptions. But verification of the assumption is always necessary. In psychology the statistical verification of the assumption that there is extra-sensory perception is dismissed as a piece of self-deception; in physics it would be accepted as proof of a theory. [W]

‡ ‡ ‡

Both physicists and psychologists—and psychologists are completely dominated by physical methods of experimentation—would accept clairvoyance and *telepathy* if the "laws of nature" were not violated. In other words it makes no difference whether the distance that separates the subject from the cards is three feet or three miles. *Light, heat, radio waves, magnetism, every form of energy with which we deal in everyday life diminishes in effect as it ripples out into space—diminishes in accordance with the well-known inverse square law.* But not the *"force"* or whatever it is that is involved in extra-sensory perception. In the new experiments we have another seemingly outrageous violation of physical law.

‡ ‡ ‡

[Consider] how animals sense the friendliness or unfriendliness of people. Cats, dogs, honey-bees, lady-bugs, cows, horses, they do not talk but they know. . . .

Do they register—as do radios—energy waves emanating from things, from people, stones, distant storms, earthquakes—or from something less material—immaterial spirit from which matter-energy takes its rise. . . .

The cat that understood an earthquake was coming. . . . Mocking-birds and cats. . . . Black-birds and their young. The little sparrow that couldn't keep up and beat its wings in order to evoke sympathy in the other members of the flock . . . is so much language necessary? . . . "The horses smell him, they know him, his friendliness, his temperament" . . . instinct . . . telepathy. [*W*]

‡ ‡ ‡

Apparently, the "vaporized atoms" of a person or animal can change physically with the differing mental conditions of the person from whom they emanate. Fear of a dog, say, will affect the vaporized atoms or odor of the person from whom they are emanating in such a way and to such an extent as to cause a dog to detect the fear of the person and so feel encouraged or free to attack him. On the other hand the vaporized odor-atoms of a brave—a fearless person convey to the nose of a dog that fearlessness and cause it to avoid the person—at least give no sign of enmity.

Ectoplasm?

In his fascinating book "Forty Years of Psychic Research" Hamlin Garland refers to mysterious emanations from the bodies of clairvoyant psychics which are sometimes luminous and sometimes invisible. An emanation of this sort is known to psychics as ectoplasm. *It would seem to be emitted as an electronic force capable at times of most amazing performances.*

Ectoplasm has been said by some investigators to have exerted power sufficient to lift a table from the floor while a strong man was doing his best to hold it down.

What I have personally seen of alleged materializations causes me to feel that human knowledge is very far short of any understanding of the constructing and guiding forces of human life. [*Or*]

T.D.

[The word *ectoplasm* is here used in the popular sense employed by mediums and not in its simple, scientific, or biologic meaning. Dreiser had attended séances with mediums during his days in New York. *Editor's Note*]

‡ ‡ ‡ ⸱

A small group of physicists headed by Professor I. I. Rabi of Columbia University created a flutter of excitement in an assembly of scientists at Columbus, Ohio, recently by announcing the discovery of what they termed *hitherto unknown rays totally unlike any others previously reported. These rays are said to emanate from human bodies as well as from other sources, including microscopical particles of matter.*

They are further declared to be of a nature that might account for the telepathic transference of thought from one person to another and also for some of the manifestations attributed to clairvoyance and second sight.

Dr. Alexis Carrel, in his book, "Man the Unknown" says, "It is certain that thought may be transferred from one individual to another even if they are separated by long distances."

If this be true it seems likely that the transmission is affected by means of electromagnetic waves. But there is said to be nothing in the Columbia experiments to indicate how the rays might carry information from one person to another. Still it may be that further research will reveal important consequences and potentialities along this line of scientific investigation. [*Or*]

‡ ‡ ‡

A trance or sleep—what difference. It means that all your "individual" personal "intelligence" or nerve receiving apparatus, against which endless exterior stimuli are striking are, for the time being, silenced. Nothing from the outside is being carried to, and registered by, the brain mechanism. You are like a hen with her head under her wing. But the chemo-physical apparatus of your body is in full swing—your heart is beating, your lungs the same, your blood flowing, your stomach digesting. Only directed by what? Your resting mind?

Every cell in your body is directly exchanging electrical impulses with its immediate contacting cells. So all is electrically connected. And what can the apparatus of the body do when it is thus working apart from your entranced or sleeping "mind"? For one thing, in case of any mechanistic break or chemic disturbance in the stomach, organs, glands, or whatever, it can wake the "mind" up!—cause it to *register a pain* and so wake it up. But how come—with only a "sleeping mind" to do with? Is the whole mechanism "thinking"? Or, is "thinking" nothing more than nervous registration of electric or chemic or electro-chemic disturbances of one kind or another—first registered at a nerve end in a finger, an eye, an ear, a nose, a palate, a stomach, a kidney, a liver, a bile gland or whatever—and later distributed like telephone messages mechanistically distributed in a telephone center. Or is it that it is *electricity that is "mind"*? Also that it is on guard everywhere?—erects its own mechanisms of all kinds, according to environment or is ordered or compelled so to do (but by what?). And, once having erected the same, is in charge of their proper functioning until they break—or cease?—are released from their guises as protoplasm, cells, organs, blood, brain, matter? And resume their primary functions as atoms, electrons, protons, or, in other words, magnetized or gravitationally controlled and directed *energy*—or *electricity*—positive or negative?

But can this suddenly liberated energy—which may be "mind" act for a little while in your vicinity as a "ghost" or "spirit". For certainly ghosts *are energy* in some form if everything else in the universe is. And D. H. Lawrence, thinking of this, wrote in his essay on Hawthorne's *Blithedale Romance:* "But some unit of force may persist for a time, after the death of an individual—some association of vibrations may linger like little clouds in the etheric atmosphere [ether or space, T. D.] after the death of a human being, or an animal. And these little dots of vibrations may transfer themselves to the conscious-apparatus of the medium. So that the dead son of a disconsolate widow may send a message to his mourning mother to tell her that he owes Bill Jackson seven dollars; or, that Uncle Sam's will is in the back of the bureau; or say 'cheer up, Mother, I am all right'." [*Or*]

Color

Color is a material thing since it is a phase of light or energy and hence to all possessing sensitivity to color it is a sensation. This explains the various affects or emotions, pleasant or unpleasant, which colors have upon us.

Why should white give us an impression of coldness, red be of an inflamatory character, green prove restful, and blue cause some human temperaments to take a contemplative and sometimes idealistic turn? Blue has been rhapsodized by poets and individuals throughout the centuries. Through the eye comes the color as a frequency of light and arouses these feelings and emotions or others. [W]

Light

No one is particularly drawn to a dark, lonely street—even though safe enough. Millions are drawn to brightly lighted streets. They are particularly drawn where there is color plus design—as to Broadway or a World's Fair. Or to a city like New York or Paris. Now this is not something invented by the human mind. All the discoveries in connection with tropisms demonstrate this. Some things are chemically so arranged as to be unable to endure certain phases of light; moles, diatoms (?), deep sea fishes. But all things have to have energy waves which are after all—each and every one degrees or phases of light. In the darkest depths of the ocean creatures that have no contact with light—sun-light as we know it—manufacture light within themselves—and if that were not the product of energy waves invisible to the human eye what would it be? [Or]

‡ ‡ ‡

Without light life as we know it would be impossible; colors are but the dispersion of white light, found as the original form breaks down and recombines into new forms. Any color which we see, in a flower, in skin, in trees, on a wall is physically caused by the fact that the surface of what we see absorbs every color from white light but the one which it reflects or throws back. The color medium for example in wall paint which looks green is really only the reflection of green in whatever light falls on it. That is why surfaces change color depending on the kind of light in which they appear. Other factors which affect the color of a thing are its shiny or dull qualities. A glossy surface can reflect colors which if it were dull its color medium would absorb.

Heat can affect the color of a thing. For example, an iron can be heated till it can absorb what its original color was and give off a color which it could absorb before, red.

Perhaps, inasmuch as many of our most obvious sensations and in fact most of our life has to do with recognizing colors, sensations and since they affect our physiological processes so profoundly, our life is bound up inextricably with light, so much so that perhaps our life is only a form of light.

‡   ‡   ‡

The city of London, in an effort to reduce the number of suicides from Blackfriars Bridge, painted that gloomy old structure a bright green. Suicides declined by more than one third. Did the green alter the mind or mood of some of the disheartened? Or was it the absence of the effect of the black—traditionally associated with tragedy and death. One thing is sure. Colors do not always register the same on all organisms. What registers as a dark green with one may be a light green or grey with another. Not only that, but it has been shown that animals and insects do not register color or form or sound or distance in the same way as does man. Hence it is by no means clear what emotional responses, if any, they evoke in these creatures, and how alike or unlike they are.

In the case of man—the two halves of the sex mechanism called man—we are in a better position to judge the effects of color, because structurally and chemically each man mechanism is closely related to every other.

What follows here as in the case of taste and smell and feeling and hearing is that there is rarely if ever exactly the same response. Blakeslee had shown this to be true with taste and smell. Noble has shown it in connection with insects, birds, and different animals, commercial and official organizations of various kinds, color printing, railroad engineering. The officers and men of the armies and navies of the world have made it plain that color as well as sound and feeling are not precisely the same in any two people. There are coincidences, fairly accurate and in large numbers, but not precise duplications. The import of this truth is enormously increased by the fact that color— all types of color—have their emotional effects, and in most cases described as mental. The color called magenta, on some, has been proved to be exciting in the gay sense. On others relaxing, quieting, or stabilizing. Violet produces melancholy in many. Yellow stimulates the nerve system, makes it more durable. In 1928 Alonzo Stagg, the football coach of Chicago, fitted out two dressing rooms for his team, one in blue for rest, and one in red for stimulating contentiousness. The harmonious blues, purples, greens, blacks, and other colors in stained glass windows of churches, cathedrals, are generally credited with evoking awe and reverence. To say that any verbal expression could be found for these effects would be transcending fact. No one has ever furnished their verbal equivalent. Therefore the effective force of them is not related to so-called thought. The reaction is direct and has nothing to do with reasoning, just as when a person pulls away from a too hot object.

It could be said of these same windows that they are restful and healthful which are not necessarily aspects of things. And it has been physically proved that purple light alone is a splendid soporific, while blue calms the nerves and restores vitality. Agriculturalists have shown at experimental stations that seeds which take eight days to sprout in sun-light will develop in two days under blue glass.

Again, caged birds are stimulated by grass green. Snakes can be hypnotized by yellow. Among men, gray, puce, russet, green, or brown are physical sedatives. Crimson lake, royal blue, fawn are nerve restoratives. Violet or chrome are nerve stimulants. Turquoise and scarlet are physical recuperatives, and olive and green are mental recuperatives.

Transmutation
of Personality

LIFE IS NOTHING LESS THAN A CONSTANT TRANSMUTATION OF personality. From infancy to death there is the physical alteration as well as the mental—the changing of the body and of the reacting powers of the entire nervous system. A child reacts to one set of stimuli in its environment. At puberty it reacts to another. At twenty-five, to another, at fifty, to another; at seventy, to another.

T.D.

‡ ‡ ‡

A grafted twig may modify its stock to the roots, just as an adopted child or a windfall of money may alter the entire character of a family.

‡ ‡ ‡

Consider Saints—individuals who like St. Augustine, Saint Francis and others, from [being] one kind of individual up to thirty years, changed to an entirely different type. [*Or*]

‡ ‡ ‡

Consider a Nigerian Head Hunter who changed in his life time into a Harlem apartment house janitor or Pullman car porter.

[T. D. himself had an experience with Nigerian Head Hunters, from Africa, who danced in his studio, and one of them later married his maid. Also others remained in Harlem and became absorbed into American life. *Editor's Note*]

‡ ‡ ‡

> Canst thou not minister to a mind diseased,
> Pluck from the memory a rooted sorrow,
> Raze out the written troubles of the brain
> And with some sweet, oblivious antidote
> Cleanse the stuff's bosom of that perilous matter
> Which weighs upon the heart?
>
> *Macbeth*—Act 5

Yes, in some instances it can and has been done. A fixed mental state altered or erased. A given type of temperament altered. And also by chemicals, hormones, etc. [*Or*]

Metrazol

Metrazol—a drug which produces convulsions, but which, before it does that, frightens a patient beyond the power to picture his fright to another. Some suggest the fear of a frightful death—a conviction that they are going to explode like a shattered electric bulb. The drug is a camphor derivative. It causes a lowering of the flow of blood to the brain. Others feel that everything of the real about them is suddenly falling away from them—and they themselves are falling into an endless nothing—and at the same time disintegrating. It is at present used to dispel illusions of depersonalization—such as where one feels himself to be turned to stone or ice or not to be existing or to be another person. [W]

‡   ‡   ‡

Medical science has at all times pursued the aim of changing the personality of the individual. For if it be true that every illness works great changes in the body and temperament of an individual, making him weak or thin, or querulous or despondent or wholly helpless and substituting often an entirely altered viewpoint, medicine, at times, by ridding him of the disturbing influences of this illness, checks or cancels these changes and restores his former state, or something near to it. Not only that, but social changes affecting the environment of the individual will do the same. Discharged from a position of seeming or actual import; some honor revoked, some avenue to fame intercepted, or a fortune lost with all that it means socially if not physically, and your so-called individual can and most often will wither and shrivel, an entire temperamental reaction of one kind being replaced by another, so that an audacious, bumptious man will grow nervous and cautious, experiencing fear and despair. Your spendthrift may well become watchful of pennies; your haughty soul humble, your liberal and even kindly temperament, embittered. In short thoughts, which are mere registrations of exterior stimuli, will so disturb the chemisms of the digestive and nervous systems as to effect despair and death. And yet we think we make our lives and control our temperaments and their compulsions or deeds. [Or]

T.D.

‡   ‡   ‡

In times of emergency, such as fear, anger or collapse, epinephrine (same as adrenalin) drives the sympathetic nervous system to mobilize all the physiologic forces of the body into readiness to ward off the enemy. Then epinephrine drives men and men drive their armies and navies. But what drives epinephrine?

The One General Personality

The Universe is represented in every one of its particles.

These appearances indicate the fact that the *universe is represented in every one of its particles. Every thing in nature contains all the powers of nature. Every thing is made of one hidden stuff; as the naturalist sees one type under every metamorphosis, and regards a horse as a running man, a fish as a swimming man, a bird as a flying man, a tree as a rooted man.* Each new form repeats not only the main character of the type, but part for part all the details, all the aims, furtherances, hindrances, energies, and whole system of every other. *Each one is an entire emblem of human life; of its good and ill, its trials, its enemies, its course, and its end. And each one must somehow accommodate the whole man, and recite all his destiny.*

‡ ‡ ‡

The temperament or personality of a man can be changed completely or partially through the stimulus of drugs, liquor, etc., as we all know from our observations of others, and from our personal experience. It is nothing unusual to see a man, ordinarily of calm even temper, kindly and good-natured, become a raging, cruel, uncontrollable person when stimulated or intoxicated by liquor or some drug. What is more, medicine today can change the mental and emotional characteristics of a person by the injection of certain gland stimulants—making a repulsive, gross, sluggish, and idiotic child, into a normally functioning being.

The personality then must be something like the body, only having more intangible and complex possibilities. For example, the same body can swim, walk, dance, wink, play a game of cards or baseball, write, talk, etc.—all these possibilities being latent in the same body at the one time, but only one certain set of possibilities being emphasized in the action or position of the moment. The body reacts to stimuli and so does the personality, and what is more these two interact, and are interdependent, making the complex and varied individuals that we know.

If the personality can be changed by the application of drugs, gland injections, and so on, it must also be influenced by the other personalities with which it comes into contact. Consider the impact of a strange personality on a group of people—a stranger coming into a group of friends—immediately, an adjustment has to be made, not only for the integration of the group as a whole, but for each individual in the group. The relation of the members of a group to each other, and also their internal reactions are conditioned according to every person, and his relative force of personality, in the group. Perhaps it is one reason why human nature seems inconsistent to us that we fail to take into account the dynamic and non-static force of personality; while it does not seem in the least strange that the material form of the body should at one time swim, another walk, another fly, according to the proper stimuli.

If it is true that thought is at last being hunted down to its essence of electrical charges, then it must be true that each person must give out, not only in the more easily sensed material reactions of sound, speech, appearance, etc., but as a sort of energy wave, his characteristic personality charge. And thus it can be explained why certain people seem to occupy positions of more importance and more influence and to attract more attention than any of their overt actions would allow.

Unconsciously we have known this always—that people had a force outside of what could be explained with reference to ordinary sensation.

‡ ‡ ‡

This matter of personality which each so-called individual assumes that he has, and which he, more or less unthinkingly assumes that other people have, is a peculiar and rather insubstantial something, to say the least. For, in one sense, people are practically what they look at, or on, in life or art or whatever. For instance, a lie or delusion can be, and often is, a truth or fact to the person who believes it—a person who is seemingly as sane and fair-minded as you yourself think yourself to be, and, when guised as a revelation by its inventor, a lie may, as many people know, exert the power of a great force over a vast number of people, changing their so-called personality in no small way, as, for instance, the Arabians, after the appearance of Mohammed and his assertion that he was the divinely ordained prophet of God, who became his fanatic followers ready to burn or slay or both any who refused to receive his word as true. Thus a mild and peaceful people, accustomed to tend their flocks and herds, were changed into a critical and watchful group or nation bent upon hunting out and destroying what to them had become the stubborn and hated unbeliever.

But this matter of personality and its transmutation into something frequently quite different is often enough much more subtle and arresting than the matter of changing from one faith or social belief to that of another. For instance, the distinctive male and female personalities civilization believes to be inherent in the individual are, in part at least, socio-nationally as well as chemico-physically produced. That is, the Mendelian law functions as to the production, via mating, of two persons or their descendants in some one characteristic such as black hair and blue eyes or a defective foot or hand design, but not more than that, whereas the distinctive male and female personalities of an entire people such as the French, the English, the German, the Italian and the American, may, or rather have, developed specific characteristics relating mostly to physical color, design, height, quality of hair, color of skin, etc., etc. In America, for instance, without conscious plan, and despite a notable admixture of races and peoples, you still have the American type, distinguishable anywhere in any racial assemblage which includes a number of contrasting types deriving from various lands and nationalities. In America, again, without conscious plan, but none-the-less surely, American social conditioning is doing away with the idea of male domination, whereas in Europe, and due to the rise of Fascism, women are being forced back into an older and more extreme type of subservience, the while Communism is endeavoring to liberate all, and, in that sense, to make the two sexes as alike as possible—each free to develop his or her mental or social capacities to the utmost of its possibilities.

But what I have described thus far is really one of the mildest phases of such transmutation of personality as I have in mind. For, as to that, a large number of scientists and psychologists are inclining to believe that a greater part of the personality differences between the sexes have been artificially cultivated—consciously or unconsciously by parents who have been striving to have their sons as masculine as possible—that is according to such pervading social standards as they are confronted by, the while they seek to prevail upon their daughters to emphasize their femininity as definitely as possible. Plainly this tends to bring about a pseudo, or at least an over-emphasized, femininity which is as false as it is irritating to some.

But this matter of transmutation of personality is by no means as simple as the above illustration would suggest. For, truly enough, the customs and laws that govern or guide us from generation to generation change with the passing of time and the coming into the world of new generations, and apart from these new generations and such new laws as their conduct suggests, these said laws and the conduct they are created to deal with have had no previous existence. It follows that a certain degree of transmutation of personality must be taking place with the coming and living of new generations, else why the change in or evolution of law? Only changing laws change our actions, and these, in turn, finally alter our characters or personalities, and then we, with altered characters or personalities, proceed to further change our laws, etc. etc. etc.

But the above is one of the slowest and mildest phases or aspects of character or personality transformations. For the fact is that in the face of this down or in pouring of stimuli from all of the various elements of the universe ejected in electronic or ionic form from one or another of the endless suns of the endless sidereal systems that are constantly spraying space, and hence our frail and passing sensory organs, the varying atoms and molecules of the same—to say nothing of the sensory organs of endless other creatures and things, if not in precisely the same way, all organisms are changed or transmuted. In so far as man is concerned, they are being stopped and held—these electrons or photons or light particles—by the human atoms and electrons in their path.

But this spells change of everything in and to man, as well as nature, for man has no power to do other than react to stimuli. So he changes, but not voluntarily. Yet, since his sensory organs have but a brief duration in time, it follows that they cannot endure as sensory pictures in man or nature. They fade and pass. All things do. Only the continued organization and distribution of stimuli from somewhere keeps life extant—or, for life, substitute our matter-energy. These are and must be extended in space and time in order for life, as we know it, to be. And because of that, life is constantly passing from deep to deep. There is this constant transmutation of personality—as, for instance, you are transmuted from youth to age, from birth to death, from ignorance to knowledge, from weakness to strength, and vice-versa.

However, this transmutation of personality does not, by any means, relate to man alone. In fact it relates to all matter. For in the crust of the earth there are certain radioactive elements, such as radium, uranium, thorium and actinium, which are continuously changing from one form to another, from higher to lower "rank", because of a constant disintegration of their atoms. Thus, uranium disintegrates into lead, the change taking place very slowly but at a different rate which, so far as we know, does not vary by a hair's breadth from one era to the next. For this reason, today, geologists can tell the approximate age of a rock by calculating the amounts of lead and uranium it contains. Indeed this radioactive clock is the best method yet evolved for measuring the earth's age, and it reveals that the rocks under our feet are at least 1,850,000,000 years old. [Today, this figure would be considered too low.] In fact, evolution is nothing if not the story of the transmutation of so-called personality or its reality into something different.

Thus, today atoms of chlorine can be made radioactive by bombarding them with projectiles. An 80-ton atom smasher turns salt into a radium substitute of probable value (so say the scientists in charge of the smashing process) in the treatment and cure of cancer. Its promise in the latter field, according to Dr. A. J. Allen, lay in the fact that it could be used to extend experiments already begun by Dr. E. O. Lawrence of the University of California, who had previously discovered its ability to isolate neutrons—the uncharged nuclei of atoms—which previous tests had shown to be four times as selective as radium in killing cancer cells without damaging normal ones.

However, this is but one out of scores of illustrations of this ever present and ever operative transmutation of personality process. Indeed evolution is nothing if not the story of the transmutation of personality from amoeba to man. For instance, the familiar tadpole and the larva of the salamander or the frog still preserve the structure of their fish-ancestors in the first part of their life in the water; they resemble them, likewise in their habits of life, in breathing by gills, in the action of their sense-organs, and in other psychic organs. Then, when the interesting metamorphosis of the swimming tadpole takes place, and when it adapts itself to a land-life, the fish-like body changes into that of a four-footed, crawling amphibian; instead of the gill-breathing in the water comes an exclusive breathing of the atmosphere by means of lungs, and, with the changed habits of life, even the psychic apparatus, the nervous system, and the sense-organs reach a higher degree of construction. If we could completely follow the psychogeny of the tadpole from beginning to end, we should be able to apply the biogenetic law in many ways to its psychic evolution. For it develops in direct communication with the changing conditions of the outer world, and so must quickly adapt its sensation and movement to these. The swimming tadpole has not only the structure but the habits of life of a fish, and only acquires those of a frog in its metamorphosis. So there you have transmutation of personality ranging over millions of years.

But in this connection it should be noted that birds and flying insects did not invent their wings, consciously. They began as hoppers, extending their hop by spreading fins or membranes. The flying fish does not know anything about flying. Pursued by a bigger and faster fish, it simply breaks through the surface into the air where it keeps right on making swimming motions, much as a dog swims by making running motions in the water. The flying squirrel, on the other hand, pursued by an enemy, or pursuing something, and leaping from tree to tree or bough to bough, probably stretched the skin between the front and hind legs until the same assumed their present plane-like surface and so provided a glider power almost the equivalent of wing flying.

And again, apes and monkeys became aerialistic, but of the trapeze, not the air, variety. For, from bough to bough they could fly through the air with the greatest of ease but for strictly limited distances only. In fact, some of the ape family, finding that climbing to the top of the tallest tree wasn't getting them anywhere, in their onward and upward urge, came down to earth and took another start, and, after a million or so years, achieved their ambition, being, as man, able to look down on the hawk, and the vulture, and ousting the wasp. And the whale had feet and teeth before it took to the sea, and whale-bone, the latter a slow transmutation of bone and teeth, one might judge, for the modern whale embryo shows traces of teeth and bone before it develops whale-bone.

In connection with this, and strange as it may seem, it is not to the fossils of prehistoric creatures that the defenders of Darwin's evolutionary theory turn to substantiate his evolutionary deductions, but to living animals such as the whale about which we have just been talking. Thus there is man himself in whom are rudimentary organs such as the appendix, and a bit of what was once an extra eyelid, which tell of passing organs. Then there are the manifest similarities between legs for walking and wings for flying. It is no accident that the bones of feet and wings are the same in number and general design despite the degeneration or development of toes and the like. So we are forced to assume that specialized organs have somehow developed from a common fundamental type.

Organisms are very variable. If a whale, which is a mammal and not a fish, can develop from what must have been a four-footed animal, everything is possible in evolution. Embryology, in connection with the whale and other creatures, offers such examples of descent. An embryo whale calf has the normal number of upper teeth that a land mammal would have, but they disappear before birth, so that the upper jaw is covered only with a plate of horn. Baleen whales (the kind that furnish whale-bone) have sockets for teeth as embryos, but the grown whales have only whale-bone. More, some snakes have rudimentary hind-legs in the embryo stage. All these are changes with which man has had nothing to do.

Transmutation has so many aspects as to quite stagger one's credulity or power of belief. For instance, lobsters, crabs and centipedes are truly enough related to the insects. For, arthropod, the latin word for insect, means joint legged, and all of the above creatures belong to this phylum or classification, for lobsters and crabs closely resemble spiders, and yet they live in the sea. The problem is, did the spider take to the sea before it became a lobster or crab—or was it the lobster and—or—the crab?

But let us drop creatures of the land, the sea, the air for the time being and turn to the ninety-odd elements of which matter-energy—the earth, the sea, the sky, or all sidereal matter apart from space; is composed, and inquire as to this matter of transmutation there. And do not forget that you, as a product or aspect of this same matter-energy, are included in this. For, if when you die the atoms or electrons of which you are composed should disintegrate, which would mean that they would change into pure energy, and if—and this is a purely speculative idea of my own—this energy should, for some reason, coagulate as a force, you would, thereby, become an immense power or unit of energy capable (assuming that thought is a phase of energy, which many now believe), although bodiless, of continuing to think—imagine the possibilities of observation, conclusion, interest—assuming that there were endless other such disembodied and yet *thinking* units of energy to be observed by you!—perhaps even confer with! Imagine! For science has already established as a fact that from the change or disintegration of the *smallest* amount of ordinary matter, immense amounts of power are formed. And so, who knows what follows?

One thing we do know, however, and that is this—that the transmutation of various so called elements—gold, silver, sulphur, bismuth, lead, into something other than themselves—can be achieved by the cyclotron, a machine which uses a $200,000 eighty ton magnet to produce ten to fifteen million volt rays which, when discharged against gold, has changed it into mercury—however, not mercury into gold. The machine was made by Dr. E. A. Lawrence at the University of California. Again, in 1936, by the same cyclotron process, artificial radium was made at Cornell. And atoms of chlorine can and have been made radioactive by bombarding them with volt rays, and yet again, by bombarding the metal bismuth with heavy hydrogen atom cores. In fact, fifteen different elements have now been transmuted into something else by the same process. J. M. Cork, N. Halpern, and H. Tael of the University of Michigan, produced two forms of radium called by them E and F. Bismuth, as most know, is an ordinary metal. Its turning into radium is as striking as changing a baser metal into gold.

However, these transmutations, and many others, such as transmuting aluminum into silicon and back again, rhodium into paladium, aluminum atoms into radio phosphorus, etc., are merely additional illustrations of transmutations that are very common today. Thus, air and oxygen, when subjected to a temperature as low as 459 degrees below Fahrenheit zero, change their characters. They become liquid, like water, and can be poured. Also in that state they can be said to have individuality. Only these cold individualities are maintained against a warmer environment that tends to evaporate them. Thus, not only can the air disintegrate them, but heat or shock will explode them—change them to fire or heat. Opposed to something such as earth, stone, wood, iron, these tend to break or disintegrate this opposition at the same time that they produce heat and sound. Thus their one time individuality as liquids being dispelled, they merge with other individualities only to create other individualities, only no one of them permanent or eternal. In sum, this endless process of transmutation was once pictured by the Greeks as expressing the presence of a God—Proteus, the Lord of the Universe. Certainly the Universe as an individual something, if it is, can be said to be Protean.

However, it is not just elements or metals that can be bombarded with aluminum atoms or alpha particles or radium or high speed particles of helium or slow neutrons, but extreme cold, it turns out also, has an amazing effect on certain metals and materials. Thus, at 15,000 feet above sea level, drinks (whiskey, gin, rum—in fact, alcohol in general) double their effect or "kick". Worse—or better—50% of the alcohol consumed at night, at this altitude, will be coursing through the blood the morning after. What is stranger still, the mind, with no drinks at all to affect it, tends to forget little things of the moment. However, when a person has become acclimatized the after effects of alcohol do not last so long, worse luck.

But this is just one phase of the transmuting power of cold as regards metals and various things. It is said to be so cold on the planet Neptune that rubber in that atmosphere would be as brittle as china; cloth could be broken as easily as can be a thin stick; and mercury, which, as we have seen, has been derived from gold, can be shaped into a hammer and so used,—so hard has it become.

But if these things and much more can be done to metals by cold or atom smashing, how much more can be done by heat? Well, carburization turns a soft iron wire into steel in one minute. The wire is heated in a hydrogen atmosphere to prevent oxidation (rust). Then the hydrogen, bubbling through alcohol, picks up alcohol vapor. This vapor contains carbon which interacts with the hot iron to make it steel. The Westinghouse people devised an exhibit of this to show the new importance of controlled atmospheres in hardening commercial steel parts. . . .

However, over in Butte, Montana, millions of pounds of copper are annually separated from water pumped out of the copper mines there by the simple process of pouring it over reservoirs filled with tin cans, scrap iron and minor portions of other metals, which, in a very short time, are thus transmuted into copper! The chemical reaction of the tin and iron to the copper laden water is amazingly speedy, 95% of the transmutation taking place in about 20 minutes!

But if such transmutations can be achieved so speedily in the instances of metals confronted by copper water or extreme cold or heat or by hurled and speeding atoms, what is one to say of man and his chemicals or atoms or molecules or cells or ions of which he is composed, and which, in their turn, are far more persistently assailed and devastatingly disarranged or disrupted than are the atomic constituents of any metal. Germs! Germs! Germs! Gases, poisons, in inconceivably minute organisms that flourish on or in the various organs or substances of the body, and so producing a fair proportion of the endless ills to which the flesh is heir to,—physical or nervous and hence finally the physical conclusion of the existence of the human body—that fatal process of transmutation that is more arresting to man as such than all the others combined. Only, thanks to the development of biology, chemistry and physics, in the last three hundred years, the world has been presented with an entirely new group of transmutations that are as arresting, if not more so, than all these thus far related.

Thus one John Hunter, an English physician of that day, who had bargained with an undertaker for the body of an Irish giant, one Charles O'Brien, who had just died at the age of twenty-two, and was eight feet, four inches tall. Needless to say that Dr. Hunter was biologically and chemically interested to learn what it was that had caused the young giant to grow so tall. And so great was his interest that, although the undertaker demanded $2500 for the body, the physician bought it. His theory seems to have been that the pituitary gland of the brain had something to do with the boy's size. What he found, on dissecting the body, was a pituitary almost as large as a hen's egg, whereas that of a normal man would have weighed hardly more than a half a gram. Subsequent researches into the functions and effects of the gland on the human body caused it to be asserted that *acromegaly*—an abnormal enlargement of the hands, feet, nose, lips and jaw, was due to a tumor of the pituitary. Also that the pituitary glands of various dwarfs examined (some of them only eighteen inches high!) showed all of their pituitary glands to be relatively small, and in some instances partially atrophied.

However, in order to test this power of a hormone or gland or an extract of the same to pass into the blood stream, and, on reaching one or another organ of the body, to cause the same to react in a different way to what or how at first it did, or normally would have reacted, and so, in many instances, alter the entire temperamental reaction of this, that or the other given creature in whom it was to any process previously regularly exercised by it, Mr. Gee, an American scientist, extracted the testes or male sex organ of a rooster, and, by so doing, caused the flesh of the bird to become much more tender than that of the normal male. More than that, he found that there were other arresting and more psychic effects. Thus the previously courageous, combative rooster changed, after a time, to a timid, peaceful, maternal bird. It seldom crowed, and, in some instances, even took care of chicks like a hen. Another very noticeable change related to its head furnishings. Its former large comb and wattles became smaller and the bright, exuberant ornamental feathers of the male became less colorful, and so it remained, a completely transmuted rooster.

But this is but one of many, many instances of transmutation of sex or character or color or design in nature. After the first world war an American soldier was seized with sleeping sickness. Only after this sickness had passed sufficiently for him to be about, his beard ceased to grow, his voice became high pitched, his breasts enlarged until they had to be amputated, and he gave up masculine in favor of feminine pursuits and interests, so much so, that when last seen by various doctors and attendants, he was sitting in a bed in a ward in a hospital contentedly knitting. In this particular case, according to a general medical conclusion, his illness resulted in a glandular disturbance of the sex organs, which same brought about this transmutation of sex.

However there are instances of transmutation which appear to have nothing to do with glandular disturbances of any kind. Take, for instance, the new case of smoke-blackened moths of certain industrial cities where, according to Donald Culross Peattie in his volume *Green Laurels*, "Powerful chemicals in the air make dark deposits in the pigments of the wings, and when these moths are removed to the country air, their descendants continue to produce melanistic or dark offspring!" A process whereby, according to Peattie, "Purely external factors, the environment, the very air we breath, can reach fateful fingers into the very germ plasm, change the orders in them, affect heredity and produce new races."

But before the notation as to the blackened moths, had been Gudernatsch, who had fed bits of thymus to tadpoles which, thereafter, had proceeded to grow to enormous sizes without ever changing into frogs. Also Riddle of the Long Island Biological Laboratory, who had given extracts of oxthymus to pigeons, with defective thymuses, had reported a remarkable effect. For these thymus defective pigeons had been laying yolks instead of complete eggs,—yet, when given the thymus extract, laid normal eggs. In sum, their defective organisms had been transmuted into normal ones. And after him, in 1937, it became known through the Press that at the California Institute of Technology new types of fruit flies were being produced by bombarding the eggs of the same with X rays. And, at that time, some one of its distinguished personnel had suggested that "were it not for the type of social, as well as religious barriers then and there holding, plus the long time between generations, human characteristics of infants in utero, as well as their sex, might well be altered in the same way."

Be that as it may, it is a fact that the sex of a female sword fish can be changed to male by the injection of a compound of testesterone. Also that when the last trace of metal manganese is removed from an other wise balanced diet, female rats lose their maternal instincts. For, out of a group of fifty-nine rats so operated upon dietetically, only one of the mothers built a nest, collected her young, and hovered over them. The others refused and their litters died of neglect. Yet when as little as 0.005 per cent of manganese was added to their diet, the mothers returned to their natural careers. As for male rats deprived of manganese, they became sterile because their sperm had lost the ability to move about!

So at last we come to this—that transmutation of personality is positively the outstanding law of life, so much so that even the mountains and the plains, to say nothing of the cities and the hamlets, change men, transmute them from one thing to another. Thus the Himalayas, being unlike any other mountain range for size, change those nearest them. For, unlike any other mountain range, they present jagged undulations of enormous height, and they seem to speak to men in deep tones, although occasionally they speak with the roar of their avalanches. And yet, at the same time, they so loftily ignore man as something puny and unimportant. And they have nurtured and made sure the most important of humble men on our globe. In fact, their overpowering effect has made many men too humble, so that even today they try to efface themselves from an earth looked down upon by clouds that sit on the thrones of Gods.

India! Its brooding Buddhas and Brahmans! Its Mahatmas, and motionless Pundits, and yearning Gandhis! [*Or*]

The Problem
of Genius

A MAN OF GENIUS, LIKE EVERY OTHER HUMAN BEING, IS LIMITED
by his environment, hence by the ideas and knowledge of the times; he
cannot perform miracles. He can only excel, and usually in a unique and
creative manner, in a function which others master to a lesser degree. But,
the occurrence of genius is beyond our control. It is a gift out of heredity;
its curve of distribution is based on the operation of multiple genes. And
the environment of its day may as readily frustrate as further it: Not all
genius is recognized. That which is extremely suited to its hour achieves
recognition, is applauded—comes to be recognized as *genius*. [*Or*]

Inventions

Are inventions and discoveries independent of any necessity in life—important, apart from human need or desire?

Necessity is the mother of invention. Did it compel nature to invent life?

While in Boston, Edison became familiar with the Charles Williams factory
for the manufacture of telegraph apparatus. One of the Williams men helped
Edison with the construction of the model of his first patented invention—an
apparatus for quickly recording votes in the House of Representatives. *When
Edison demonstrated it in Washington, the politicians explained that it would
be unwelcome, because it would destroy the system of obstructing legislative
business by calling for votes which wasted time.* After this experience Edison
decided he would not attempt inventions unless there was a definite market
for them. This made him the first great scientific inventor who clearly conceived
of invention as subordinate to a need for the same—i.e. to the demands
of commerce. *He abandoned the traditional theory that inventions and discoveries are independent creations, having no necessary connection with other
affairs.* [*W*]

The Myth of the Creative Power of the Individual

It would seem, from the history of art, that nine-tenths of artistic capacity,
at least, depends upon tradition, and one-tenth at most, upon individual merit.

All the great flowering periods of art have come at the end of a slowly maturing tradition. [W]

‡ ‡ ‡

Geniuses are made as well as born. In terms of Nations, one environment evokes hereditary traits and actions which other environments would suppress. In England, at the beginning of the century, for instance, a man might have risen to be an admiral of the principal navy of the world—or the Prime Minister of the greatest empire. But where else? He might also have become Vice-Roy of India—but any where else? In the Arctic? In the heart of Asia? In Africa on the Equator?

In the Arctic men fight cold to their constant disadvantage. In the tropics, heat to the same end. In more favorable climates great nations arise—great opportunities. In less favorable—few opportunities. Sunlight in reasonable quantities develops life. In immense quantities it restrains.

Thoreau said: "Who produces a perfect work is obedient to laws yet unexplored." [Or]

‡ ‡ ‡

If Mozart, therefore, plays the piano at the age of five as well as the ordinary piano players after years of practice, it is asked how or where and when this child has learned what others learn at a much later age? He has had no time for this since his birth. There is the ancient suggestion of pre-existence. And that involves the existence of piano or some technical musical instrument at some earlier period. There are a number of people who testify to recollections of previous existences. Genius is also explained as the receipt, telepathically, by a supersensitive temperament of the ideas—or thoughts of many, working or thinking in one period of time concerning a given problem—and by it organized to a practical or artistic end. [Or]

Fore-Knowledge

Before cosmic rays were discovered Madame Curie, the discoverer of radium, was referred to by Geitel, the German Physicist, in the text of a report of a discussion of this subject before the German Physiological Society as "*suspecting* the existence of a penetrating radiation disseminated throughout the Universe". As to this, Harvey Lemon, the physicist comments in his work on cosmic rays: "Such amazing insight as this is nearly always associated with genius." [Or]

‡ ‡ ‡

The parents who formed Tolstoi's thinking *after his creative work was done* [!] were Jesus, Plato, Rousseau, Proudhon, and Schopenhauer. And he in turn seminated, in varying directions, the minds of Lenin, Gandi, Hauptmann, Henry George. Schopenhauer for his part was born of the minds of Plato, Buddha, Kant and Hegel, and in his turn influenced and gave direction to the minds of Nietsche, Wagner, and Freud. As for Montaigne, he, descended from Plutarch, influenced a host of luminaries from Shakespeare and Bacon to Franklin, Anatole France, and a host of others. [Or]

Edgar Allan Poe

Never so long as writing endures—never so long as men are nervous, vain, despondent, brittle, brilliant, shy, doubting, laughed at, adored, spit upon, misunderstood or understood—never so long as one somewhere can sing and despond, in the same spirit and because of the same reactions to the mysteries, the terrors, the hatred, the brutalities or the grandness and the condescensions and the charities and madnesses of life, will they take him out of the minds or the hearts of men—never. [*Or*]

‡ ‡ ‡

The puzzle of aesthetics, the constant quarrel over the functions of art, proper and otherwise, the relation of the artist to society, the question of what is art, what is good art and what is bad—all these questions may be important and interesting to us on the surface of our lives, in the day-to-day-here-and-now-considerations, but they are irrelevant to the question of art in reality—inasmuch, as their very formulation was based on the illusion that man is a free individual and that he creates freely,—and from this it follows that if you could only show the artist what was right and proper he could, by his own free will, produce endless pictures, statues, books, poems, symphonies, and so on.

Art

Persistences in the form of dreams and desires eventually produce our typical experiences. But our desires and their resulting dreams and experiences are nothing more nor less than chemical reactions to exterior stimuli—first registered—then "stored" and until such time as the chemic state of the body is actually most propitious—that is, most sensitive to these stored registrations, when they revive—come to life—grow like flowers or weeds in any garden, when the sun shines and the moisture is sufficient. And betimes being strong, they in turn radiate their dream forces—and these like germs or molecular pollen, fly and contacting related chemical states anywhere, in male or female anywhere, they register or impregnate or implant that related state. And so—assuming the pollen to be male, the sensitized chemism of another person female, or vice-versa there are either long distance or direct, immediate unions, as in loves, partnerships, agreements of opinion—as in the "marriage of true minds"—or as nature impregnating the sensitive chemism of the artist. [*Or*]

‡ ‡ ‡

What is art but a frozen form? So many notes on a bar, so many words on a page, so much paint on canvas, such a form of stone or bronze, so many lines on a sheet of paper.

It is in other words, as any other real object of nature, passive unless sensed by someone or something. Music, black notes on a printed page becomes the unbelievably sweet song of a spring morning. Is this magic? But surely. Here is the dead sprung to life.

Here is a painting. So much gold and blue and red streaked on canvas. It is a woman, lying on her couch, a secret, sensual smile on her face. What is she to you? Nothing, you never heard of her. If she ever lived, she has been dead these many hundred years. Yet she evokes a mood in you, something intangible and lovely. That form presented to your view for your sensation, for your imagination, brings into being a new combination. Your magic combines with its magic—a new form, intangible, and having no material reality, but yet something real, inasmuch as you have seen it and it influences you, is made.

The artist when he wrote the poem you read, or painted the picture you see, or designed the temple you stand in, or formed the image of a God in marble was living in a world of actual experience which no one else ever lived, or can live. The picture, or the music, or the temple or whatever was for him a synthesis of experience, of reactions, and is for you a potential world of reactions. The difference between what he put into that form and what you bring to it when you experience it may be great. It probably is. It is impossible for any two experiences of art, even for the same person, to be exactly alike. The form which the artist creates carries a charge of experience, potential for the observer. This charge has possibilities limited only by the concreteness of the form. It is possible for the observer to react completely to the concrete expression. Perhaps. But the observer whether he is an artist himself or merely an ordinary person with no artistic pretensions can sense it. He can get as much from the form as he has himself to give. In other words, his artistic appreciation is not so much limited by art as such, as by his own mechanistic abilities, his own memory, his own reactions, his own possibilities of connection, formation, extension, temperament. [*Or*]

‡   ‡   ‡

It is because man is not individual but truly a mass representation of a formula or type—a full length presentation of what is actuating large numbers of people, their hungers, ambitions, lacks, defeats and what not else, that one can select—one here and one there—and present them in courts, in the newspapers, on the stage, in the moving pictures, in paintings, in the novel, as typical. Yet however "individual" the so-called individual, thus presented, he still remains typical of thousands and millions—in part at least—and by reason of this fact is able to move them emotionally—either to sorrow, anger, hatred, admiration, etc., in the same way that he is moved. If this were not true, how could a character in a book or play or painting appeal—and often so movingly and even violently—to millions upon millions. Consider, for instance, "The Man With the Hoe," Shakespeare's Macbeth and Hamlet, Moliere's Tartuffe, Goethe's Faust, Thackeray's Becky Sharpe, Tolstoi's Anna Karenina, Balzac's Pere Goriot, Dicken's Oliver Twist, and David Copperfield. In these, as in various world heroes, its soldiers, statesmen, philosophers, poets, inventors, discoverers, every unit of the mass sees itself, either as it would prefer to be, or as in some way or part it is—happy, miserable, strong or weak, fearsome or brave, resourceful or stupid, but always, as in life, in this earthly environment, common to all. Hence, as you see, even in his dreams man is not individual. He has mass dreams and mass ideals. [*Or*]

Genius in Nature

But there is another phase of this problem that is not so clear. Neither spider nor insect, as Fabre, and a number of other naturalists have definitely demonstrated, has any such thing as conscious wisdom or reason. Both do too many things in too automatic and wholly uninstructed way to permit any human being with his limited senses to credit them with forethought. In short, many of them burst upon the world from an egg, a wax cell, like the bee, a silk pocket or pouch like the young of spiders—and with both mother and father this long while dead. Yet immediately they proceed to do amazing things—walk, run and sun themselves in order to get strength, climb grasses or bushes or small trees to the topmost twig or blade in order to pay out upon an unobstructed breeze a thread of silk, and of their own spinning on which they may sail forth in the world, like some Columbus on a caravel, in order to reach a fresh field of operations far from the immediate region which would otherwise be too crowded by the other young spiders. And once there, wherever, to begin a career of hunting, mating, home building, and web-spinning, but without any earthly training whatsoever. Out of an egg in a purse into a world of which seemingly it could know nothing yet with an inherited egg-perfected equipment for doing all the wonderful things that a spider can do. And generation after generation doing the same thing through thousands upon thousands of years (millions). Yet built and trained by what? Vaguely we know some of the methods and materials used. For one, the chemical synthesis called protoplasm which consists of various combinations of elements plus sunlight, plus oxygen, plus water. But, as we well know, knowing *that* much we know nothing. For here is a creature that can spin silk finer than any silk man can make. And not only that but pay it out, loop it, fasten it, here and there, use the wind to rest it on, and if short of silk, eat all that it has paid out and internally reform it into new and spotless silk.

Not only that, but in building and rebuilding its amazing web-traps of accurate geometric design which withstand wind and weather and also in tunneling and curtaining its underground caves (the black bellied tarantula) which task involves, as do some of our most modern subways, curves, levels, side-chambers and the like, and also excavation, the removal of pebbles almost of the weight of the spider itself, the measurement of width and heighth and depth of walls, and excavations from which stones came, and repairing the same, it exercises if it does not know, the science of engineering mathematics. More, in this matter of weaving, it appears to have the science of weaving as well as draping after the fashion of the interior decorator, at its finger tips—exquisite webs, purses, lids, hangings, all coming from the same atelier, its belly, and all being deftly and effectively placed. Not only that, but like the gladiator of the Roman arena with his trident and net, it can and does measure the distance, calculate weight and the like for it can not only spin, throw its net, but accurately enmesh anything from a bee to a preying mantis, and in most sturdily designed nets which it weaves almost as swiftly as it throws them.

There is even more of craftsmanship and technical skill here than meets the eye, for this machine-like insect, like the thrower of any net or flyrod, any hook or baseball, calculates distances with an accuracy which in a human would be considered technical skill of a high order. In addition to this, it appears to understand the anatomy of any insect whatsoever that blunders into its trap. For it knows the exact spot in the cervical genglis of a bee, grass-hopper, wasp, or preying mantis to strike with its poisoned fangs in order to produce the instantaneous collapse of its victim. That done, it knows at which points in the anatomy of its victims to insert its sucking proboscus in order to extract the particular fluids of the veins or the brains on which it lives.

In the world of men, of course, such technique does not come with the new born infant. Neither is it intuitively acquired. Hearsay, contact with those who know, training, either by tutor or by technical schools or colleges is required. Unlike men, however, on its arrival on earth, the spider appears mechanistically to know. It has distinct understanding of or reactions to the forces of nature. In building its net, it appears to take into consideration not only the direction of the wind, but its force, also the particular angles at which a net must be strung in order to be fully effective and these angles of course vary with the nature of the environment in which it finds itself. Also the tensile strength of the threads which it tests and doubles or triples as the force of the wind or weight of itself and its victim may require—as to all this implied in the way of what we call intelligence, when you remember that all bushes or grass blades or weeds or tree-twigs are not placed just so. The spider must take its web-building opportunities just as it finds them, just as any engineer or architect or excavator does. And so it does and effectually, generation after generation but without visible instruction. Read me this riddle if you can.

Genius and Unity in Nature

I don't know how much I assist in the economy of nature when I declare a fact. Is it not an important part in the history of a flower that I tell my friend about it? All beauty, all music, all delight springs from this apparent dualism but real unity.——Thoreau.

Also hunger in the bee and odor in the flower, the bee's necessity for food and its sensitivity to honey or perfume brings the bee into the beauty problem. More, the transfer by the bee of the sex pollen of men-flowers from the male to the female plants brings the problem of beauty into the problem of the evolutionary creative power of nature—suggests a technical economy in arrangement and construction which brings up the question of mind in nature—that is—is nature or the universe or this creative force mental? The only clue we have to that is this; that if man had devised and operated such an intricate system as this—at once economic and artistic as well as creative—he would speak of it as mental—and himself as a genius, at once artistic, creative, and economic. [*Or*]

T.D.

NOTES ON LIFE

Part II

The Theory
that Life
is a Game

RECITE NATURE'S HELP OR GENEROSITY TO MAN—EVERYTHING that he has. (The Lord giveth and the Lord taketh away.) With the food and sensory reactions of the first living things—even the energy of the living things—began Nature's beneficence. That it was coupled with accident and death merely demonstrated that life as we know it—the life of give and take, of struggle and achievement, pleasure and pain—the general intensity of life as set over against death, or change, was intended. In other words, *life is a game* and was plainly intended to be so; suffering and death, at every stage of the evolutionary Life-process is limited—held at the minimum, considering the total result—enjoyment of life—achieved. [*Or*]

‡ ‡ ‡

Some temperaments register these things more than they do the accidents and cruelties of life. They are favorably stirred by them.

‡ ‡ ‡

The present state of civilization is said, by some, to be a measure of the success which man has achieved in utilizing his environment and adapting it to his needs. By others—those who like myself deny to him individuality, individual thinking, free will, individual creative power, possessions, responsibility, memory, etc.—it is either the planned results of a universal mind or the unplanned results of a will-less machine, even though to some at times it does not seem to be.

For myself, I am free to say I suspect a stupendous mentality, solitary and eternal that with powers exhaustible or inexhaustible finds necessary to itself both activity and rest, the creation of illusion and the exercise of reality, a mental content to the expression of which are necessary contrast, memory, forgetfulness, rest and activity, variety and unity, chance and surety, mercy and cruelty, love and hate, joy and sorrow, order and disorder, change and stability, ignorance and so-called knowledge, strength and weakness, courage and fear, secrecy and its opposite—openness or frankness—in other words, contrasts with limitations forever.

‡ ‡ ‡

One thing to consider in connection with this theory is this, that nature in creating her vast stores of minerals did not—probably—have man or his needs or emotions in mind. (Or did she?) Any how it seems more *reasonable* from the man mechanism point of view, to assume that she was intent (if intent) on solving her own internal problems and not on providing wealth for the human race—or beauty, or emotional responses to so-called beauty.

Yet in the case of the precious stones from gold and silver to crystals and diamonds and rubies, they are looked upon by man (possibly by some animals—birds) as beautiful and so valuable. They evoke, as all know, an emotion or reaction called a response to beauty—color etc. Yet without light, form, color and the mechanism called man built to respond to such things, how could they seem either beautiful or valuable to him.

Hence there arises the question—was man or all protoplasmic life forms constructed to respond to such things? And were they constructed to evoke certain emotions in him and then at the same time satisfy them? Or are both accidental and not mental—that is, purely mechanistic developments—mere accident or chance—sound and fury signifying nothing? Yet if something were planning such a game, as this life seems to be, forethought (such as this might possibly be) would not be out of order. Or is this mere mechanistic error! [*Or*]

                                                                    T.D.

Death, Justice, Mercy, and Cruelty

All change and all death involve not only mercy for men but justice. While birth and growth serve to supply organized life with not only social energy and skill—man being born with these attributes as well as with that sensitivity to proportion and order which results in social peace, prosperity, ease, education, the arts, beauty, music, etc.—still others (enough to keep the game called life functioning and operating fairly smoothly) are born with reverse and opposite qualities. They are stupid, violent, greedy, cruel, disorderly. However, these meet not only with opposition from the first but are, their effects, modified by the first.

Also in connection with this, change, illness, weakness, death gradually overtake them and often when they are at their worst . . . the height of their skill in whatever it may be . . . cruelty, disruption, murder, they are so disposed of. The evil and destructively ignorant die and are replaced by those who are not so or, at least, slowly grow to be so, since they are not effectively so when they arrive.

It is also true, of course, that the good, creative, useful die sometimes when they appear most to be needed. And it is they who furnish the material for the unjust or evil (if any) to work on. Without them there would be nothing wherewith injustice, cruelty, fraud, theft, murder, and the perpetration of the same could be contrasted, . . . the two types and the materials they provide being, along with ignorance and wisdom and any other qualities or types of reaction, the materials wherewith the game of life can be played.

‡ ‡ ‡

Vanity arises from necessity for contest. Each creature must contest with something else. A cat vies with a bird to see which can outwit the other. The chase among all animals is not only a necessity prompted by hunger, but a pleasure depending on victory. Loss can also prove a pain for one, pleasure or joy for the other.

By various scientific methods Psychologist Edward L. Thorndike has shown that less than one-third of all we spend goes to keep us alive, while over two-thirds goes to keep us amused and socially important and to prevent our being laughed at or regarded as queer, or homely. Of the $700,000,000 spent annually for cosmetics and beauty parlors, he shows one-seventh goes to make us look and smell right, one-fourth for courtship, one-third to do the "right thing" socially, one-eighth to secure inner self-approval, and one-tenth to secure domination over others.

Take another phase of this same thing. In any game—and *Life is a game*— pride enters as an element necessary for victory. This is true of business, as well as in contests of any kind, games, principally. Each contestant not only desires to win the game for his side or school, but each individual member of a side wishes to prove not only his importance but his superiority as a contestant over all other contestants. Without such spirit or vanity on the part of each, no game would be worth seeing. [*Or*]

The Black Widow Spider

The black widow spider during a single summer lays five sacks of eggs—two or three hundred eggs to each sack, a thousand or fifteen hundred spiders—in order seemingly (not certainly for no one knows that) that a certain number of the Black Widow Spider family shall survive. But then along came a little fly, *Coquillet* in science, which has discovered let us say, that its larvae, if placed where they can eat the young spider eggs, will grow and flourish just as we have learned that if we eat endless hen's eggs, or young chickens, or young calves, or birds, or fish or their eggs (shad roe, caviar, sturgeon eggs), we will grow and flourish. So little Coquillet the fly arrives, after the black widow has hung her sack so that the sun and the rest of nature may ripen them and cause them to grow, and fixes her eggs upon the surface of the sack, since her eggs mature and the young larvae come out before the young black widows in their eggs can appear. And once out, they eat the Black Widow eggs nearly all, so that out of a thousand or fifteen hundred Black Widows perhaps no more than three or four will survive. To be sure, this is apparently enough to keep the Black Widow family going. Also the Coquillet family. And perhaps some other families that live on the grown Coquillets or their eggs. But why? To keep this living scene as it is? To make contest? Activity? Drama? Beauty? Pain? Death? Change? Does anyone know that? Can you give a (seemingly) more intelligent reason? [*Or*]

‡   ‡   ‡

Insects worry. Bees, ants. The struggle for existence is a worry to every struggling thing. Release from that struggle is pleasure—rest, motion; motion, rest. Insects sing only when not disturbed. Also when not hungry. Also when there is the hope of satiation in sex or food. They sing at their work when the work is agreeable. They flee when afraid, showing that they experience the emotion called fear. They fight to live, to obtain food, to defend their young, showing not only fear but courage, satisfaction in victory, knowledge of how to fight, etc. Their mating and survival processes indicate intelligences not so different to those of man and the animals. [*Or*]

‡   ‡   ‡

Nature surely could provide enough food and shelter for ants without war and strife—yet does it do so? The amount of food necessary to support all the ants in the world for the fifteen or less years of their life without toil and war is probably contained in a million bushels of grain. And nature, if it *would*, could easily arrange for that. As minute as they are, as little as they eat, as small as is the space they occupy, they must be preyed on by all sorts of insects struggling for life and subsistence, and more, by rivals of their own or related species—murder and sudden death, battles, slaves, endless work to gather a store of food and protect the same, reproduce their species, care for and feed the young.

In fact, in order that they may have the minute life that they have, there must be struggle, adventure, contest, enmity and friendship, love and hate, greed and charity, waste and want, safety and uncertainty, ignorance and knowledge, courage and fear—in fact all of the things that go to make a good game, and the enjoyment of the same. Else no ant life and so no ants. And here in place of the word *ant* you may write spider, wolf, wasp, grasshopper, mouse, rat, fox, dog, bird—every creature that has ever reached the state where collectively it sought to live, reproduce, and enjoy itself as a living organism. And yet it did not and could not make itself. It was made and in its particular form and with its particular needs and instincts by forces above and beyond its comprehension. [*Or*]

‡   ‡   ‡

Life is for pleasure and not for misery or death.

Observing the life of which we are a part with the sensory equipment provided us and for all of its appearance at times of extreme cruelty or brutality or the reverse, it still appears to be nothing more than a game, mechanistically or intelligently devised and/or a game intended to be played. The principle of the game is no different to the principle in any minor game played by man, whether it be that of football, baseball, hockey, or any game where antagonists of relative strength, sometimes with the same, sometimes with different equipment, are opposed to each other. In sum, the individual is equipped in a certain way, that is, with a form, a degree of energy, and five, possibly six, senses. With this equipment, he is faced by other individuals of relatively the same equipment, and the contest is not merely one for survival but for joy out of the contest. For if this life game is not for pleasure I fail to detect what else it is for, unless it is to benefit in any way the totality of energy or creative power out of which it takes its rise? I cannot see it or think it. Its achievements apart from sensory pleasures or the struggle for them here or now are *what?*

Be that as it will, the outstanding characteristic of this game, like that of every subsidiary game devised by man in imitation apparently of the great life game, is contest, with a view to victory over some rival contestant who loses. In fact, upon his arrival on earth, the individual, whether man or animal or insect, is faced by the problem of subsistence, survival, and pleasure as opposed to escape from pain or defeat. For all, but more diversely for man than for animal, this involves not one but a series of contests or games from birth until death, or until the individual or active unit called man is worn out by the process. At birth apparently one enters upon the game of testing one's strength or right to survival against the right or will of various rivals as opposing natural elements, whether in the form of man or elements to inhibit, modify, or destroy. This game or contest is conditioned by success or failure as to health, strength, beauty, fame, success, in understanding, and in the prosecution of understanding, desire, plus love of contest, and the results to which these give rise. In other words and because of these various contests, many types of games are devised or they automatically arise. They are the games of discovery or success in science, art, law, medicine, architecture, trade, writing, painting, engineering, navigation, exploration; only by us they are called professions. And the contestants enter them not only with the purpose of subsisting but of triumphing in the game, and more, being applauded for that triumph. Not only this but without these various contests or games the totality of this life game would have no meaning. Its awareness of itself as life arises from contest or a game, and without such contest there can be no sense of life.

Furthermore, the whole process of living in this unit form as we find it here has the earmarks of a carefully planned game, just like any lesser game devised through this same creative force operating through man. That is, whether we sense it or not, it has been limited as to time; approximately seventy years is the limit of the game. In that period only certain goals and no more can be possibly achieved—subsistence, victory over disease, victory over physical weakness or handicaps of any kind, victory over ignorance and one's fellow contestants for pleasure, fame, love, power, and applause.

The danger of defeat is the associated element in this game of course, and as in all games it is interesting to note that defeat is by no means always destructive or even too painful, let alone fatal. To be sure, out of a large number of contests, there are a number that end in death, and death itself appears to be one of the risks devised and calculated to give the game its extreme thrill. That it does not always follow upon contest is natural and human; often it is not even involved. And in connection with this life game of his, or rather some of the series of games or contests of which it is composed, man may well live, and does, to contest in other and later games and on occasion wins. Few lives are composed of an unbroken series of failures.

Not only that, but in this life game provision against too great suffering has been made. For instance, no form of suffering can be carried beyond a given degree. The sensory reactions of his body do not permit that, although why he does not know. Thus at a certain point in every contest where the power to endure through suffering is involved, suffering itself, beyond a given degree, becomes impossible. Reason gives way. The sensory nerve chains unhook and pain is not reported. That is, unconsciousness invariably and speedily relieves too great pain. Even death by slow torture cannot be protracted beyond a limited period. Either the ability to endure or the will to endure ceases, consciousness takes flight, and while the body may be mutilated, the sensory powers have no part in it and will not return to share anything more than a limited or endurable process of recovery or attempted recovery. It is even true that of this planned contest that the contesting units are not even equipped to endure or rather enjoy ecstasy or pleasure or reward beyond a given sensory limit or goal. Neurology has already satisfied itself that intense pleasure like intense pain is inhibited by unconsciousness. Thus the satisfaction or pleasure reward that can spring from a given achievement through contest, i.e., wealth or fame or power or love, has obvious sensory limitations. One can only sense so much of a given reward or result of victory. The rest is beyond the yardstick of the mind, or, in other words, the limitations of the sensory responses of the race or its units to perceive or sense. In short, observing life as a whole, neither limitless joy nor limitless cruelty or brutality nor anything *limitless* is either intended or permitted. What is permitted is a limited sensory swing between so-called "extreme" pain and "extreme" joy. These swings range on either side of what is in mathematics known as a mean or equation, in philosophy as the golden mean, in physics as dead center. Past this dead center in either direction the sensory responses appear to be allowed only measured distances or responses—an early calculable top of pleasure and a rather easily calculable bottom of pain. That these ranges or swings will yet be mathematically calculated, and in terms of energy, is certain.

THEODORE DREISER

Special and Favoring
Phases of
the Solar System

WE HAVE BECOME ADAPTED TO LIFE NEAR A STAR OF MODERATE temperature, as we are conditioned to register temperatures, and that emits more visible light for our type of eye than any other kind.

But there are other stars with surface temperatures several times higher than that of our sun, up to 50,000 degrees in extreme cases. With a star of this type for a sun, we would have to adjust ourselves to radiation of entirely different composition from sunlight. For although such a star would give out more rays of all kinds than the sun does, the great bulk of it would be far out of sight in the ultraviolet, quite invisible to eyes like ours.

And we could no longer speak of golden sunshine for there would be none. Instead it would have a ghastly bluish tinge—like the glow from the lamp in a photographer's studio.

‡ ‡ ‡

The modern chemist is reminded by his researcher of the astronomical hypothesis that man's whole body is full of the same chemical elements as are present in the atmosphere and in the rocks originally derived from the sun. [*Or*]

‡ ‡ ‡

Consider air plants (Southern Moss, Gold Thread, Mistletoe), spiders that grow by sunlight (Fabre)—they get no nourishment, presumably from anything but the sun shining on them. Snow flakes take form from cold—not heat. Plant and flower forms spring from chemicals planted in solutions at a given temperature (LeDuc). A seed of any plant or animal can be nothing more ·than a chemical combination favored by special chemical and physical conditions such as prevail here on earth. [*Or*]

‡ ‡ ‡

Clipping:

Sunlight has proved better than artificial heat in purifying bees-wax for high quality candles and cosmetics. Solar heating, according to C. S. Bisson of the

California Agricultural Experiment Station, not only helps remove impurities but also bleaches the wax. Pure bees-wax will burn with practically no smoke, but that gathered from the hive contains some pollen and bee glue which tend to produce soot.

How does it do this? By electronic extraction very likely—the drawing away of the electrons and atoms that compose the color and the impurities.

T.D.

‡ ‡ ‡

The "wealth of the sea" lies in the fact that in time sea water attacks and dissolves nearly all known substances. It has dissolved many of the precious metals from their ores and of course holds in solution many, many chemical salts. On the stability of its present chemical formula, dependent as these are on the earthly and *solar conditions* environing it, depends the lives, forms, colors, if not the energies or atomic structure, of all its inhabitants, animal and vegetable.

T.D.

‡ ‡ ‡

Mild mercurious chloride, a non-poison, will be changed by sunlight to mercuric chloride, a poison. It is customarily kept in wooden boxes or brown bottles to prevent this happening.

‡ ‡ ‡

Solar light and heat consist of little bullets of energy. As far as the earth is concerned, enough of them strike a city in a single hour to wreck it completely if they all could be put to work. Also, if the solar energy which falls on a city block could be changed from heat energy into mechanical energy, it would be enough to wreck a ten story building every hour.

Again there are certain rays from the sun that would be deadly if they could ever reach us men and women—not by any means all animals, insects, or vegetation. They would blister the skin and blind all of us if we had to stand them for only a few days. But before the beam can reach us, ozone gas, whether accidentally or intentionally distributed from 25 to 40 miles overhead, stops the blinding ultraviolet light as effectively as a stone wall.

Sunburn and tanning, the first our only legitimate complaint, are caused entirely by a few invisible ultraviolet rays that just manage to escape absorption by the ozone. The immediate reddening of the skin is a temporary effect produced by the heat from the visible and the infrared rays. But the latter penetrate much further into the skin and, for no reason known to man, are of real value in the treatment of sprain and bruised muscles.

Again, certain ointments discovered and collected by man are fluorescent. That is they will glow in the sunlight. They absorb ultraviolet rays and then, promptly, emit them again, but usually in the form of visible light. Their protective action for the human body roughly corresponds to that of ozone for the entire earth. [*Or*]

‡ ‡ ‡

It may be that the real solution of the power problem lies elsewhere than in those physical laboratory devices that are intended to capture sunlight and develop electrical energy directly from it. One source that has been suggested by more than one scientist is plant life—the utilization of the energy that is annually or periodically stored by all those plants that grow quickly in the sun and so store energy quickly.

Think of grass or any plant or tree, and how, when dried, it can be burned—turned into heat, or great energy. Think of the enormous waste of energy (from the human point of view) when a forest burns—the dreadful and wasteful forest fires! Each year there is fifty times as much energy stored in plants as the world uses (C. C. Furnas, Assoc. Prof. Chemical Engineering, Yale University). Many a Dakota farmer has warmed the family through the winter by burning hay. Western threshing outfits used to use straw as fuel for their engines.

Our first railroad engines used wood. Until sugar cane waste became valuable as a raw material for insulating board, all steam boilers in sugar plants were fired with the squeezed out stalks. And think of all the grass and brush and leaves and "trash" that are annually burned off estates and lawns and yards and open lots to improve their appearance. Assume, for instance, that all that were collected and stored to be sold or used as fuel for plants or to be converted into insulating board or synthetic wood!

Yet if all our present corn crop were converted into motor fuel, it would only supply half of our present needs. Also it would injure the coal, gas, and electrical business as these are now, unless they controlled and used the corn. It is undoubtedly possible today to breed plants that will be far more efficient in their energy converting (photosynthetic) power than they now are. In fact, because of genetics, there is no evident reason why the energy conversion efficiency of a plant cannot be stepped up ten times and so give us fields of stored carbohydrates growing with a luxuriance that will put even the carboniferous age which gave us our coal fields and mines into second or tenth place. In sum, we can grow more coal every year than we can use. [Or]

Want and Plenty

The solar energy falling on one square mile of any arid region is equivalent to about a million horsepower. This would be a year-round average, for night and day, summer and winter, clear and cloudy. One mechanical or electrical horsepower operating continuously night and day for each American, or ten manpower.

Now, harnessing the sunlight that falls on only about 200 square miles of the Mohave Desert all the year round would supply our nation's present demands. Not only that, all the sunlight which falls on the earth's surface in one minute would supply the world's present heat and power requirements for an entire year. Yet this excludes all the other minutes of the sun's radiation that falls on the earth and is used by man mechanically—that is, in connection with his machines.

And furthermore it excludes all of the sunlight that does not fall on the earth at all—the sunlight that lights an area so many billion times greater than the entire surface of the earth that it is beyond his so-called mental power to conceive. And by [man], since it appears to be of no immediate service to him, it is looked upon as wasted, whereas from a solar point of view it might be that the small portion that falls upon the earth and so makes him possible, is, by something else, looked upon as wasted. For of what particular good or use is he to the sun? Can he imagine any? [Or]

‡   ‡   ‡

Can it be called upon as convincing proof of the constructive and directive intelligence of the mechanism called life that not only has *man* taken his rise among and, therefore, obviously from exterior stimuli, as has been demonstrated by Loeb, Pavlov, and the entire science of biology, and that he is exteriorly controlled and directed thereby, but that he is most carefully shielded or insulated against other forms of stimuli which would most surely tend to disturb, disarrange, and in many cases certainly destroy the limited response equipment which he represents?

Consider the high electric fields of energy through which he moves and which, were he not sensorially insulated against, would disarrange and destroy him. The gases to which he is immune! The high frequencies of sound, of light, of heat against which he is protected, either accidentally or designedly—but all within the mechanical order of the solar system as well as the universe. This second arrangement of insulation, and so of physical and nervous protection, is as important as energy direction and control via exterior stimuli. The two are inseparable concomitants or factors in the life mechanism which permits of the existence of man along with all the flora and fauna of earthly life. By the same token, this argument applies as well to suns and planets, solar and sidereal systems—in sum, the entire arrangement of island universes called by man, in the English language at least, the *universe*.

T.D.

The Necessity
for Contrast

THE ENTIRE REALM OF PHYSICAL NATURE HAS A DUAL PERSONAL-
ity. The tiniest particle of energy known and of which everything is composed
has a dual personality, partaking as it does of the characteristic of a particle
and a wave. The *wave particles* of the electron are much smaller than the
wave length of light and yet give them the character of light: Use of them
by the ultra-electron microscopes permits of the visualization of much smaller
objects than can be seen through the most powerful microscopes of the lense
and ordinary light variety. [*Or*]

‡ ‡ ‡

What would life do without the contrast presented by *stop* and *start?*
[*Or*]

‡ ‡ ‡

All elements or atoms or electrons or protons, or any combination of
them—either matter or sidereal system or man—could not, insofar as the
organized life we see, by any possibility be of equal authority or wisdom
or both and at the same time have the world of creation function as we
see it. For in the life of man, as in the life of all creatures and the solar
and sidereal systems, we see nothing if not differences and hence contrasts
of endless variety and significance or lack of the same: the giant island universes
as compared to the lesser ones, the giant suns as compared to the lesser
ones, the immense coagulations of matter as compared to the trivial ones.

Always differences, differences, differences, contraries. Little, big, hot, cold,
fast, slow, strong, weak, bright, dark, newness, oldness, few, many, ignorance,
wisdom; creatures that crawl, fly, walk, swim, stay still; elements and gases,
metals and stones that vary in weight, color, durability, usefulness; a world
of vegetables that feed man, bird, beast, and insect.

And all appear to be, and in fact are, ordered or *compelled* arrangements,
or structures, or forms—gravitation and/or magnetism ruling the various
electrons, protons, atoms, molecules, and/or the various combinations and arrangements of the same, of which they be composed, wherever and howsoever.

And at the same time, we do see attractions and repulsions, affinities and oppositions, positive and negative charges or temperaments, and, what is more, that to have one you must have the other or Life as *man* knows it could not be.

‡ ‡ ‡

Before anything can *be*, not only the possibility but the compulsion to simplicity, also to its contrast, complexity, must *be*. Simplicity and complexity are, of course, degrees of the same thing, yet separateness of appearance and of effect are both necessary to creation, evolution, dissolution.

‡ ‡ ‡

If it were not for the wide range of contrasts to which the organs of sensation are compelled to respond in life—the sufferings as well as the pleasures, the disasters as well as the miraculous successes and achievements—what would become of music? song? poetry? the dirge and the Hosannah? the tragedy and the comedy? in short, all art in all fields? The song that you whistle or sing is about what? Sorrow? Joy? Some hoped for but as yet unrealized dream? Some past or recent failure or sorrow?

All of them, of course, and without them, there could not be the contrasts, the delights or at least comforts, at bottom the restful feeling of resignation, tinged with melancholy though it may be, that is in all art and without which it cannot be.

For art—music, painting, poetry, sculpture, the comedy, the drama, the humblest song—merges all of the contrasts of life in a rhythmic unit of one kind or another—the never absent rhythm of the universe, which at long last makes a song, poem, art form out of everything. And with this, if no other, it seems to seek to console the sensitive organisms it has evolved on earth from man to amoeba, with rhythm, sound, color, odor, taste, the delight of form and motion registered in such ways as it has devised for their registration. [*Or*]

T.D.

‡ ‡ ‡

In a world that presents nothing if not contrasts, in which we can only be aware of ourselves because we are confronted by an endless variety of things and persons which are obviously not us, but other than us, where we are only aware of heat because of the possibility of contrasting it with cold, light because of darkness, and so on, it is odd, and often smacks of the naive and fantastic, to harken to the innumerable voices in many lands calling for the "liquidation," as one phrase has it, of vice, crime, prejudice, intolerance, and what not. As though there were ever a day in which those names were non-existent, or ever will be. The things that count to any man, and in the terms of those qualities listed above and others like them, are the contrasts of this moment, himself and other men, his house and another's, his job and another's, his state of mind and another's, his past moment and his next one.

On the other hand, it is true that ignorance at a certain deep level has been modified, the quality of sensory darkness diluted. But has the dilution done more than to permit ignorance to keep within hailing distance of the van of intelligence which measures the distance of the rear guard? Although evolution is a fact, and progress in a perceptive sense as well as a technical one is plain, ignorance maintains its distance as measured by the van at any period. And those who do not know are, at this hour, innumerably greater than those who do, as everyday living as well as the collection of evidence of our social statisticians forces us to realize.

The stuff of life is this feeling of contrasts and involves a constant struggle to do away with the painful, or socially malevolent, or evil, or whatever name is given to that side of the equation which is hated and feared. Our potential ability to pick flaws, dream an illusory better dream seems limitless.

And thus the naivete of the educated humanitarians, the intelligent world-settlers, such as came together at the Harvard tercentenary conference [1936]! Naive because the illusion of this moment forces them into a struggle which is at once hopeless and inevitable, their concrete or intangible plans, their good and beneficent gestures, successful though they might possibly be in their immediate and finite conclusions, can never solve the ultimate essential problem of the existence of contrasts, and so the ills of humanity.

How can this be otherwise in this mechanical world in which the final conditions have been fixed and forever?

The sensory stimuli which environ man and which cause his sensory reactions, insofar as he can judge, immeasurably surpass his nervous and organic powers to respond to them. Endless ages of matter-energy have plainly erected a material super-structure or environmental state of such stupendous proportions as to dwarf and make fearful any sensory unit, particularly of the earthly or protoplasmic order. And yet, the protoplasmic process brought into being on this earth suggests an evolutionary building up and fitting out of a mechanism suitable for registering in consciousness the matter-energy universe as a whole. But this does not seem to happen instantly or ever completely. There have been ages and ages of what to a super-being might seem experimental and explorative efforts; so many millions upon millions of organisms have come into being and have failed, either instantly, or after a period. And all of these, if one were to accept the registered conclusion of the man-mechanism as a standard of judgment, have been topped by himself, the man-mechanism. He thinks of himself as the most sensitive and responsive of systems, reacting more swiftly and accurately to such interior and exterior stimuli as the universe presents than any other of the protoplasmic forms which have appeared here on earth and with which he recognizes a distant kinship.

But now, here is the interesting thing: one might safely deny this man-mechanism's deductions; and there are endless protoplasmic mechanisms—mammals, birds, fish, mollusks, bacteria—which, as man has found in *his* process of registration, have powers of sensory response which far outstrip man; and these same powers, as again, he must register, are plainly the expression of the compulsion of matter-energy to form, activity, and gratification, just as are his own. In spite of these realizations as to the qualifications of other species, man is accustomed to rationalize his position into one of dominance by the reflection that at least he is in a superior position when it comes to the question of surviving and conquering the other species. Yet, even here, there is no standard for measuring this superiority, either in terms of the individual or of the race to which he belongs. Bacteria, possibly, could be said to sit in judgment on a man-mechanism or at least to evaluate it, when they destroy it. By the same measure, the shark is obviously superior to the man it cuts into pieces in the water, and a snake, when a man dies from its poisonous bite. As you can see for yourself, there is no first point of departure for these measurements, no sure measure or rule. Man and all the other species seem to have a characteristic in common which far outweighs their relative differences and superiorities. They are, all of them, their registering mechanisms, driven by the creative forces which they merely register, far beyond their capacities to register or to prevail, one against the other, except perchance, and without any surety of procedure or conclusion. All of them are driven and compelled by their unwilled environment operating on their will-less selves to do as they do, and after the briefest possible space of time, pass away into that which they have ceaselessly and unsuccessfully been compelled to register and prevail over.

In consequence, it is of no real importance what man thinks he thinks about anything. It is of the very greatest importance how the mechanism called life compels him to react. For that, by a slow process of its own, and but little of it clear to the man-machine at any point, seems to be slowly evolving, and by reason of contrasts and not otherwise, into a more and more complex and sensitive mechanism. But even as it proceeds, its gains or advances are only made known because of that which has not gained or advanced so much.

For example, consider the engineer who, in planning a bridge, takes into account certain laws of nature and the laws supplied him by the empirical sciences and by physics in particular. And the logico-mathematical instrument he employs is essential for every type of rational, planned activity. This is true not only in constructing machines but also in organizing human associations and activities, for instance in the field of economics, for planning both individual enterprises and large scale undertakings. For without this instrument, it is clear that civilization as we know it today would not be possible. But on the other hand, while some men or minds are capable of using this instrument and planning after this fashion, others are not. And this individual defect of the many tends to give rise to the control and dominance of the few. The intellectually weak, but nonetheless chemically and physically motivated beings (all the mechanistic products of nature itself) are directed and not infrequently (in fact quite generally) deceived by their emotions, their desires.

For these seek fulfillment. But without a logico-mathematical understanding of and reaction to the laws of nature to guide them, they count on vague, illogical conceptions of charity, kindness, goodness, and the like to guide and supply them, or save them, on God and morality, on social law and "justice" (as applied to others, not themselves). They are like the naive player of any game who expects that his opponent will make just those moves or mistakes that will further his own plans; and sometimes he does, to his wonder (chance being the natural factor it is). But not often. Their expectations, inadequately founded, are usually followed by disappointments in the behavior of others; yet the failure of their hopes, instead of leading to the corrections of erroneous assumptions, frequently become the occasion for a childish reproval of opposing groups, and in the names of variable yardsticks, such as morality, justice, imaginary divine command, etc. To be sure, these in their turn have the backing and the authority of vast organizations or masses of the equally deluded, but for this very reason are of no more authority than those who appeal to them. Back of all lies the unstable equation called life, which must have both ignorance and wisdom, good and evil, morality and immorality, kindness and unkindness, order and disorder for it to function at all as the thing we call life. For if all could exercise the logico-mathematical faculty equally well, where would be those differences, those contrasts and the exchange or work they involve in maintaining this unstable equilibrium which is essential to what we call life?

But all cannot; your mechanism which reacts fairly accurately to logico-mathematical data is but one out of many. The others, and through no willing of their own, being purely mechanistic developments of the law of contrast or that function to which the spectacle called life is due, have no power of registering accurately such stimuli as make for the logico-mathematical approach toward life. They can only wait for and make use of the logico-mathematical engineer, scientist, chemist, mathematician, doctor, lawyer, statesman, etc., who does not make himself by any means but is mechanistically set forth by nature equipped as he is, and be used by as well as be served by his superior (if they are) skillful reactions. Indeed, to be what he is, as you can see for yourself—engineer, scientist, chemist, architect, statesman, doctor, lawyer, philosopher, mathematician—it is absolutely necessary in the world of the mechanism called man that he be confronted by and, more, be made possible by those who cannot be any of these things, but to whom these things, services, arts, etc. are useful and, more, necessary. Where would your doctor be except for patients too ignorant of medical science to be of help to themselves; ditto your engineer, assuming him to be minus those ignorant of engineering as a science. Ditto your educator, chemist, physicist, lawyer, and what not; to be what they are, they must be surrounded by

those who are *not* what they are, but who still need or can make use of
the services, skills, etc. which they represent. No medical ignorance on the
part of many—no doctor. No chemico-physical mathematical ignorance on
the parts of hundreds of millions—no physicist, chemist, mathematician. In
other words, no ignorance—no wisdom. For only division, contrast, unequal
proportions of the same things make possible the spectacle which we call
life. Nonetheless, you will find the wise berating the ignorant, although except
for the ignorant they could have no least claim to wisdom, no one to berate
or direct, or control, or inform, no power to feel superior as creatures
(mechanisms) set over against the inferior. Similarly, the strong, the weak;
the cunning, the simple—even though the simplicity of the simple makes
the life and the success of the cunning possible. And so it goes throughout
the vast dualistic system.

Indeed, if you will but once get it straight, illogical thought is as important
a factor in determining human behavior and the picture or experience we
call life as is logical thought. And those anti-rationalistic tendencies of this
day which preach that reason, exact verified knowledge, should not be
over-esteemed are not without their roots in fact. More, various organizations,
religious, financial, governmental, that have long profited by the ignorance
of the many are to a degree mechanistically correct and necessary if we
are to have this spectacle called life. For that very great miracle called
abolishing ignorance or mental differences can never be effected without
abolishing knowledge as a conscious thing.

But instead of realizing that the confusions in practice and doctrine which
are to be found in society, science, and art—in short everywhere—are characteristic of life (an inherent and unescapable aspect of the mechanism), many
of our so-called logico-mathematical geniuses believe still that ignorance,
as a contrast to knowledge, can be abolished, that all can be made equally
wise and intelligent, which is nonsénse. If that could be done, life as we
know it would not be. More, many also believe that these painful differences
flow from an over-evaluation of the intellect—the logico-mathematical instrument we call exact verified knowledge—and that a halt might be called
there. Imagine!

And, in spite of the improvements and advances that have been accomplished
in this man-machine through the compulsions of contrasts, it is not clear
whether the end is to be his own greater ultimate delight, or greater misery,
or some intermediate equation. For along with all the improvements, is he
any happier than he was, or than the fish in the sea, or the birds in the
air, or the vegetation of the fields, the electrons and protons of the ultimate
atom?

Who is to say that? What evidence is there to guide us to any other
belief than that our imaginary human minds are other than innate aspects
or expressions of an immense matter-energy synthesis—a concatenation of
cosmic actions and reactions—which we dare not assume to be measurable

by the sensory responses characteristic of us? For while it includes all that as registering and expressing machines of its devising can register and measure, it includes or rather is that which we neither register nor measure. And while we may describe or react to that which environs and affects us either favorably or unfavorably as good or evil, beautiful or ugly, important or unimportant, destructive or constructive, and so forth, here we cannot know and therefore cannot say or see how these contrasts or distinctions can be operative elsewhere. Our knowledge, after all, is not only finite, but worse, equational—a rough balance, unstably maintained, between our here markedly limited stimuli and our registering capacities of the same—those, for instance of heat and cold, length and brevity, heavy and light, to say nothing of ranges of sound, odor, taste, feeling. But who can say whether or how these may be chemically or not chemically registered elsewhere?

We cannot know—yet. In consequence we can only wait and measure and guess in such ways *as we are mechanistically constructed and motivated so to do, and not otherwise.* Which means that not we but something else of which our environment and its stimuli, and we also, are but as a minor fraction, may continue to direct or motivate us toward or away from a solution—who can say? And more, which may as readily motivate us entirely away from, rather than toward, a so-called logical solution; in sum, to our eventual passing without any solution of any kind. Might that not well be? [*Or*]

T.D.

‡ ‡ ‡

Supposing all were adjusted, no one committed any crime, no one was immoral; due to the arrival of equity, there were none put upon, no poor, and no idle and at the same time no over-privileged rich; each by a certain amount of pleasant labor had enough to get along on, and each realized that according to just needs he was equitably provided for and neither insulted or fawned upon—So what? No more wars, because no more inequitable struggle for power. Well, what would each have to do and how would he feel? Well, one man, H. Gordon Garbedian, in his book "The March of Science," comes forward with one picture. Here it is:

When our technological civilization ultimately attains its maximum development, two or three hours of work a day may be enough to provide us all with a plenitude of the necessities of life. Since there will be enough of everything to satisfy everyone, there will be no longer the economic or hunger incentive for competition and war—men and women will spend most of their lives in leisure, in doing the very things they want to do most; climbing mountains, organizing expeditions, to little known lands, writing long epic poems, creating music for their own entertainment (and possibly for that of others), becoming amateur zoologists, or indulging in any other hobby which may suit them best. . . . There will be fewer travel books written, for men and women will be able to satisfy at first hand their curiosity about the dancing girls of Bali, the Chinese Wall, child marriages in India, castles along the picturesque Rhine, the ancient Coliseum of Rome or the carefully aged wines of Paris.

But for myself, I cannot help asking what about people with lesser or greater capacities, mentally and physically. Can all be made physically and mentally strong or will there still be, via the factor called chance, some at least, mentally weak and physically weak, and what about them? Will there be no superior or inferior musicians or painters, poets, engineers, scientists, captains of industry or of state craft, and if so, how will they look upon themselves? Will the life around them, once freed from the need of toil and the fear of hunger or defeat, supply the necessary incentive to further research, or will the desire for applause, public notice and acclaim serve to urge them on to discover and achieve as in the past? Or will they by any chance feel that enough has been done and that they would rather play golf or climb mountains or go to Bali?

But assuming that they will not—how about this matter of applause due to their continued interest and labors and the fact that for outstanding achievements they are likely to attract more attention than their fellows? Will that be all right? Will there be no least trace of envy—to say nothing of a possible struggle or contest here and there for the right or the opportunity to share that applause—and no shade of hatred, in case the general public, financially free to attend to such matters, should refuse one his estimated measure of applause and yield to another whom he considered less deserving; no heartache for instance, on that score. It is a logical question, practically as well as philosophically worth pondering.

And apart from especial achievements of this kind in various fields, how about, for instance, the present beauty and ugliness among women, and their natural desire (all of them) to be beautiful, and when not as beautiful as one or another, as sexually and mentally attractive, to yield to jealousy or sadness or a desire for revenge of some kind—if not on any particular individual, then on life in general—to feel their life is after all (the money problem settled) as equitable or as perfect as it should be. And how would that be socially adjusted?

Could all women, via biological processes of the future, be made beautiful, and if so, would men be as much interested in this matter of female beauty as they are now? If not, what would become of the intense and at times decidedly exciting desire for it among women? Might it not fade? And with it the present intense drama of having or not having it? What about all the Hollywood beauty stars? Would they not disappear and with it the present day furore in connection with their glamour? What about the dream of being a stage or picture beauty? Of winning fame and fortune, as well as love and wealth, by reason of the Helen-like lines of one's face and body? What! no thrill as to that in any woman's life? All being beautiful equally or relatively, and the ancient money ills to one side, no longer to be worried about, would there be a Jack for every Jill, and would that arrangement be as satisfactory or more so than this present day inequality in this matter of the possession of beauty?

Who is to say? For while it may be possible and even comparatively easy—present breeding and improving arts being what they are—to make beauty as common as large potatoes or larger heads of lettuce or asparagus, yet the matter of interest, zest, appeal is something not completely guaranteed by unvaried perfection. For ennui, dissatisfaction with any given type of anything, even any perfect type, is almost conditional in nature. There is quite always a revolt against the usual and quite always in favor of the unusual, the necessity for change, physical and chemical, in order to have motion, activity, life. And with one level of beauty holding, as against rare beauty opposed to frightful ugliness, and great desire on the part of many for beauty as opposed to ugliness—who is to say that this extreme contrast might not provide more life interest than unvaried beauty?

In short, it seems quite obvious to me that in every instance or situation where it is proposed that some wrong or lack, or this or that, be abolished or reduced, it follows that there is involved an unescapable reduction in the intensity or zest or vigor of life.

The Necessity
for Limitation

Limitation of all things as illustrated by the sense of the passing of time and the end of all things (death) involves a seeming intention on the part of the Creative Force to enforce a degree of equality as between the strong and the weak, the just and the unjust, the merciless and the merciful, wealth and poverty, etc. [*Or*]

The Rhythm of the Universe

Everything fritters away into the infinitesimally small and is recombined into the enormously large, which in turn reverts into the almost inconceivably small again. [*Or*]

‡ ‡ ‡

Duponts have a sound or energy amplifier that amplifies—by 100,000 times—the sound of beetles feeding on leaves.

Our eye registers only one-tenth of the total amount of light. Other devices register it all.

Feeling can be registered the same way, also taste, odor, poisons. . . .

To be different, everything has to be limited. [*Or*]

‡ ‡ ‡

At what point does number (more than one of anything) becomes unintelligible (unthinkable) to the human mind.

Three hundred chorus girls are not necessarily 10 times as exciting as 30. . . .

One girl is appealing to a youth but three, five, ten or fifty, a hundred?—where does appeal, understanding, delight pass into reduced interest, slight interest, indifference, lack of import, and finally blurred and meaningless registration. [*Or*]

‡ ‡ ‡

There is nothing that is really helpful or harmful save relatively—that is according to the amount of quantity or degree of it used. Nor is it helpful or harmful (good or bad) save under special conditions or particular environments—social, chemical, physical, legal. A grain of poison may be fatal to an insect—not to a man. A type of food may build and sustain one kind of creature and not another—an insect say, but not a cow, a horse, a bird. All foods and poisons, for instance, depend for their usefulness or serviceability not only on heat and cold, dryness or wetness, but on the presence or absence of the organisms which can be benefited by them. Also on the amounts that can be obtained or used. A grain of corn will not aid a horse or man much. It might sustain a small insect or bird for a long time, etc. [*Or*]

‡ ‡ ‡

How poisonous is poison? Well, that depends on the size of the creature poisoned. Also the amount of poison used. Also the vitality of the poison itself. Also the immunity of the creature bitten to a given poison. Thus, the poison of a small spider such as prey mostly on flies—a tiny, tiny droplet will kill the fly almost instantly, but a man or horse or pig or snake or rat, no. It is not enough.

Yet, on the other hand, the droplet of a small black widow spider such as flourishes in America may prove fatal to a man or child, and to some animals. In general, scorpions and some spiders are dangerous or fatal to man in proportion to their size, age, and the warmth of the climate that they dwell in. But, of course, *more* of the same poison of any venomous species—spider, snake, wasp, hornet (enough)—will most certainly kill a horse, an elephant, a man, a rat, a snake, etc. Quantity, plus venomicity, plus or minus immunity to given types of poison is the answer.

You or any creature may be killed quickly by a number of drops of cyanide of potassium—the above conditions still holding. But dilute a drop or two of the same poison in a glass of water with ice, add sugar to suit and you have a refreshing and harmless drink—I mean man has. A pig might not touch it. Nor yet a horse or dog or cat or bird. So what is its true "reality" in nature. It is a real poison to what? A delightful drink to whom or what? Time, place, size, form, weights, measures, distance, nearness make this or that real or unreal.

‡ ‡ ‡

Even an extremely small thing like a single living cell or disease virus particle is immensely larger than an electron. Hence an electron can pass through it. If it were not, an electron could not pass through it.

The truth or fact that *limitation* is a necessity or condition of the universe is demonstrated by this fact that if anything is larger, something else must be smaller or you could not know either small or large. And so something must be limited as to size, or weight, or color, or speed, or number if it is to be contrasted with anything else that is larger, heavier, brighter, redder, faster, or whatever.

Without limitation not only on one side but on both sides (limitation of the larger as well as the smaller), there could be no contrast, no variety, and by the same token no interest, and so no life as man or a human being knows it. Dr. Erlich showed that if the syphilis germ was to be destroyed, there must be found something smaller that could penetrate and destroy it—and that *was* discovered. [*Or*]

Gold and Silver

In order to be different, to be seemingly individual, to be *one* as opposed to many, everything must be limited—must not be illimitable. And that is nothing more than an observation of universal law.

Gold, in quantity, can be a fortune, a hundred ton block if necessary. Or it can be a tree-like *lode* with branch-like veins in a mountain. Or, broken down into smaller quantities, it can be money or jewelry. Reduced still further, it can be dust or a thin film or even so little as an atom, which can and has been, in solution, administered as a drug—the one-time gold cure for the liquor habit. Also, scattered through the universe in atomic form, it can be a gas but in each instance, as you see, in order to be anyone of these specific things, it must be limited—that is, delimited. It cannot be all of these things at the same time—not the same delimited quantity of gold.

But this, as you can see, is true of all the elements—from silver, lead, iron to carbon, helium, strontium, whatsoever you will. Silver, reduced to a trace, can be used as a germicide, a tankard, a frame for a picture, a ring, a plate, but definitely limited as to quantity and form, no one of the elements nor yet all of them together could possibly furnish forth the universe as we know it. Given limitation, you have variety. Without it, not any. [*Or*]

‡ ‡ ‡

Preachers, doctors, lawyers, engineers, specialists in all fields, as well as carpenters, brick layers, plumbers, plasterers, etc. illustrate the necessity for limitation. All are called to do a little—not much—and are spread out, as is a field of energy in which electrons and protons, positively and negatively charged, fulfill their respective duties. Consider atoms in fixed positions in all molecules—the characters of all the endless varieties of substances depending on their being thus limited in position and function.

"He also serves who only stands and waits." [*Or*]

T.D.

‡ ‡ ‡

In order for there to be contrast, there must be limitations. That is, each man or animal mechanism or organism must be cut off in some ways (but by no means, in all ways) from all others. Insulated. Otherwise, where would be the illusion of individuality, personality, temperament? So-and-so must *seem* different. You must really walk among puzzles and mysteries for life to be mysterious, surprising, irritating, destructive.

But how to achieve this? Nature does this by environing each mechanism separately, with stimuli related, but never exactly the same. You can see this when you consider the differences of being reared in the mountains, in a valley, in China, India, Norway, in the Arctic, or at the Equator. Next, consider hereditary differences brought about by ancient and, to what we call *consciousness*, forgotten or frozen stimuli of endlessly varied character. Next, the structural as well as organic differences of the world you move in. And to variations of which, never exactly the same, the organism called man or animal is subject. Lastly, permit only part of the registrations of one to be sensorily registerable by another, and at once you have the necessary *limitations*, and at the same time, the unescapable and yet partial likenesses and differences between organisms which give you life in all its color, variety, mystery, surprise, and drama. [*Or*]

‡ ‡ ‡

The wear and tear of life—very frequently joined in the thought of man with his inefficiency or incapacity as a machine—is correct insofar as it concerns him as an exteriorly driven mechanism, but not otherwise. For if man wears things out, and in the process, wears himself out, it is not of his own intent to wear them out, but an integral factor or condition of any use he makes of anything. Nature, not man, except as an implement of nature, is the force or entity that does the wearing. And you are to consider in that connection the earth, the stars or suns, the sidereal systems or island universes, all of which, if the theory of the dissipation of energy is correct, are being slowly but surely worn down and falling into the dust or final etheric sea from which they took their rise. But [on the contrary] for purposes not only of life, or of action, variety and change, without which this sense or scene of life could not be in us, this wear and tear, or waste and disorder, may be—and no doubt is—as essential as order, stability, permanence, etc.—the elusive, hypnotic qualities with which, due to the brevity of our own lives (relativity) we endow the really swiftly altering scene which we contemplate. [*Or*]

T.D.

The Necessity
for Change

[A long, completed chapter for this heading was published in *Hey Rub-a-Dub Dub* and so is omitted here. The short essay on Proteus expresses this, one of Dreiser's favorite themes. *Editor's Note*]

While the bodily natures of citizens are being fitted to the physical influences and industrial activities of their localities, their mental natures are being fitted to the structure of the society they live in. But as climates and environments differ so do the industries and hence so do their people. And all is constantly changing.

T.D.

Varietism

Consider the necessity for change in contacts—people tire so quickly of each other if forced to remain in contact too long. A woman very often prefers a variety of men to one man. A man, more often than not, prefers a variety of women to just one. Marriage, except for the presence of children— growing and so constantly changing as well as, in the first instance, presenting a variety of temperaments—becomes to many women and men a bore. Very often only a religious theory or social pressure (custom, taboo) as well as joint property interests, or lack of means—sheer necessity to live as cheaply as possible, pool all earnings—will keep a husband and wife or a group [from] change.

Change, variety, the lure of the outside, the unfamiliar, the strange, the different, is the thing that presses heavy on sameness—as the outer air upon a vacuum. [*Or*]

‡   ‡   ‡

Human beings are always fascinated by what horrifies and disgusts them. The reasons are obscure and doubtless complicated. Why do certain of the elements and chemicals have their affinities as well as their antipathies or vice versa. There is the quite universal craving for *change*, due very likely to a chemical weariness or sameness.

207

Why is light in such a hurry? Here on earth in this time-limited thing we call our life—the petty compulsions and doings that make up our days—monotony surely rules and oppresses.

Most yearn to be stimulated, excited, thrilled, even to the point of committing suicide if they are not. For it is more life, not less, that suicides are seeking, and in the determined absence of which they prefer to die. In consequence, for some, the horrifying and disgusting are a source of strong emotion, and they are sought, pursued even, for that reason. But it is also true that with our carefully limited—one might almost say niggardly nervous equipment—we are quickly satiated, filled up. Our organism cannot stand much, neither of hot or cold, weight or imponderable matter, hunger or satiation. Our eyes, as we say, are bigger than our stomachs. Our enjoyments turn to pain; our intensities, to an irritable desire for rest. Rewarded either too much or too little, we faint, fail, and even die. [*Or*]

[*Proteus*]

The secret of the Universe is that it has no place to go. Being all in all (I am that I am), it can only change itself, transmute its totality into endless forms with endlessly varied objectives or desires, moods, aspects, pleasures, sorrows, successes and failures, dramas and tragedies. To achieve this, it must veil itself by making each of its creatures sensorially incomplete.

Memory must be for a day ("beyond which memory runneth not to the contrary"). The duration of each creation or creature must be brief—no time to learn or even doubt much. In order that there may by happiness for itself .in each of its transmutations and in all of its endless disguises, the misery of no one of its creatures must be too great, nor the joy. All must be ended at a given degree or point. And as death for all. Only so much pain, so much heat, so much cold, so much weight, so much deprivation can be endured by any. Each dies at the point where its degree of planned durability is reached ("He giveth his beloved sleep."). But in doing so, the creative force is giving this same peace to itself. For it seeks change within itself: interest, joy, sorrow, beauty, strength, wisdom, adventure, etc. But in order to have these to the fullest measure, it must invent their contraries by which each may know and measure the other. And, as we see, there is no such thing as illimitable cruelty or joy or sorrow or poverty or plenty or strength or weakness, but invariably, everywhere, an equation or balance by which all things are given pause, whereby all are restrained, measured, weighed so that no one thing shall have too much, no least thing too little, for otherwise it will cease and return to its source ("I am the vine and ye are the branches." "I am in my father and my father is in me." "In my father's house are many mansions."). For in these things—all of them, as is obvious—is the Creative force itself—Its will to change as well as the power to change—but not wholly, since it is Maker and Ender of all of these things, and since Nature's limit to change, alter, disguise is not to be sensed by any of the creatures by and through which it chooses to express or pleasure or weary itself. Hence, because of all these things, it seems obviously to be a thing apart from that which it creates; however, not entirely, since it chooses thus to express itself in part, but rather something which has the power to assume endless such disguises and at the same time the power to end them and be that which can be something else when it chooses.

The vast wisdom of the Greeks who symbolized *Change* as a God—*Proteus* the God with the power to endless(ly) alter himself into something different!
[*Or*]

                                                                          T.D.

The Necessity
for Interest
and Reward

THE SUPREME MIRACLE OF CREATION IS, FOR MAN, THE THRILL
of expanding life. Is it true for the Universe? [*Or*]

‡   ‡   ‡

We humans are much like fish that swim in an ocean which they call
their "world," yet are dimly aware of another world up where the light
shines. If they were mathematicians, the fish might make a few interesting
and valid conclusions about that luminous world above, into which, occasionally, a bold porpoise or dolphin may look.

We are compelled to speculate, to synthesize, what little data we can
gather about the ultimately (or so it seems to man) impenetrable universe
around us. It is, at long last, a chemical or physical compulsion. We cannot
escape interest or sensation. And the built up organs by which sensation
manifests itself to man and animal may be the ultimate creative process
at work in and through us. And because of it, this compulsion to respond
which evokes what we name *interest* is the only possible way of learning
something about the universe and, more, our Creator. [*Or*]

‡   ‡   ‡

The interest which a percentage (by no means all) of the living people
of the earth, who, on an average, live but forty-five years, take in the so-called
progress of the race is not to be explained by any benefit that they, individually
or collectively, can possibly derive from any such endless progress, if it came.
They will not be there to see or react in any way unless the dead live;
and as for the few who appear to sense and proclaim this certain progress—where
will they be?

What might explain the interest of the few is not anything that they truly
see as of value to themselves, but rather the possible and even highly probable
profit that the force now motivating them, as mechanisms, and which will
continue so to motivate them throughout an immense future, might derive.

For this force through them (as mechanisms) might well enjoy self-expression on this planet throughout millions and millions of years, but perhaps not otherwise. For, as you can see for yourself, not these, nor the current population of which they are a part, can possibly live more than a minute fraction of all the time required to see this progress, which is by no means certain. Whereas it, the creative force or forces, *can* [see it], and *through them*. Indeed, their seeming interest may be nothing more than the shadow of the real interest of the creative force itself, which is using them as mechanisms for the achievement of peculiar and special experiences of its own. [W]

‡   ‡   ‡

Suppose for instance that a man has a business proposition before him. He must decide whether to take it up or not. He must consider the several factors in connection with it as far as he is able, and after considering these he will make his decision. This is called conscious, practical reasoning. To make this more specific, let us say that the man has an agreement with some auctioneers to auction off some of his goods. In the agreement, the man says he will pay the auctioneers so much for their work, that he will pay for certain expenses such as carting, cataloguing, advertising, in connection with the auction. The auctioneers say they will perform the service of auctioneering, but they do not say just how. The problem the man must decide is this. Will it be worth it to him to dispose of his goods by this means? His first reaction is no, it will not, as the matter stands. In the first place, rare books, the value of which has never even been approximately determined. In the second place, the agreement reads in such a way that the man feels that while his end of it is specifically noted, the part which the auctioneers intend to play is not sufficiently described. He wants further mention in the agreement of just how the auctioneers intend to dispose of the goods. And he must have some idea of the amount of money which the sale will bring in.

To go backwards, just what is it, specifically, that are the man's problems? He says, if I can get some idea of the amount of money I will make from the sale, and if I can get the auctioneers to specifically describe their services in the agreement, then I will take it up. But when he "wants some idea of the value of his goods at sale," what does he want? He has a vague, hazy notion that the goods are valuable, although he couldn't translate that into money. He has asked his friends, and they say that the goods are worth anything from 5,000 to 50,000 dollars. Already, based on his ideas of money, his experiences of money, earning it, and paying it out throughout his life, he has some notions of value. But these notions are not rooted in reasoning, and especially not in *his* reasoning. They depend on the price the group has set on his work, and on the things he must buy to live. And ultimately these depend on the primitive notions of exchange, so much corn for so many knives, and so on—a ratio set by nature, and which we accept, in the very beginning, without reasoning at all.

The number of peaches on a tree, the number of trees in an acre, the rate of multiplication of natural things, the length of time a man must work to get tired, the amount and kind of work different kinds of men can do—these we accept, and base our reason on that; so, when the man's experience teaches him that 5,000 dollars net from the sale is not sufficient value, but that 10,000 is, he has no sound logical basis of his own reasoning to set this notion in, but only certain assumptions, built up out of a continuous experience of his own and his group, but no intrinsic facts, relating directly to the books and their value, which he can put his finger on. If the books, when they come up for sale, should bring five hundred dollars, that would be a fact, but he would be greatly disappointed, because in spite of all his logic, and all his friends' logic and all their reasoning, and all the factors they take into account, they still know nothing of just how the books are going to strike the public at the day of the sale—whether each individual who might be interested in buying one of them is going to be struck with a desire, an emotional want, an immediate reaction, such as a woman feels when she sees a hat she wants, or a baby feels when it sees a bright colored ball—which, the total sum of which individual desires, is going to bring the sum realized from the sale into the man's scale of values.

Now for the second thing the man wants done before he will agree to the sale, the stipulation as to how the auctioneers are going to conduct it. He wants the things that are never, or almost never, put into contracts. He wants the auctioneers to conduct the sale with flair, style, clever advertising, efficient and unslacking effort—all of which things are not matters of logical reasoning and which cannot be judged with reason or logic. Again we are faced with a flux of values, all of which depend on a whole lot of reactions, much experience, many equations of value. What is flair—you know it when you see it, just as you know blue is blue, a tone of voice, a wave of the hand, a manner of walking, atmosphere. The same for style, and the same for advertising—something which has immediate, and unreasoning appeal. As for efficient and unslacking effort, the man knows only in a general way what that can mean in the auctioneering business.

Well, and in conclusion, just what, supposing the auctioneers are willing to stipulate more specifically just what their services are going to be, and supposing the man is satisfied a priori that the sale will be justified from a money point of view, what will the man get out of the sale? In any case, he will get a logical deduction of a sort, a fact which he will have to consider no matter how illogical it is basically, and that will be the amount realized from the sale, which in the long run will depend on many other people's logical deductions with regard to buying the books for sale or not. If the sale brings 500 dollars, he will experience great disappointment—an emotional and unreasoned feeling which he may be able to rationalize into indifference by the reasoning process of, "Well, after all, that's something," or "it doesn't matter," or whatever. He will have to have some feeling about the sale.

Success, if the amount runs over 10,000 dollars. Moderate satisfaction if not quite that much. Elation and surprise if it runs over 20,000 dollars. . . . All of which leads us to believe that it is the emotional basis from which he started, and the emotional basis on which he ended which were the prime movers in the situation as far as he is concerned. After all, as you must admit, the money itself, the 500 dollars, or 5,000 dollars, or 50,000 dollars which he must realize from the sale, is of relatively little importance to him in this particular case (although they may be in other situations) compared with *how* these amounts of money fit in with his ideas of money in general and with his illogical notion of the value of the books, conceived a priori, in particular. And yet it is a logical end of the cash itself which his methods try to insure, in spite of the fact that his mind is moving from the emotional state of desire to the emotional state of satisfaction or frustration. [*Or*]

‡ ‡ ‡

The fact that nature, the creative force, via the evolutionary process, could and did and still does evolve the endless variety or forms of creation—male and female—men, animals, birds, fishes, insects, flowers, and what not, and, what is more, chemo-physically arranges it so that each should not only optically visualize the one the other as male and as female, but because of this difference of form and color, among other things, be sensorially and so sexually attracted one to the other in such a way as to cause each to function structurally, and not only structurally but accurately structurally, so as to bring about an accurate reproduction of the species, is not only proof of an immense chemical and technical science involved but a startling illustration of the chemo-physical—or perhaps I had better say the chemo-technical as well as physio-technical—use by nature of form, color, motion, odor, sound, energy in the form of heat, light, etc. in order to bring about the desire and/or emotion which man calls *love* but which in connection with beasts, birds, insects—all flora and fauna, in short—he speaks of as *instinct*.

Among other things it should make plain to man that the male and female sex forms which, at their best and so for the duration of the mating or reproductive period in his realm, he holds so highly—provoking as these do in him the emotion called love, the reaction or sensation called beauty, as well as the desire and fever and very often sacrifice that accompanies the actions compelled by these—constitute but two of quite endless forms or designs which nature in its chemo-physical laboratories is forever capable of producing, reproducing, and changing.

And this raises the question of how important in nature this particular love and sex reaction of man and, for that matter, all other creatures is, seeing that nature uses it to produce so many other types of creatures—endless varieties in fact. Also, how much and for how long man, given this knowledge as well as free will, would or could react to the particular male or female form that at this present hour so moves, emotionalizes, and entrances him—how long it would continue to compel him to act as he does. [*Or*]

The Necessity
for Ignorance

IGNORANCE, IN ONE SENSE, IS THE TRUE GARDEN OF EDEN. It
is the realm of rest as opposed to the realm of unrest. It may well offer
more marvels and delights than wisdom. At least, it is necessary for that
"progress" in wisdom and knowledge, for without it there could be no reason
for wisdom or knowledge. You do not seek something that you have or learn
something that you know. [*Or*]

T.D.

‡　‡　‡

Knowledge can only be set over against ignorance. Without ignorance
to overcome wherein would lie the importance of knowledge? By what would
it be measured? With what could it be contrasted? What would it abolish?
The truth is, the two form a single living vail [value]° and the one cannot
be real without the other. Both must be modes of expression of something
that includes both, but is not either. Plainly they are implements wherewith
a game can be played. A game of seeming or pseudo-reality as opposed
to something which includes the real and the unreal. [*Or*]

°[Here, Dreiser used the word *vail*, old form of value. *Editor's Note*]

‡　‡　‡

There is evidence that prehistoric man used the horse for food, hide, and
bones, some hundred thousand years before he thought of riding him.——Dr.
Johann Keeler

One thing is certain, that for the purpose of life as we know it or as
evolution shows it to have evolved, ignorance (very, very, very slowly banished
ignorance, illusion is an equally good word) is a very essential thing. For
if the sum of knowledge that we know as life were capable of being imported
to an instantly evolved or perfected mechanism—call him man or what you
will—the spectacle and pleasure of evolution would as instantly be dispensed

with. There would be no need of any such thing as evolution, or the slow and interesting discovery of anything. In fact, the amazing spectacle of the Universe could be dispensed with, and man would become the equivalent of the creative force—no need to do anything but *be* in its essential immateriality. [*Or*]

T.D.

‡ ‡ ‡

How many billions of people are kept interested in life by their ignorance of life's processes. The great question of *Why* as well as *How?* A struggle for existence is easily generated by nature, which has made all of its processes as secret as possible.

Christ said, *Seek and ye shall find. Knock and it shall be opened unto you.* But not without labor, curiosity, awe, danger, hunger, cold, heat: the promise and possible fulfillment of all the evolved appetites of men, animals, suns, and planets. But not without work, movement, energy. In other words, nature has invented a game of hide-and-seek in which *all*, whether they choose to be or not, by the ignorance thrust upon them and the appetites and hungers they did not invent, are compelled to participate. [*Or*]

‡ ‡ ‡

If you are to have a varied and colorful world with many things to wonder over, many things of which to stand in awe, many things to fear, many things to admire, many things to study and puzzle out, and concerning which to instruct or educate or inform others, it follows, in the first place, that you must be a limited and uninformed and different sort of mechanism to those about you; next, the other mechanisms must be endlessly varied and [of] strictly delineated forms which are different to you and to each other, and that involve processes of which you are ignorant, just as they must be ignorant and even fearful of the processes or mysteries which are you. Otherwise, no awe, no wonder, no strangeness, no ignorance, and no knowledge, which decidedly make possible the process or procedure or reaction now known—to man at least—as life. [*Or*]

T.D.

‡ ‡ ‡

If the universe were a finite thing and if its forms did not change, then knowledge or whatever it is that becomes known or felt in conscious or unconscious form could at last dispel ignorance, in truth, gradually overcome the unknown.

However, there is reason to believe that the universe is different from us in that it is an infinite thing, and that like us, the various parts of it change forms constantly; its infinity in combination with its changing form present an absolutely unknowable spectacle. Knowledge, therefore, is paradoxically enough only a form of ignorance; and increasing knowledge also increases ignorance in proportion, in some ways analogous to geometric progression. Knowledge, therefore, could only have been absolute at the beginning of things and so now has a relative absoluteness at the moment it is acquired, but no longer.

Our insistence on the existence of general truths does not make them truth. This insistence is only the form of our compulsion, for practical purposes, to give form, law, and order, corresponding to our existence as finite beings. Individuals, groups, societies, etc. are very finite things in comparison to the whole of which they are a part, and by analogy, they have this compulsion to make all things fit into their finite scheme, in regard to everything of which their finite senses make them aware. Therefore, we deduce laws, limiting the operations of what we see; we give properties to matter, energy, space, time, all infinite things, and their combinations, only to find that in spite of all our efforts to know and put things in order, we become aware not of conquering knowledge, but of increasing ignorance. The anarchy of the infinite and ultimate must, it seems, reject the forms and molds and laws into which we try to put things to make them like us, or our so-called minds.

So it seems that to share this point of view is a kind of defeatism for the struggle for knowledge, as Socrates said when he asserted that he was the wisest man because he knew that he knew nothing.

‡   ‡   ‡

Ignorance cannot be static. To endure as ignorance, it can be only partial ignorance, for complete ignorance in the face of universal knowledge (that which keeps this amazing universe operating) is ever in the position of "danger", if you choose, of being dispelled by some portion of this greater knowledge (being changed to a lesser degree of ignorance) and so a greater degree of knowledge. More, if this were not true, the ignorant would forever be in danger of ceasing entirely—the organism which could not respond to this change, dying, disappearing. In fact, in order to keep this *game* or *show* of *diversified* life going here on earth, at least, it is necessary that there should be—up to the point of destruction—greater and greater degrees of ignorance just as it is also true that it is also necessary that there be set over against this greater ignorance (like sunlight on one side of a revolving planet and darkness on the other) greater and greater degrees of knowledge in order that the two in opposition may provoke the various evolved organisms possessed of lesser degrees of knowledge but with the capacity for *acquiring* greater and greater degrees of knowledge to acquire the same. This brings about change of activity plus sensory interest plus all that sensation and interest tend to give rise to.

In fact, in order to keep this game or life process functioning, it is absolutely necessary that there should be change from the lower or less sensitive organisms to the higher or more sensitive, although the reverse process may, at times, provide interest as well as energy or life. In other words, it can only be that ignorance be set over against knowledge or soon there would be neither knowledge nor ignorance. Ignorance would stay the unchangeably ignorant and eventually end them, and knowledge would improve those organisms dominated by ignorance but capable of being improved or changed by knowledge to the point where those which were once ignorant would be wiser. And yet, in connection with the constant development of wisdom in others, still comparatively ignorant, the once wiser would be still wiser. In other words, knowledge that shows to be ignorance when confronted by greater knowledge is still capable of acquiring knowledge and so ceasing to be ignorance—but only relatively, as I have just shown.

In other words, the creative principle which is assumed by man to govern in life on this planet and to be demonstrated by evolution is one of change from lesser sensitivity to greater sensitivity and/or from lesser complexity to greater complexity and so, necessarily, from lesser wisdom or apprehension to greater wisdom or apprehension. But this is to say that unless this process is interrupted by terrestrial as well as sidereal or cosmic processes as yet unknown to man, the time would come when increasing knowledge constantly dispelling human ignorance and greater complexity replacing lesser complexity and, assuming for argument's sake that there is such a thing as universal creative knowledge or wisdom, basic and operating in and through the universe, the time would come, I repeat, when man himself or some later phase of him would, in some form, automatically and (might one dare say) consciously blend with this ultimate something if not *be it?* Whether this is true or not (this last speculation) certain it is that both ignorance and wisdom, if not endlessly evolving in the above described manner, are the chief and obvious factors or principles or tools or rules in this evolutionary process or life-game here on earth, if not the only ones by which it can be played, but which thus employed bring about all the change and along with that the contrast and color whereby this whole process is made endurable and so durable, or vice versa.

‡   ‡   ‡

There seems to be some evidence to the effect that the form which Proteus, or changing force, takes in us is some kind of increasingly organized and accurate reactions to outside forces or things not strictly subjective. This only means, though, that even as we increase the sum of knowledge, which we call these stored up reactions of the individual and collective organization called intelligence, we are also increasing the sum of *ignorance.* If Proteus is potentially nothing more than an infinite and innate capacity for change, then, increasing intelligence, so-called, really does not mean progress in any absolute sense, but is only a manifestation of Proteus which seems to be affecting us and making possible life as we know it here.

If Proteus or nature is infinite in a third dimension, not the obvious shift of plane from ignorance to knowledge, but in the content of those two, then indeed we can never have progress or even purpose. In other words, science with its knowledge which it has taken out of ignorance (in other words changed the *form* of the fact) seems to find in changing this form that that is all it can do, that the content itself is unconquerable. [*Or*]

The Necessity
for Secrecy

YOU SAY TO YOURSELF EVERY DAY, PERHAPS EVERY HOUR OR MINute that life is interesting. But stay for a second and ask yourself why is it interesting. "Well," you say, and you proceed to give a thousand reasons: murder, sudden death, love, the hope of advancement, prosperity, reward, success, friendship, sex, food. But why do these things make it interesting. Because they do. They cause you to read, to feel different kinds of sensations, some pleasant some unpleasant, some thrilling, some boring. But why do they do that? How? Ah! That is something else. Why? How? You do not know and, more, no one can tell you that. It is a mystery—*The* mystery—the strange and astounding and cruel and beautiful mystery of life. [*Or*]

T.D.

‡ ‡ ‡

Your future must be veiled—hidden from you—if you are to be interested and intrigued by it. [*Or*]

T.D.

‡ ‡ ‡

Life is secret, nearly entirely so, in all its phases. Nature reveals her secrets to no man, save grudgingly and peradventure. Why is this so?

Because it is a fighting world—each pitted against the other. Revelation would mean death, defeat—secrecy means preservation. We cherish our own secrets and try to find out those of others.

Self-revelation—does this spring from some fear that other people will ferret out our secrets anyhow and that it is better to confess?

The Platypus

Man thinks he taught himself how to build a house. He should study some of the houses of animals and insects: for one, that of the duckbill platypus—a freak creature, if ever there was one—bird, fish, mammal, reptile all in one. Unlike most other creatures, he builds or burrows two types of residence, one for everyday use or resting, and one for nesting. The resting burrow is the all year round home and usually a semi-circular excavation with one to three sleeping chambers, completely unfurnished, and often a very long entrance tunnel. This male resting burrow is never occupied by the male and female jointly, and only occasionally by two friendly males. The female nesting burrow is much more complicated and shows engineering as well as architectural skill. It is built by the female during the mating season. Tunnel and all, it is usually twenty-five feet long and ends in a circular nesting chamber which in most instances is only a foot in diameter. Tunnel and resting room are flat on the bottom with a carefully arched or, in the case of the room, domed top. Although this is so gracefully constructed, no loosened soil is ejected. Rather, as soon as the animal has burrowed a few inches, it contorts its body and manages to compress the loosened soil into a mere fraction of its former bulk. It also spreads it quite evenly along the whole length of the tunnel and room.

Inside the room, the female builds the nest of grass and leaves and in this lays two eggs about as large as those of a pigeon which, thereafter, for twenty-one days, the period of incubation, she guards without ever leaving the chamber. Her arresting engineering skill is displayed before the egg-laying by the construction of a truly amazing series of ten or more "pugs" or earth plugs, or sealed doors, not unlike those occasionally used for sealing mines. The first one is put in place only a short distance from the entrance and results from the female loosening the earth circle-wise and compressing it into a "pug" or door with which she stops the outward side of the passage. This leaves a smaller circular room just inside of it. Two to three feet farther on she will repeat this, only, at the same time in each case, changing the direction of the tunnel so as to deceive any trailing enemy into burrowing straight ahead, instead of turning to right or left, as she has done. When ten of these are constructed and the course of the passage has been many times changed, she is ready to begin her twenty-one day vigil without food.

Later, when her young have appeared and have developed, as they do, enormous appetites, she has to make journeys to the outer world. Yet each time she goes, she laboriously digs through and replaces each pug or door not only as she goes but as she comes! Human beings hire architects, not knowing how personally to construct a house, most of them. But here is the freak animal of the world that does. Both male and female know how to construct and engineer. [*Or*]

‡ ‡ ‡

There are the strange Leaf Butterflies (Kollina Albofasciata) of Southern Asia, which, on the underside, are colored just like a dead leaf, though they are bright above. Wings folded, they look like a dead leaf, and so escape some of their enemies. However, in connection with this, the butterfly cannot be charged with having sufficient creative power to invent this deception. The endless numbers of its species are born thus equipped.

It follows that the evolutionary force that brought this about either invented this safe-guard or else the creative energy back of the evolutionary force did so. In the latter case, you have the primal creative force guilty of deceptive subtlety.

It appears that if the evolutionary life of this earth must depend on the existence of many creatures, nearly all of which can serve as food as well as objects of interest (the chase plus the delight of reproduction being among the chief evolutionary interests), it follows that the creative impulse, whatever its nature, must have brought this about, and intentionally so.

For to assume such an evolutionary effect as accidental, mindlessly unintended, is to assume the entire process as mindless and even fantastically so—a deduction or reaction to which the human organism is not chemically and physically, or as we say, mentally, capable of responding. [Or]

T.D.

The Necessity for Ignorance—Secrecy

Can nature be said to be deliberately concealing anything? Is it possible that all is not known to itself? An answer to that is that certainly to that part of itself which is man, all is not known. And more, he appears to have done much wondering and groping or seeking and failing. But, on the other hand, these very impulses to wonder and grope or seek—where could these have come from? Out of himself alone? Or out of the forces that evolved him or permitted his evolution or growth?

If so, a deliberate attempt at concealment would be charged since the impulse to grope, or seek, has been reworded in many ways. Man, along with all animals and life-forms, the very universe itself, has evolved. Whether with much pain or little is neither here nor there insofar as the argument of concealment is concerned, since it *has* evolved—come to know—that is shown (seemingly) more and more. Only, was there ever a time when all was not shared by all? *Seek and ye shall find/Knock and it shall be opened unto you.* Out of which supernal depths of authority and knowledge did these rainbow promises spring? [Or]

‡   ‡   ‡

Behind the problem of secrecy, of the known and the unknown, is another one, perhaps one that will make the problem of secrecy clear. And that is the very problem of knowing anything.

For instance, it must be obvious to all of us that we do not need to know or care to know much of anything about other animals, or the ways of electrons or protons, or about other men and how they live. We can really get along quite well without knowing or understanding any but the smallest bit of information about ourselves or other people.

Our body goes along from day to day without our bothering or thinking about how it works. Nobody knows exactly how it does, anyhow. And this state of ignorance is not new, it has always been. And there is reason to suppose that it is practically universal. In fact, if it were not for the constant competition and conflict, the flow of change, rise and decay, it seems probable that one thing could get along quite well without knowing anything about anything else.

If, for example, there were a certain group of sea animals who were anchored to a bank in a river which constantly washed into their waiting mouths the food that they had to have to live, those animals wouldn't need to know anything about other animals, and they wouldn't need to have any secrets themselves. Those animals could stay there indefinitely, since there wouldn't be anything that might destroy them.

Right here, it should be pointed out that secrecy outside of the animal world is more complicated to discuss. Whether the difficulty of probing the atom is because the atom has developed a defense policy of keeping its organization to itself or whether we are just poor at observing and analyzing is a question.

The Necessity for Youth and Age, Old and New

IF IT WERE NOT FOR THE OLD HOW WOULD ANYTHING APPEAR NEW. How would we know newness if we had not seen oldness. There must be the juxtaposition of these two in order for us to have life as we know it—see it as it now is. This matter of contrasting everything appears to be an integral and unescapable part of the formulae called Life. [*Or*]

‡ ‡ ‡

Intelligence springs from experience—in many cases ancient experience inherited; in others, by direct contact with life. It is possible that inherited ancient experience can be wiped out, insuring thereby a return of barbarism. Current, immediate life experience might possibly by degrees replace the loss of ancient inherited experience—maybe. But it could also prove a slow and maybe never wholly successful process. In the western world, for instance, the high civilization of Egypt, which was maintained for nearly 4000 years, was almost entirely lost to succeeding generations by being confined to a small class of the more intelligent of the population—the purpose of which was to prevent its "wrong" or dangerous use by the ignorant or evilly disposed. Again it is possible that greater civilizations than any so far recorded by man have been and, for other or related reasons, have gone. [*Or*]

‡ ‡ ‡

If life is to appear *new* to an evolved (or created) and limited organism or mechanism, the *old* must be forgotten or it must pass, disappear. Since often that does not take place quickly enough for a time-limited organism such as man, the organism itself must die and be replaced by newer, inexperienced organisms carrying no previous registrations of the immediate present. That done, all *old* things (the things that seem *old* to *old* people) will appear new, fresh, strange to the *young* person—the new born. It can be born new in old things, but they will appear new. [*Or*]

‡ ‡ ‡

As the antique order of an old house becomes the disorderly decay of a newer age, so with changing ideas. The refreshing tides of seasons, years, and generations succeed each other, not without sadness and despair and suffering for what was, but mainly with welcome and gladness for the vitality and promise of what will be. To some it is necessary to find out these new directions, build new forms, be the van of circumstance; and to some is necessary blindness and the sterility of age and decay. This balance is a part of the universe of which our puny ideas, theories, and proclamations are only a reflection, but a necessity, or so it seems. The seeming of what is new is only possible through the seeming of the old. The eager delight of a fall wind takes its rise from the ennui of summer heat. And who does not thrill to the arrival of what is untried and promises power and delight? [*Or*]

THEODORE DREISER

‡ ‡ ‡

Obsolescence, more than mere supply and demand, is the governing factor in business, i.e., manufacture and trade. When technological improvements or discoveries are accompanied by improvements in distribution—travel facilities, transfer facilities, and techniques of selling, *business* or *exchange*—social changes are expedited.

Business, as all know, depends on things being eaten or worn out or wearied of or destroyed in some way, so that manufacture, farming, invention, discovery, etc. can replace them. And these, taken together, spell life, change, color, romance even. Among all the agencies employed or at work to bring this about, nature comes first. It is the great destroyer, because it invented hunger, thirst, ennui, or boredom with this or that, the nervous weariness that rejects the long continued presence or enduring of anything—a face, a mind, a speech, a manner, a style of clothing, an environment, in fact the unchanging continuation of anything.

Nature also directly wears things out by rain, snow, cold, heat, fire, drouth, attrition, war, the attacks of insects, microbes, what not, at the same time it is the collective as well as the creative impulse invented by nature and enforced by hunger, cold, thirst, and the weariness of contemplating decayed or worn things that brings about the invention, manufacture, industry, and trade that replaces all the old, destroyed, wearied of, or eaten with the new.

And today, as ever, it is the engineering activity, along with a corresponding development in sales technique and transportation methods, which is putting new life into business and opening new frontiers at the same time it is supplying the ordinary demands as they previously were. At one and the same time, it is supplying the old ones and, at the same time, developing new ones.

It is a process that at last having consciously gotten under way may make a better state, a better or at least an easier living world, providing the technique of state management—socialism, communism, or democracy—advances at an equal rate. For social craft, skill, or wisdom, plus invention and so change, are necessary to make not only good business but a good state—one that will cause its associated units, the people, to feel that it is worth having and so keeping. [Or]

T.D.

‡ ‡ ‡

It may be—and properly—questioned how many human brains actually reach full maturity. Many obstacles stand in the way of full development, such as physical, social, educational, or economic handicaps. Religions, castes, tyrannies, tyrants, and inherited taboos and fears have endlessly blocked the way. As Edwin Markham put it:

> Tradition lays its dead hand cold
> Upon your youth—and we are old.

[Or]

Scarcity and Plenty

CIVILIZATION IS GOING THROUGH A PERIOD OF WASTE WHICH IS due to swing to rigid economy. Cycles of economy and waste, according to Sir Flinders Petrie (noted British archeologist), cover about 130 years. Waste began in 1535, 1660, 1790, 1920. The more austere periods revived in 1560, 1690, 1820.

A larger cycle relating to civilization and its advantages as set over against its absence and the absence of its advantages were noted by Sir Flinders, who studied Egypt and drew some conclusions from it. The archeologist found that every 1,115 years or thereabouts the Egyptians repeated an experience of developing the arts, mechanics, science, and lastly wealth, after which other races broke in for plunder. Then came centuries of mixture, and then the cycle was repeated with a new dominant element. Civilization, according to Petrie, is now in the wealth stage of this cycle. [*Or*]

‡   ‡   ‡

If control of chromosome doubling by chemical means (Blakeslee's Colchicine) proves of general application, as seems to be the case, the plant-breeder will be able to work with greater precision in his efforts to *control the evolution of economic forms* both of plants propagated vegetatively and of those reproduced by seed.——Blakeslee

This in connection with *tray* farming spells what? More abundance? More people? Better people? If it ended wars for subsistence—if wars are for subsistence alone and not for reasons of vanity, self glorification, a special place in the sun, a better social state—then peace *might* appear and endure. But who can say that the struggle for subsistence is the whole answer. [*Or*]

T.D.

[T.D. had added under above:]

Enough food will not settle anything. It will not make an ugly person beautiful; a short person tall; an emotional person unemotional; a dull person vivid; an ignorant person wise; an indifferent person interested. It is no cure at all.

‡   ‡   ‡

It has been practically estimated that every cubic mile of ocean water contains about $25,000,000 worth of gold—enough to provide every person in the world, if anyone wanted to do that, with three and a half million dollars.

But sea water contains in even larger quantities, lead, zinc, iodine, copper, nickel, iron, radium, tin, bromine and silver. The Dow Chemical Company of Wilmington, North Carolina is at this writing (1939) and at that place extracting 15,000 pounds of bromine daily from sea water, which is used to take the knocks out of gasoline. At present, though, the cost of extracting these other elements from water is so great that no profit would accrue from the undertaking.

But should the day come when economical means for getting them from the ocean are worked out, dry land mines would be of no further use.

‡   ‡   ‡

There should be a chapter as to scarcity and plenty covering the vast natural waste of fruits, grains, meats, vegetables, as illustrating human ignorance of what is of value to human subsistence. The lack of forest preserves, animal preserves, suitable granaries; the ennui that enters upon tastes; the greed that seizes more than is needed and holds it until its use to anyone has vanished (Dog in the Manger), possessions for show rather than use.

Sunlight would feed us and warm us and furnish us with endless power if we knew how to capture it. The rains of a country would obviate drouth almost anywhere if properly stored. Insect evils could be overcome. But humanity is not only lazy but, more frequently, feeble and, still more, incompetent. In most directions, waste ceases only when extreme necessity enforces it, but as a rule (and due to ignorance or feebleness) not even then. Plenty follows exaggerated gifts by nature to individuals of strength, quickness of mind, cunning, cruelty, inheritance without effort, and the like. One would think it was a scheme on the part of something to present a spectacle rather than an equitable system. [Or]

‡   ‡   ‡

Lives that are drab and colorless must be deficient in joy and power. Dirt and soul-deadening work or environment, streets and houses that present one gray uniformity are breeding places for disease and ugliness and that sensory reaction we call mind.

The opposite state to the life that is starved of color and radiance is the life that is lived amidst a riot of color dissonances where wealth is merely the channel for insensitive display, and color, which like form should be and is one of the eternal phases of beauty, is prostituted.

‡   ‡   ‡

Think of all the money stored in banks that at some time or other represented actual human labor, reinforced in many instances by helpful creative thought.

Yet once done, both the work and the thought, there it lies, from time to time transferred, by the death of someone, to another who never did do anything—some silly who could not possibly retain it and wastes it on other sillies until perhaps at long last it reaches some real worker for more actual labor truly performed.

In the main, however, its original worth is long in truly dying. For about you, everywhere, you see ample evidence of work—true labor—performed by endless dead men who lived anywhere from a year to thousands of years ago. Individual laborers with the help of tools, of course—the work of earlier dead men—built the pyramids of Egypt, Mexico, India. They built the ancient roads of the world and the new ones. All of the buildings that abound—new and old—they built. The great canals, the ancient cities, the ruins of which remain, the temples, the shrines, the mausoleums. Think of the dead hands that put together the Taj Mahal; that placed the giant figures on Easter Island; that prepared the entire structural world in which we live and which we daily use.

We complain, all of us, of the little that we have, how poor we are, how little we earn, and often enough (too often) in an intimate contact and use, sense that is true enough and a subject for social reproach. On the other hand, think of the immense social wealth bestowed upon us—the things we use, wear, look at, react to with a sense of comfort, admiration, joy, that we never, never paid for, never contributed to with anything in the form of labor and yet that we use constantly. But without a thought ever of the dead men and their hands and their strength that built them.

Yet beyond them, again, think of nature, the endless processes by which all of these came to be, and ourselves, and the earth we stand on, and the sun above us, and the sky and the stars, the animals, the birds, the trees, fishes, flowers which we never made, yet we ever use, so often without tending or serving. If we live and share any health, and the least of means to support ourselves, are we truly poor? And if not, are we grateful?

THEODORE DREISER

‡   ‡   ‡

Scarcity and plenty applies to the emotions and memories—pleasant and unpleasant, helpful and retarding, or destructive insofar as the human beings and many animals are concerned. And they are stored—the pleasant ones—by the human and animal mechanism, perhaps by all evolved forms, for the definite purpose of making the life process agreeable and so bearable and so more endurable.

For certainly without them—the stored memories of the more pleasant and wholly thrilling incidents or phases of the past—the passing hours of many would not be worth the ticking. Indeed the absence or presence in sufficient quantity at varying periods in individual lives of memories of a pleasant if not unnecessarily of a brilliant or thrilling character accounts for their current strength or weakness, sickness or health, agreeability or disagreeability, even their ending or continuing.

Indeed scarcity or plenty of such memories, not to mention a plenitude of disagreeable or misery-evoking registrations of the past, governs the productivity or non-productivity of many in quite all fields whose products would be of the greatest import to society.

To realize the truth of this, you need only note how constantly and easily the attention taken (and required) by some passing physical duty of the hands, some practical labor of the mind is, almost without notice to the individual, transferred to some more agreeable thing not necessarily of the current moment, but out of yesterday or yesteryear or even the exceedingly long ago—as the distances of one's past are measured.

You may be tying a bundle, or oiling an engine rod, or calculating mathematically a metal strain at a given point in a bridge tower. Yet out of your stored assortment of past registrations of things agreeable or beautiful or emotionally valuable will come a face, a smile, a village streetcorner, a lighted window, a bird song, a sickbed, a graveside, or a lone seashore with rocks and waves, but each in its way holding something of soothing beauty, not unlike the melody of a song.

And each and all, because of a stored supply of the same, which interstitially as described above, break and ease the monotony of less vivid and/or more wearisome or painful things. In fact they constitute a kind of riches, but supplied not by the so-called mind and its "thought" but by life, which has not only evolved and arranged all these experiences but the endlessly evolved mechanisms which by their presence, changes and contacts make these experiences possible. And all the chemo-physical mechanisms and/or arrangements within the creatures or machines called men, animals, birds, trees, flowers, etc. make the registration and storage of these experiences, as above described, possible. [Or] (Rome)

[Dreiser has referred to memories of Rome, here. *Editor's Note*]

Strength and Weakness

Myth of Individual Strength

STRENGTH, PROVIDED ITS OPPOSITE WEAKNESS IS PRESENT, IS the equivalent of possession—Power. But since to be strength it must be joined with weakness, its opposite, it is of itself a myth. For possession that depends on the existence of something else is not absolute but conditioned, subject to alteration. So is it, also, with Power. [*Or*]

‡ ‡ ‡

It is obvious that *strength and weakness* are either designed or eternally fixed and unescapable as an equation, for in the first place one cannot be known or measured without the other—all weights and measures so obviously existing and balanced in nature.

Furthermore, without design or plan, or the equivalent of it, unrestrained strength could not possibly coexist with unprotected weakness. Unrestrained strength would obliterate unprotected weakness so that there would exist only unrestrained strength, which is unthinkable.

You could have no thought and so no word such as *unrestrained* without the existence of sensorily registrable restraint, which would at once imply weakness on the part of unrestrained strength or the unescapable presence of strength and weakness.

‡ ‡ ‡

The phagocytes of the human blood stream, selected by some mysterious process of the human body to surround and destroy invading germs, many of them, sometimes most, dying in the contest—the human organism, all the billions of cells they were defending dying in consequence—seems to indicate that war—attack and defense—is an integral part of the protoplasmic process of life.

Just the same that some units of the blood—primarily cell members of the cell body politic of the human body—should be thus predestined to soldier service and the chance and the duty of dying, while others by reason of other service, pleasant or disagreeable, are not so drastically predestined, raises many questions.

For instance: (1) Why these and not others? (2) Does that establish the necessity for cruelty in life if we are to have life as it is? (3) Is it just? (4) Is it *moral?* (5) Is it possible to have varying types of organization, animal, vegetable, mineral, or commercial without defensive arrangements and processes especial and peculiar to each organism?

A study of nature—the evolutionary process—seems to make very clear that the answer is *no,* insofar as both defensive and predatory war are concerned.

Here strength is of no avail—in connection with being compelled to be a phagocyte—but very important in a phagocyte *as* a servant to the body, or cell state. [*Or*]

‡   ‡   ‡

Nietzsche's will-to-power and his call for a superman is, to me, ridiculous. The will-to-power is not in [all] men, any more than is the will to weakness. The force in nature that divides itself into positive and negative, into male and female, also divides itself, or is automatically conditioned so to do, into the weak and into the strong. To be sure, as Nietzsche points out, the strong in the main resent and even abhor the weak—slaying them freely, devouring them or their substance in order to perfect their own strength and its security. On the other hand, so to do, they must have them (the weak). Otherwise, out of what would come their strength, and worse, before whom would they strut and stare, and by whom be applauded? For the strong are their rivals for power, and hence their enemies, and will do battle with them. . . .

‡   ‡   ‡

Thrice armed is he who hath his quarrel just.

What gives courage to the human or animal organism is the sensation—not the absolute knowledge—of adequacy to face and meet what is to be.

But the sensation is nothing that is willed by our so-called *minds.* It is, more likely, the chemical generation of energy due not only to some immediate exterior change or need for strength to survive physically, but usually long preceding that, the registration by the organism as a whole of various environing conditions that suggest not only danger to life or limb, but the greater danger that lies in the absence of the general physical well-being of the individual at any and all times.

There is not only that however, but in addition, the general *internal* chemo-physical order and well-being of the *internal* organism as a whole; also the nervous or energy registration of the same by the central nervous system of that organism, which manifests itself constantly in *feelings* (not *thoughts or ideas*) of strength, energy, gaiety, desire for movement, to dance, run, sing, play in some manner or other.

And this, as we all know, is not anything that individually we *will* to do but something that, on the other hand, we are moved to do—a fact which is most clearly illustrated by a child's desire to run or hop and skip. So too are the play or energy movements of young animals—dogs, cats, lambs, colts, and what not.

Courage or strength is usually added to—and entirely mechanistically, as you will note—by the sudden appearance of danger, even though the individual's power to overcome the same is not always sufficient. He does not always "mentally" sense whether it is or not. Past experiences which have resulted beneficially for him are even likely to move him to oppose his strength to some danger which will result in his undoing. He is just as likely to be misled by his past experiences as to be correctly and safely led by them.

They sometimes move him to contempt for something which should by no means be contempted. There is also, at times, a wholly honest sense of unfairness or cruelty on the part of another toward some person not intimately connected with his or her interest or advantage which causes either [or both] to struggle and even lose or die before either will yield.

Again personal greed often enough causes a weak organism to contend and suffer for that which a correct registration of the environing conditions or possibilities would cause it to register a self-saving fear—a fear that would cause it to withdraw from any contest for that which it most greedily or avariciously desires. [*Or*]

                                                                              T.D.

Courage and Fear

Do NOT FORGET THAT NATURE, NOT MAN, IS THE AUTHOR OR IN-ventor of fear, as it is of courage.

The forms and forces that have frightened each other in times past—forms of beasts, birds, fish, men, savage and civilized (but with arms); the forms called fire, ice, rain, snow, clouds, waterspouts, torrential rains, lightning, and thunder, and color, plus the negative phases of these positive forces called dark, hunger, thirst, weakness, silence, distance, shadows, drouth—these, operating upon and through the mechanisms called men, animals, trees, birds, and what not, have evoked in them what we know or sense as both fear and courage.

And except for these, and by no other means, could they have come into being or could they now persist. But man did not create them. Nature—the life force, matter-energy—operating in and through time, space and form and color—produced and maintained and maintains these things, because without them life could not be or function, for it is these two along with the nerve reactions called pleasure and pain that give life its reality or meaning and without which it could not be.

‡   ‡   ‡

Our lives are muddled because we compromise ourselves constantly in a fruitless effort to live by antiquated conventions and stupid social prejudices.

We're afraid of what people will say, so we live by the standards they set for us, sometimes at a frightful cost to ourselves and to others. We bungle into trouble and think it is selfish to get out of it. In other words, forces other than ourselves direct us. [*Or*]

Admiration of Bravery Abolishes Fear and Creates Bravery

Admiration for bravery, strongest in those who are fearful and wish they were not, brings about interest in bravery—brave acts or gestures.

These in turn, widely propagandized (for profit) by the press, radio, movies, as well as the builders of armies, navies, aviation fleets (hero builders), appear to bring about, evoke, compel the simulation of courage in those who have it not, or cause it to grow, "step up" a little of it into enough, so that today one witnesses endless manifestations as well as varieties of courage or its imitation.

Individuals in all walks of life—men and women, soldiers, sailors, criminals at death, suicides, etc.—whether primarily courageous or fearsome, can be and are stepped up to the place where they are able to sing, dance, or gesture their way to and through a brave or seemingly brave or self-sacrificing deed, consciously or unconsciously. [*Or*]

T.D.

‡ ‡ ‡

The love of power is the embodiment of fear. Men desire to be in control because they are afraid that the control of others will be used unequally to their detriment. [*Or*]

T.D.

Blackbirds and Fear

A little while ago, I had to go out and feed the blackbirds. I had been listening to their mournful *hunger note* for some time but had neglected to respond to their call. When I went out with the raw oatmeal, I found a row of little rascals sitting on my front wall, their yellow serpent eyes fixed expectantly upon me. I like the cockiness of these birds and the way they point their bills skyward in search of possible enemies. They are always on the alert. No one can catch them off guard. They put no trust in anybody or anything—today, they are almost as much afraid of me as they were five years ago when I first began feeding them. They know their onions. They are not nearly as easy to be tricked as many humans. Wild nature was and remains their teacher. And man, for all his illusions, still deals with, is, in sum, a creation and symbol of its wildness. [*Or*]

T.D.

[This must have been written in T.D.'s Hollywood garden, near the last year of his life. *Editor's Note*]

‡ ‡ ‡

The prevailing popular opinion that the forbidding and weird or monstrous aspect of unfamiliar insects is correlated with their capacity to contend and conquer or destroy any or all of their enemies is not quite correct. As often as not, a weird or horrific or powerful aspect is nothing more than a defense mechanism on the part of a creature that emotionally (that is chemically) senses its own energy lacks and mechanistically (via physical construction or fortification) seeks to create an illusion of strength and even ferocity.

‡ ‡ ‡

A caterpillar is crawling adventuresomely along the ground. In order to see what it will do if disturbed, you touch it with a twig or small stick. Instantly it stops and convulsively abbreviates its length and thickness as if seemingly awaiting some shock or disaster, which it must resist as much as it can, and so remains "playing dead" as the phrase has it, in order to deceive some caterpillar devouring insect or bird, which it appears to assume is at hand. If not further disturbed in any way, it will, after a time, often as many as five minutes, relax its pretended death tension and move away as quickly as possible. If at this point it is disturbed a second time, it will repeat this pretended death scene and so on through a third and fourth until either slain or released from its misery. Fear, of course, is its guiding impulse. The simulation of death its one subterfuge.

But of course the caterpillar is not alone in its sense and expression of fear any more than it is in its absence of courage. For both courage and fear are in fact forces or feelings that only grow by accumulated experiences of successful or unsuccessful dealings with difficulties and dangers, and these are either proofs of individual strength, agility, endurance, subtlety, or the absence of the same, and no one will deny that perpetual failures resulting from incapacity of one kind or another produce discouragement and fear in insects as well as humans. Also, that repeated triumphs provoke courage or a readiness to encounter difficulties and what is more, difficulties of a somewhat larger nature than others that may have preceded it.

Both courage and fear are far more varied in their particular aspects than any generalization such as the above could possibly imply. Thus it is Hume, the Scotch philosopher, who asserts that the first idea of religion arose not from an intelligent and comprehensive contemplation of the beneficent works of nature on the part of man, but from a decidedly anxious concern on his part as to his needs and wishes for peace and pleasure. Also his dread of future misery, his terror of death, his thirst for revenge, and his need for food and shelter. Also, other practical and earthly concerns, which no particular individual out of his earthly strength and devising could possibly assure for himself. Naturally enough, as philosopher Hume sees it, such inability might have caused him to conceive of a higher power to which he might appeal and so—religion.

Be that as it may, courage and fear are represented in life by an amazing variety of actions or compulsions—mental as well as chemical or physical—on the part of animals, insects, plants, in fact every conceivable form of life—animal, vegetable, or mineral. Thus testosterone-protionate, a hormone, when injected into men, is said to relieve some of their inferiority complexes, just as will a number of drinks of whiskey, or any number of drugs—opium for one, hasheesh for another. Injected into hens, testosterone-protionate makes the most fearful of them brave—that is, those most picked upon by other hens, to turn and pick on them or others, and so truly to dominate them. Again, mother love, which usually implies courage in the fullest sense in mothers connected with their young, may be stimulated in animals by injections of *prolactin*, the milk-producing hormone, so that courage is here seen to be subject to two chemical forms—prolactin and testosterone—so that the absence of one or the other might imply the absence of that almost indefinable and yet most important thing called courage.

Again, a plant like the sensitive plant, an American fern, the leaves of which, when touched or plucked, exhibit a tendency to fold together as though aware of injury or pain, a reaction that suggests pain or fear—and this in a plant! But then, in this connection, consider all thorn-bearing trees or bushes such as the rose, the hawthorne, the blackthorn, the honey-locust, and the common cactus, and then ask yourself why, in each instance, *the thorn?* Are these plants or trees or bushes so conscious of the rudeness of life—its so often brutal destructiveness—as thus to desire, and what is more, to proceed to arm themselves against life's destructive invaders? And is that not a very human type of form or fear?—as distinct and human as is the form of armament, for instance, indulged in by our police, our soldiers, and, for that matter, our nations that keep themselves armed with a standing army? And are not all like the thorns of the rose based on fear? Is the rose not afraid?—and justly so? I think so. And so are the police, the various nations, and their armies.

However, as one looks about us in life and notes the quite endless varieties of fear-courage manifestations such as the horns of the bull, the savage nose horn of the rhinoceros, the tusks of an elephant, and the equally savage tusks of a wild boar, the claws and teeth of a cat or a tiger, the fighting hooves and teeth of a stallion, the immense teeth of a shark, the stored electric bolts of the electric eel, to say nothing of the self-protective box of the armadillo, the turtle, the horned toad, and the deadly poisons of the various snakes, to say nothing of the various insects—bee, wasp, hornet, spider—their endless variety of nets and traps and paralyzing stings, one wonders at the fears as well as the necessities, the wisdom, as well as the labors and courage, that have provided all these with their various devices and methods of survival. Yet it must follow that the evolutionary force that brought all these about either invented them, as well as the amazing variety of creatures and their amazing devices for survival, plus their courage as well as their fears, or else the supreme Creative energy and wisdom that we worship as God so did. In which case, we had best pause and attempt to reflect, for we are practically charging it with deceptive cruelty, a charge which a created mechanism such as man is scarcely in a position to make. For he cannot be sure that he knows with what intent this entire process was got under way—Good or Evil? For most certainly it appears that a high proportion of the endless variety of creatures which constitute this spectacle find it of sufficient interest, not only to desire not to relinquish it, but rather to continue the struggle so long as they are the victors and not the vanquished. And yet it can be said, of course, that not having made themselves but having been made as they are, it is not they who have the privilege of wishing or deciding, but rather this Supreme Creative Energy that must be charged with the invention as well as the retention of this amazingly dramatic as well as semi-tragic program. For, as all know, not all are slain and devoured by any means. There is everywhere, and in connection with every specie, that very considerable percentage that enjoys its youth, or nearly so, unharmed, being protected and fed and fended for by its elders; and again another considerable portion, that for reasons of youth and strength, if not physical desirability as food are better able to feed and at the same time protect themselves than are those who, older and stouter and so less agile, are at the same time more desirable as food and so much more sought after than are these youngsters who are living their best years in comparative safety.

Nonetheless, sentient man, the so-called lord of creation, cannot help but wonder at, and, to a high degree, trouble over the destructive and internecine phases which life as a whole presents, not only to himself in his personal labors to live and be, but to all the creatures, to say nothing of the materials or substances of his immediate as well as general environment, be they animal, vegetable, or mineral, which are seen to wear, rust, age, and break or collapse so that they require of him constant attention and labor in order that the passing stability he knows something of may not wholly vanish before his gaze.

But darkest of all, of course, is this never-ending evidence of contest and struggle between all the creatures of one's immediate environment for the privilege of living and being. For here, at my feet, in a sandy portion of my garden, is an ant lion (by some known as the oolie-oolie bug) that is busy about the, to him, seemingly engaging labor of digging a small pit in which to trap unwary ants which he enjoys as food. The hole is nothing more than an obtuse section of a cone about one-third, at worst, or best, one-half as deep as an ordinary thimble. And its side walls slope quite gently, so much so that if made of ordinary earth they would offer no obstacle, let alone danger, to any hurrying ant either hurrying from or returning to some adjacent hive, for the sloping sides would then be firm to the tread of any ordinary insect from one to a dozen times the size of the common ant.

But what the ant lion is about at this particular time is the business of making the side slopes of this small excavation as friable and unstable as any side slope could possibly be, and to do this, from an immediately joining sand surface, he is progressively selecting the largest and smoothest sand grains he can find and carrying them to the thimble-like cone, one side slope section of which appears to be firmer than the rest. At least it is to this section of this inverted cone that from moment to moment he goes and returns to, a selected sand grain in his grasp. And with this sand grain, due possibly to some particular design of his feet or possibly a peculiar lightness of tread and skill of balancing himself, he is able to descend to the bottom of his lair and then up again, meanwhile placing the latest grain in its, to him, most advantageous spot. For his plan—as sufficient time given to watching will prove—is to make this entire side slope surface as collapsible as possible, so much so that once he has completed his labor and hidden himself under a number of grains at the bottom of the cone, he can lie there unseen until some unwary ant, coming from or returning to one or another of the, by him, conveniently selected ant hills, finds itself unthinkingly, and before it can stop itself, descending into this trap, the side slope sands of which immediately tumble inward and so downward upon the luckless ant, the while the lurking ant lion emerges from his lair and pounces upon the unintentional intruder, a pounce which quite invariably ends in death to the innocent and industrious, if not over cautious, ant.

But does not the entire insect world exhibit murderous tendencies as well as intense fears of other insects or other creatures such as birds, spiders, snakes, lizards, toads? An example of probable fear is displayed by the puffer, which swells up not to swallow the enemy as some fish do but to defend itself against him, the exterior of the swollen skin presenting small, strong poison tipped spines which makes successful attack almost impossible. As a defense device this looks to be most brilliantly thought out and to suggest that nature has the only mind and is the one and only creative genius of all that is. It may be and probably is a fear development as the puffer is not predatory in any important sense.

But one wonders at the primal source of so much aggressive planning and slaying on the part of creatures of all types and descriptions which are required to kill and eat in order to live, and that at the same time indulge in so much defensive preparation in order that they may not be slain and eaten.

And in that connection, I am thinking of *Mason Mygale* and *Clotho*, two spiders which lure insects as craftily as possible with their spun nets and at the same time make for themselves (*Mason Mygale*) a burrow or hole in the ground which she equips with a lid or trap door undistinguishable from the color of the soil, and moving on a hinge which she keeps closed until she is ready to trap and slay for herself; and next *Clotho* who erects a silken tent supported by a multiplicity of arches one and all alike, to say nothing of a front as well as a rear door so that should any predatory enemy find entrance, he may be led astray by the multitude of arches, the while the pursued Clotho proceeds to vanish through one or other of the doors. On the other hand when pursued on the outside, Clotho runs quickly to her tent, opens the chink with a touch of her claw and disappears. For after her the door closes of itself, yet is supplied in case of need, with a lock consisting of a few threads. So also the rear door. Thus almost anytime, and inside or outside her tent, she can await the pursuers labors in peace. On the other hand her own victims being rarely so resourceful die at her hands!

And then the *Walking Stick* that, living on other insects, alights on any branch of a tree and folds itself so as to resemble a brown twig of the same. The object? Woe to the insect that, believing what it sees to be a twig, draws near enough to be seized and so captured. Only more interesting is the thought of the underlying creative process that can and will trouble to devise an insect that can make itself resemble a twig and then use the resemblance to deceive and destroy another insect!

Mercy and Cruelty

IS IT POSSIBLE TO PROVE THAT LIFE, THE EVOLUTIONARY PROcess, is not as grim as it seems? Nature begins with the infinitely small, supplied in unlimited and almost insensitive quantities and from these, that is through their use as not only proof but as implements of service, builds up the larger and so varied forms we know, all flora and fauna, but, in so far as sensitivity is concerned, in an ascending scale. In other words, can we prove that nature is not brutally cruel but as kindly and careful as the labors of construction will permit?

‡ ‡ ‡

Man's lust for wings, anymore than that of animals and birds, is not to fly away from trouble. It is a part of the animal instinct to conquer and loot its universe, first of food and then of anything else that can possibly be used.

‡ ‡ ‡

Evolution is generally looked upon as a moral manifestation of the unknowable. Something good is on foot—there is a "divine, far-off event" awaiting man, although exactly *why* is not clear. Only the great Huxley remained the doubting Thomas. What good, he asked, did it do the ancestor of the horse, slow moving, defenseless, a prey to all fleet-footed animals, to be told in his death throes that one of his descendants would one day win the Derby?

Again, a seemingly hungry and therefore predatory animal is by great nature provided with prey, or food. This seems to imply cosmic cruelty as well as (by antithesis) cosmic mercy, but neither may be involved. The life process—to be at all—may necessitate both, and the sum of one may balance the sum of the other.

‡ ‡ ‡

I am standing at the edge of a small bay, safe upon a wall. Below me the smooth unruffled surface of an incoming tide. At the surface or so near that all are visible like a knotted net spread just under the surface, I see

239

hundreds upon hundreds of small fish as varied in size as my fingers. All
are peacefully moving, wave-like ranks upon wave-like ranks. So calm, so
peaceful, so restful in form and motion. But—I lift my hand above the water.
Instantly commotion—an immense, water splattering dash for the depths.
Instantly—all gone. Only little fishless ripples where they were.

But why the fear! The terror! How come all dread even a hand in the
air a score of feet above them? It is possible that it is identified with a
bird of prey, a gull, fishhawk, tern, heron? It must be. And yet so new
is the world—a few months at best. Mercy—cruelty. How come these are
interpreted here so quickly and so instinctively. Do atoms know? Molecules?
Protoplasm? Do they fear—and so soon? And how do mercy and cruelty
equate here?

The Grasshopper and the Ant

"Never does the grasshopper go to the door of the ant-hill with piteous
cries for something to eat, promising faithfully to pay back the loan with
interest; on the contrary, it is the ant that, pressed with hunger, begs of
the other." So concluded the great French naturalist Fabre after many years
of entomological observation, some of which is recorded interestingly in
Marvels of the Insect World.

This is how the grasshopper extends his largess. On hot summer afternoons,
when other insects look in vain for cooling drinks among faded flowers, the
grasshopper, better equipped for deep drilling, never is at a loss to find a
refreshing beverage. With his gimlet beak he need only bore into a sprig of
juicy shrubbery to find a veritable well of delight. But no sooner does the
sap begin to flow than his thirsty colleagues of the insect world, with the
ants in the vanguard, rush to share the lucky strike and show their deplorable
manners.

Here you have an ant that knows where and what a grasshopper is about
—that the boring he does means food and goes to get it. A grasshopper
that knows how to bore for water or a juice and get it—also knows the
various grasses and green grain foods he can attack. He certainly sees and
hears.

‡ ‡ ‡

Apart from religious dogma, the general theory of the realist throughout
history has been that life is a brutal and cruel procedure; that it lives on
murder, is "red in claw and beak"; its dominant characteristics being pain
and strain. Whether it seems true or not true depends, to a degree at least,
on the amount of evidence of pain or escape from pain which the particular
individual sensorially registers, either through the eye or the body in general.
In consequence, not only is opinion greatly divided but such evidence as
is recorded is disputed.

Even wars with all their attendant horrors are by some held as good and
even glorious, whereas others condemn them without stint. As for disease,

it is held to be mitigated by many things, and there is the expressed hope of abolishing it. So too with inequity or so-called human injustice—man's inhumanity to man.

Of course the existence of both good and evil are generally admitted. And by some, the first is stressed; by others, the second. Personally, such evidence as has been reviewed by me causes me to feel that the entire living process in general, but not in more than a percentage of individual cases, strikes a balance; that is, all details being accounted for, they would show at least 50% of pleasure and 50% of pain of the same volume and weight, for that mythical being, the average man. In the case of the individual, no such comforting balance could be struck. His ills would be greater or less according to his strength or weakness, luck or ill luck.

In nature there is no exact division of anything: the rain falls on the just and the unjust; the strong are fairly balanced by the weak and the weak can be an affliction or a benefit to the strong and vice versa. You see something of the weight and the solidity of this argument when you consider that, insofar as nature is concerned, the animal that suffers by being slain is there and then roughly equalized by the animal that does the slaying and rejoices in its profit. But this is not only true in the animal kingdom but is actually true of humanity. The very individual who will complain of the inequitable treatment received from others will himself on occasion practice inequity and rejoice in the benefits his inequity achieves for him. Hence the inequities he benefits by must be set over against the inequities he endures. Even the extremely understanding and just cannot avoid balancing the advantages, satisfactions, and gifts, if any, bestowed upon them by nature against the inescapable ills and afflictions that go with the life process for them and others from birth to death. Anyone who took pen in hand and sought to list the evils which have befallen him would be automatically compelled to check them against certain benefits and, in only rare cases, if any, would it be found that there were no benefits or satisfactions to register.

In this connection, one would have to examine carefully much of the data that is listed as unmitigated cruelty. One animal slays another, and the assumption of the spectator is that enormous pain goes with this process. But the biologic data relating to the amount of strain that a given nervous system can endure belittles and makes very doubtful the quantity of pain endured in any form of death, either as the result of murder, accident, or disease. Murder in the animal kingdom and for the purpose of food or because of the inherited instinct to kill is almost invariably swift and, on the part of the victim after the first clash, may not even be accompanied by consciousness. Birds seized by cats, though dead, are frequently found to be unharmed. In connection with executions, there are any number of recorded cases in which unconsciousness has preceded the execution of the person.

No death chamber record is without illustrations of this. In 1892, in the city of St. Louis, I witnessed the execution of a wife-murderer who had to be carried to the gallows and was limp and unconscious at the time the trap was sprung. And, I, myself, struck by an automobile and realizing that death impended—as was afterwards proved by the fact that had the car moved an additional twelve inches, I would have been crushed—was nevertheless relieved of all thought and pain by unconsciousness.

Death by freezing is without pain. All forms of instantaneous death involve no suffering except for the living. Much sickness, to percents which some day may be carefully calculated, [is] without serious pain. And in the case of all operations conducted under present anaesthetic conditions, pain is largely eliminated again. If there is any one thing that biology has fully demonstrated, it is that the sensory pleasure and pain reactions of all animal life up to and including man range from the infinitesimally minute to the immensely greater degrees witnessed in man.

Not only this, but the experiments of the mechanists from the inception of the thought to the present day have fully demonstrated that the lower forms of life do but dimly and in very limited ways respond to danger or actual destruction. Among other things, the brevity of their lives ranging from a few seconds to a few days greatly limits the possibility of nervous experience, good or evil, pleasurable or painful. And only as life proceeds from physical and nervous structural simplicity to complexity, from brevity of life to length of life, does the power and possibility of nervous suffering increase. However, since most forms of animal life are of brief duration and their nervous systems, as compared to that of man, of extreme simplicity, it follows that there is here full evidence of a mechanistic regulation which modifies the charge that immense cruelty is involved in the fact that life lives on life. For while an infusoria may consume any quantity of minute water forms, the consumption is little more than a chemical, and so, from the point of view of nervous registrations, an unconscious or painless procedure. A fly consumes untold numbers of minute living germs as do various insects. A bird in one lifetime will consume hundreds of thousands of lesser insects, and millions of birds, of course, are disposed of by other creatures as well as by cold, but the charge that enormous natural cruelty is here involved is certainly open to debate. That there is suffering, no one denies. That it is consciously planned or rejoiced in remains to be shown.

T.D.

‡ ‡ ‡

When I use the phrase "nature," or "God," I mean to convey the idea that the enormous revelations of Science in regard to nature indicate a necessary balancing of forces, which at one point of man's limited grasp appear evil and at another point good, but, in order to achieve the seeming reality called life, both of which are necessary.

It follows that, under these conditions, no intentional cruelty can be attributed to the creative force or God, as you choose.

THEODORE DREISER

Beauty and Ugliness

BEAUTY IS PEACE. THERE IS NEITHER STRESS NOR STRAIN WHERE it holds, registering itself, whether briefly for the instant, or for hours or years. It is constructive, building. Any single thing—a flower, a song, a color, a form, a word, a mood, the smile of a child, a friend, a lover, the look of an eye, bearing affection; and so beauty returns and returns, brightening drab hours, modifying stress, relieving sorrow, lightening burdens, physical or nervous.

It is a great force expressed as sound, color, forms, but most of all, as combinations of these that address all the substances of the body, as these in their turn and in the combination called *you* respond to them. United as beauty, they are your reward for living and struggling as well as your comforter, the one thing that, amid the seemingly unescapable ills of life, sustains you. Whether they are the sum or only a portion of the forces that create or make possible your being, they are your reason for being, the things for which you pray and with which, if at all, you are rewarded.

One might say, seek beauty, but whether you can or will so to do, it is everywhere seeking you. Though your head is bowed with care, still will you hear and see. It calls and there is that in you, attuned to it, which makes it impossible for you to refuse to answer. [*Or*]

T.D.

‡ ‡ ‡

Why is it that we consider anything beautiful or anything ugly? Some say that beauty is pleasure, some say that it is the perception of the general in the individual, some say that it is an intrinsic relation or harmony between the perceiver and the perceived. Some say that it is selection, some say that it is a synthesis or comprehended relation. Why are not all these answers reconcilable and true?

Many say that ugliness is chaos, is practicality, is unintelligible welter of unrelated forms, is pain. Why are not all these true also? [*Or*]

[This is near the end of a long essay on *Need for Contrast,* not used. *Editor's Note*]

‡ ‡ ‡

Beauty is the sole form of reaction or response immediately and wholly within the sensory range of a crowd or mass anywhere, as it is proved by flowers, colors, tones, sounds (the ringing of a bell, the lowing of cattle, the singing of birds, sunsets, dawns).

Spectacles, processions, involving these, invariably attract the masses. Vestments, jewels, decorations, youthful forms—all appeal and often divert and save masses from the sensory impact of less pleasing and restful forces or stimuli. [*Or*]

T.D.

‡ ‡ ‡

Some one has said that bird-song may express emotion but cannot be beautiful since it has no objective content. But how does one know that? Nor its objective—possession of the female? If so, the critic is right. Assuming that it *is* something, is it either of these that makes the bird's song beautiful? [*Or*]

Beauty of Form in Nature

The artistic form of the snow crystal! From whence does that form come? Dr. Lela E. Booker of the department of chemistry, Columbia University, in the process of extracting Vitamin H from rice polishings, obtained a cluster of Vitamin H crystals of microscopic size that resemble snow flakes. When a thin coat of water freezes on a sidewalk or a window pane the loveliest leaf designs are formed, designs like those of the banana palm and others. Blown snow in very cold regions frequently takes the Christmas tree form. These are seemingly mechanistic yet apparently not evolutionary forms. But if so, where and in what form do they exist? Or, are they instantaneous evocations of other forces in combination, like LeDuc's chemical flowers, shells, birds, or bugs. [*Or*]

T.D.

‡ ‡ ‡

Atomic and molecular patterns are now known to underlie everything.

‡ ‡ ‡

What is the force that draws such beautiful frost flowers on a window pane or on the stone slab of a sidewalk. It is art. It is beauty. If a human being did it, he would be counted an artist—possessed of a fine mind. But this energy that does this? Is it mental? Is it immaterial? [*Or*]

‡ ‡ ‡

Probably the most beautiful of the unicellular denizens of the ocean are the Radiolaria, the favorite of Haeckel among the protozoa. The protoplasm of these tiny creatures is a microscopic foam. Their specific density is such that a slight warming of the sea on a sunny day causes the bubble of froth to expand and the creatures to rise. When the weather is cold and the sea stormy, the bubbles contract and the creatures sink to calmer and warmer depths. The peculiar beauty of these organisms is due to the precisely symmetrical and delicate designs of their skeletons. They show an amazing variety of form and arrangement of their silicious spicules. In some species, the skeleton consists of many delicate radii joined together by concentric spheres perforated in polygonal patterns. Their empty shells form vast suboceanic deposits, and more than half of the known varieties are fossilized. [Or]

‡ ‡ ‡

Geometry, that is to say, *the science of harmony in space,* presides over everything. We find it in the arrangement of the scales of a fir cone, the art of an orange, the sun or the moon, the arrangement of a spider's lime-snare, the ripple of water, the waves and ripples of desert sand, the spiral or snail's shell, the ordered arrangement of rose petals, the orbit of a planet, all phases of flight or motion. It is everywhere, as perfect in the world of atoms as in the immensities of space. Whether this indicates the presence of a Universal geometrician, who has measured all things, or a mechanism, without consciousness except through man of its own surpassing grandeur, is certainly not for man to know. [Or]

T.D.

‡ ‡ ‡

Art is the impact of environment on such human mechanisms as are chemically sensitive as well as mechanically adjusted to the refinements of such an environment, and so capable of registering them. For the purpose of their registration in such accepted forms as paintings, sculpture, poetry, music, literature, there must enter such tropisms as Loeb describes as heleo—stereo—chemo—etc.; in other words, the compulsions or pull of various forms of beauty which throughout man's evolution have shown themselves to be for him among the most powerful of the evolving forces—sound, color, form, odor, the tropistic compulsions of which are obvious.

Insofar as man is concerned, these make not only for registration and re-registration in the artist, but also for the desire for copies of these (registrations and re-registrations by other men), a desire, the reverse effect of which is a compulsion and acts as such on the artist, and on themselves. This in turn provides applause and material reward or payment to the artist for its satisfaction. [Or]

‡ ‡ ‡

The world of imagination is the world of eternity. Generations come and go. And the deeds of the same—multitudinous and confusing. But the other taps the rank growth and decaying mulch of endless time and endless worlds. It blooms on high—a gorgeous bloom tinted with reflected hues and moods to which this world approaches and of which it knows only through it. [Or]
[Dictated to M.T. Published in *Direction,* 1938. *Editor's Note*]

The Physical Nature of Beauty

BEAUTY—physical beauty, even when it is the outward covering of a dangerous nature, is none the less a real force which acts and accomplishes as any force acts and accomplishes. And where the beauty of women is concerned, man is no more than a sensitive registering machine—like a radio for instance—responsive to minute waves and can no more escape registering and responding to those waves or the beauty of a woman, the particular type of beauty that his temperament is attuned to respond to, than can a radio fail to respond to the particular wave length at which it is set to receive.

In that sense again, the beauty of a truly beautiful woman is like a current of electricity that will light a lamp—in short, all lamps that are so constructed as to be lighted by that current. Thus men—men of many varieties of temperament—when brought into the presence of a beautiful and sensuous woman, and when not changed or modified by other temperaments that may be present and in opposition to them, swiftly and even wildly find themselves responding to the current or force that the beauty of a truly beautiful woman is.

The eye of a man is no more than a photo-electric cell attached to a machine which, when played upon by the electric ray or beam which the beauty of a beautiful woman is, starts the machine. He cannot escape being started—reacting. The beam of beauty emanating from a beautiful woman cannot fail to start him any more than an electric beam striking the electric eye or photo-electric cell of a machine electrically controlled can fail to start it. Man, radio, machine are attuned to given rays. [W]

T.D.

The Sunlit Sea

Whether we see the same sunlit sea to be smiling frankly or in treachery would depend, one would think, on the chemo-physical synthesis as well as sensitivity of the receptor mechanism at the time of the registration, plus the chemo-physical characteristics and compulsions of the earth, sea, and sky at the particular moment of registration—that is, how bright the sunlight, how blue the sea, how dancing or still the water, how safe or brisk or harsh the wind.

For light, color, motion, form, all environmental and determining forces in their own right here meet with and impinge on not only evolved and internalized and mechanized chemo-physical compounds which, via heredity and the subtle and yet definite direction of timeless and universal law, have already been conditioned and limited as to their responses. I am speaking of men.

And even those responses are often greatly and unpredictably modified by internal arrangements or disarrangements—that is, favorable or unfavorable synthesis of not only the humors of the blood, the order or disorder of the respective organs and glands or their chemisms, and not only these but the favorable or unfavorable nature of past registrations of water, light, color, and motion combinations as these relate to the sea.

If all should chance to synthesize harmoniously at one and the same time, the man mechanism can experience a happy hour or happy days by the sea. If not, if any one of the literally thousands of possibilities should intervene— a bad breakfast, an insult, some delayed memory, or piece of bad news, even a pin-prick, or unsatisfactory thought—presto, the blue sunlit sea may remain so and even be added to, insofar as beauty is concerned, but its registration by the particular man mechanism will be blurred or even completely invalidated, and may even take the form of a compound irritation. [W]

T.D.

‡ ‡ ‡

It may be, and no doubt is, a fact that in all these seeming contradictions and repulsions, subjections and dominations which apparently throughout nature characterize all of its activities, nature is doing nothing more than organizing and reorganizing itself, its totality, according to such states and moods as it contemplates or is moved to desire.

Two of such states or aims which a human being with his five limited senses may readily detect are change and self-enjoyment. There is nothing but change and an obvious search for satisfaction, more joy, on the part of all sensate creatures, most likely on the part of all energy.

A third [aim] may be the achievement of *beauty;* or, again, that may be nothing more than a concomitant and unescapable, or another more conditioned phase of the other two. Whether one or the other, certainly nature, insofar as detectable and interpretable by man, seems almost inescapably constrained to achieve this third and last also. [*Or*]

T.D.

‡ ‡ ‡

There is such a thing as passion for things of a high plane—a love that is for the seemingly good and beautiful. Some react so deeply in this way as to believe that if this passion were developed more in man in general it might displace to a degree (some feel even entirely) his animal passions—sex, food, personal as well as material display, his love of power and/or fame—and so make him happy even though he did not believe in a God. And it is asked by these, "Cannot man be happy in making others happy, regardless of whether or not there is any other reward here or hereafter."

But the answer to that is that there are these other passions in conflict with these higher ones. And man being a chemical as well as a physical structure—an unstable equation of the same, constantly changing from birth to death—the chance of the displacement of the higher by the so-called lower is ever present. In fact, chemically it seems impossible for anyone to keep one passion or desire so aloof from all others as to be possessed only by that one. Dr. Alexis Carrel has suggested the possibility of racial progress providing that the sciences (chemical and physical) provide a social laboratory or laboratories on the scale of the Catholic or Mohammedan faiths where, chemically and physically, man might be so treated as to evolve the higher (if any) type. How he would evolve without the slow but sure development or change for the "better" of his universal and planetary and so his social—that is animal, vegetable, and mineral—or energy environment is not clear. [*Or*]

T.D.

‡   ‡   ‡

Nature not man, save where he has been chemically organized so to do, beautifies everything. From the darkest rain to the sunshot rainbow; from the spring-fed rill and mountain framed turquoise lake to the filthiest pool and the muddiest commerce infested harbor or river—beauty! beauty! beauty! No insect, no bird, no tree, no flower, no fish, no animal, no silent, evasive reptile but manifests in its structure, movement, color—or if not that last directly then indirectly, that is by contrast—its homogeneity with as well as unescapable compulsion to convey art and loveliness in all the various forms in which these are known to and registered by man. And (in) no way does he create, nor ever has he done more than to copy that which chemically and neurodynamically he has been constructed and most carefully adjusted to register.

Beauty of color, beauty of sound, beauty of motion, beauty of stillness, beauty of reaction in animal, man, bird, fish, tree, flower—either in the form of quiet and restoring mood or stressful emotions—are all the beauty, gifts, or conditions which nature unescapably arranges and bestows upon all her creatures, from germ or atom or electron to the mightiest of her island universes, their glittering or slowly decaying suns and planets and meteors. Man, on occasion, has thought of himself as an especial recipient of these favors—one, above all other creatures, especially organized to respond to this all pervading essence of beauty. But he errs. Nature has not arranged for the presence of favorites. All are an integral part of itself and its art and in that sense share the totality of its exquisite essence which is beauty. And nothing more and nothing less. [*Or*]

T.D.

July 17, 1941

‡   ‡   ‡

It was Lao-tsze who made clear that the Universe is to be apprehended through feeling not "thinking," that illusion to which sensory reaction to exterior stimuli has given rise. [*Or*]

T.D.

[Written under picture of two seagulls in flight. *Editor's Note*]

‡   ‡   ‡

For thus have come to be all organs that respond—an eye to see, an ear to hear, a tongue to taste, a nose to smell, a touch to feel—and more, that synthesize the same or rather permit them to enter and endure and harmonize themselves, so that at long last we not only see, hear, feel the new and passing strange, but find it harmonizing itself with all that has gone before in life, with all that via evolution and *heredity* has been stored in us, so that when beauty enters it is joined and harmonized with all the beauty that has ever been, not only to us in our particular heredity line, but to all life that has been so full and wondrous as to make our evolution chain, make life as we know it.

And hence the sorrow at night fall, the joy at dawn, the thrill of a sense of freedom vouchsafed man by the sight of the flight of a bird in clear, bright space, or the wind in the trees, or the movement of water hurrying onward to the sea. [*Or*]

On The Dreams of Our Childhood

We cannot be sure that the dreams of our childhood are utterly without substance. Later years in a world in which the larger forces of life are perforce subordinated to a given form of existence—namely that which we see and feel—is calculated to weary our bodies and harden our souls. We no longer see clearly nor feel truthfully. But what of that?

I had almost said "larger" but for the sake of argument will substitute "fairer" vision which the world presented to our eyes in childhood. We cannot forget, nor can we ever utterly ignore, the wonderful feeling of sweetness and light which filled our days. These were the hours in which this seeming too grim world took on the radiance and the softness of dreams. The earth was so fair, the sky so blue. In the immediate circle of our vision were trembling strange visions of beauty and delight. The wonders of color and sound, of which, for all our boasted knowledge, we still know nothing.

Those were the days of the morning sky and the heavenly winds, those were hours of the multitudinous voices which call and call, filling the open mind and the fresh heart with evidences and the feelings of beauty and delight.

But our later years have modified our feeling. An organism built for a little while has lived too long. Something has come over the burden of our flesh to seal it and harden it with the evidences of things as they happen to be but now and here. Tomorrow we may die. Tomorrow our body may be dissolved and our spirit released. Think you that then we shall know aught or reck aught of that which we here call life? This tremor of sound and fury; this clattering of bricks and stones. The things which we collectively call chattels or merchandise—our houses, our lands, our implements—all travail merely, shadows of something else. We must know that the tomorrow of our spirit is looser and freer than this.

And this is but that our childhood teaches us. The evidence of the sun in the sky, the birds in the air, the touch of fresh forces there, then, were enough to convince us of the joy of living. No argument was required, no thought. We were happy. And this will come again. Tomorrow, the day after, the next day, the next year, surely, certainly we will go back to our own. The waters will be glad to receive us. The winds, to admit us to their glorious company. All the sweep of the fields, all the breadth of the sky, all the galaxies of the suns and the planets of infinite space, these will be ours eternally. Did you think you could really die? Hearken to the voice of your childhood. It will teach you how wonderful, how incomprehensible are the secret and permanent blisses of the world. It will show you how to be happy. You need but to live, or die.

Theodore Dreiser

[This little essay was found in a box of subsidiary writing from Dreiser's Tenth Street days, judging by paper, blue type, etc. It seems appropriate here. *Editor's Note*]

Order and Disorder

LET US SAY THE UNIVERSE IS NOT SUBJECT TO ANY FORM OF MORAL surveillance, and it may not be. But there is law, universal and (insofar as man, to date, knows) permanently operative. However, there is something else that may be looked on as a substitute for universal surveillance and that is the splitting up, by something, of all forms of matter and energy into units, almost infinitely minute and certainly enormously great. And the endowing of the same or their various surfaces with positive or negative energy, which gives to each the power to reject or attract that which is like it, its *like*. Hence to cause to be balanced everywhere a definite amount of positive as well as a definite amount of negative energy. Now call the one good and the other evil, according to the effect or effects produced by too much of either, and you have good balanced against evil and vice versa. And there is nothing of which science knows at this time that overcomes this balance. So, if there is no god, no surveying and controlling intelligence, there is yet this universal balancing and proportioning of positive against negative, or what may seem good to one against what may seem evil to it and vice versa. Now it may not be possible for most to either grasp or, revere, let alone worship, this idea. Cardinal Newman is alleged to have said, "It is not natural for the human heart to love God." But love or no love, it may be compelled, and in truth is, to respect the validity as well as the social and, should you choose to look upon it as such, the "moral" value of the universal balancing of too much of anything by a sufficient quantity of something else which will forever prevent it from permanently (really never more than temporarily) unbalancing order and substituting for the same, disorder.

For everywhere, if we are privileged to accept the deductions of physics and chemistry as reasonably conclusive, disorder is forever surrounded by order, and in due course order dispels it; whereas nowhere is there any proof that order anywhere is wholly surrounded by disorder, or that it ever has been or can be dispelled by the same. Order—as opposed to a considerable amount or tendency toward disorder—yes. But disorder as overtopping and setting at nought *order*, local or universal, there is no scientific data which serves to establish that.

T.D.

‡ ‡ ‡

Few if any of the arrangements that go to make up society, the state, the social arrangements of animals or insects can be said to be permanently orderly or disorderly, although it may be that *order and disorder* are but two phases of a larger process that is truly *orderly* in a larger sense.

Thus, in order to have progress or change and so contrast, which nature seems to desire to achieve and so does, it would look as though the given reproductive order and desire for dominance on the part of any one species or thing has necessarily to be interrupted by another, in fact many others, in order that the reproductive and self-protective and hence eventually dominating force of any single species may not exclude the presence and at least partial success of the others on which, of course, depends the spectacle we call life—with all of its varieties and so desirable contrasts—and the drama and delight as well as the terror and death or change that, at present at least, accompany the same.

Thus, some man must get rich and then other men must get richer and absorb or destroy him. The sons of great masters must be weaklings and so lose or dissipate all that was assembled and held by their fathers. The strong man must grow old and be removed and defeated by the younger man who has yet to lose his strength. Animals must be eaten or driven off and so starved by other animals in order that these second animals may survive, but they in their turn must yet again be defeated by others in order that those others may survive, perhaps for some cosmic reason for self-expression in terms of variety of form, color, taste, energy, and self-entertainment.

In sum, there must be variety in order to have contrast and color; also contest and change in order that there be interest; also death in order that there may be new life—progress. To the ignorant but seemingly orderly individual of one species seeking to preserve itself against the members of other seeking species, this might look like a cruel and even disorderly process. But to the super-force ordaining and regulating the same, it might well appear as a valuable and spectacular and happiness-giving success. [*Or*]

T.D.

‡ ‡ ‡

Neither chance nor law or order can be proved. A struggle between law and order here and in the universe can be proved. Large bodies of anything, by their magnetic pull or speed, compel certain seemingly *orderly* results—that is, they compel the revolution about themselves of satellites or lesser bodies, prevent their flying off at a tangent and wrecking or joining something else. But what compels them to compel such revolutions on the part of satellites?

And from the satellites' point of view may this compulsion to revolve about a larger body be a disorderly proceeding, brutally interfering with their privilege to rove *where* and *when* a body of matter such as a satellite *pleases?*

Certainly, except for this restraint or compulsion on the part of a larger body, there is this tendency to fly free until some major force is met up with, which seems to indicate an opposite if not an equal force to this pull of a larger body which is said to establish order. In other words, there is an anti-order.

But suppose, instead of the word *order,* or this something which is sometimes referred to as divine order or a *will* to order, one puts the word compulsion or restraint. So then what? For here on earth, by man if no other mechanism, a compulsion is looked upon as a denial of freedom—a contradiction, and a disagreeable one, at times, of the seemingly equally strong compulsion or impulse to be rid of restraint, be "free". But what is that? A denial of order? A tendency to disorder, or at least an opposition to some form of established order, whatever that may be?

No man on earth can say as to that or whether it makes for more order or more disorder or a continuance of the balance of the two. For certainly order seems to maintain itself via an innate tendency or condition on the part of large bodies to control or compel smaller bodies to rotate about them, and disorder to come about because of an innate something in these smaller bodies, lack of size or weight or whatever, not to do so unless compelled by this so-called gravitational pull, which they, in their turn, exercise upon still smaller bodies. But what is that? Law? Order? Or disorder (in equal quantity and volume) opposed to order? No physicist has yet answered that. And no philosopher. And yet for answer, might not one suggest that they are the equal and opposite halves of something which seemingly requires both, perhaps not so much to *be* as to express itself, and that as nothing more, or other, than *order/disorder.*

T.D.

Good and Evil

WE COME INTO THE WORLD WITH THE BURDEN OF ENDLESS PAST errors upon us and not of our making, unless we have some deathless but unconscious, psychic part in it all, of which we are not, of course, aware. And in addition, we carry subconsciously arranged appetites and compulsions of which we are not the conscious authors. At once, in connection with these, begins not only the problem of adjustment due to the struggle which results from the compulsions to exist and gratify these pre-arranged appetites— the same struggles for the same reasons on the part of all, since all are similarly, if not exactly, environed. And from the very outset, these struggles as readily result in death to the individual as life, and, more, each mechanism is certain to end in death or mechanical collapse in sixty or seventy or eighty years due to the manner in which the body or machine is constructed. Plainly it is unable to endure more than a limited period of strain. [*Or*]

T.D.

‡ ‡ ‡

The mythical Christ is credited with the prayer: *Lead us not into temptation.* Whatever its source, it is a vague conception of the mechanistic character of life, for it presents the so-called individual as helpless in the face of forces (temptations) which motivate or project him in one direction or course as opposed to another direction or course—in this case assumed to be evil.

For evil needs must come, but woe to him by whom the evil cometh.——from the *Gospel according to St. Matthew.*

[*Or*]

‡ ‡ ‡

We seem to be divided in ourselves, against ourselves, as witness our troubling over what is good and what is evil. But actually this has never been the result of any true individuality or individual thinking on the part of man. He is a mechanism built to respond chemically or sensorially to exterior forces which are both good and evil, or neither.

For what man or animal is to say what they are? *They are.* And he has been constructed by them to respond to them in the ways which he does. Was it his fault in the beginning that he killed to eat? What established his hunger and thirst? Did either he or his animal forebears know? Does he know now? Decidedly, he does not. It is true that he can cease eating meat today, providing his sensory responses or reactions to the sufferings of animals move him so to do. And where they move him so to do, he does. Where they do not, and unless his meat-digestive processes go awry, he does not. And until they do so move him to do, he will not, because he has no choice to do other than his chemic or sensory reactions compel him to do. [*Or*]

‡   ‡   ‡

Even in the materialistic or purly mechanistic philosophies of such thinkers and experimenters as Spencer and Loeb, you will find references or rather appeals to the individual to consider himself, the results of his conduct, and to guard and control the same as though this same were after all, to a marked degree, within his keep—a thought, a conclusion that is wholly beyond the will of the individual, as both Spencer and Loeb prove.

In his *Study of Sociology* (London: Keegan, Paul, Trench & Co., 15th edition, page 198), Spencer writes, "Nothing like a high type of social life is possible without a type of human character in which the promptings of egoism are restrained by regard for others."

But of course the regard for others is not individual or personal in any strict individualistic sense. It is a reaction peculiar, not to any so-called one individual, but rather to billions and billions, and throughout a great period of time, and brought about by experiences of what others will do to one if one's promptings of egoism are not restrained. And that is a mechanistic or chemico-neuro response and not the result of so-called thought or mind.

T.D.

Who Am I That Speaks?

Call Life—God. Or call God—Life. Either way, it is the same. By its, or his, or her stark powers, physical or mental (we know them now to be the same), are men and all things brought to form and being. Rat and king, germ and behemoth, tribe and race. However small, each minutest mechanism, however huge and seemingly important or trivial, by Life or God or nature is each timed and manipulated. Once an English royal family wrote above its walls. "God is my right." So might any man, any rat, any germ, any star. Life is my right. Life is my authority. I am as good or ill as Life ordained me to be, neither more nor less so—an implement of it. Be I either evil or good, seek neither to disdain nor ignore me. An expression of Life, I move and have my being. Because of Life, the mean and great, the ugly and the beautiful are and do, but not otherwise. Murderer or saint, humanist or devil, through them as its mechanism, its mouthpiece, it says or does what it wills. Along with every other of its creations, they present it. In me, perhaps minutely, no more than one atom or quantum of its endless self; in others, be they Gods or suns or sidereal systems, only something more of it, but not all. Make way. [*Or*]

THEODORE DREISER

‡ ‡ ‡

According to Theism, which pictured God and his creation as entities distinct each from each other, the human subject was outside of the deepest reality in the universe. God was from eternity, complete and sufficient unto himself. He threw off the world or the universe as a free act, as an extraneous substance, such as a toy balloon, prepared to float, which you might manufacture and throw out of a window. And as for man, he threw him off too as a third substance, extraneous to himself, and, for that matter, the world he had just thrown off. In sum, God is one; the world is his creation, and so is man; but he lets the world or universe live longer, one of them as an abode for man, who is to repeat himself until a day of judgment or such time as God is tired of it and his creature man, and decides to resurvey them, and decides whether he will save or destroy them.

The worst of it is, as many have pointed out, that although he made these things, he is in no sense implicated or involved in anything that follows because of his creative act. To be sure, he is thought to have put man in a garden with all that was necessary for him, and man was to be guided by rules prepared for him. He was at liberty to eat of everything save the fruit of the tree of knowledge, although the meaning of the tree or its fruit or its allure for man or why man should have been created with a desire to eat of it when he could just as well have been created without such a desire (the tree might even have been made distasteful to him) is not explained.

In other words, man is made an outsider. God is not heart of his heart and reason of his reason, but a magistrate who creates without explaining and then punishes or breaks or slays his creature or toy if anything goes wrong.

But this implies stupidity or cruelty or both—the actions or inane blunderings and maunderings and murderous temperament even that of an idiot, one whose actions can affect us, but who can never be affected by our reactions, angry or supplicatory. And what is more, it has operated as a force in the world, operating in time and place as law, since man has been ordered here and there to worship God or Jehovah or Allah on these terms and regardless of the ills inflicted. As William James (*A Pluralistic Universe*) puts it, "Conceptions of criminal law have in fact played a great part in defining our relations with him (God). Our relations with speculative truth show the same externality. One of our duties is to know truth and rationalist thinkers have always assumed it to be our sovereign duty. But in scholastic theism, we find truth already instituted and established without our help, complete, apart from our knowing; and the most we can do is to acknowledge it passively and adhere to it, although such adhesion as ours can make no jot of difference to what is adhered to. . . . Truth exists *per se* and absolutely, by God's grace and decree, no matter who of us knows it or is ignorant, and it would continue to exist unaltered, even though we finite knowers were all annihilated." Ignorance of the law or truth is no excuse, and so our earthly legal codes insist and function to this day.

In the evolutionary or mechanistic conception of life and its sources, as that reads today, the situation is radically different. No personal entity or man-created God of whom he is a likeness is acknowledged or admitted. We are not only environed by but are an integral part of a vast mechanism, the unexplained origin of which does not alter the fact that out of it has evolved man, a mechanism, compounded and constructed of and, what is more, operated by the very chemicals and elements or forces found operating in and throughout the ponderable and, in part, visible universe of which man is a part, and which, better still, is a universe of law, of weights and measures, of ladder-like elements which ascend from a definite base or unit, primarily the hydrogen atom; and yet as separate elements and combinations of elements and by reason of (unexplained it is true) attractions and repulsions, [these elements] combine to make or be and function as the endless suns, their planets, the sidereal systems or isolated island universes, which we register with chemically and physically sensitive bodies and eyes that have come out of the same.

But of this it is not written that it is all-wise or that its processes, insofar as they relate to man or the evolved creatures of earth, or that said processes are entirely merciful or successful as man interprets success, or that apart from man, it is a realm of peace and order in which, to change the phraseology of the Bible a little "is no variableness neither shadow of turning." *It may be*, but physics and chemistry do not attempt to intrude human moral conceptions or compulsions or illusions upon the universe at large. It is. Insofar as we can see and weigh and measure, it does or acts as intended, and there-upon follow such physical and chemical laws or reactions as can be verified here on earth—not elsewhere.

Mainly there are problems and factors not yet resolved, although the progress of such resolving is, at present, constant.

The Problem
of Knowledge

KNOWLEDGE CAN ONLY BE AWARENESS OF THE LAWS OF NATURE
or life and of nature's skill in applying the same to the creation of forms
functioning within and according to its laws (The acquiring of knowledge
is the beginning of wisdom). *Why* its laws came into being, man does not
know. He has surmised (guessed) that it might be to bring him and all other
creatures into being and make all happy. But much suffering and despair
causes him to doubt this. *How* its laws came into being, he does not know
but surmises, or has surmised, that they are *from everlasting to everlasting.*
But that is a surmise. He does not know. Hence, he must return to the
first sentence and end there. [*Or*]

‡ ‡ ‡

Why is it that energy, as expressed in human and animal vitality, requires
changes and contrast (they are not always synonymous) to maintain what
humans call *interest*—that something which all of us require (including perhaps
nature itself) to escape from boredom or all but suicidal humdrum. Neither
humans nor animals made this necessity. It is no invention of theirs. *It is*—as
the Russians say. But how does it come to be? Is ultimate energy responsible
for it? Or is it a condition or quality or characteristic of matter-energy?
Science offers no explanation. Philosophy is silent. But must it be? Is there
not a *how?* Must we be content with an unanswered *why?* [*Or*]

T.D.

‡ ‡ ‡

Intuitive knowledge can and has been lost: 1. By the lack of realization
of its value by the one in whom the intuition was evolved. 2. By the lack
of a receptive environment. Knowledge and its reception and growth is not
unlike the *Parable of the Sower.* Perhaps Christ, in speaking of the *Kingdom
of Heaven,* was referring to supreme, ultimate, underlying knowledge. [*Or*]

‡ ‡ ‡

The *Kingdom of God* cometh not by observation. Love can place (reach) the witness for itself, in the hearts of all men. [*Or*]

‡ ‡ ‡

Kant himself found that the secret of things lies in the inspiration of the human *conscience* rather than in the cunning decrees of the human *intellect.* What is *conscience* and what is *intellect?* [*Or*]

‡ ‡ ‡

Complete knowledge of the nature and functional processes of the Creative Force operating and expressing itself in and through matter-energy (if matter-energy is its only form of self-expression) could only be *granted* to any creature or mechanism, such as man or a solar system or an island universe or a single sun, by the processes or *thought existent in said creative energy.* Certainly [such knowledge is] not to be thought of as existing *in* or to be independently *achieved* by the toy or mechanism or creature of said primal creative force or energy, whatever the nature of that toy or mechanism as devised by said primal energy might be?

Knowledge less than the totality of Creative Wisdom could not seemingly exist outside of itself and operate as independently as the primal energy man contemplates appears to do. [*Or*]

‡ ‡ ‡

In recent years most of the philosophers (at least those of English speaking countries) appear to have been dismayed by the difficulty of discovering any consistent rational pattern or order which could be responsible for the complications, the paradoxes, the errors, the absurdities, and the outright contradictions of human motives and behavior. No less a thinker than Immanuel Kant likewise expressed the belief that a *plan and purpose probably direct the course of man's history, but admitted bewilderment at the thought of attempting to discover its nature.* Evolution throws no light, nor history. They do not indicate any clear objective. A procession of forms, one derived from the other or many others or the environment, all at each period have confronted. But bound where, meaning what? Religion has an answer—heaven? Science none. It offers *what is* on the altar of speculation. [*Or*]

T.D.

‡ ‡ ‡

Chemists, physicists, the world of medicine, as well as others, cooks and street-cleaners included, are constantly dealing with endless combinations of matter, chemical as well as physical in their nature. These chemical (at bottom, atomic) mixtures, always being discovered by researchers, taken apart by them, and suspected of being or proved to be the cause or cure of some ill, are unquestionably just that—for everything, infinitely small or great in relation to something else and under particular environments, must be the cause of some ill or disturbance or its cure. For, being atomic, hence energy at base, they have the significance and authority of all energy.

T.D.

‡   ‡   ‡

Julian Huxley says science has two inherent limitations. First, it is incomplete, or, as befits it, partial; and, if you please, because it only concerns itself with intellectual handling and objective control. Next, it is morally and emotionally neutral. It sets out to describe and to understand, not to appraise, not to assign value. Indeed, science is without scales of value: the only value which it acknowledges is that of truth or exact knowledge. It is, therefore, equitably correct because it studies all reaction, sensory and emotional or chemical and physical, and classifies them for what they are—action/reaction. It is so greatly concerned that it dissolves illusion and puts the operation of life on its proper chemical and physical base.

Knowledge of this last type is also power—the door to immense forces which cause the process of evolution to continue. [W]

T.D.

Cosmic Rays

Longer than the infinitesimal electrons but smaller than protons, the mysterious "cosmic rays" are flung earthward from somewhere in the outside universe with energies estimated at several million volts. They lose a part of their energy in collisions as well as ionization through the atmosphere which they encounter here. But nonetheless, arrived at the surface of the earth, they have penetrated several inches of lead.

With prolonged losses of energy, however, they suddenly reach a point where, with still several hundred million volts to their credit, they break up. It is a ray cataclysm. Once so broken, their fragments may be stopped by a plate of lead a centimeter or less in thickness. The final catastrophic smash and loss of energy is out of proportion to other earlier losses on their earthward journey, and physicists are now trying to determine what happens when this disaster occurs.

For this purpose, two cloud chambers are used, one on top of another. In the upper, smaller chamber, the speeding particles are subjected to a strong magnetic pull, and the curvature of the particles' path under the pull of the magnet is photographed. From this its mass and energy can be computed. In the lower chamber, layers of lead, aluminum, and other metals are arranged in the path of the particle. Photographs are then taken of the effect of the layers in slowing up the particle. Also of any results from disintegration caused by collisions. Accurate measures of mass and energy are possible only with those that have been slowed down to speeds of ten or fifteen million volts. Most of the particles reach the earth at speeds that defy all human traps, or else, because of sudden disintegration, they fail to reach the earth at all. More, a very small percentage of the particles reaching the earth can be then registered and investigated.

Query: Do they strike all stellar bodies? Atmospheres varying so greatly on different worlds, what becomes of them? What novel blends, if any, are effected? [*Or*]

‡ ‡ ‡

Striking among the chromosomes in the nucleus of a single generative ovum and knocking out of a gene chain one of the color spots or character traits, such a cosmic ray or energy seed emerging from possibly an illimitable distance in space can nonetheless change the entire character of a man, animal, tree, flower, vegetable, or even bacillus. Striking in the gene chain of an ovum, it could produce an Alexander, Caesar, Napoleon, Newton, Jesus; perhaps it could alter the entire course of earthly society for a thousand or more years; perhaps change its entire complexion for a still longer period. [*Or*]

The Black Dwarfs

Twenty years ago (1920) astro physicists were weighing the Universe!—obtaining its atomic weight! They did not know then of the existence of the *black dwarfs*—or "Cinder" stars—of which now it is held probable that there are countless numbers. These are stars that are cinders or the remains of exploded stars—those giant stars that by exploding form (1) a new nebulae and (2) a black dwarf or cinder. These dead stars or cinders, after they cease glowing, give off no light and in consequence are invisible even to the most powerful telescope of today (1940). Yet, while they continue to glow, they are visible and so are known to exist. Yet they were not known and could not have been weighed in 1920 or earlier. However, like all matter, they have their atomic or energy weights and must be included in any weighed universe. Hence, the ascertained weight of the universe of that day had no basis in fact. Yet it was "awefully" accepted by readers of that day as truth or knowledge. [*Or*]

The White Dwarfs

The surface of these old and highly dense stars becomes white hot (because of shell collapse and condensation), but the total radiation they emit is low because they are so small. Such dying stars, called *white dwarfs*, can still exist for quite some time, but they are very stingy in their lost energy resources. They have no future in front of them and sooner or later they are bound to freeze "to the bones," and form cold, dark bodies, wandering aimlessly through the vastness of interstellar space. *Just how many of these wanderers there are scientists have no way of knowing, for they emit no light and thus cannot be seen.* [*Or*]

‡ ‡ ‡

Consider the deaths of the day anywhere, make your own list this morning. Here is a somebody, an expert publicity director who knew all about achieving publicity for millions. Here is a distinguished jurist, full of knowledge of the law in America at least. Here is a famous educator, charged with methods of distributing knowledge; here the discoverer of the wireless; there a railroad executive, risen from the ranks to be president of a great and useful system. Here a famous editor, respected as such by all; there a great actor; here a poet, or painter; there a navigator. And all stored with special and often thorough knowledge of some one thing, such as few have—history, biology, chemistry, engineering, architecture.

But knowledge, the vast knowledge that each represents or failed to represent in its fullness—is that lost? Gone? Or is it still extant, like the birds' knowledge of how to fly, the bees' knowledge of how to build a hive and store honey, a tree's knowledge of how to gather its substance and live, the wasp's and spider's knowledge of how to build a paper house or a silken web and to kill, eat, mate, and rear their young? All most certainly possess knowledge, for we call our discoveries in connection with an animal's or insect's or bird's or worm's life-procedure or technique *knowledge* and store it as such in our libraries. And if information as to *how they do* is knowledge to us, how much more so is it to them or to those forces that bring them and their procedures into being.

However, the point is not that it is knowledge as we use the word, but that such knowledge is not the exclusive possession of anyone or thing, but of life. And that it does not die with one bee or one ant or one man or one nation or one race, but goes on as a part of the creative functions that bring all creatures into being, and dies only with the death of all of them, if it does so die. Rather, viewing the universe as well as evolution on this particular planet as a whole, one may guess that particular knowledge is everywhere—in the elements and chemicals that make the universe as well as our solar system—and as such is deathless, now manifesting itself as does invisible moisture when it is changed by heat into a cloud or by cold into visible moisture. In short, it is a protean thing, now this, or that, but always, basically, if not the ultimate substance of the universe, at least a manifestation of it.

T.D.

Education

Education is relative—very. For instance, in Australia each Stone Age hunter must have an enormous amount of land to support him and his family. Game is scarce; so is water. Besides, these fine brown fellows with their spears must know in infinite detail the habits, varying with the seasons, of animal life. This takes great intelligence and knowledge, which anyone must respect. It is not savagery any more than knowing how to farm or install plumbing or electric fixtures is savagery; in fact, it is more difficult and requires more so-called mental ability than the average plumber or electrician dreams of. He goes by a method and practice book or has someone to teach him. So has the Stone man. And put down in Australia or some parts of Africa, the average American or European would not last a week.

More, we talk loftily of our organized society: its civilization, morality, charity—this and that. The Australian Stone Age man meets his problems as thoughtfully and considerately as any American or European anywhere. Over there, scarcity of food has required a balance between population and food supply, and these people have met it by various forms of eugenic control. In times of great stress, they kill their own children, which causes the so-called civilized European and American to hold up his hands in righteous horror. But the American or European (the American or European in high financial and social positions I mean) will gladly send millions of boys, mostly underpaid and underprivileged at the time this is done, out into the wilds of a scientifically prepared no man's land where the improved murder techniques of war, worked out in laboratories and universities, can slaughter them by millions. And all to settle—for the overprivileged, not the underprivileged—the question of material precedence, who shall be first Lord of this or that.

But this is not shocking to "civilized" America or Europe any more than are ten million men out of work for years, and, who, because of enforced idleness, have no chance to practice what they know and are slowly but surely losing their value to others and so to themselves as workers. They and their children can, because of undernourishment, physically decline and die, so long as a top group, as in England, France, America, can be comfortable, well-fed, well-clothed, much talked about as lords or captains of this or that. In contrast to this (although for practical reasons), these Stone Age men do not kill their old people, because they are valuable to the community, having needed knowledge to impart. However, here we have long gotten past all that, having replaced the old by the school, the university, the technical laboratory, the labor apprenticeship, and so on, and so making it possible, and more, necessary for them to go jump out of a window, the annual tax budget of the sixty families coming first, a thing not to be increased.

In sum, educated and "civilized" Europe and America (their modern industrial and financial overlords) consider that they have an immensely superior approach to life—a "culture" which is socially helpful, humane, progressive, this, that. And they look down upon the Stone Age man who, having been islanded upon an underprivileged continent, has still brilliantly succeeded in educating himself to his environment and so preserving himself. For, with their advanced "thought" and techniques, the American and European can advance upon and displace or enslave him, at the very least "mentally" upstage him, as alas the American has done with his really marvelous Negroes.

At the same time, they manage nicely to forgive their brutal youth-murdering wars, their savage industrial cruelties, their unspeakable slums in the midst of their wallows of wealth, their wage slaves, child labor, forgotten elders and children—strutting the while and vaingloriously under the sun with their unspeakable lunacies concerning social superiority, and personal precedence, the *better than thou* complex. And yet, because of their ignorance of the necessary and really splendid knowledge which the Stone Age man has at this hour in Australia, Africa, the frozen North, they, put in his place and even though given his physical equipment, would perish swiftly.

So what is education? And what is civilization? If you want to find out for yourself, try a different environment where none, or few, of the things you find so necessary are, and yet, where so-called savages live and maintain themselves in strength and their kind of wisdom without which you and your education would die.

Go to the Australian wilds or the Arctic and Africa and see.

THEODORE DREISER

The Equation Called Morality

THERE IS NO MIDPOINT BETWEEN GOOD AND EVIL THAT CAN BE fixed upon as the changeless and proper stand of morality or right conduct. There is, to be sure, that indeterminable ideal called the Golden Mean. But that mean which seems the changeless and proper one is no more than the point we have taken on the road which leads either to indulgence or self-denial. And what two individuals could agree on that point. [*Or*]

Morals

They can be called the rules that must govern under special conditions in order that anything may *be* and function.

There are no morals in nature. Cannibal cells are primarily injured cells. Spiders, beasts of prey. Let the buyer beware. The rain falleth on the just and the unjust. The ooley-ooley bug. So-called morals are rules established by social agreement for the comfort and possibly the development of species, but never to be universally applied, since that is a dream, an ideal to be referred poetically to some world far from ours "where moonlight and music and poetry are one."

Nonetheless, under given conditions the necessity for compromise or equation holds. The "honest grocer" is the one whom a profitable reputation for honesty induces to continue to give fair weight and strictly fresh eggs, milk, fruit, etc. The dishonest one is one whom necessity, including political parasites or grafters, plus poor logic (a deficient reasoning faculty) has driven to cheating.

Then there is the usurer (money lender), pawnbroker, trickster, but no moralist or immoralist who is not made by nature and the pressure of difficulties (chance). The average so-called immoral woman may be a glandular defective. Ditto a moral woman. Ditto a courageous man. Ditto a coward. Ditto a thief or kleptomaniac. Where are morals in war? If religion did not promote morals and rewards, what would it have to sell?

Just the same, there are *relative morals*—morals or rules that must govern among spiders, cannibals, prostitutes, thieves, politicians, and whatever. Religious theories require, for practice, rules of some kind, and they are looked upon as necessary and moral. [*Or*]

‡ ‡ ‡

A machine, to be a machine and function, must abide (as it does) by chemical and physical rules or laws. Those rules or laws are the same as the rules or laws or morals or taboos of men and animals, the same as the rules of a game, if there is to be a game. Disobedience means the destruction or injury of the man, animal, tree, vegetable—or the injury to or breaking up of the machine or the game. [*Or*]

‡ ‡ ‡

Force, energized by ignorance, suffering, need, hope, faith, illusion in any form, is sufficient to overthrow chicanery or subtlety since the possessions of these are never sufficiently numerous to physically match those who are not subtle or clever. The former, like the Lilliputians, do succeed in binding on occasion the stolid and drowsing Gulliver—*the mass*—with their endless silken webs, but only so long as he fails to sense that he is being bound. Once he wakes or even turns in his sleep, all their threads are swept away. [*Or*]

T.D.

‡ ‡ ‡

The moral instinct has been identified with the instinct to serve. If it is an instinct or compulsion provided by nature (not the individual), where is the morality, and Rene Quintion, the French philosopher/soldier describes the moral instinct as directed (by nature of course) to an end beyond the species to which the individual belongs, and as being in some way, perhaps, the determining factor in evolution. He adds his conviction that beyond the merely animal instinct to fight (game-cock, bulls), there is a fundamentally social instinct which finds its expression in war. It is his neighbor's life that a man must fight to defend since his neighbor is fighting to defend him.

The moral drama, which we may equally call the drama of history, lies in the conflict between the instinct to serve and the instinct to live at the expense of service. [*Or*]

‡ ‡ ‡

No love without hatred. No heat without cold. No black without white. No good without evil. No strength without weakness. No light without dark or shadow. No truth without falsehood.

In short, life as we know it is compounded of opposites. There can be no sense of life without them. At bottom, these appear to be the principals of a contest or a possible contest ideationally conceivable as necessary if the ultimate something which the Hindus called the Nirvana and physics and chemistry call creative energy should wish to change from still ether to life. In other words, all of these opposites or qualities, while not an essential or active part of the ultimate *still* force, remain necessary to life as we know it, or said life cannot be. Whether beautifully or not, as we its mechanistic parts see it, it involves certain conditions or rules or means by reason of which, and seemingly none other, can it be. They are listed above.

Speaking of God, or the creative energy as we know it, the Bible says, "He is of eyes too pure to behold evil." And, for the sake of argument, admitting this, the while we contemplate the physical and chemical rules of the world that we see and sense, we would be forced to conclude that life is not the best expression of force, but only its active phase. Viewing these rules of life from this point of view, they would appear to make it possible for the Creator, without prejudice to his ultimate purity and goodness, to still express himself as life, since, when all is said and done, it has no reality, but is a passing illusion. In that sense, good and evil, while an integral if not an unescapable part of the ultimate being of energy in its quiescent state, would still be the finality or penalty attaching to any activity. In other words, good and evil, plus all of these other equations listed above as life, would be no more than necessary balances in such a game, as we see here, useful as illusions but not as a fact.

In which case, life, with all of its so-called strains and tortures and brutalities, would still comprise no censure to the ultimate quiescent force. For that force, as the mechanist argues and even as the Christians hint at with their heaven and their forgiveness of sins, would be no more than a harbor into which the strains and unreal contrasts of the game would ultimately vanish.

In fact, that, as I see it, would provide not only life as we know it but the sinless wisdom of the ultimate energy as dreamed of by the religionists, the heaven of the dreamers of the all-good. He or it who is "of eyes too pure to behold evil." [W]

T.D.

‡ ‡ ‡

The walls of the stomach are lined with several layers of plain muscle. When food is present, producing normal extension of the stomach walls, the muscles are quiet. In a few hours time, in the adult, the food begins to pass into the small intestine. This leaves the stomach empty. Immediately, and without any willing on the part of the possessor of the stomach, it begins to contract rhythmically. These rhythmical contractions are called hunger contractions, and in all languages and in all times, some word indicating hunger has, because of these contractions and not because of anything else, come into being. Furthermore, these contractions make the animal mechanism, be it whatsoever it may be, insect, tiger, rabbit or man, to search for food.

In that highly mechanized thing, the society of man, it has become a crime for men to steal, let alone kill, to get food, and yet these muscle motions drive some of them, on occasion to do that, just as they drive the fox to the barnyard, the rat to the trap, the tiger and the lion to the water hole where weaker creatures come to drink. Since the vast majority of animal species are not organized socially as are men, among them to steal and to kill each other are not crimes. They are evolutionary victories, just as are the successful wars of rival societies. Ethics or morals are not involved, and cannot be. Yet among lions, on occasion where one has killed and eaten and another is hungry and prowling about, the first will permit the second to finish what he has left and, in that society of men, which as yet has but dimly responded to perhaps only now developing social compulsions, there is sympathy for the hunger striker and the hunger murderer, law breaker though he may be.

But this sympathy reaction has a much larger implication than might at first appear. It introduces the question: does the mechanistic system called life involve, and that purely mechanistically, kindness? Does it, whether it wishes to or not, whether will is involved or not, establish a balance, even roughly, between too little and too much? Suppose you test it for yourself in yourself.

We will assume that you are sitting in a restaurant near a window and are comfortably supplied with what you desire in the way of food. The muscle walls of your stomach are at rest. But outside the window, at that point, there appears, let us say, the face of another mechanism like yourself. Also, it wears an expression which, due to your past registrations of expressions of that kind, or those of others, you identify with the reaction or emotion or compulsion called hunger. In other words, this eye registration of yours in connection with the mechanism outside is something which conveys to or evokes in you a registration or sense of hunger as afflicting, or at least, characterizing the mechanism outside. At the same time, in certain cases at least, it is likely to evoke, what shall I say (there are various words for the possible evocation), sympathy, pity, sorrow, compassion, compunction? Whatever it is, however verbalized, it, let us say, moves you to rise and go to the mechanism outside and either invite it in or at least provide it with a modicum of what you are moved to consider will satisfy the hunger compulsion which the expression of the outside mechanism has conveyed.

At the time you do this, however, you may have the feeling or registration that you *will* to do it, and, hence, not do it. Yet either impulse or decision, so-called, would not be *willing* on your part, in any sense of the word. It would be nothing more than responding, either weakly or strongly, to the stimuli provided by the expression on the mechanism outside. If the expression were sufficiently stimulating to your organism, you would automatically rise and do as described. If it were not, or if your organism were insufficiently equipped to register its import, you might have a faint impulse to go, and yet sit still, but you would not be *willing* to do either. Besides the cost of so doing, the labor, past registration of ungrateful beggars, or stories concerning them as told by others might be, by now influencing you, hence. You would be doing one or the other according to the power of the compulsion.

But don't think that we are through with this problem or query as to the possibilities in nature or matter-energy or the universe of some mechanistic equivalent of the slowly evolved English word *mercy* in nature. For, now you must ask yourself, does the mechanistic registration on the face outside the window really cause the organism to rise or respond, and if so why? As to this *why*, we have said that there are names for it, words that appear to explain why—pity, compassion, etc.—and their equivalents in many languages.

But these are words, mere verbalized symbols of a force that compels what?—an equation of some kind between too little and too much? Is it the same thing for instance as warmed air rushing to where the air is cold and blending with it and so tempering it, and cold moving to where it is hot? But that is a physical law and not only on this planet, but throughout the universe. And it maintains a rough balance or equation between great heat and great cold, everywhere. But if you ask the physicist why, he will tell you that the *why* is the nature of all physical law—to every action an equal and opposite reaction—a law which seems to be in the very nature of things, and for which there is no explanation, but which *is*, and which pervades everything.

Hence, if you ask the mechanist why the man inside the restaurant goes outside the restaurant, he will say it is a compulsion, a physical law, that there is no *will*, only physical and determined action and reaction. Just the same, you are not to forget that on that law, if it is a law, has been built all the notions or doctrines or dogmas that relate to so-called justice, pity, so-called sympathy, compassion. That is, it has given rise to what we know of ethics, morals, religion, duty, mercy, love. It has brought into being such maxims as "Do unto others as you would be done by." "An eye for an eye and a tooth for a tooth." "They that live by the sword shall perish by the sword." It has also given rise to the parable of the Good Samaritan, the Beatitudes, the Sermon on the Mount, and Mohammed's word as to the "son of the road." It has established the very crude and seldom exact system which we call justice. As a matter of fact, it is the basis of all social law and relations. Nonetheless, whatever the shadows or errors or dreams to which it has given rise, it remains, as you see, a mechanistic compulsion.

T.D.

The Myth of Morality

We will say that you are sleeping not too soundly at one or two o'clock in the morning, and suddenly, somewhere in the dark of your residence, you hear a noise. The thought of burglars arises, and if you are courageous you might get up and move in the direction of the sound! But at some point, you are suddenly confronted by a masked man with a gun, probably a searchlight, and are commanded to put up your hands while he binds you, and proceeds to remove your silver or gold or whatever, and then makes his way out.

Current morals and most of the legal authorities on the criminology of the day would tell you that you have been confronted by, and are dealing with, a criminal very different to yourself morally, emotionally, socially, and in every other way. Wilfully he is a thief, whereas for your part you are either naturally or wilfully (and here, by the way, as you may often note, if you choose, no trouble is taken to distinguish between the two) a man of honor and good conduct. At least you are in possession of some property, whereas the other may not be, usually is not. More, it is legally, and hence rightfully, yours. Besides, in that passing myth called the individual mind, morality and property are, if not one and the same, at least interchangeable.

However this may be and whatever your particular evil tendencies or crimes may be, at least you do not go about at night with a gun entering people's houses and taking their silverware. Of course, if you were a stockbroker, you might be gypping someone out of his stocks and bonds; or if you were one of the owners or at least controlling heads of one or other of the world's powerful corporations, you might, through the connivance of government officials, courts, members of Congress, various State Utility Boards, some lawyers, and your fellow directors and investors, be daily and hourly, and penny by penny or dollar by dollar, exacting from a vast public—the assumed owners of all natural privileges—an undue reward for the monopoly services you render. At least, wealth via monopoly comes to you and is restrained from reaching others. Yet, according to law as well as mass opinion, you are not honest or honorable in so seizing and witholding special property and then unduly taxing the mass for the use of these, because under most of the provisions of current government—constitutions and such—you know that it is agreed that those who govern do so only by the consent of the governed, and that they, and not you as a monopolist, are the owners of the vast privileges of any given country, and you but a steward whose business it is, and for a proper reward of course, to administer these conveniences of life for the benefit of the public.

Nevertheless, by reason of the idea that the man with brains or ideas or creative power is entitled to enormous privileges and returns, and the man without enough of them is not entitled to much of anything, you feel morally sure that you are entitled to this extraordinary profit and that it is not robbery. Or, whether you so hold or not, but because of your wealth, ill-gotten or well-gotten, you feel that you will not be punished for having secured the same by whatsoever process. Usually the thought, mood, illusion with which you respond to this matter of your possessions is like that. Yet, whether you know it or not, you are really a victim of the "might makes right" idea—an influential and motivating force in you—just as the absence of might or capabilities of any profitable kind in your burglar makes him the victim of the notion or reality that he is being put upon—unfairly deprived of resources and happiness by powers over which he has no control. In addition—in his case, due to the type of mind he has (and of course it was not made by him) plus the chemical impulses which he receives from either over-stocked or undernourished glands of various kinds—he is motivated in the direction of revenge; whereas your so-called mental equipment (which you did not make), which is directed by glandular impulses in the direction of trust-making and money-gathering, causes you to move in the direction of self-protection, or, in other words, toward personal if not general social security as one of your inalienable rights. It is not of course, except by reason of social contrast, fully lived up to by all. But let that pass.

So, of course, when you are confronted by the burglar and he is confronted by you, you naturally do not understand each other. He looks upon you as wilful, selfish, and brutal, and oppressive, and as holding much more than you need to be happy; whereas you look upon him as a man who, whatever his lacks—mental, financial, physical—wilfully refuses to see that he owes a duty to the society of which he is a part and that he should not only go to work and earn the means wherewith to be the kind of man he would like to be and to live the kind of life he would like to live, but also that he should join with you in protecting you and himself in the possession of what either of you by that process might achieve.

But, as you see, neither of you are in possession of an ideal standard of life. It does not exist, or at least is not practiced, and never has been anywhere. Nor have either of you the ability or the mental or physical equipment wherewith to conform to the same, assuming that it did exist. Nor have either of you the personal wisdom which would permit you to solve this physical-chemical mix-up which we call life. It is possible that the forces which make and present you both to each other in the way you just found yourselves at midnight might sometimes weary of the show—the stage play which they have prepared and which they are so interestingly conducting—and decide to end it. Whereupon both of you—you with your homes and lands, your idea of honor and position and duty, etc.; he with his lack of the same—would both disappear. For it, all of it, is a stage play, nothing more— sound and fury signifying nothing.

For—and to begin with—there is no such thing as a being who comes into the world predecided upon being a thief or a murderer or a saint, any more than there is a being or creature who enters predecided upon being a banker, a minister, or a corporation head, or a good man. What comes into the world is a mechanism not built by either your mother or your father, nor even the generations preceding them, but by life and circumstances, all life and all circumstance, and they are things not to be solved here. They are compounded of forces and elements and mechanisms as yet unguessed by man.

And not only that, but the mechanism which you dimly sense as yourself, or at least think that you do, is exteriorly regulated, just as the modern radio plow in the field or the radio motor boat on the water is operated and regulated either by the man in the farm house half a mile away or the other man in the radio tower. And you, just as they do, turn and twist and go and return in this direction and that, subject to wave lengths preceding from a radio tower somewhere. And make no doubt that the atoms, the molecules in you, just as those in the radio plow and motor boat, react sensorially to the forces which make and control them. All are motions of matter-energy and cannot therefore be influenced by human will even in the instance of matter forming a part of the human body. What their sensations of relation with the rest of nature or life are, that of course we do not know as yet. Certain it is that their sensations of unity and individuality and the motions they make are not of their willing any more than are all those of you or your burglar. Literally you are victims, you two, confronting each other in the night; or, if you wish to put it another way, motivated mechanisms which yet do not know why they are motivated mechanisms or why they are where they are. Like cat and dog, flower and germ-pest, bird and hawk, you are so.

Neither of you originally intended to be burglar or rich man, or so to meet. Neither believed, intended, or had any knowledge that some day he would be in the condition and under the circumstances which might compel him so to be. Both were shunted into these respective positions by life or fate. And as non-volitionally you came out of non-understandable circumstances—a past about which you know nothing—so again, after having met thus in this mythical and yet dramatic fashion, you return to it. And the time seems certain to come—the mysterious processes of nature and change and disillusionment being what they are—when here will be no least record in any essence anywhere of either of you, neither as to this joint stage appearance or in any other way. And more, it is not only entirely possible, but plausible that in the endlessly changing welter and play of forces, the society in which you thought you were entities, plus the period of time in which this appearance of you both was made, will merge and be effaced, leaving no trace of all that was so dramatically enacted. Like a letter or a word at one time drawn in water, they will not be. [W]

The Compromise
Called Justice

IN PRACTICE, AND FOR MEN SINCERELY SEEKING *JUSTICE*, THERE
will be little peace on earth except the peace of the soul.

‡   ‡   ‡

We are what we are and can only find happiness in expressing and developing
those potentialities which we happen in this here and now to possess. [*Or*]

‡   ‡   ‡

It is said of justice that it holds a balance in which all things are impartially
weighed, the one against the other. In life this is not by any means always
true. In the universe—as regards its suns and galaxies at least—it would
seem as though the life treatment is impartially accorded all.

‡   ‡   ‡

Green grain will grow as well if not better for the presence as fertilizer
of the tortured and slaughtered bodies of a wronged man or woman or animal
or insect or tree.

"The rain falleth on the just and on the unjust."

[*Or*]

‡   ‡   ‡

You will note that the rich and strong have never wholly triumphed anywhere,
nor have the weak and so poor been obliterated. One is the hand maiden
of the other. Some must be feet, some hands. [*Or*]

‡   ‡   ‡

Many people, for instance, are accustomed to argue thus: "If all things
have followed from the unalterable laws of the universe and the universe
or its laws by which we arrive here are good, how is it that so many imperfections
have arisen in nature—corruption, for instance, of things till they stink;
deformity, exciting pity or disgust; confusion, cruelty, crime, etc."

But the perfection of things in the universe is not to be judged by their
effects, pleasant or unpleasant, on man. Decaying meat is not pleasant to
smell or behold, but as the inevitable chemical result of changes in the equations

273

which make protoplasmic life possible and, more, as the unescapable reaction of one element to another under given matter-energy conditions, it becomes agreeable and even awe-inspiring—the more so since it involves a mystery of action which is not only universal, but entirely beyond the range of the human mind.

Nor are such things—murder, cruelty or beauty—more or less perfect in nature because they delight or offend the human senses or because they are beneficial or prejudicial to human nature. [*Or*]

T.D.

‡ ‡ ‡

Do you really think that anyone on earth deserves constant happiness? On what is that mood based? Evidently the desire to continue sensations that are intensely agreeable. But since these can only be experienced via their contrasts, unhappiness or a median state in which is neither happiness or unhappiness, it is obvious that the desire is an aspect of disproportion or unbalance, and, life being what it is, an unstable equation, it cannot possibly endure.

Besides, unmanageable changes, both physical and mental, insure the passing of a number of phases such as those depending on youth, illusion, strength, etc., and are replaced by those of maturity, middle age, old age, besides all that those last imply—indifference to the earlier anticipations of youth relating to love, means, success, fame, power, etc. For with age comes the sharp recognition of the brevity of all things and the certainty of failing faculties and death. [*Or*]

T.D.

‡ ‡ ‡

In life it is not necessary to be logical or consistent. There are of course, certain fundamental considerations—customs, taboos, laws—that one dare not, without danger to oneself, disregard, and *they are not*, except by the stupid or the hopelessly incompetent. Apart from that, every case can be weighed on its merits, and, as a rule, it is so weighed. [*Or*]

T.D.

[In this or another connection, Dreiser had filed the well-known quotation from Emerson: "A foolish consistency is the hob goblin of small minds." *Editor's Note*]

‡ ‡ ‡

Justice is an opinion. Therefore, it is variable, more or less indefinite, flexible, and ambiguous—according to the person or people expounding "justice." Many people imagine that laws are founded on and designed to promote justice. This is often an erroneous conception. Laws are founded on custom and are mostly born of political expediency—an answer to some pressing question concerning mass necessity, need, self protection, or what have you. In the main, justice is *at best* an incident or by-product of something else—the idiosyncrasies, often enough, of the judge or the secretaries or regional attorneys who are assumed to administer or secure fair play or "justice" to one individual or others who chance, *justly or unjustly,* to be accused of injustice or crime. [*Or*]

‡ ‡ ‡

Ours is an interdependent world. There is no freedom other than that of Newton's 3rd law, which runs "for every action there is an equal and opposite reaction." This does not always appear to be true, as for instance, when a man stabs and kills another man or steals his savings. Life cannot be returned to the dead; the stolen money is not always recovered by the loser. Nonetheless, there is, in the case of the knife blow which brings death to one, a repercussion in the minds or registering sensibilities of many, which brings about often enough revenge—either immediate, as where friends or relatives strike; or legal, where because of the sense of inequity evoked in others, laws are passed to prevent such wrongs, or such laws (the penalties provided by them) are enforced. Or there arise feuds or vendettas; or these failing, investigation, prompted by the deed, reveals that the seeming crime was, in its way, a crude and sometimes ill-balanced, but not wholly unjustifiable, attempt to right a previous wrong, to effect a crude balance or equation between evil and good, mercy and cruelty, and the like. [*Or*]

T.D.

‡ ‡ ‡

But this same law (Newton's third law; "For every action there is an equal and opposite reaction") is at the bottom, the rock bottom, of all our weights and measures. Consider the scale that we use in so many material trade reactions, where goods or materials are measured out by the ounce, the pound, the grain or gram; or, on the other hand, by the inch, foot, yard, mile. In all of these transactions is it not true that there is, if not an equal and opposite reaction, at least or worse, a social expectancy of that same, said social expectancy being based on all the laws or rules of barter and exchange that have governed since the interdependency of men was sensed by the first men compelled by necessity to barter, the one with the other. "With what so measure ye mete it shall be measured unto you again." "Are not two sparrows sold for a farthing. . . ." To be sure, in the affairs of men with their refinements of exchange—that is, handsome buildings to provide, displays to be made, shipments of goods to be arranged for and guarded, wages of agents and servants and salesmen to be calculated, difference in rates of exchanging, and the varying value of the money or gold unit in various lands—the equal and opposite reaction (equivalent) is not easily calculated. Nonetheless, when all risks and labors are calculated and the differing services to differing peoples in all times and lands considered and weighed, their varying instincts and pleasures being as accurately satisfied as possible at the time, it is not impossible to believe that a rough approximation of Newton's third law has been achieved; indeed, that throughout nature in all time, there has been holding, if it is not necessarily true that it will continue to hold, a very close approximation of Newton's third law, the factor called chance to the contrary not withstanding. [*Or*]

T.D.

‡ ‡ ‡

Nature, profoundly ignorant of our sniveling ideas of justice and equality, vastly pampers certain animal species, while showing herself harsh and indifferent to others; now the male is favored, now the female, upon whom the greatest mass of superiority is heaped, and upon whom likewise the cruelties and disdains.——Remy deGourmont, *Natural Philosophy of Love,* p. 36.

Our ideas of justice and equality spring from the personal or unit instinct or desire for self-preservation. To preserve ourselves as against all others even when we are seemingly struggling for justice for another, we declare for equity as against inequity because equity, an exact half, is the least we are willing to take. *More,* gladly, we would take, and do, providing no ill is to follow or we are not restrained. But equity—*50 for me as against 50 for you*—is the least we will take without opposition. [*Or*]

The Salve
Called Religion

[Dreiser uses the word *salve in its original, older usage and pronunciation, like salve in salvage or salvation.* Also used in chapter 25. *Editor's Note*]

RELIGION IS AWE IN THE PRESENCE OF AMAZING AND NOT UNDERSTOOD forces. It is also fear of these forces and a longing for peace and quiet. It is also a sensory response to order and a reaction to beauty, the origin of which it cannot explain but the presence and continuance of which it prizes.

It is a dread of dissolution and a desire for continuance, with the dream and even hope of some method of achieving it. It has allied with itself structures, forms, codes, vestments, and unsubstantiated assertion, all based on the above reactions. And all slowly either vanishing or being transformed into their proper qualities and values or lack of values by the progress of exact and unbiased science. [*Or*]

T.D.

‡ ‡ ‡

If religion is an opiate, so are all Emotions. [*Or*]
[Comment on the Marxist slogan, "Religion is the Opium of the People." *Editor's Note*]

‡ ‡ ‡

They are always looking for the soul of man. Why not instead the soul of life—Nature? [*Or*]

‡ ‡ ‡

For what is a "soul" but life itself—a fragment of God. [*Or*]

‡ ‡ ‡

By observing Life, Lao Tze meant that Life—all the creations of the Creator, all His manifestations—was registering itself upon the senses of all His creations or creatures and that thus, and so, all were learning of their Creator, nature or the universe or Tao, and in no other way. And that in no other way could they learn. So, their minds, their senses, their emotions, their so-called thoughts were nothing more than reflections of the substances and forms, their energies and motions and reactions through which He has chosen or been compelled to express himself. Their minds are limited shadows of the one Greater Mind. Their being, parts of His Being, but by no means the whole of it.

If religion truly reflected this great truth and its followers were capable of grasping it, we would have an end to inordinate individual vanity and the brutal effects of social and financial greed upon the masses of mankind. [*Or*]

‡ ‡ ‡

"The Lord Giveth and the Lord taketh away". . . . However stern the process, would not most be willing to say, "Blessed be the Name of the Lord?" At any rate, few are willing to prematurely end life. They do not truly wish to die. Hence, they must value this life experience accorded to them by Nature. [*Or*]

T.D.

‡ ‡ ‡

It is regrettable that the *Wu Wei* doctrine of Lao Tze's should have been interpreted to the Western World as non-activity or "Do-nothing." That was due, probably, to translators educated in the highly industrialized countries of the West. It seemed to them, maybe, to offer to the eager and often strained and defeated pursuer of fortune and fame a unique and fascinating Utopia, a spiritual couch on which to recline.

But the true, wiser meaning of Lao Tze's *Wu Wei* (Do-nothing) offers no such easy mattress. On the contrary, it is a doctrine of non-striving in the sense of resisting actively and successfully the illusions of mental and spiritual growth or achievement via the amassing of material wealth or earthly distinctions, honors, or powers. These are the things that are to be actively resisted in the sense of one's refusing to succumb to their allure and, instead, in their place, to cultivate moderation, simplicity, self-restraint, and repose. But not to the end of doing nothing for anyone—neither yourself or another. Rather, what it implies is not only the active maintenance of these qualities in oneself and as against all other material and sensual allures, but the vital (that is, spiritual) presentation of these same not by words or argument but by silent forceful example, and, where necessary, aid to those who are to be aided in the most selfless and so helpful way. [*Or*]

‡ ‡ ‡

Clipping:

"We are living in tremendous days," the Bishop said. "We see today in large parts of this world an open return to paganism, and we see with this a deification of the State, a brutality and cruelty, a contempt for the rights of the individual and a racial and religious intolerance and persecution which seem almost incredible.

"The present world situation is showing us that men cannot leave God out of account and retain their faith in the dignity of human personality and the sacredness of human liberty and human life.

Science Seen at its Worst

"We are seeing now that our boasted advance of science and of modern knowledge is worse than futile without corresponding spiritual faith and development. Modern science has given us many blessings, but modern science has given us also the bombing airplane, the murderous submarine and the hideous invention of poison gas.

"There is at this time more sorrow and suffering and fear in this world than there has been for centuries. . . ."

The impressive order and control of the universe must probably be symbolized in some way so that the limited minds of many will in some dim way sense some of its significance and be impressed thereby, so that a portion of its order will hold in their lives and they be saved from the certain disaster that follows the failure to abide by its laws. [*Or*]

T.D.

[This undated clipping out of a newspaper from before the Second World War still applies today, especially as commented upon by Dreiser. *Editor's Note*]

‡ ‡ ‡

When man realizes that he is a planned and created mechanism, the handiwork of his creator; and that in the *plan*—the totality of its structure and movement—is discernably no *intended* evil, at least not to man himself, the extension and instrument of his creator; that there is in the mechanistic process a balance and proportion, which seemingly without imbalance or disorder involves and permits of love and hate, mercy and cruelty, sorrow and joy, good and evil, ugliness and beauty, truth and falsehood, justice and injustice, ends and beginnings, strength and weakness, courage and fear, ignorance and wisdom, frankness and secrecy, plus interest and ennui, one can, without religious or dogmatic delusions, experience awe, reverence, gratitude, and, more, love for so wondrous a process or spirit, whichever one chooses to emphasize. [*Or*]

‡ ‡ ‡

It follows that man as well as all phases of nature are materializations of energy, and hence of that from which energy takes its rise. Furthermore, such being the case, he can only know either what he is permitted to know or that which energy chooses or is self-compelled by its own laws to express in, by, and through him and all the other forms in and through which it materializes itself.

Therefore, materially and energetically in so far as nature is concerned, there is a God, and all the forms of nature are his or its ways and forms. And its evils and its goods or contrasts are possibly necessary for this phase of its expression. Whether there can be other phases, man, as an infinitesimal part of it, cannot know. Nor can he know God. [*Or*]

                                                                                    T.D.

Problem of Knowledge

Sometimes I think that when people are thinking or talking about Christ or God or Allah or the Divine Spirit today, they are "thinking" of or, better yet, reaching to the great Creative Force that the scientists—their physicists, chemists, biologists, astronomers, geologists, and what not—refer to so cautiously as Matter-Energy, or the Universe. For at least many of the things that the New Testament, as well as the Old, calls for or (feels) close at hand (such as the power to) "Heal the sick"—Well, is not the modern scientific world seeking so to do? For pay you say? Pasteur, who found the cure for rabies, never worked for money. Neither did Roentgen, who discovered x-rays. Neither did [Jenner] who found the cure for small-pox nor [Chagas] who sought the cure for sleeping sickness (the bite of the Tsetze fly). Nor yet Copernicus who sought to reveal the wonders of the heavens; nor Newton who noted the apples fall and announced the law of gravitation. Nor Rutherford who changed matter into energy; nor Harvey who discovered the circulation of the blood; nor Einstein who formulated the law of relativity. Signs and wonders? What else are these? And what miracles have they not performed and what miracles will they not yet perform. And if they are not thinking of these things when they are thinking of or talking about God or Christ or the Divine Spirit or what not, they ought to. For these things are not of men. They are merely revelations of Creative Energy *through* man, no more and no less. [*Or*]

                                                                                    T.D.

                                    ‡   ‡   ‡

It is silly to pretend that man has no reasons for feeling grateful to the forces of nature that brought him into being and that have preserved him and his fellows, the animals and birds and insects and trees and flowers, over so great a period, even though throughout the entire period of his days he has been assailed by many ills—war, pestilence, hunger, deprivation, and the fears and hatreds to which these have given rise. See all the rhapsodies in the Bible. The songs of the poets: the stories of adventure, the pleasures of love, the delights in books, plays, pictures which present life—its ills as well as its delights—the pleasure men take in eating after hunger, resting after weariness, being made well after being sick, meeting with their fellows in amiable contest or thrilling even over war and in war.

In fact, man has ample reason for feeling that he is looked after by nature as a whole, even though he quarrels and contests with his fellows, for, he can see that his quarrels and contests with his fellows are over what nature provides and how they are to be divided among them, not that nature in the large cruelly denies him a reasonable method of subsistence. He can see for himself that he can throw waste on the ground, and the elements or chemicals of nature will dispose of them so that they shall do him no harm. Fire will cook his food and warm his hut. The sun will rise and make a bright day, and the rain will fall and nourish his crop. His cattle, trees, bushes, plants, and grains will grow and yield him food, clothing, shelter. He has a stomach, and hunger which he did not make, and the food nature grows will satisfy it. He has eyes to see and ears to hear and many sights and sounds of the world, most indeed are agreeable to him. Nature, not himself, has taught him to sing and dance and admire. He works and grows weary, but sleep restores him. He has a sexual mate and can have children. There are roads or paths, the rivers, lakes, stars, the sky, and the mountains, and their valleys, and he can wander forth into strangeness and take comfort in beholding that which is new and strange—things which [he has not made nor grown], but to which he can respond. In fact, the burden or cares of life rest not wholly on anyone. They are divided among the races of men—the animals, birds, fishes, trees, flowers—and these over the endless generations who breed and labor and bequeath their labors and holdings to others, and life has given him, or sought to, a span of years and the instinct to prolong his days. And usually his sorrow or complaint is not that life is not good, but he is not given all that he wants of it—endless years and these without satiety or hunger or sorrow. [*Or*]

‡   ‡   ‡

In all times and in all places, religion must be entirely freed of ulterior and extraneous aims. It should not pile up wealth. Its ministers and priests should by no means live luxuriously. There is no need of dogma or special revelation nor any schools or colleges or orders to interpret the same. Vast costly temples for worship—costly to build and more costly to maintain—are not needed, particularly where their maintenance evokes financial strain on the worshipers.

Above all things, religion should be completely divorced from government—the economic and social duties of the state. It should not undertake education or reformation in the legal or punitive sense in any form. Nor should it practice medicine or hospitalization, nor the relief of poverty in any form. Those are the proper functions and duties of any well conducted state because, for their proper fulfillment, they require the educated and intelligent and sympathetic understanding and cooperation of all of the people.

If anything, religion should seek to inspire such intelligent cooperation—not to replace it by seeking itself to be the state, its executive arm as well as its social conscience. In other words, it must be pure, not defiled with those human ambitions that involve the necessity for power and the right to execute the practical social duties of life. At its farthest reach, it should do no more than to interpret those laws of nature, its quite mystic weights and measures, which, accurately interpreted, lead to balance and proportion in life and so to a measure of peace and happiness for all. [*Or*]

T.D.

‡   ‡   ‡

The religionists of different periods of the past have apparently either looked forward to the appearance in their midst of a Messiah or Savior (or redeemer of a given people, the Messiah of the Jews); or have conceived of a God or creator as present at the time (Christ, the Great Spirit); or as having lived in the past (Brahma, Buddha, Vishna, Osiris, Jove, Wotan, Thor); or as immanent, that is, indwelling or inherent or intrinsic or incarnated as God in nature—"His works." "God is all in all."

But this last is not at all remote from the present scientific attitude toward nature; i.e., the Universe (matter-energy in space-time), its laws and *evolutionary processes*, where these are at all distinguishable in the galaxies of space, as well as (and somewhat more particularly) suggesting a creative process (intelligent in so far as man is capable of defining intelligence) existing in and directing the evolutionary process as this same is known to man here on earth (Ontogeny, Ontogenesis).

For, of course, as this particular volume is designed to show, man is an evolved (a very leisurely evolved) mechanism, mayhap even an invention, but a very leisurely invention, that has, over an immense period of time, been gradually improved if never perfected. [Consider] Thoreau's tree that was finally enabled to grow by being protected by a ring of bushes. [*Or*]

‡   ‡   ‡

Where is God? Why you're in Him. He is not only in and around you but you—what you call you—are a physical and chemical expression of himself, just as is a whale, a star, a planet, a disease germ, an ant, an emotion, a lust, a fever. And what would you be and where if it were not for his endlessly varied totality expressing itself in such endless variety as to cause you to feel that you are individual and different, as he most certainly is.

But how different?

Something withdrawn and separate and special? A creature apart and looking on you as a creature apart—something different and less and so unimportant as to make it a matter of indifference whether you live or die, are happy or unhappy, old or young, strong or weak, rich or poor, cruel or generous, beautiful or ugly, lonely or bathed in affection or showered with attention. The endless variety of himself, his disguises, has confused and deluded your particular extension of himself into thinking that he is not in you and you are not in him, part and parcel, atom by atom, electron by electron, an integral part of his totality. But you are: Examine all of the knowledge of the world and seek to discover that you are not. It will only demonstrate to you that you are. [*Or*]

Religion

The nature of God, or the Creative force that appears to operate directly through matter-energy as well as the laws and spatial conditions environing the same, is, in fact, the only reality—universal creative reality—the rest being no more than modes, and these same possibly very limited ones of its immense powers and possibilities of self expression.

As for man and the perfection of his so-called thought, which he thinks *he* achieves here, it is in reality nothing more than his chemical and at the same time mechanical reaction to exterior stimuli—stimuli from form, light, color, sound, heat, cold, movement, and what not else. Indeed these furnish proof positive that his so-called thinking is nothing more than his very finite reaction to these infinite stimuli, arriving seemingly from immaterial space in endless variety.

In sum, that infinite stimulus, together with its evolved mechanisms which we call men, insects, trees, flowers, birds, animals, vegetables, fishes, worms, germs, etc., are nothing if not its devised or evolved instruments and intended by the same Creative Force—immaterial (as compared to the devised clay or energy with and through which it works)—to cause each and every one to desire and enjoy as well as suffer an endless variety of illusions (no two alike) of an unreal yet seemingly real reality, which in all instances is dissipated by death.

"For to admire and for to see"—For there is just enough of its real self or substance in all of its products to cause each and everyone to grow into and experience this illusion for a period, in many cases of scarcely more than momentary duration, in others for relatively longer periods—seventy to one hundred years, rarely more. In fact all may have been intended as a game, may even be a passing dream of the ultimate substance itself. [*Or*]

T.D.

The Hidden God

If only there were some kind God whose sanctuary were in a Church or many Churches or in the pure sweet places of the hills or the mountains! Yet only in the troubled heart of man is this dream of Him.

Contemplating wild nature, as we must, the dream is groundless. There is none who in our extremity cries, "Come unto me ye who are weary laden." Nature, machine-like, works definitely and heartlessly, if in the main beautifully. Hence, if we, as individuals, do not make this dream of a God, or what He stands for to us, real in our thoughts and deeds, then He is not real or true. If you wish a loving and helpful God to exist and to have mercy, *be* Him. There is no other way. [*Or*]

THEODORE DREISER

[Late manuscript. *Editor's Note*]

His Face

One dare not say that he will not show his face. He will show as much of himself to all these expressions of himself as he has been able to make it possible for them as limitations of himself to comprehend, with not so much pleasure in the dull dragging sense of a mild, scarcely changing reaction to a limited fraction or degree of himself, as with an increasing and intense and changing registration by which they taste of his immense infinity and wild variety—registrations wherewith and by reason of which they go wild with imaginings, enthusiasms, passions sensational and destructive—lusts, fevers, dreams—all that the steadily developing organism will bear. His Face! It is fever. His strength and emotions—They are death to us—Death *into a life* (ours) that is past all our understanding—and the limits of which He Himself has fixed. [*Or*]

                                                                        T.D.

[Late manuscript. *Editor's Note*]

‡   ‡   ‡

The push toward (by some it is described as the striving for) rational conceptions or comprehensions of anything and everything on the part of man is thought to be one of his noblest attributes. If anything, it is a noble attribute of the forces that bring him into being and maintain him here. What else has, what else could, evoke such *striving*?

Ants, bees, animals, insects, plants, germs, even protoplasm plainly strive toward "rational" procedure—that is, such procedure as will keep them alive, warm, housed, reproduced, defended against enemies, etc.—though (by man, who has no more rational procedure than they have) they are not granted *reason*. However, in his age-long quest, or at least by the struggle of the forces that make and keep him here, he has been able to secure what he has, call it freedom, comfort, satisfaction, beauty, peace, strength, etc., only through better technical mastery of his environment.

But what gave him the environment to master? And what built him up out of the protoplasm to be what he is and to do what he does? Himself? Tosh! Boloney.

You are back to the creative forces alone, which long ago in nature evoked wonder, awe, curiosity, fear and which man thought of as Gods or devils or, at long last, a God, even a loving God. And to man the creative forces are as a God—certainly functioning in the place of one. And as loving as any reasonable affectionate Creative force or forces could be expected to be. For they have implanted in him or built into him, as you will, all of the emotions, desires, strivings, satisfactions, thrills, loves, hates, fears that he is capable of. And while no particular individual is as yet safe, even though the race as a whole may be thought to be fairly safe, still a great majority of them endure quite comfortably for a time. And they love life—which is to say, they love the outward face or *show* of the forces that bring them here. So that though many or all do suffer much or little, rage at times, cry and die or slay themselves, still it is never because they want less of this *show*, of which they are a part and so often curse, but more. They love it. They rage at being given so small a share of its comforts, pleasures, delights. So that sanely and truly they can be said to love this thing that is as God to them. And so to love God. If this is not so, what else is it or can it be?

And yet they cannot comprehend Him, or those Creative forces. And for the very good reason that these forces have not as yet built man or anything to that point where he or it can register them in their totality. They are as yet little more than evolving structures. And may always remain so—changing, changing, changing, both the Creative forces and this which they create. For without this process, where would either be? And such being the case, we may ask: Is it necessary, worth-while—when the scene is as it is, or seems, so moving and beautiful to the mechanisms constructed to respond to such particular scenes or environments as each so satisfactorily respond to—is it necessary that an ant should evolve to a greater, all comprehending ant? Or a fly? Possibly. But not necessarily. For, may it not be that it is all no more than a revolving process of change for the creative forces and the things created, so that the created may ever respond or react to and even, betimes, behold some phases of the Creative or, if you like, its Creator. And the *Creative* or *Creator* in their or its or His turn, if you like, behold the things which they, it, or He have created—forever and ever.

Why not? Why more? What more? [*Or*]

THEODORE DREISER

The Problem
of Progress
and Purpose

SOCIETY NEVER ADVANCES. IT RECEDES AS FAST ON ONE SIDE as it gains on the other. Its progress is only apparent, like the workers of a treadmill. It undergoes continual changes: it is barbarous, it is civilized, it is christianized, it is rich, it is scientific; but this change is not all amelioration. For every thing that is given, something is taken. Society acquires new arts and loses old instincts.

What a contrast between the well-clad, reading, writing, thinking American, with a watch, a pencil, and a bill of exchange in his pocket, and the naked New Zealander, whose poverty is a club, a spear, a mat, and an undivided twentieth of a shed to sleep under! But compare the health of the two men, and you shall see that the white man has lost his aboriginal strength. If the travelers tell us truly, strike the savage with a broad axe, and in a day or two the flesh shall unite and heal as if you struck the blow into soft pitch; the same blow would send the white man to his grave.

‡ ‡ ‡

How does one reconcile the problem of progress with the fact that the search for knowledge is mainly a kind of war on other forms of nature? Vivisection, for instance (murder)? Also a form of prying or detecting where prying and detecting happen not to be wanted.

Take the first name of the machine called the cyclotron, which was originally called the atom smasher. Atoms have to be smashed in order to reveal their secrets, in order ultimately to advantage man. But if his progress or development were actually intended, why the necessity for contest, murder, endless bickering in order that he might succeed at the expense of something else?

T.D.

‡ ‡ ‡

Life, the instincts and necessities it has evolved in and which it expresses, if not always satisfies, through you, is the author of purpose, if there is any, and progress also. And you, and almost every other person in life, will agree that life without a purpose is meaningless. You must have a purpose or, who or what are you?

Life—Nature, matter-energy, space-time—has provided you with a number of aims and without any let or hindrance from you. One purpose you have from the beginning is to get something to eat; and another, something to wear, at least to keep warm with, if you do not live on the equator. And a third purpose or desire which springs from interdependence and swiftly transmits itself·into what on earth is known as a purpose, possibly provided by heredity and if not by heredity then by your sensory reactions to actions or conduct of others, *is to do as others do*, live as they live, dress as they dress, go where they go, be what they happen to be—doctors, lawyers, generals, bankers, presidents or vice-presidents of this or that, writers, painters, poets, ministers, millionaires, scientists, and what not—and anyone of these in turn becomes an end. And if you achieve it, presumably you can die content.

More, there is a general feeling abroad among those who have such an end in view (that is, a purpose) that one who achieves any such end, if even only approximately, should be pleased to die so well-placed, seeing that so many others are finding it, their purpose or end or very often just the matter of existence, so very difficult.

But see how this works out. Your non self-evoked, non self-created purpose or desire, a thing not originated by you but forced upon you by life, proves very often (not always) a delusion, sometimes a trap, which does for you completely. [*Or*]

T.D.

‡ ‡ ‡

In emphasizing the *progress* of man—not that of the insects, fishes, birds, animals and all floral life that has preceded man—the fact is always emphasized that life has slowly evolved, during several billion years of time, from protoplasm (or the chemo-physical elements which preceded protoplasm, to which, later, moisture had to be added in order that protoplasm might be) and that later, at some point, a few hundred thousand years ago, man in his ape or other *barbaric* forms might appear. Also, that when he did appear, he was densely ignorant of all about him—clumsy, fumbling, brutal, savage—that somehow nature via environment was slowly but surely permitting if not guiding his evolution or progress to a still greater and—us. However, we further read that left-over prehistoric tribes in New Guinea, which consist of not more than a dozen or two people to a tribe, do at this day miserably trek here and there from one part of the primeval forests of that area to another, living in constant danger and fear of slow starvation or sudden death, as helpless and hopeless a group of "men" and "women" as one can (today) imagine.

And, more, that they are totally ignorant of the immense resources of nature about them and in space—no least inkling, at this day and date, of all the vegetable and animal wealth of other lands; no knowledge of the coal, the iron, the free heat of volcanoes, the electricity and light, and gas and steam that we know of today. In sum, they are, as they were a hundred thousand years ago, excellent examples of the slow evolutionary process that, nonetheless, has served to evolve man.

But with all we know today of the miraculous and seemingly eternal wisdom of nature, which before ever these slowly evolving and much too tortured forms of earth had begun creative life or nature had previously brought into being the endless universe that was to be about them, also that even in the construction of protoplasm, to say nothing of the endless forms to which protoplasm, via its prearranged environment was to give rise, it—nature, the creative process—had manifested nothing less than miraculous genius: all power and all wisdom in preparing a universe in which an evolutionary process could later come about. But, if so, why should these later creatures of its strange devising have been (and for what reason, if reason there be in nature), still be, subjected to this slow and obviously torturous process of evolution and of living. Is not that passing strange?

To be sure, the religionist has said God moves in mysterious ways his wonders to perform. The philosophers stare and offer no better thought than that it (this process) may involve some divine, far-off event that will somehow justify all this—the endless suffering, murder, and cruelty of the past. But will it? Can it?

Why life preying on life? Why hunger, cold, starvation, death? Why the endless sweat under weary loads? The endlessly terrifying shapes of prey lurking each about the other to devour and destroy? For plain it is to the biology and physics and chemistry today, to the microscopy and surgery, electro-chemistry and electro-physics, and all the "advanced sciences" that even now we are but dimly permitted to comprehend that their immense constructive resources were in full force in the world at the time protoplasm came to be and even since. In fact, they themselves, as they swam or crawled or slunk about the world of this Genius-Nature's devising, were in themselves marvelous chemo-physical illustrations of its miraculous skill in the matter of chemo-physical construction and action. In sum, by sheer genius, they were devised so to act—to pursue and be pursued, to slay and be slain, to suffer cold, hunger, heat, drouth, thirst, misery, fear, death, plus the reproductive urge, which, if anything, might be looked upon as the reason for their being. But in themselves, no immediate remedial wisdom, nothing to save them from any of their desires, fears, pains, and death—nothing. Theirs but to do and die, giving place to others to do the same.

But the answer is always made that there has been progress; that men, animals, insects, birds, fish, vegetation of all types have evolved, improved, enjoyed themselves. And that might be looked upon as a sound argument, providing the short-lived individuals of any species at any single moment of their or the species career or duration had known anything about this evolutionary or progress idea. But they did not—nothing of their evolutionary past or future. They came, suffered, struggled, reproduced, died—and this in endless procession over a billion or two years! So that truly the best that anyone today could say for it (those of sufficient information and wisdom to comprehend the thing as a whole) would or might be that it suggests nothing of greater import than a game that might possibly be entertainingly and enjoyably indulged in by organisms constructed of fairly indestructible atoms, electrons, protons in molecular association and combination. But by what else? The Creator of the Energy that is expressed by these forms? Or by the energy or essential something that is behind this energy and out of which it takes its rise? If so, we have the thought, or pleasure, or shall we say passing entertainment not only in the construction of but also the subsequent activities of these mechanisms of which it is the inventor and subsequent sponsor. And if so, what are we to think of that force? The mechanistic answer to that would be: we are to think what it chemically and physically constructs us to think, no more and no less.

But of what import is that?

‡ ‡ ‡

If you recoil from this conception of man as a machine, let science convince you that you are not degraded and that perhaps the race may achieve a far higher destiny, because all that we sum up in emotion, consciousness, love, and nobility will ultimately be explained in terms of mechanism, chemical reactions, electrical effects, and other responses to the *external* world. Pavlov for one said:

I am deeply and irrevocably convinced that along this path will be found the final triumph of the human mind over its uttermost and supreme problem [The universe will explain itself to and through its mechanism—T.D.]—the knowledge of the mechanism and laws of human nature. Only thus may come a full, true, and permanent happiness. [*Or*]

‡ ‡ ‡

In connection with the progress and purpose of man as one of the many species of nature, neither science nor philosophy are completely agreed, and never have been, that man is progressing and that he is destined to some superior state or fate which no other creature can anticipate. Nevertheless, man's personal hope has been that some such superior destiny awaits him, not only here on earth as a species, but, if one accepts the religious dogmas of the modern as well as the ancient world, that he has a soul, and according to its faith, rather than its social and humanitarian efforts here, it is destined to a glorious and everlasting future. Moreover, today, dismissing religion as a factor in the argument, a considerable fraction of scientific thought favors the idea that man is progressing at a rate entirely apart from any other creature in nature and that such changes as we see, social and scientific, foretell, if not determine, an advance that no other creature can hope to share. In other words, we are going somewhere, and that somewhere is to out-run all our wildest fancies as to the good, the true, and the beautiful as these are connected with ourselves. And in substantiation of this, any reporter of the world's progress can cite volumes of startling discoveries in connection with the process or the "how" of life and, with general applause, can offer these as proof of the approaching accomplishment of an ideal, though just [what] form that is ultimately is not quite clear. A man like Arthur Compton, the co-discoverer of cosmic rays, asserts that it is fair to assume that God or nature is not only working through but with man to achieve man's superiority. Millikan also is convinced that there is cosmic law and purpose and that the prime direction of these can be seen in the achievements and evolution of man. Eddington, Keith, and Julian Huxley also are partial to this view.

To many, however, the substantiality of this argument is not evident, for although we can see, insofar as the scheme of things on earth is concerned, that man appears to have achieved an outstanding creative success, for a part of his number, this success is measured by himself, and according to his past experiences in sufferings and defeats, and what he can find out about his earlier history since he parted company with the ape. Since he grants no such powers of concentration and interpretation to any other creature, it is obvious that his word and his word alone must be accepted as his authority. No other creature, he asserts, speaks, writes, sings, or invents, or "thinks" to the same degree that he does, nor has any the data that he has now assembled for both thought and invention. In connection with animals, data supporting this view from the human side is considerable and cannot by any process of logic be ignored. However, there are other factors in connection with the name progress which have to be taken into consideration, and they are very troublesome.

In the first place, man knows nothing of the existence of any other system of creatures outside of the earth. He has no evidence of the existence of any other solar system just like this, and there is considerable evidence—ample as a matter of fact—demonstrating that no such condition as permits the existence of man here now operates on any other planet in our system, and he has no warrant for assuming that there ever has been. As a matter of fact, light and heat and energy and time seem to vary so greatly in space that no assumption as to the possibility of the existence of a protoplasmic base such as that that has produced man and life here on earth could be more than possible. At the same time, there is no reason for assuming that no other form of life outside of the protoplasmic type dominant here exists just because the protoplasmic type is the only one we know. It would have to be granted and is by some that elements might be combined somewhere else in space in such a way as to produce beings of some type and a kind of life—sensory, perhaps, as is ours, beings reacting, remembering, associating, etc. And it might even be possible that the erection or appearance of these forms might take place without evolution, since they might spring almost instantaneously from a chance conjunction of chemicals in a given medium.

For instance, consider the growths that Le Duc produced by combining chemicals in colloidal solutions, growths that grew and behaved in very much the same manner as do our plants, birds, fish, flowers, and shells.

Dismissing the possibility of differences of opinion as to the possibility of a universal supremacy, for man in nature or God's working with and through him here on earth to effect his evolutionary triumph, what seems to have been entirely overlooked is this—that the evolutionary process, which has resulted in him for one thing, is something which has not yet been proved to have contemplated what is now here or the enduring triumph of any species whatsoever. Furthermore, it cannot logically be shown that the evolutionary process, excluding man's presence entirely, would not have and did not have various values which did not and do not now depend on man's presence. For, in different calculated periods of time, endless creatures and endless creations—such as the atom, and the molecule, and protoplasm, and all of the forms accounted for and not accounted for, but to which these have given rise—did arise and did, possibly, constitute as valuable a phase or phases of life as that which has existed since man evolved. In other words, it is possible to conceive of an evolutionary process here on earth without any men that would be as enjoyable to the basic elements involved in their creation and being as it would be or is with man included. Protoplasm itself, in its humblest form, that of the amoeba, presents as vital and intellectual and aesthetic a process as anything that has since been achieved by the so-called progress of protoplasm. For protoplasm as such achieved with its arrival motion as well as those appearing and disappearing structures within itself, its phantom walls and channels, and those forms of matter described as sticks or threads that within the plasm instantly organize, and dissolve, and reorganize with a speed and a mystery which offer to the so-called evolved mind of man something so startling that it cannot grasp the "how" let alone the why of it, nor whether it is pleasurable or the reverse, or "thought" or what, and this in the lowest of the evolutionary forms. But if today this process staggers and thrills the evolved observer, who is to say to the elements involved in the amoeba itself that the amoeba is not as advanced and as self-conscious and as self-comforting an achievement as any that has occurred since? Furthermore, this can be said of protoplasm that cannot be said of man—that it is the basic implement in the construction of an inconceivable variety of structures past and to come, seemingly an instrument for the erection of the same, structures no one of which, nor even the like of one of which, man as a so-called independent mechanism has been able to create or even to share, in any least way, in the creation of the same or to understand the ultimate meaning or purpose of the same. Furthermore, man's significance as an evolved organism depends not on himself as a lone organism which has evolved, but on himself as a part of a vast evolutionary system consisting of endless organisms, in contrast with which and by reason of which contrast alone, he achieves his significance as an individual organism. Sweep all but himself away leaving him with his evolved efficiencies, and what would his world be like? Where would life be? And without life, where would he be? Take away its birds, its fishes, its animals, its trees, its flowers, the planet, and the solar system itself, and what significance could man have, and with whom?

However, waiving all this, let us assume that he progresses to what or where, ultimately we need not at this moment consider. For the time being, it is enough to note that as he progresses he changes. We have evolution to indicate what he has been like in the past, and already there are extant descriptions of what he is to be like in distant periods to come. His head is to be larger and his hands smaller and different phases of him are to be eliminated or added to, so that the creature we know as man need not ultimately be any part of the finished man product of the future any more than the lemur is an arresting part of the man family now. To be sure, the structure and faculties of both are remotely connected, but no more. Not only that, but the forms and processes by which he now lives and with which he now dies, his own inventions and the creations of nature, are not guaranteed as enduring along with him. As a matter of fact, it is definitely assumed that they will not last. His present devices, like the primitive forms that preceded them, will have gone, and neither he nor his new inventions or creations can be predicted. Consider the machineless age of three hundred years ago and the machine age of today.

It is obvious that man is capable of destroying some existing forms of creatures. He has already done so. It may be that he could be instrumental in preventing the appearance of some others. But since he is constantly changing and the earth and the evolutionary process also [and in ways beyond our comprehension], just what his powers will be in a position to concern themselves with is nothing that can be predicted. Lastly, the appearance and disappearance of endless forms of varying sizes according to the temperature and the moisture of any given period offer no assurance of man's endurance. We know of ice ages and, roughly, of what they effected in the way of reductions of forms and numbers. Curiously, nothing is ever said of heat ages, but since there were ice ages may there not have been heat ages? And what about the forms that might have existed before their arrival and might not have existed after their departure? One cannot deny the possibility. And if such did occur or can occur, is it not obvious that all present forms of the evolutionary processes might cease and that the process might have to begin anew?

The Myth of
a Perfect
Social Order

THE PROSPECT OF A PERFECT SOCIAL ORDER IS A MYTH. THERE will be a social order; it will be constantly changing and probably constantly interesting, even increasingly interesting, but it will not be perfect, because I look on life as a progressive game that is being played for some purpose, probably for self-entertainment.

To make the entertainment continuous means that it must change, but regardless of the change, the rules of the game cannot be abandoned, and there is no evidence in physics or chemistry or the controlling dynamics that the rules are changing.

Incidentally, I hold that there is no evidence to show that this game, as played here, is planned to solve anything. For all we know, such a play process may be in progress under different chemic and dynamic disguises on all of the endless planets and suns. [*Or*]

DREISER

‡ ‡ ‡

"Men must either be governed by God, or they will be ruled by tyrants."——William Penn

What should be pointed out is that men are automatically operated by nature; that a balance is automatically struck between good and evil; that the creative force pours creatures of contrasting sensitivities and reactions into life; and that good is oftentimes met with evil, but that evil is as frequently met with restraining good, to the degree that a wave-like procedure of order/disorder is effected. But only as much disorder as will emphasize the value of order and promote progress or at least change, interesting and so gratifying change.

In fact, this wave-like procedure or order/disorder/order is likely to show that while the periods of disorder are much more intense than those of order, they are shorter; and those of order are longer in duration and more comforting and constructive. [*Or*]

‡ ‡ ‡

Do we get a higher standard of character—morality, intelligence, wisdom—in the rulers of states than in the people of states? [*Or*]

‡   ‡   ‡

It is clear to me that if the masses cannot "think" for themselves, as is so often asserted, meaning "think" in the sense of *thinking correctly*, they can and certainly do *feel* for themselves—and feel most often much more correctly than their alleged leaders would have them, correctly enough in many instances to turn and dismiss or destroy them.

Another word for feeling is emotion—that is, heightened feeling. *And do you not often witness an emotion that does not convince you of its correctness?* But is that not mind or the response of mind to something? If it is not mind responding, what is it?

Consider an emotion evoked by a Statue of the Virgin Mary, or a crucified Jesus. [*Or*]

The Perfect State

The perfect state will never be static. It is something that will always be an organism that is active, in the top heat of creating something, and, what is more, by reason of that heat of creation, anticipating a delight which is then and there present, but which is added to by the illusion that that delight is to be postponed until the creative process is finished, which it is not. The perfect state always *is*. It is never *to be* save in the imagining of it as something afar off and that is yet to be accomplished, reached. [*Or*]

T.D.

‡   ‡   ‡

And there is still the task of getting human beings concerned with government, with matters which affect the social body as a whole, and that of course is the essential problem. There are human inertia and human selfishness and egocentrism to contend with. There is a natural, and at times very disturbing, heritage of individualism in all spheres of thought and action, in every day attitudes, to overcome. Again, the implanting of a deeper social sense in the young, if that is possible, will be necessary if there is to be any emergence into life and action of people who are not wholly "rugged individualists," which is another description of the heartless isolationist, his indifferentism. But that means organic instead of compartmental education—a deeper emphasis on the fact that each creature is a member of a social organism, that man does not live to himself alone and never has, that to a degree, whether [he] responds to the fact sufficiently or not, he is his brother's keeper. [*Or*]

‡   ‡   ‡

Marx thought that the economic and the psychologic problem of man cannot be attacked at one time; that the psychologic problem could wait; that, so to speak, two different revolutions are necessary, and the economic-social revolution has to precede what Moreno has called the psychological or creative revolution of human society. [*Or*]

‡   ‡   ‡

Clipping:

In the Soviet Union, all factories, all mines, railways and shipping, land and trading organizations are the property of the people as a whole. The economic and social life of the country is planned in the public interest.

The family is greater than the state, babies are more important than battleships, devotion and lowliness sink deeper into the soul than political fortunes or economic strife, and in the end our happiness lies not in wealth or place or power, but in the gift and return of love. [Or]

The Herd

There is a peculiar, glowing satisfaction to most people in being in the presence of thousands of other human beings. In union there is strength. The average man is fearful of solitude—an evolutionary heritage. He likes to rub elbows. To be in contact or in the presence of others, he will subject his body to a lot of unpleasant jostling, his eyes and nose to clouds of dust, the fenders of his car to many a bump and dent. [Or]

Equity

"Everyone can certainly have an equitable share of what is necessary to them providing everyone helps every other."——The Daily Worker

Is this true? What are the real wants of each? And what are the "equitable" wants—those that society at large will be willing to provide. Would society provide Oscar Wilde with boys; a varietist with many girls or boys according to her or his sex? Would Rockefeller have had his great desire, wealth; and individualists like Stalin or Napoleon or Caesar, power? Could an artist satisfy his real taste? An architect? An engineer? A philosopher? Could beauty have all the men she would attract, would not the homely one have to be content without any?

T.D.

‡ ‡ ‡

There is a cycle in government by foxes and government by lions. The foxes hold their power by skill in chicanery; they thrive in ages of commercial speculation and intellectual skepticism. The lions must eventually overthrow them, ruling by force and energized by faith or illusion, until in time that government in turn is itself undermined by a slow infiltration of new foxes.

‡ ‡ ‡

No class of society will willfully commit suicide for the sake of another. It may bring about its own death by greeds, illusions, inhibitions, as well as the death of others, but never willfully. It could not even collectively will to do so, for where there is not free will for the individual, there is certainly none for the mass. As birds, fish, herd animals, etc., act collectively and from outside pressure, as well as fears externally provoked, so do classes and masses. [Or]

‡ ‡ ‡

Is there an antipathy to regular, sustained labor which is deeply rooted in human nature? Or is it merely to undue labor or strain? How explain the idler, the loafer, the dreamer who does nothing at all, accomplishes nothing?

Apart from self-sustenance and reproduction, what do animals and insects accomplish—herds of wild horses, millions of wild fowl? [*Or*]

T.D.

‡ ‡ ‡

Every culture is based on compulsory labor and instinctual renunciation. It is, therefore, inevitably evoking opposition from those affected by these demands. The means of acquiring culture and the culture itself, once it has been acquired, have both to be defended against the rebellious and destructive passions of the members or sharers of culture.

So, in addition to the difficulties attending the acquiring the means of a culture, there is added the necessity for defending it. There must be introduced persuasive as well as coercive measures, not only intended to reconcile but to compel them to assist in maintaining a cultural order. I say *must* be introduced, but what I mean is that apart from the will of man and conditionally and hence compulsorily, they are introduced.

That is, a culture does not arrive by the thought or will of anyone, man or group of men. It is evolved, through men—by forces which they did not create and which direct them through their appetites, their desires, their ambitions, and their fears which they do not create. In short, culture is the residue of a struggle for existence on the part of many—the many who have become the many by reason, by appetites, and compulsions over which they have no control. [*W*]

T.D.

Rich Man's Sons and Daughters

Because of the peculiar feeding activity of the caterpillar or worm-like grub that is the second stage in the life of the butterfly, its third, when it appears so gloriously arrayed to flutter about for a few weeks in the sun and reproduce its kind, is really comparable to that of the rich man's son or daughter—the rich man who idolizes his children and seeks only to make them happy.

For the caterpillar does all the feeding both for itself and for the butterfly that later it is to be, leaving the latter free to devote itself to love—the conception of the race and the perpetuation of the same in the sunlight or moonlight of the glorious harvest season of the year. Work they have to do, of course, the female in particular, for her duty is to produce eggs and, more, to scatter them far and wide on the proper food plants, so as to insure the largest possible crop of butterflies. All her efforts, all her emotions—and they are many and diverse—have to do with the proper performance of this duty.

But one thing neither she nor he need do and that is to struggle for food. The caterpillar has done the feeding for both, and that, perhaps, is why we think of them as dainty ornaments of the woods and fields and gardens, flitting here and there and sipping nectar from the flowers. But feeding, as the student of the genera knows, is in most cases more of a diversion, and many do not feed at all, at least do not feed on flowers. The male seeks his mate and fights his rivals. The female, once mated, proceeds to look after the future of her young before she dies.

‡ ‡ ‡

Among other things, man is crucially involved with the problem of evolved races and nationalities now on earth—their present reactions to life and to each other. At present, due to many advances in travel and exchange, as well as knowledge and exchanges of various kinds, there is the often expressed thought of an international, and better still, if it is better, world brotherhood where all quarrels over all differences of every kind are to be reconciled, harmonized, freed from contention.

But all men, as well as animals, do not see eye to eye, are creatures of evolved differences, predilections, inequalities due to past struggles for self-maintenance. Yet, if a perfect state or social organization is to be achieved and maintained, a larger measure of tolerance than has yet appeared in the world will have to appear or be developed.

For instance, the Negro's particular temperament and life desires (unless there is to be but one kind of individual on earth) will have to be socially harmonized as is with that of the white man; that of the Jew with that of the gentile; that of the inhabitant of the Arctic to that of the citizen of the tropics.

Also, unless friction is to arise, science must be reconciled with religion, i.e., the quarreling sects of the uninformed with the intelligent communicants and subscribers to the wisdom of evolved ethics. Also wealth with poverty, ignorance with wisdom, strength with weakness, etc.

But these, as I have said, are as yet evolved conditions and situations which may not be thus wholly reconciled without removing from life the contrast, interest, color, zest, together with a large number of employments, duties, pleasures, activities, and the like which depend on these various contrasts for their existence and meaning. For in life, as we know it now, ignorance is opposed to knowledge, and without ignorance, knowledge, its spread and usefulness, could have no meaning. Wealth cannot mean anything without poverty to contrast it with. One would not know what wealth was unless one knew of the lack of it; similar with strength as opposed to weakness; order as to disorder.

If you advance from one condition to another, just as from one position to another, you have to have present or in mind the knowledge of the new condition to which you have advanced. In other words, no low, no high; no rear, no front; no back, no forward; no heat, no cold. And under these circumstances, exactly how a social condition without sharp and at times even painful contrasts is to be achieved is beyond me.

T.D.

‡   ‡   ‡

[This was taken from earlier political writings. Dreiser had filed them in this chapter on *The Myth of a Perfect Social Order*. He would no doubt have revised them somewhat for the present day; however, they are still valid and pertinent to our times. *Editor's Note*]

Insofar as the United States is concerned, Washington, Jefferson, deTocqueville, John Quincy Adams, Andrew Jackson, Abraham Lincoln, James Bryce, and both the Roosevelts have warned America that individual lust for power and possession, unless equitably curbed, could end only in the disestablishment of our attempted democracy and the re-introduction of autocracy and/or fascism. Due to our uncurbed individualism ever since America was discovered, resulting as it did in our wars with England, Mexico, the South, and the seizures by the unrestrained individuals among us of such resources, powers, and privileges as money, and subtlety, and selfishness could accomplish, we have at last reached the place where our monopolies, trusts, and holding companies, still masquerading as individuals and lovers of democracy and social equity, are in possession not only of most of our national powers and resources, but of international connections and resources which now set our national democratic machinery at nought. We have the form but not the substance. And what deTocqueville and Bryce, to say nothing of the others, predicted is at hand. Our corporations are more formidable, more authoritative than our government. Where the government taxes the individual one dollar, the corporations, jointly if not severally, tax ten. And, in addition, with profound contempt for the people and the government, from whom and which they presumably derive their authority and most certainly their means.

Of course, they blazon contempt for our people and government because of the fact that our people and government meet them with stupidity or indifference or both and have permitted or winked at, and in many cases even aided, this illegal seizure, or thefts and robberies which now permit these octupi to spread their tentacles and to control not only America but the primitive and partly civilized countries of the world and to tax them also. If you doubt this, consider the Standard Oil Co., the beef trust, the International Telephone and Telegraph Corporation, the Power Trust, the automobile monopolies, the steel trust, the coffee trust, to say nothing of the railroads, General Electric, Westinghouse, etc. Where they do not actually control, as in lands that are just being opened up to civilization, they have joint financial relations, which give them control of resources and power far beyond their native land. You have only to think of Venezuela and its asphalt, Chile and its copper, Bolivia and its tin and oil, Nicaragua with its possible canal route and its fruit plantations, Mexico and its oil, Cuba and its sugar, Paraguay and the Chaco, also with great oil reserves.

And yet, they speak of the need of preserving the individual and his rights, also, our primary democratic union, and speak of themselves (the Standard Oil Co., A. T. & T., the steel trust, etc.) as simple, two-handed American individuals, with their spades and shovels in hand. (Is that a laugh!) And whether they wish to or not, the American people have not as yet awakened to, let alone arrayed themselves against, this menace. . . .

[A few dated paragraphs omitted here. *Editor's Note*]

What our corporation masters most desire and contemplate with great pleasure is the jungle—the lion stepping forth to find its easy prey. The "king" of beasts or men roars and looks abroad at the herds frightened and in flight. It is useless to introduce here the fact (if it is a fact) that these lords temporal are unconscious of what they do and of where they are going, that as individuals they have good intentions and good will toward all. For the perpetuation and progress of democracy, it is far more important that they be accepted at their appearance value—what they appear to be doing as self-willed, self-motivated individuals. As such, there is not room for them in any scheme or dream of democracy. They will and must be stopped by those who believe that democracy is possible and that it is a humanely agreeable relationship to be maintained, or they will stop democracy.

Make your mental choice now. If you wish most to live in a world of moderation, having and holding in limited and harmless ways, having and holding as men in the happier times and lands may have held, you cannot possibly permit or endure any of these incursions and the unrestricted materialistic displays of want on individualistic power and parade which now in America, as elsewhere in the world, are all too manifest. Men should not return, as they already are returning, and, in many places, are already returned, to the awe and cringing, and the fear, not of equitable authority, but rather of inequitable authority and power. Today, on the lips of almost all Americans are such words as the chief, the big fellow, the boss, the *king* of this or that—from potatoes to oil companies—and, instead of open statements of belief and confessions of faith in a simpler and more equitable world, there are all too many fearful whisperings as to the danger, as to the limiting power of such things (social reforms) on strong, creative men and their right to incentive. But do not Americans know that this is the open road to the blatant and chiefly ignorant and brutal lover of power and show—the strident dictator or king?

The newspapers, who or what controls them? And what do they say? And what are they doing? Our courts and judges! Only listen to their corporate preachments! And how long since was it that they were preaching and enforcing the right of the large corporations to 7% on every dollar of its graft and plunder? And our legislatures and legislators and their political leaders and bosses, do they really concern themselves with law and duty as these truly relate to the welfare of the people, or is it with the welfare of the corporations that they busy themselves? Our officials and executives, from presidents to police! Consider that insolence, the arrogance, in the assumption that all worth and authority emanates not from the people but from the financial masters who mostly have inherited, not created or pioneered, what they now control and by reason of which they tax. Are they the pioneers, the discoverers, the inventors, the developers of the resources and utilities of the country which they now direct? Those other ones, that older breed, selfish and greedy, were at least personally courageous, industrious, and self-sacrificing. And at least they rendered initiative, ideas, and labor for what they took! On the other hand, these who claim authority and power—and by reason of inherited wealth—are the ones who, to maintain themselves in show and separateness, will gladly betray the masses, their subsistence and their lives. One need only watch them to see.

In conclusion let me say, if Americans, at least such of them as believe in the democratic ideal of social equity, value a land and a time of equitable human relationships, they should not let these savage individualists win what they wish. Now, not later, they should spy out and punish their machinations. Either they should seize their wealth or restrain their inequitable uses of it. Only so can a great country be saved to its ideals, its land, and its resources. A great people possessing such a dream would so struggle.

Laughter

Humor

HUMOR IS NOT INVENTED OR DEVISED BY MAN. IT IS MECHANIS-
tically improvised by life as is automatically reacted to and memorized by
man and thereafter set down by him—copied. Long before the humorist
appeared humor was—in the evolved and of course mechanistic procedure
of life. It is even chemical—as are both sorrow and joy, for a little whiskey
(chemical enough, that) will make many laugh, feel gay—others cry. The
drug benzedrine sulphate will make most cheerful; another drug or chemical,
prolochis will make others loving and/or pitiful—that synonym for sorrow.
Automatically—by no will of your own you encounter and see humorous
or ridiculous things all of the time. And mechanistically, by eye or ear, register
them, and you do not think, or will or decide to laugh. Without thinking,
or willing, or deciding you *do* laugh. As you so often say *you cannot help
it*. And you cannot. Try to sometime and see how you make out. [*Or*]

T.D.

‡ ‡ ‡

It [humor] must be a surprise. It must involve caricature. Some familiar
orderly thing must be anachronistically presented or represented in order
to make one laugh. Consider a clown. Consider a lie—a greatly exaggerated
lie—so exaggerated as to be ridiculous: Baron Munchausen, Gulliver, Gar-
gantua. A little exaggeration will produce a smile, a little caricature also.
[*Or*]

T.D.

Much humor is based on what you either know or assume to be a fact
and some erroneous or true contrast to what you know or think on the
part of another.

This to a degree emphasizes the necessity for ignorance.

T.D.

‡ ‡ ‡

Jokes and witticisms are repeated over and over to new generations. The process is so mechanical as to suggest two cog wheels, the oncoming cogs or jokes of one wheel fitting smoothly into the oncoming receptive grooves of the other.

‡   ‡   ‡

Things are only ludicrous when judged by some human standard (Relativity), the norm of anything—courage, fear; strength, weakness; sorrow, joy; love, hate; order, disorder; wisdom, ignorance; mercy, cruelty; beauty, ugliness; etc.

‡   ‡   ‡

Only placing before the eye or ear or nose or the sense of taste or feeling the contrary of the expected or accepted (like hot where you thought it was cold) is the sense of the ridiculous or humor in the form of laughter or a smile evoked.

‡   ‡   ‡

"The loud laugh that bespeaks the vacant mind"——Goldsmith

Not only wit but the sense of humor are arrogated to an exceptional mind or temperament. This [is] an assumption, but one without foundation of humor. There are endless grades and shades of humor and as many responses. Birds have humor as I have. Dogs also. Monkeys appear to have it. Penguins also. [*Or*]

‡   ‡   ‡

Humor depends on knowledge of environment, of the subject as well as the object of humor. To enjoy a joke, you must know the entire environment or setting of the source of your humor, or these must be explained to you. Hence verbal descriptions, or drawings, or both. Example:

The Pittsburgh rooster that crowed every time a smoke cloud lifted, thinking it was dawn! [*Or*]

The Penguin

A bird that has wings but cannot fly; that not only has a keen mind, but also a keen sense of humor and a flair for showmanship that easily ranks him as the Charlie Chaplin of ornithology:

The favorite stunt of Paddlewings II is to stand on the very edge of his diving board in an attitude simulating drowsiness. Head rolling over on his chest, he will sway forward, then catch himself just in the nick of time, to the pent up 'O-o-h' of the spectators. Again he sways, this time a trifle further just to put the crowd on tenterhooks and draw others from distant parts of the building. Finally, accompanied by a great roar of delight from the watchers, he will swing just too far and sprawl into the water on his chin with all the studied clumsiness of a circus clown. A few swift turns around the tank and he climbs back on the landing to get ready for the next performance, which will be repeated as long as the noon crowd is on hand—and not one minute longer. [*W*]

‡   ‡   ‡

To cover a good deal of ground only to come back unwittingly to the starting-point is to make a great effort for a result that is nil. So we might be tempted to define the comic in this latter fashion. And such, indeed, seems to be the idea of *Herbert Spencer:* according to him, laughter is the indication of an effort which suddenly encounters a void. Kant had already said something of the kind: "Laughter is the result of an expectation which, of a sudden, ends in nothing."

Comedy

Comedy can only begin at the point where our neighbor's personality ceases to affect us. It begins, in fact, with what might be called a growing callousness to social life.

‡ ‡ ‡

It might be said that the specific remedy for vanity is laughter and that the one failing that is essentially laughable is vanity.

‡ ‡ ‡

Laughter is above all a corrective. Being intended to humiliate, it must make a painful impression on the person against whom it is directed. By laughter, society avenges itself for the liberties taken with it. [*Or*]

‡ ‡ ‡

All clowning—all attempts at achieving the humorously ridiculous by exaggerating or abnormalizing the normal—is obviously a purely mechanical procedure. The normal ear or nose or mouth or forehead or eye of the clown is made huge or otherwise distorted or discolored in such a fashion and to such a degree as to startle without unduly straining or frightening or saddening the past sense registrations of the normal in connection with these same.

But it need not always be consciously sought or achieved by any means, for nature, because of the necessity for contrast, automatically achieves laughter—a loud guffaw, as when any evolutionary form swings too widely from the more pleasingly constructed or beautifully colored or voiced species.

Thus a crow or a macaw or cassowary encountered by a human being in the same environment with himself and a true songster of any description is more likely to produce laughter than any other reaction, particularly where their voices are closely related in time. They are exaggerated departures from some temporary norm which has been mechanistically built up in man.

So, too, with apes, chimpanzees, baboons, and men met in a zoo. Although, under the circumstances, the reactions of the first three to man are not clear, definitely those of man to the others is one of amusement due entirely to mechanical registrations by man of seeming clown-like distortions of his own structure and features, which to him, via evolutionary processes, have come to seem normal.

These reactions on his part are not, of course, self-devised or created moods on his part any more than the seemingly grotesque figures and gestures of the apes and baboons are self-created. All are evolved mechanisms. And the laughter of men because of these others—as seemingly wild exaggerations of themselves—are merely evolved chemical and physical reactions, due entirely to the evolutionary processes of nature.

In other words nature is the inventor and designer of humor and its result or effect, laughter. It makes the clown and the mechanism called man that laughs at the clown.

The universe, either by will or some unescapable condition which prevents it from being and doing other than it does, evokes its own sorrows and joys and then, fantastically enough, indulges in them, as extra natural, the sources of which it does not know. And if one asks why, one's answer might be "as an escape from inaction, stillness, nothing-ness." [*Or*]

‡ ‡ ‡

Life itself suggests that it is little if anything more than a game. Hide and seek. Consider how protoplasm, that mixture of extremely complex chemical compounds organized (how? why?) into a nucleus and a surrounding cytoplasm, but only appearing here because of the earth, the sun, the balanced relations of the 93 elements which compose the same, the existence of the universe itself or matter-energy, space and time, heat and cold, moisture and dryness— how this thing, primary in all evolutionary biologic life, is constructed and operated (not self-constructed and operated) by the universe about it (seemingly more immediately by its particular environment) first to resist, to a degree, destruction by its environment and to preserve itself by absorbing self-maintaining nutriment and rejecting that which is not self-maintaining or destructive. But, of course, being first provided by nature with an environment in which it could appear, live, and/or function, such environment would of necessity contain or be stocked with such nutriment as a chemical and physical mechanism called (by man) protoplasm would require to permit it to function as protoplasm. Also, it would require that the said protoplasmic substance or mechanism be constructed in such a way as to not only require said nutriment, but to be able to capture and absorb, that is digest, or convert it into such other forms as would serve to energize as well as rebuild or maintain the structure or mechanism called protoplasm.

Also, before its being worn out in this process, to permit it to reproduce—not itself—but a duplicate or triplicate or scores of itself, as the mechanism called protoplasm is known to do. But now, all told, what is that? What does it suggest to man if to nothing else in nature. A game? Or a great program of some kind? Some enormous adventure, since all human or biologic life has this protoplasmic base and no other? But a program or adventure on the part of what? Electrons? Protons? Atoms? The enormous magnetic force that holds the electrons and protons together in the arrangement known to man as the *atom?* Or the 93 elements composed of atoms and known to man as *matter,* but that same compiled out of units of energy deriving from the sun and/or all the sidereal hosts known as island universes or the universe?

And did these—and do these still—need this protoplasmic expression or chain called man and animal or flora and fauna here on this minute ball called, by man, earth? Taking the universe as a whole (assuming it were possible for minute man to conceive it as such), the *thought* (reaction) is fantastic! What, this scruff! this scale or excrescence on the surface of so large (comparatively) a thing as the earth important to the universe or the solar system even? To what end? What to be achieved thereby? If not some passing entertainment on the part of a minute (the minute) number of electrons, protons, atoms, and their super structures of the same called molecules, cells, organisms, et cetera, involved in the evolution and production of all the past and present forms, since protoplasm was permitted to appear and which now includes the organism or mechanism called *man!*

But what about all the forms or organisms, protoplasmic in their origin, which have appeared and still *are* appearing, but endless numbers of which, depending on the physical and chemical state of the solar system and its various satellites, including *earth*, have appeared and disappeared—conditions of heat, cold, moisture, drouth, variations in the chemical constitution of the earth's particular atmosphere permitting.

But this last has been and still is a decidedly variable thing. Let even so (universally speaking) infinitesimal a thing as a comet of a particular chemical constitution and radiation sweep too near and presto, the possibility of endless varieties of evolved forms appearing as well as disappearing, as plainly they have appeared and disappeared in the past. Even the rocks—our seemingly too, too solid mountains—that now are above the waters of the earth and again under them, and that in some heat age are as subject to flow as is water, whereas in some ice age, of which there have been many, they become most durable, nevertheless serve to reveal that, during their stay as solids, endless creatures have come and gone, beginning first, and as usual, as protoplasm and then evolving like the pretty five-toed horse until, at the size of a gazelle, it became recognizable as the horse of modern times—the servant, the pleasure, as well as the labor slave of man. But, on the American continent, curiously enough, arriving, evolving, and disappearing during a period of a number of millions of years, but *without* the presence of his later companion and master, man: being permitted, in short, to arrive, develop, and disappear without ever having seen a man—Indian or otherwise—knowing man as a companion and later a master in Europe and Asia, from which continents he was actually transported into the astonished gaze and service of his American continental successors and masters, the Indians.

But the horse is only one of literally millions of forms or organisms, animal, vegetable, mineral, that have appeared and disappeared over hundreds, perhaps thousands, of million of years.

Man's current museums give but a faint suggestion of creatures of every conceivable form and description that have arrived as variations of earlier protoplasmic forms and have—pari pasu—taken to the air, the water, the land, actually passing, changing chemical and physical conditions permitting or compelling, from one to the other, quite indiscriminately. The whale once walked on feet. Today even, fish climb trees! The manitou (sea-cow) once grazing on land, now suckles her young in salt water. Birds were snakes or fishes; fishes, snakes or birds. Change, travel—tropistic, instinctive, osmotic— have brought about all of these.

But because of some universal necessity? Or compulsion? Or *idea of advancing* the nature or wisdom or skill of the universe as a whole?!

What phantasm is this?

Why, these—*all*—are will-less, directed, evolved, and constructed organisms which arrive by permission of environment, not otherwise; and change and/or disappear by reason of environmental changes and not otherwise.

And as for *purpose?*

Kind heaven, what purpose?

Observe what they do? How they arrive! How long they endure—and why? What changes, if any, they affect or have affected!

Have they not gone? And were they not here?—they and their continents and seas?—their heats and colds?—their floral and faunal associates, the endless variations of the same over periods of so-called "time?" And have they not gone and are they not succeeded? And is the universe still extant?

Import? Progress? Purpose?

To what end?

Pleasure?

Self-entertainment?

The entertaining of itself via the device we know of as a *game?*

If not that, why?

How?

Is brief man manufactured to aid the universe in any of its (to him) inscrutable purposes? To be, say, a greater, more useful, more intelligent, more "humane" universe? To help it, for instance, to "go places?"

Is that, perchance, why it has proceeded, in these latter days, to manufacture *humor?* For if *Life* (the mechanism called life) does not manufacture humor, what does? Actually and mechanistically, it causes man to laugh at himself—and so, by implication, its *Creator*, whether that same be especial and limited in its significance or universal. [*Or*]

                                                                                        T.D.

Music

MAN IS THE PHYSICAL AND CHEMICAL INSTRUMENT THROUGH WHICH nature, or the life forces, has brought music, as he knows it, into being. Save as a sensitive responding instrument, he did not create it. It is as a sensitive, responding instrument only that he knows it.

Consider birds, bells, water sounds, wind in trees and mountains, insect humming, all natural sounds:

> The Tuning Fork
> The Wind Harp
> The Harp
> The Mouth Harp
> The Jews Harp
> Accordion (Dutch Pull Out)
> The Bell
> The Musical Cup (Sings when filled with hot water, Owned by
>   Mrs. B. Marshall, Ravenna, Ohio)
> Glasses filled with different quantities of water
> The Tinkling Rill
> Wind Sounds through chinks
> The Organ
>   [Or]

‡ ‡ ‡

As many as fifty different qualities may be obtained on different notes from one violin—a complex that defies mathematical study and makes actual electrical analysis necessary. The differences are too slight for detection by human ear, but they cannot escape the electrical analyzer, and they doubtless play their part as a whole in making a good violin sound as it does.

Yet the listeners think of any sound as a separate and in no way complicated thing. More, they think that the tone of a violin comes from the string, as bowed by the player. In reality, it comes from the vibrating body and the vibrating air within.

‡ ‡ ‡

We have verbalized the sounds and the colors, the light and the darkness, the beauty and the ugliness, the kindness and cruelty, defeat and success of which music is another—an emotional unverbalized expression. But by means of our previous verbalizations, we receive and emotionally accompany the emotions which all of the above in some form or other (never anything wholly beyond our sensory experience) have evoked and expressed themselves through the musician—a sensory mechanism like ourselves. [*Or*]

‡ ‡ ‡

Everybody turns to music for happiness, for comfort in their sorrows. Some music will make you laugh. Music will certainly ease heartache. It will not cure hunger or supply a meal, but it will soften the want of it. More, it will illuminate some problem, as that of *sorrows* of another, the peace that some temperaments achieve, the anger, the despair. [*Or*]

Sorrow and Joy

How would you have music without sorrow or joy. . . . [*Or*]

‡ ‡ ‡

Music it is that is the sensory synthesis in us (in man) of all ancient colors, sounds, delights, fears, deprivations, agonies, irrevocable victories, irreparable defeats, whereby we, as races, tribes, early evolutionary forms, and late, have risen or sunk, succeeded or failed, loved and lost or loved and been repaid. Yet, although gone, these are still vouchsafed us through music, its rhythmic record and reflection.

Hence Pan with his pipes, Apollo with his lyre, Zeus with his bolts, Thor with his hammer, Syrinx with her reed, Tantalus with his fruit. And Beethoven, Bach, Brahms, Tchaikowsky; Praxiteles with his chisel; all music, all poetry, all art, which speaks through no single mechanism called a man, but through races and peoples to this hour, until races and peoples and life, as we are granted to know it now, are no more. [*Or*]

T.D.

‡ ‡ ‡

A composer, sensitive to the moods and movements of life, is moved by the same to compose a sonata, a dirge, a dance, a symphony, a song. That is, there are evoked in and through him reactions representative of the above, plus the impulse to evoke and express them.

His medium, today, is a series of symbols representative of the keys or strings and frets or apertures and stops or blows and resonances upon and from a series of humanly evolved instruments.

These instruments, as well as the symbols or musical notations which represent the sounds which these instruments make when struck or picked or blown, are in their turn material representations of earlier and past moods or sensitivities or reactions of the mechanism called man to the various stimuli that, throughout many ages of time, have played upon him—sunlight, moonlight, the wind, the rain, cold, heat, hunger, food and feasting, danger, escape and peace, birth and death. The cries of the injured, the shouts of the joyful, clouds, birds, water, still or in motion, the sounds of forces in operation, thunder, lightning, the crackling of ice, the explosions of volcanoes, the rumbling of earthquakes, and the tinkle of running water.

Why does the nature of the composer react to produce a certain sound to suggest a certain mood, and why does the listener think that this sound, this combination of sounds, is like a mood?

It is because man, since his earliest days and even before he was a man, when he first developed hearing at all, noticed that certain events, such as pain, such as joy, such as a storm, in fact any of the above, were accompanied by expression in noise, cries, the inarticulate sound of emotion, with no form in words, nothing so sharp and defined or definite as that, but expressions of part of the man—a tone of voice, a rhythm of speech, a cry or yell, a sigh, or weeping, the roar of the wind, or the escaping water, the thunder, the lightning, bird-song, the contented rustle and singing of the grass in the summer breeze.

He found that with his own voice, he could make a sound, sing a song, like the trees, like the mood of nature, which could evoke in him and in his hearers the same mood. And when by accident, in the course of time, he came to notice that by blowing in a reed, he could evoke the same sweet or sad tune, or by blowing in a shell, or by beating a drum of animal skin, or by shaking nuts and shells together, he could produce the vibrations of nature, isolate nature in musical moods. That he could come closer to the flow of emotion which words can only approach. That he could vicariously express and recall himself and others and his environment through the sound which he could issue from his own throat and through the instruments which nature provided for him.

And as he developed and "invented" other devices, so he developed these of music, which are now today so complex, and so he has more possibilities to express more completely and fully, and to imitate the flow of nature. . . . [Or]

[A longer version continued here, but was not completed. Editor's Note]

‡   ‡   ‡

One person listening to a simple melody or the profound and moving changes of mood and action in a symphony finds himself, if he troubles to inquire or investigate, reacting differently to the different tone and form phases of the melody or symphony than does his neighbor. One person listening to one phase or movement of a given work may find himself emotionally or technically responding—tuning fork wise—to a sound as well as a color and motion picture of a regiment cavalry on the march, whether in orderly forward hurry or strained and intense anticipation of danger and yet with the courage and zest, even, to meet it; or, on the contrary, the same regiment in intense and disorderly and nervous flight from the field, with perhaps the enemy in fierce pursuit; whereas a seated neighbor, of a somewhat different sensory reaction to life as well as differing post-sensory experiences, might be visualizing and, of course, feeling the approach, rush, thrash, strain of a great and destructive wind or rain storm or hurricane, together with all of its whistling, creakings, crashings, groans, and cries of frightened creatures in flight as well as the squeakings and fierce grinding of rocks, woods, and metals hurried and whirled and triturated one against the other in space. This would depend to a very considerable degree not only upon the actual experiences of the listener in times past, but also on his private readings of scenes of a related character; or, if not those, then on past auditorial receptions of the narratives of others who had seen such things; or against his own recollection of stage presentations of related occurrences, together with of course the value of the technical and emotional interpretation of the conductor and his musicians. For all of these, barring the possible gifts of heredity, would be requisite to any possible understanding of the music whatsoever. Yet, third, fourth, and fifth persons can be imagined who . . . [*Or,* unfinished.]

‡ ‡ ‡

The artistic temperament and the scientific temperament are quite different. A great deal of art has that sort of unrecognized expression which psychiatrists call the symbolization of repressed desires or needs.

For instance, you become a writer of moving novels, plays, or poems because the things you would like to do or be in real life, or the things you deeply feel, are, insofar as your knowledge goes, nowhere else expressed in plays, poems, books, pictures.

In consequence, and because of the existence of various art forms which do not express what you feel or need but *do* express the needs or experience of others which nonetheless help or interest you, there begins to form or grow in your subconscious, out of registrations of things in life which stir the unsatisfied feelings or desires of you, a poem, play, book, picture, or musical symbol, which, if ever externalized—that is, given existence as a book, play, picture, poem, or musical composition—will in some measure cure the misery that your particular lack has set up in you.

Yet for a long time, maybe never, this internal symbol will never be externalized by you. If it ever is, and assuming that potentially or chemically you are a Keats, a Beethoven, a Van Gogh, a Michaelangelo, or a Shakespeare, you are likely to write an "Ode to the Skylark," an "Ode to a Grecian Urn," a 5th or 7th Symphony, a *Hamlet* or a *Macbeth,* a *Crime and Punishment,* or sculp a *Moses* or a *Dawn* or *Dusk* or paint the winds and waters and fields and peasants of your native land as did Van Gogh or the Dutch painters of the sixteenth century.

Beethoven, for instance, facing the fact that he was going to be deaf and suffering the emotional storms and pains internally generated by the same, suddenly symbolized the same in his music.

Just before this ill assailed him, he wrote in the Mozartian manner. Afterwards, when already deaf, he began anew with the Eroica and continued with the 5th and the 7th, his soul struggle symbolized in his music.

Life created Beethoven, his deafness, his emotional misery. And so life, through its mechanism Beethoven, and its broken ears, wrote Eroica and the 5th and 7th—in sum, all that followed his deafness, and for that matter, all that went before. [Or]

T.D.

‡ ‡ ‡

The 9th symphony is played, and you are greatly moved. Because of the inpouring harmonies, it would seem as though you were afloat on wide restful wings in an empyrean of peace, of light, of bliss—all ills of the flesh and of life fallen away.

Yet at another moment, and because of an inpouring storm of harmony, dark, disillusioning moods sweep all the first away. The inconsolable grief of not one but the endless millions of the ages gone is upon one. You sink, you fail. An inexplicable despair seems to check the heart, clutch at the throat. Oh, that this should pass!

Yet another shift of sound and Spring has come. It is morning, dawn! A sky of delicate silver and fleecy pink clouds. Youth is. No trace of disillusionment. A fresh green meadow on which to run and play. Litheness of body. Lightness of heart. Heaven on earth. No loneliness. No sorrow. Light and delight.

But whence this? With what words, if any, is this communicated? How strange that sounds, endless variations of sound, registered by evolving man through endless ages of men, animals, birds, fishes, trees, flowers, insects, stones, water, in the sky and in the sea, should gradually have come to be synthesized in this way by man in this orchestra.

Well, first possibly, after grunts, gestures, coarse imitations of natural sounds, at last came real sounds, words, true vocal copies of natural sounds—winds in trees, among the rocks, through chunks of stone. Then the spiral conch, the pipe of reed or straw. Latterly, the thongs of tightened bows, pulled and released to hear the musical whirr. Then bows of two or more strings—the harp. Lastly, the world of slowly evolved and diversified instruments discovered here, forgotten there, but yet, in part at least, at last assembled, as here in this orchestra.

And more, there is each and everyone's eager, yearning attempt to reflect in sound not only the sounds of nature, but the feelings or moods evoked by those sounds in that other instrument of hers—man, his gayeties and griefs.

And, because of these, in and through him, those notes that today symbolize the sounds as well as the finger positions and movements necessary to control the stops or chords that will best evoke the musical equivalents of all that he feels and has toiled to produce. [Or]

T.D.

[Five lines of this essay are repeated in the following *Note* with different continuation. *Editor's Note*]

‡   ‡   ‡

But whence comes this? With what words, if any, is this communicated. How strange that sounds, endless variations of sound, registered by evolving man through endless ages of men, animals, birds, fishes, trees, flowers, insects, stones, water, in the sky and in the sea, should gradually have come to be synthesized as such [music] by nature, and once so synthesized, be reacted to or reflected by all other organisms so that, as Thoreau so accurately and exquisitely phrases it, "We are grateful when we are reminded by *interior evidence* of the permanence of universal laws"—as for instance, that a flower shall be constructed *so;* a stone, or sun or bird or fish, *so,* all conforming to a given environment, the result of a given, basic something called energy or mind (if you choose) in its last indissoluble and controlling form. And that we, as disparate evocations of the same—we, things that have evolved out of it—shall respond to it *so:* as a leaf or water to the wind; as darkness to light; as cold to heat, or vice versa; as sound to silence; as a little thing to a big one, with pleasure or pain; that which is uneven to that which is even; that which is loveless to that which, most of all, needs to love.
[*Or*]

The Essential
Tragedy of Life

[These two headings, representing chapters which Dreiser had listed for his *Notes on Life* Nos. 23 and 25, were already finished essays which had been published in his earlier philosophical book *Hey Rub-A-Dub-Dub,* as was true of a long essay called *Change.* In a complete edition of Dreiser's *Notes on Life,* these chapters might be repeated, but here, because of limited space, and the importance of the two concluding chapters, containing completely new material, we do not wish to include anything already published.

However, Dreiser had since collected new *Notes* on the same subjects for possibly expanded chapters. We are presenting shorter pieces, showing in his own words, what these headings represented for him. In this way, his thought is rounded out, even here. *Editor's Note*]

To me the most astonishing thing in connection with man is the same vanity or power of romanticizing every thing relating to himself so that, whereas in reality he is what he is, a structure of brief import and minute social or any other form of energy, left by his loving Creator to contest [with] billions of inimical powers, and significant only insofar as he or they are interlocked with others in some larger unity, either (for illustration) as the soldier in an army or its delegated commander or as a delegated or acknowledged representative of some moving or mass or race impulse. Nonetheless, he has this astonishing power of viewing himself as a tremendous force in himself, a god, a hero, an enduring and undying figure of glory and beauty, as significant almost as the Creator Himself, in whose image and likeness he is supposed to be made!

The wonder! The beauty even!

Sometimes I think all this is the almost inevitable result of something inherently weak but with one clear power: that of visualizing or perceiving strength in other things and so, by contrast, its own weakness and, by reflex action merely, attempting to salve° itself against its own ineffectiveness by imagining itself to be that which it may never be—a victor, a Colossus bestriding the world, an undying potentate ruling forever—and so gaining strength to go on. For individuals are never masters in any remarkable way. They merely, and at best, borrow or direct the energies of many, and in the main to no important result to themselves or those whom they seemingly direct. A Napoleon slaves and starves to the end that he may die on St. Helena and bring considerable profit to many who never heard of him and care not at all. A Caesar toils endlessly at organization and the development and preservation of Rome only to be stabbed to death in his fifty-sixth year, practically unrewarded. A Hannibal slaves for Carthage, enduring endless hardships, only to die by his own hand. The category might be extended indefinitely. And yet the world is full of laudations of the powers of man, their satisfactions, their vast, vast rewards and glories, while so many decayed steles and temple doorways and data unending bear testimony to their utter material and subsequent mental futility.

And when I say this, I wish to make it perfectly clear that I am by no means confusing the race with the individual or vice versa. What a race may do and what man may are two very different things. The race, representing the totality of active, creative push of dynamic forces from without, may be, and insofar as one can guess, becomes at times relatively successful. The God or force or forces using man in various aspects here and now (two billion men at the present moment) may be and no doubt is finding self-expression through and in him and may well be, for all one can tell, tremendously satisfied with the result. But in what way does that, or can it, add to the comfort or bliss of the particular individual? Endlessly repeated, an oyster-like copy of every other man that has ever been, a mere minute portion of something the significance or import of which he cannot even surmise. . . .

Herein lies the pathos, and this is the outstanding fact; that man is essentially a creation or mechanism, accidental or not as you wish, of a force or forces which, insofar as anyone can determine, is or are far more than he in his wildest flights of fancy suspects, the thing which he most craves to be, individual, enduring, but of which he is only a part and of which he is constantly seeking more—*life*.

[°Again, Dreiser uses the word *salve* in its original usage and pronunciation, as in *salvage* or *salvation*. Also used in title of chapter 20. *Editor's Note*]

Equation Inevitable

ALL OF US HAVE SOMEONE OR SOMETHING NEAR BY WHO RESPONDS
to influence or to whom we respond, in a world otherwise so impersonal
and impenetrable; something not only to balance themselves against or to
be balanced by, or, by reason of need of additional strength, to blend with,
or to control or be controlled by, and use or to be used by, as implements
or an implement, or additional forces, for purposes of one's own or those
of another or of many others.

Some have pets, some children, some servants, some a religion, or a God
for whom they do and by whom, in one way or another, they are done
for.

To be sure, many do not realize this even though to others it is quite
obvious, chemically and physically sound and scientifically correct. Some
have astrology, some love, some money (that still undisturbed token or symbol
of force) that at a word or movement can be exchanged for the goods, chattels,
services of life that Proteus-wise it represents and from and by reason of
which they take or give strength, and in return are taken from and given.

The more of anything or many things—if they truly represent needs, emotions,
desires, either to receive or give—the more stable the temperament or body
of the giver or receptor; the less of this equation he or she maintains, the
more unstable and declining is his state until, at last, there is nothing.

THEODORE DREISER

Balance and Disbalance

When you are fighting against disbalance anywhere—extreme cruelty as
opposed to adequate punishment, extreme reward as opposed to adequate
reward, particularly where others are denied it—you are fighting on the
side of the enduring and equalizing condition of the Universe as a whole,
its balance, its law and order as opposed to a wild, colorless, meaningless disorder, of which it knows nothing.

All is order everywhere, the weight and measure enforced in connection with all things, from the given number of electrons required to make a given atom, the number and variety of atoms required to make a given molecule, the number of molecules required to make a cell, the number of cells required a given measure or protein—be it a muscle, a bone, a nerve, a hair, the sounding chords on ear, or the photo electric nerves of the eye—all spells but one thing: order as against disorder, precise weights and measures as opposed to not enough or too much—by which same order would be prevented, a given electrical material or *"mental"* or "emotional" end achieved. . . .

Think of a stalk of wheat, a blade of grass, a tree, a house, flower, a bird, a worm, an insect, or a manufacturing or building process of any kind, whether the same be in the sea, the sky, the earth, or the sun, it is one and the same—*a preceding impulse to erect something orderly,* even though, in so doing, it may be transgressing and breaking down and removing something, that which another preceding impulse to order had placed where it now chooses to be, to present itself as the chosen and current expression of beauty and force as that may be.

T.D.

The Problem
of Death

THE "DEATH OF MATTER"—THAT IS, OF ATOMS—MEANS ONLY THE transformation into pure energy in the form of electric power, heat, mechanical force, or what not. From change or "death" of the smallest amount of ordinary matter, immense amounts of power are formed.

Insofar as man and some, perhaps many, animals are concerned, Wonder, Awe, Fear, Illusion, as well as the hope of knowledge which has brought science into being, all take their rise from this fact. Also Religion or Theory.

It suggests at first an immaterial control of a material thing by something, although it may well be that this Matter-Energy is at once material and immaterial and, like the Genie in the bottle, has the power to will itself to be anything that it chooses. [*Or*]

‡ ‡ ‡

Does the fear of Death prove that Life is worthwhile? [*Or*]

‡ ‡ ‡

The seeing eye and the "feeling" heart or brain (sensating) are, in spite of many things, inextricably involved with that which lives and changes forever, for they represent some of its phases here and are its instruments here.

That which so placed itself in the organism as not only to *sense* but to observe and reflect on such sensation, after the fact, need not die with the body. It is in fact extant in all living things even as you "die" and is producing more organisms such as you are. [*Or*]

Absolute Heat and Absolute Cold

Death is held by some to be nothing more than a cessation of impulse on the part of energy, which now moves to construct something and now rests—the power to rest or to construct being ever present; the power to cease absolutely or disappear completely, which would be death, being absent.

This power on the part of energy to move to combine or construct or to rest seemingly ranges between an absolute zero of cold, 284 degrees below

Fahrenheit zero, and 15,000,000 degrees of heat above, which, according to such physical knowledge as at present holds, may be looked upon as "absolute heat."

But energy itself at absolute zero does not cease or die. [*Or*]

‡   ‡   ‡

Metaphysically speaking, the connection between sin and death that is expounded in many primitive and modern religions has an analogical basis in scientific fact. For example, sin in the spiritual sense corresponds to wearing out or a state of non-utilizable energy in the scientific sense. Death, therefore, corresponds to a state of energy transference, from one form of matter-energy to another.

This is obviously true in the case of the body. In the case of the "individual mind," if there is such a thing, it is also true. For the individual mind or consciousness or motivating force is really a part of the enormous well of energy which comprehends and creates all things and which, as far as we know, does not die, but has infinite and all embracing life.

‡   ‡   ‡

It would seem, even today, as though the dead gave us energy. How much we draw from them! They are really the base on which we rest, the foundation we erect, whatever is "new" buildings, "inventions," laws, "discoveries"—most correctly we use the phrase "additions to knowledge." Precisely, current or live knowledge is only possible by reason of frozen knowledge.

Consider science, philosophy, music, literature, architecture, social arrangements, religions, governments, or states of all kinds. Like the coral islands of the Pacific, built by the minute coral insect working through endless ages, so like-wise is man a compound, resting on and in greater compounds. [*Or*]

‡   ‡   ‡

You fear death. But to what have you been alive? How? What portion of knowledge—total knowledge of matter-energy, space, time, with all of its conditions, qualifications, achievements—have you been a part of? And why, since you know what is here to be the merest wisp or rumor, if so much, of that totality, do you cling so fearfully, desperately to it when outside of this little stage play, rounded by a sleep, is all reality—the ultimate essence or base of it all? Can you not see that it is ignorance and the fear that ignorance inspires which cause you to cling so desperately to what is here? You are like one in a dream, yet the *you* fears to die a dream death and clings feverishly, as I personally have, to an imaginary or dream life. It is no more than that. And though you may not be able to wake completely, yet you can come to that point where by reason of the evidence of the unreality of all that is here, you will cease to fear its dissolution. And after that, at worst, you can but experience another illusion; at best—and perchance—reality. [*Or*]

THEODORE DREISER

‡   ‡   ‡

The Fear of Death is at times partially abolished—

In his *Studies in Human Life*, Professor Elie Metchnikoff inquires what is the "disharmony" which, when we know death is inevitable, makes most feel such horror or despair at the thought of death. And he shrewdly explains and comes to the conclusion that, through no fault of our own, we die too soon, or we fear to, before the time (that is) when death will seem to us to be a good thing, a desirable thing.

In other words, we fear to die before we have exhausted our capacity for living, our taste or zest for living. But this is because chemically at one state, nature, earlier, has planned or at least brought about the fact that we are more zestful.

Consider the growth of the thymus, or of the sex gland, which reaches its highest development during the period of our greatest reproductive efficiency, and after that, and seemingly because of sex satisfaction, child creating and bearing and rearing periods, which continue strong for a number of years, it gradually decays and withers away.

And also consider along with that, the mentally creative periods that come with the same or follow it for many, in the fields of trade, adventure, invention, science, education, letters, painting, music, politics, government, and what not—the *dare and do* years—and all evoked by the chemical and physical reactions of the human machine to heredity and environment. But these compulsions finally fulfilled, if not completely exhausted, consider the calm or relaxation that comes for many and automatically after we have done what we wanted to do, or at least a part of it, and not before. Then and not before, strangely enough, death is not so terrible. The rearranged chemisms of the body that no longer react so vividly to exterior or inherited stimuli make the activities and the *"to-do"* of the world seem less important.

From somewhere (a chemical reaction this too, I take it) comes the feeling that one who has seen so much, done so much, lived so long—in each case as much as the other fellow, or if not quite so much then almost as much as the next one, even he who comes here—will ever see, fear, feel, do, know, achieve; a feeling that somewhere in the scheme of human and mayhap even animal, vegetable, and atomic life, lies an equitable or at least semi-equitable apportionment of things, that to none, possibly, was ever a great wrong intended, and more, that in the endless strife and play of the forces that are without and beyond man, may exist or arise new combinations of matter-energy under endless forms, and with as yet unsensed and endless variations of reaction (In my Father's house are many mansions) which might in some way tend to reward us.

These feelings cause us to live in part at least in anticipation of other great or at least sensory ways. And so, some at least feel this recession of the horror of death. Others, like Metchnikoff, appear to feel that if only we can extend the at present too-short duration of life, man's life, man will come to a time in this extension—not necessarily great—when he will feel "full of days" and satiated if not exactly tired of life, mayhap even that. And so peacefully he will lay himself down, not regretting if not exactly welcoming the end of passion, struggle, adventure, applause, and where life has been too severe, even welcoming its conclusion.

The optimists, the dreamers of social progress and some strange impending triumph of the human race, will even hold that in a well-regulated society, hunger and too great strain abolished, no one will die before he has achieved what he needed to achieve and is comfortably and peacefully full of days. [*Or*]

T.D.

‡ ‡ ‡

Death has always been, if it may not always be, of value to everybody on earth at least. For instance, if no one died, what need would there be for replacement of anyone by the birth of another. The earth would soon be full to overflowing with deathless creatures, so that if more were born they would only prove a hindrance and a suffering to others.

But more likely it would end marriage and birth. There would be no need of the sex relationship except for pleasure, and for many there would be no pleasure of the possibility of bearing and rearing children, establishing a home, experiencing the joy of watching them grow from infancy to man or womanhood. And what would become of love as we know it? No courting; no need of affection of husband for wife or wife for husband; indeed, no need of male or female, but only of a neuter type, for without the need of having and caring for children, why a male or female? And without death to make birth necessary, why male or female?

Indeed without death, life as we know it could not be, for most of the features and practices attending social life as we know it would have vanished. No births, no deaths, no worry over any hereafter, no troubling over the ills of old age or the problems of youth.

Education as a feature of man's life would largely cease, for the function of education is to inform the oncoming generations who are born ignorant, and there would be no oncoming generations. The one original generation would be forever present, unchanging and sufficiently informed by experience to do with but little if any re-education. Hence, no schools or universities or teachers or professors. No increase in population, hence, no statistics worth mentioning.

No graveyards, undertakers, tombstones, funereal industries—one of our largest. No doctors (a real blessing). Probably little sickness. No fear of death. Hence, no life insurance companies.

No religion very likely—certainly none that predicted a hereafter (what need) or any heaven, hell, or purgatory. For how would you get to these places? And if not these, why churches or any such institutions as gather people together to warn them as to their souls after death. So, few if any ministers or priests.

Again, no murder or manslaughter or war even, for unless you could be killed, why war? And so, no armies, generals, war departments, war industries—in short, all our training academies and camps and forts, all our warships, war planes, submarines, ammunition and powder factories gone. Hence, no war scares, war heroes, war hospitals.

In sum, death is so important a part of life, so extremely necessary to its present day activities, that it is a question whether it [life] could go on, would be of any interest to those bereaved of it. For without it [Death] would there be fear? And without fear as opposed to courage, endurance, etc., would there be courage or endurance, any need of either? And without these, why books, plays, poems, theatres, libraries, moving pictures, radio.

For what would they be dealing with? Love? Romance? Courageous and even heroic conduct? Endurance? Patience? Subtlety? For without ever new generations of the young of both sexes to love and bear children and train them—and without all of the above things to experience, the danger of death in particular, either in fear or with courage or with or without skill or subtlety etc.—where would any drama or tragedy come from, any mystery or romance or comedy. Where?

Would not the theatres, the libraries, even the magazines and newspapers be done for. And without the newspaper hourly reporting and re-reporting all of these things, why would anyone wish to live? And if they did not, what a dreadful ill that would be if they could not die. Death indeed! It is the most valuable thing we have, for without it—no life.

‡   ‡   ‡

A.

Involved with the problem of Life—meaning always the limited *life* we see here, plus individuality as it relates to the very limited number of forms we see and control here, plus the sense of *being* which all these energized forms seem to possess—is the mystery of death or cessation of function in and subsequent crumbling or liquefaction of the same. For we are all so convinced, so sure, that we are not only specifically and very definitely alive, if being alive means reaction to other forms of life, but, insofar as that very general or common reaction is concerned, that we are individual. Hence, that cessation of this individualized form elsewhere (as in heaven) or, that being demonstrated to be a figment of fancy of the five senses here, then [that annihilation follows, is rejected by most,] excluding the agnostic. Obvious in all of this is much of the ludicrous and the fantastic. Yet to know that there is something to discuss, we have only to recall that science has already established the oneness of matter and energy and the indestructibility—except for changes, the one into the other—or both. They merely change—the one into the other. An American scientist of no little standing, George W. Crile, has dogmatically asserted that life is electricity. But what is Electricity? The final all or a mere phase or expression of it?

The endless meditators on the mystery of life and death in India have summed up their conclusions in regard to all this in the doctrine of Brahma. Philosophically and even reverentially, they are convinced that there is a one and only life—Brahma—beside which there is no other. And, by inference or direct assertion, they attribute to it sublime perfection—a state of peace or bliss in its omniscience and omnipotence which is beyond good and evil. Yet Brahma, at peace in its timeless unity, wisdom, perfection, strength, is either volitionally or conditionally extended as all phases of form, matter, energy, throughout the forever and forever.

My own meditations on that timeless energy which is obviously the essence of all life, manifest itself how it will or when or where, lead me to the conviction that the ancient Hindu conception remains unrefuted. Time, light, space, energy, the eighty or ninety elements and their combinations, atoms, electrons, protons, neutrons, deutrons, quantums, all of the arbitrarily named phases of energy and matter into which they pass and from which they return again, indicate, if anything, but one thing: The presence of an ultimate energy or substance by turns, either as or not as, as it chooses, matter and energy—the one beside which there is no other and out of which all things take their rise.

This ultimate energy, when not quiescent, may flame as a nebulae or suns or a sidereal system, whose light or energy may traverse space through endless time. And while these latter may pass with all the welter of eager "life" to which they in their turn may seem to have given rise, yet that from which they took their rise, never. Apparently it, as some forensic meditators have imagined, is by turn resting or waking or sleeping, forever and forever.

Here on this minute earth, a seeming extension of a single man, we, by what magic of the eternal substance or thought we know not, seem tethered to the demonstrable illusion of a reality which is as fantastic as our own narrower and yet, to us, seemingly wild speculations in regard to witchcraft and magic. Men are born or, let us better say, they appear. And by what an astounding and mystical process! The sexes—"Male and female created He them." Desire. Dreams. Love. Yet which same no one of us, to this hour, has ever been able to explain. Yet once here, we, as well as all the multitudinous forms of creation which, via will or accident, struggle with each other for light, space, food, freedom, *seemingly* function and disport ourselves for a period of seeming time, in pleasure or pain, and then most mysteriously, and yet in order as to time and change and the compulsions of our various hours here, cease and dissolve before our very eyes.

And yet we still speak of *reality!* And we still think of *individuality!* And even hold violently and yet vaguely and wishfully to some hope of persistence in the mystical and unexplained forms in which, to our constant and utter amazement, we find ourselves here. Yet, a man, an animal, a bird, a flower, an insect appears and disappears by a combination of chemical and electro-physical properties and activities quite closely related at times to those which produce us, but of which processes anywhere we have only the vaguest, if so much, conception—no ultimate understanding whatsoever. And yet we dream of them as somehow durable and persistent; even as having that mystical and illusory thing, a soul. And yet with this last, and at last, after many years of speculation and meditation, I have come to agree. But not in the ordinary or conventional understanding of the word *soul*.

For in my connection with my thought, whether the material form of anything as we see it here, plus its matter, impulses, reactions, and what not, conditioned as they are here on earth, appears to be totally dissolved and evanishes without a trace, as we seem to see it dissolved before our very eyes, still that is neither here nor there. What is important is whether the creative impulse, primarily responsible for the appearance and temporary existence of that form, ceases or not. And now science as well as Brahminic thought return to assure us that it does not, since, given a one and indestructible [form] behind all forms, it could not. At worst, it would have retired into the ultimate, to be extended in what other form or forms we know not. But to die? No. Not even though the idea of such a thing as a man die, or a tree, or flower, or bird, or world, still that which could make any or all of these—tree, rock, flower, stream, mountain, sea, world—is, and that which can make a sun or a sidereal system is not dead and seemingly need not die.

B. The Myth of Death

"What is man that Thou art mindful of him? He cometh up as a flower and is cut down; he fleeth as a shadow and continueth not." Yet, while here, and by reason of the force which has been interested enough to manifest itself in the form in which he, along with billions of others, finds himself, he assumes he is individual, conceives of himself as specially created, even indestructible, not as to his physical form, but as to his soul, of which he dreams himself possessed and which is to continue after him! And in proof of his individuality and his right to persistence as an individual, he calls attention to his creative powers here on earth. Witness he can make tools, machines, buildings, books, pictures—all extensions of the creative force that is in him, but which he believes personal to himself! Manifested by a, possibly, eternal, indestructible force, he also finds himself with the power to reproduce himself, to actually bring forth others like himself. That done, and as a presentation of that kind, he conceives of himself as thinking, inventing, building, in short, creating a race as well as a social order, and of his own devising, instead of himself as an instrument or implement through which something else is doing or producing all that he sees and feels and does, himself included. In other words, he is immune, or by the creative force has been completely immunized, to a realization of what a tool or implement he is. He has even written his and its history, filled libraries with stores of *his* inventions, and the world with *his* so-called discoveries and powers. Yet, actually, in his brief hour under the sun, he does no more than react to what he finds or sees about him, as well as that which, by reason of precedent and remembered life, he is able to duplicate, alter, or add to in some slight form.

Indeed, by some inexplicable abracadabra, which no scientist and no laboratory has sensed, let alone displayed, he appears an amazing complication of creative wisdom—he and his engines, dynamos, microscopes, telescopes, spectroscopes, and the rest (inventions which fill the world)—and more astounding still, struts, probably by some permission or perhaps (and better) imperious compulsion, being filled with a quite mystical—that is, wholly illusory—sense not only of creation but possession!

What is there like unto him? *He* has invented an airplane, an electric eye, a system of music, a system of physics, a system of mathematics, a system of chemistry, and, with his interests concentrated almost exclusively on himself, he is half inclined to believe that there is no other in earthly form that is the equal of himself. And yet about him are the endlessly different and, in so many ways, superior forms of whose powers and processes, let alone the art of whose creation, he has not the faintest knowledge.

Yet, where the authority for all this? Is it possible that in the deeps of cosmic law—of the forces or rules of chemistry and physics, electro-chemistry and electro-physics—lie necessities for vanity? Illusion? Delusion? It may—possibly even—must be, vanity as well as delusion or in combination being propulsive forces.

And yet, when one considers, how farcical. For with all his assumed personal wisdom, without this super directive wisdom of which he is a shadow, could he manufacture so much as a single cell? Or be able to understand its various functions, let alone its essential sources? Never having seen a bird, could he dream out a bird? Without a mountain to behold, could he plan a mountain? Indeed, before the least as well as the greatest of all of the multiple forms which flourish and function about him, he stands, especially when confronted by a demand for an answer, in silence. The flower in the cranny, the cloud on the wind, the light on the wall, the wall, the earth under his feet, his own power to live and breathe—all are beyond his knowledge. And yet he thinks of, and at times speaks of possessing creative power. And more, an enduring soul, a persistence after death. And so, for the most part, fails miserably of any even approximate knowledge of his true relationship to that eternity of energy of which he is an integral part. Indeed, for the most part, he fails of the thought, let alone the sensory assurance which is still there, that by no means can he escape essential unity with the forever out of which he must have come and into which he must return, not as the singular thing which he finds himself to be, nor yet as a bird or flower or a worm, or even a given form of energy, but rather that essential something which is all of these, or they are not.

I will illustrate another way.

C.

There is a tree, and there is its evolutionary history, and there are its present varied forms or family connections, and there is its particular process of manifesting, maintaining, and replenishing itself.

It, too, might say it has individuality and, like every other thing, its essential soul or thought of which it is a manifestation. But is the soul of a tree the tree itself, with its roots, its trunk, its branches, and its leaves? Or are the roots, the trunk, the branches, and the leaves the manifestation of something else that is really not the tree but the idea of it, expressed through the roots, the branches, the leaves? And has that idea life? And is it mind? Or an expression of mind? In other words, a creative thought in the one thing beside which—the Hindus call it Brahman—there is no other? If not, then from whence can it have come? How persist even for a moment? For must it not be rooted in endless, deathless force or power? If so, is that force or power mind, or what? Since only negation or annihilation lie the other way, it must be that we are forced to predicate an ultimate something which, if it does not directly create, permits creation, and so is itself the ultimate life and power. Either the tree or that which builds it must possess mind in as distinguished a form as mind in any other form of so-called life here manifests itself, since it displays skills and powers as mysterious, as illusive, and as matchless as the powers of mind in any other field or form of life.

Can you make a nut? Can you make it grow? Can you line a central pocket of it with velvet and fill it with a kernel that, given similar or even relatively dissimilar conditions such as environed the parent tree, will make another tree, and another nut, or hundreds of them, each capable of reproducing a tree? If not (and you say that) you have said for the tree all that you can say for man or any other manifestation of life, so-called "material" or "immaterial," "animate" or "inanimate."

The wonder is that there is any illusion of invention, let alone creation, or even of initiative in the various things, man, animals, vegetables which, as is so plainly to be seen, are mere manifestations of energy on the part of something that uses man as man uses a machine. Having laid an egg, a hen cackles. Having interpreted something beautifully, an actor, a singer, a painter, a poet presents himself for applause. An inventor or discoverer or explorer, the same. But who is the inventor of the spectroscope, the discoverer of America, the explorer of the human anatomy or a mysterious continent or the skies—a single individual anywhere, or the creative impulse manifesting itself through life and many individuals; and assuming its impulse withdrawn, what "life" anywhere? What invention? What tree? What flower?

Hence, Life after Death (or disappearance) for any of these? The inquiry to me at least seems fantastic—as though a drop of water separated from the sea, or all water, or oxygen and hydrogen which (in certain proportions) combined should say, "I shall endure forever as a drop of water." Yet as a part of something that may forever, either at "will" (if man dare venture to attribute "will" to the all) or per willess condition, produce drops of water, there is a continuation of the essential something which makes a drop of water possible. But is that its "soul"—the "within" that is also "without"—its continuity after its brief experience of form here? If there is more than that, the answer is not yet.

My Creator

Many, many times in my semi-industrious life I have been asked by one person or another what I thought of life (!) or whether, if ever, I sought to interpret the Creative Force by reason of which all of us find ourselves present—numbered among the living? At that time my brash and certainly most unpremeditated reply was that I took no meaning from all that I saw unless it was some planned form of self-entertainment on the part of the Creative Force, which cared little if anything for either the joys or sorrows of its creatures, and that, as for myself, "I would pass as I had come to be, confused and dismayed"—a very definite statement, which, for some reason or other, seemed to register sharply on the minds of many, and which since, and up to this very day, has been thrown back at me whenever I have chosen to claim any clear understanding of any of the amazing processes that I see in full function about me in the world. And yet here they are—a minute number of them.

War and peace, mercy and cruelty, sorrow and joy, love and hate, change and stability, youth and age, ignorance and knowledge, humor and the lack of it. Memory and forgetfulness, courage and fear or strength and weakness, also the disrupting factor called chance. Also beauty and ugliness. Death or an immaterial life after this, as well as the evidence of plan and design in all things everywhere from time immemorial. Thus, mountain to rock to pebble to sand, or water to snow, to ice, to hail, to vapor, and return. Or flower to vine to tree, to bush, to weed, to grass—even the bryophyllum, plant which actually grows while you wear it, absorbing its nourishment from the air and needing neither water or earth to cause it to thrive! As for the purpose of all this—good, bad or indifferent. Ah, there! as in endless other instances, I found myself staggered by its import or a lack of the same—the *why* of it. For certainly bryophyllum is not a numerous resident of this earth nor of any seeming great import, any more than is or was the great Auk, which disappeared from this earth a century or two ago.

Truly the endless variety of life—from amoeba to man; the three-toed, dog-sized horse to his present day, heavily hoofed descendant; the one time sea-going mammal of minute size that descended or ascended to be a whale; and so on *ad infinitum*—puzzled me to the point of reading Darwin, Haeckel, Spencer, Loeb, Lodge, Crookes, and who not else, Freud, Menninger, a long list. In fact I spent three solid years informing myself as to their views and conclusions, as well as those of many, many others, which same, in my case, led to the making of the above list and my personal conclusion in regard to the same. As to that conclusion, it was that *contrast*, however attractive or disagreeable, joyful to many, or terrible to others—as for instance, extreme wealth as opposed to extreme poverty; extreme beauty as opposed to extreme ugliness; extreme strength as opposed to extreme weakness; extreme wisdom as opposed to extreme ignorance—that was apparently indispensable to this life and world-process if we are to have life as we know it.

For remove contrast and what have you? Any single thing that is different to or distinguishable from yourself? The answer is no. For, assuming that you were a male of any species, there would then be no female to contrast yourself with. Or, again, if you were strong, there would be no opposite in the way of weakness by which (that is, for reason of which) you might know of yourself to be strong—that is, different in this matter of strength. In sum, you could not even guess what the word or the fact of individual strength or weakness might mean. In fact, as to endless other things which you now recognize as opposites or contrasting forms or forces, you could not know of them. They must be different in order to be present to your consciousness. Thus, it is evil and evil alone that you use as a yardstick by which you measure any such *good* as befalls you. In other words, when you think of good in any form, you instantly think of something that is not as good, something by which you measure yours as better or, at least, some better.

For instance, let us consider poverty as opposed to wealth. For if you were poor and there were no stored wealth in the hands of others—more wealth or goods than you possess—anywhere, you could not think of yourself as poor, or any other, for that matter, all having the same quantity of whatever was.

So too, with this matter of beauty and ugliness—either in the matter of the arts or architecture or the physical design of a beautiful woman or man or animal or tree or flower. For without contrast to something not so beautiful, either something of its own specie or another, how would one know anything at all of beauty? One would not, and there is an end of that, for the variety, color, design, as well as the odor of things, foul or fair, would be gone. A beautiful woman without a homely one anywhere would be what? A beautiful woman? Who would know her to be such—herself or any other? For beauty, like all else in life, depends on the absence of beauty elsewhere to be what it is.

Yet one thing more and I am done with this matter of contrast, and that is that which relates to wisdom and its contrary or contrast, ignorance. For, strange as it may seem, ignorance, although so constantly derided by all who are so fortunate as to possess what they consider wisdom, is one of the most important things in the world to them. For without ignorance—vast quantities of it—where would their wisdom be? Whom would it benefit? For, for wisdom to function and be of the great import that most truly it is, how very necessary it is for ignorance to abound, for without ignorance, why wisdom? Whom would it serve?—those who already have wisdom?—who know and can do the things that others (assuming they exist) cannot do? The thought is preposterous. If you have wisdom, you must have someone to whom you can impart it. Actually, ignorance is an all-essential thing; otherwise, you not only *may* but *must* close your schools, colleges, universities, your laboratories, publishing organizations, and what not. For, except for those who are ignorant and will or must come to learn, where the value of your wisdom? Where? In other words, and except for its abounding existence, no more institutions of learning, no more trade schools even. No more apprentices anywhere. Wise men and women everywhere sitting silent. For to whom could they impart what they know of already, since the one to whom they might wish to impart it already knows all that they would have to say? Scoff not. If you have wisdom, bow down to ignorance, for it is the very and ultimate reason and import of all that you do know.

However, while in awe and wonder I study the various constructive processes of nature and witness, as I say, not only the very necessary contrast it involves insofar as all thinking or reacting creatures are concerned—tree with fish or bird or animal or flower or man or worm or germ or gnat or elephant or with any or all of the same—I am really most awed and, to a very great degree, made reverent by the all prevailing evidence of not only an enormous and all-pervasive subtlety and skill in the construction and arrangement and operation of all of these obviously endless forms which now either are here or are still, at this time, coming into being, in sum, only now are beginning their evolution. Or they have been and have passed, and so, in perhaps endless instances, have never been entered in the records or the knowledge of man, who, himself, in earlier and seemingly almost unrelated forms, has come and gone—whether ever to return or not, who is to say? The hairy ape! pre-*Eocene* man! The Piltdown man, etc. etc. etc.

And yet now as to these, all of them—the mechanical and chemical genius of their construction and operation! Also, the amazing variety and, what is more, the almost invariably esthetic appeal of nearly all of their design! We think of design as an art and praise this and that creature of the Creator—painter, sculptor, poet, architect, designer, inventor—as geniuses, even, in some instances, superlative geniuses, but solely because of the examples of design that they have furnished us.

Phidias and Praxiteles for their forms in stone; Michaelangelo's tombs of the Medici, or his slaves; Leonardo's conception of the Last Supper or the aeroplane. Boticelli's suggestion of spring and youth in paint—yet copied from where? Nature? Of course. Where else. And yet, do but open your door and walk into your garden or the fields, or even into the hard streets of a city with its shop or house windows! Design! Design! Design! Yet in each and every instance copied from a previous design in nature somewhere. And, what is more arresting, by a creature—male or female—itself a design of nature, itself chemically and mechanically repeated these endless millions of years. Yet often in many, many instances accompanied by a slow change in design, as though something were thinking of improving design in every direction.

As to the flowers, I have been studying them from day to day and year to year—the lily, the rose, the iris, the poppy, the morning glory, the orchids as a group—in sum, the thousands of flowers and flowering trees and bushes and water-plants and weeds and grasses; before any one of these I am moved to pause and meditate not only on the beauty of the coloring, the sweetness of the odor seemingly designed to attract some bee or hummingbird or butterfly, but above all and in the case of nearly all, the exquisite beauty or import or meaning of the design itself. Design! Design! Design! Could anything in nature be more significant? Or suggestive of thought? But on the part of what—the flower? the tree? the weed? the vine, with its richly colored and flavored fruit? the tree with fruit? the bush with fruit? Yet I have seen flowers—how many—before which the graceful design of the stalk, the utterly lovely design of the leaves, the petals, the exquisite coloring and arrangement of the petals, and the intriguing sweetness of the odor have caused me to pause and ask, how could a delicate structure such as this in so, at times, harsh a world or environment as so often prevails here and there, come to possess this structural skill, to say nothing of this extreme sensitivity to beauty in these matters of form, coloring, odor, variety of design? For has it a mind? or is the mind without or within? for if one such were to be independently invented by man and presented, say, to a flowerless world, and ignoring the fact that man has been invented by his creator, how great would be his acclaim! How great? For would it not be looked upon as a masterwork, a genius-work of the first order. And yet, behold the fields! the gardens! the varied climates of the planet and the practical use of the same that is made not by the trees or flowers out of their own wisdom and selection, but out of those, obviously, of the Creative Force itself, which has chosen to create these and all the things that are made better or happier by them—man, animal, bird, insect, what else? For who can say what else?

Yet in my garden is also an orange, a lemon, an avocado, a walnut, and a banana tree, to say nothing of a variety of tall cedar and pine, green and dark. And as to these fruit and nut-bearing trees, I have this long while been over-awed and made most profoundly speculative and respectful—really in a sense, reverently so—by the process as well as design that accompanies the same, to say nothing of the engineering as well as the chemical knowledge that accompanies the life of each and every one.

For my avocado is planted in a hard-packed body of dust-covered earth which extends down some twelve feet and requires a by no means large quantity of water to cause the tree itself to flourish, build itself an eighteen inch-thick trunk for instance, also at least a half dozen three to four inch branches, and branching from those a score or two of lesser branches, bearing in their turn heaven only knows how many minor shoots, which are used to carry how many smooth and shiny leaves—graceful as a warrior's shield is graceful. Also, in its season which endures through October and November, bearing two hundred or more round, ebony-skinned avocados, which begin each and every one as a green bud and end in November as a soft and buttery fruit or vegetable, which for flavor and taste has nothing that outrivals it. Birds and man love both and in so doing help to sustain their lives!

But what interests me in this (to some, possibly, commonplace) process is not the fact that this particular process and result is annually undertaken by this tree and successfully completed, but by mankind in general made use of, if they happen to know of it, and yet by some, thought so little of. Pooh! An avocado tree? What of it? It bears avocados after the manner you describe and they are very good. What of that? I can buy them for ten or fifteen cents apiece, depending on size. So what? [I find plenty to answer to that *what*.]

For here is one of these miracles of my Creator—Nature—which confounds me completely. For I have been thinking this long while that insofar as man is concerned, at least—also as to many animals and birds and even fishes and insects—that each is equipped with a brain, that particular organism on which we pride ourselves.

But whether they have one or not, here is this particular tree, which, out of millions of important trees and plants, arrests my attention and will serve to pose a quite amazing problem well worth thinking of. For, in the sense that we know the animal, insect, or human brain, the tree or plant or flower family has no such mechanism. Examine any one carefully and you will find that it has many things—roots, bark, or skin, a powerful or weak wooden stalk or post of varying height, which it very carefully erects in order, in due course, to carry the varying and increasing weight of many branches, which, in their turn, are to be equipped with twigs, and buds, and later, leaves, which in their turn, the buds first, the leaves last, are to be fed with a chemical fluid or sap extracted from the ground by the roots

. . . [Ms not clear here. *Editor's Note*] . . . which with sunlight and rain from above, are to make this beauteous thing with its artistically polished fruit not only lovely to look at but helpful in the matter of sustaining many creatures, birds and animals as well as men.

But this process, thus arbitrarily selected by me as an illustration of the supreme genius of this Creative Force that so over-awes me, is, as all know or should know, but one of possibly endless billions of such processes which have resulted in the endless variety of forms and creatures—animal, vegetable, mineral—which have come and gone since first this particular planet became or was made habitable for any type of form plus any type of movement.

It is true that as to design as well as utility—as predatory man has been developed to register design and utility—not all are possessed of the same esthetic or practical appeals or values as are many others. The frog is by no means possessed of the same esthetic appeal as the hummingbird or the nightingale. Yet, like the kangaroo, the giraffe, the rhinoceros, and the elephant, it serves as best apparently to provide the always arresting value of contrast, by reason of which man—and very likely many other creatures—find life interesting or at least endurable.

The fact is, however, that more than anything else in connection with the Creative Force which brings us and all other phases of life into being—at times for so little a time as, in the instance of some flowers or insects, an hour or a day; in the case of some trees or vines, for hundreds of years—is, as I have said, this matter of design. For design, however one may feel concerning some of it, is the great treasure that nature or the Creative Force has to offer to man and through which it seems to emphasize its own genius and to offer the knowledge of the same to man. Design! Design! Design! And with each astounding variation, either of beauty or practical wisdom or both. And what is of greater import to some than even beauty, there stands forth to the eye as well as to the practical, physical tests of anyone who chooses to imitate the same, the most brilliantly informed and carefully exercised engineering knowledge that somehow nature or the Creator has seen to it, *ever,* that man should see it. For whatever the height or breadth or thickness or weight of trunk or branches or roots, or the fruit or flowers of either tree or flower, to say nothing of the wind and heat and cold forces of any particular area which may tend to strain or injure or destroy the same, the Creator of the tree, the flower, the vegetable, the animal, or man, and whatever his or its beauty or homeliness, has seen to it that each is so constructed or engineered, as well as chemically and sensitively equipped, within and without, to withstand the same, at least to an arresting degree and for a given period—be it one day, one hour, one year, or three-score years and ten, or a thousand years!

In addition to that, there seems to have been thought out the advantages or disadvantages of a given soil or climate area where each may flourish or, at least, may test its strength. And although all varieties of advantage and disadvantage may prevail, now here and now there, and, although bitter

or sweet may be the lot of this or that created thing, and that often enough
(after the fashion of the soldiers of a contending yet well-equipped and
well-clothed army) is now here and now there, and seemingly arbitrarily
at times, set down to make its way as best it can; yet it is not often, as
you will note, that flower or tree or what you will is alone anywhere or
that it is not (*more* rather than less) well-fitted to make its way in the realm
to which its Creator has called it—suffering or no suffering, cruelty or no
cruelty. For plainly, if one will but trouble to look and study, it has not
only been thoughtfully but considerately devised and equipped for the task
to which it is called. For instance, behold the savage and yet stately lion,
forced by want to lurk and kill, and yet which same is *kind* to his own
kind. Again, but see the beautiful and yet anachronously awkward flamingo
or his fellow the Ibis or the wading birds in general, how carefully constructed
and equipped for the lives they must lead.

Or, and again, if one turns to the sea, behold the endless variety of creatures
from whale to shark, to crab or petty minnow, or jelly-fish, yet each and
all so carefully and, in the main, esthetically as well as practically designed
and constructed for the world in which it is to find itself. Yes, everywhere,
from pole to pole, design, as well as efficiency and chemical energy, are
ever harmoniously present so as to fit each creature not only with a chemo-
physical world *without*, but another *within* with which it is harmonized,
so as to produce not only beauty but pleasure, as well as hunger and desire
and pursuit and defeat or victory—the intricate and interesting, and yet
often enough, trying and sometimes terrible, and yet never wholly unbeautiful
structure or game we call *life*.

And so studying this matter of genius in design and beauty, as well as
the wisdom of contrast and interest in this so carefully engineered and regulated
universe—this amazing process called living—I am moved not only to awe
but to reverence for the Creator of the same, concerning whom—his or
its presence in all things from worm to star to thought—I meditate constantly,
even though it be, as I see it, that my import to this, my Creator, can be
but as nothing, or less, if that were possible.

Yet awe I have. And, at long last, profound reverence for so amazing
and esthetic and wondrous a process that may truly have been, and for all
that I know, may yet continue to be forever and forever. An esthetic and
wondrous process of which I might pray—and do—to remain the infinitesimal
part of that same that I now am.

Hollywood, November, 1943   Theodore Dreiser

Notes
by John J. McAleer

NOTES ON LIFE I

Powys Introduction

p. x John Cowper Powys (1872–1963), English novelist, literary lecturer, and natural mystic. Dreiser first met Powys in 1912. Their friendship continued even after Powys returned to England in 1934. Dreiser visited him in Corwen, Wales, in 1938 and continued to correspond with him until 1945.

Notes on Life

p. 1 Dreiser first called *Notes on Life*, *The Mechanism Called Man*. Later he referred to it as *The Formulae Called Life*. Preference shifted next to *Illusion Called Life*, then finally to *Notes on Life*.

1 Mechanism Called the Universe

p. 3 "The raw materials for the onward and upward urge for wings. . . . Winged flight, as symbolic of man's "onward and upward urge," is a favorite theme of Dreiser's and supports his interest in ameliorative evolution. The notion of soaring as a bird intrigued Dreiser even before he saw winged flight as emblematic of man's aspiring nature. See *Dawn*, pp. 60, 265–266, 352; *The Color of a Great City*, pp. 74–75. See also the allusion to "the lust for wings" in "Mercy and Cruelty," *Notes on Life* (II 13, p. 239), to "the onward and upward urge" of the lower primates (I 23, p. 171), and to passages in I 18 and II 14.

p. 4 In *A Traveler at Forty* (1913) Dreiser wrote: "I trust the universe is not mechanical, but mystically blind" (p. 18). Although a quarter of a century after he first read Herbert Spencer he still was expressing himself in mechanistic terms, Dreiser continued to find life an intriguing enigma. Eliseo Vivas offers this shrewd assessment:

[Dreiser] is not only an American novelist but a universal novelist. . . . The mystery of the universe, the puzzle of destiny, haunts him; and he, more than any other of his contemporaries, has responded to the need to relate the haunting sense of puzzlement and mystery to the human drama. No other American novelist of his generation has so persistently endeavored to look at men under the aspect of eternity. . . . While Dreiser tries to demonstrate that man's efforts are vain and empty, by responding to the need to face the problem of destiny he draws our attention to dimensions of human existence, awareness of which is not encouraged by current philosophical fashions. . . . ("Dreiser, an Inconsistent Mechanist," in *The Stature of Theodore Dreiser*, ed. Alfred Kazin and Charles Shapiro, pp. 237–238).

p. 6 "In the beginning God (or Creative Mind) created the heaven and the earth" (Gen. 1:1).

p. 6 "I am that I am" (Exod. 3:14).

p. 6 Helena Petrovna Blavatsky (1831–1891), Russian spiritist, founder of the Theosophical Society. Her *Secret Doctrine* (1888) probed unexplained laws of Nature and man's latent powers. Dreiser interviewed one of her chief disciples, Annie Besant, in January 1893 for the St. Louis *Globe-Democrat*.

p. 9 William Blake (1757–1827). "To see the world in a grain of sand" is the opening line of the poet's "Auguries of Innocence" (1801–1803).

p. 10 Max Planck (1858–1947), German physicist, originator of the quantum theory. Planck's Constant ranks as one of the most important scientific discoveries of the twentieth century. Planck received the Nobel Prize (physics) in 1918.

p. 13 "The Stars." Even in adolescence Dreiser often pondered stars and man's place in the universe. In September 1896 in *Ev'ry Month* he stated: "[Man] is working in harmony with great laws which place splendid powers in his hand and assist him to rise. A great maker of stars above is his master." ["Reflections," *Ev'ry Month* II (Sept. 1896), 2–7.] Often he slept alone out-of-doors, conscious of the wonder of the night sky, as when he traveled by himself by car into the Arizona desert in the 1930's. When he settled in California in 1938, he went often to the planetarium above Los Angeles and to Mt. Wilson Observatory, an hour above Pasadena. Here he became acquainted with Gustav Strömberg, who let him peer through the observatory's 100-inch reflecting telescope.

2 Mechanism Called Life

p. 14 "In the beginning was the word and the word was made flesh" (1 John 1:14). Even when not deliberately adapted, Dreiser's quotations from Scripture are not always exact. Usually the phrasing is close to that of the King James version however, though sometimes it is that of the Douay.

p. 14 Ralph Waldo Emerson (1803–1882), American philosopher and poet. Dreiser was introduced to the transcendentalism of Emerson and Thoreau by Mildred Fielding, a schoolteacher from Malden, Massachusetts, who guided his early career, in high school in Warsaw, Indiana, and afterwards, at her own expense, sent him to Indiana University. Dreiser's interest in transcendentalism never waned and in his last years was resurgent, taking direction from his broad philosophical inquiries into Nature and from work done on Thoreau for his book *The Living Thoughts of Thoreau*.

p. 15 Dreiser's comments on the water-lily and mosquito introduce the typical nature *Note* with which his files overflowed. Various aspects of the vegetable and animal kingdoms contributed to his view of life in general. He read Maeterlinck on the bee, Fabre on the spider, Clark on the butterfly, and investigated the many kinds of ants and their habits (cf. the early story "McEwen and the Shining Slave Makers"). An ample book could be made of Dreiser's nature *Notes* alone. The editors here have limited themselves to a few such *Notes* in each category.

p. 15 Jean Henri Fabre (1823–1915), French entomologist, famed for his work on spiders, wasps, and other insects. All his work was based on direct observation. Fabre credited wasps with reasoning power. Dreiser admired his *Marvels of the Insect World* (1927).

p. 16 Benjamin De Casseres (1873–1945), essayist and poet. A collateral descendant of Spinoza, De Casseres did not have a large following in his native America but was popularized in France by Remy de Gourmont. Dreiser admired his volume of poetry *The Shadow-Eater* (1915). In 1933, when George Jean Nathan rejected an article which De Casseres at Dreiser's behest had written for the *Spectator*, Dreiser resigned his editorship. De Casseres's death preceded Dreiser's by just three weeks.

p. 17 John Grainger, British plant pathologist (1904–   ). Between 1933 and 1943, Grainger was director of Britain's Tolson Memorial Museum at Huddersfield, then became head of the department of plant pathology, West of Scotland Agricultural College, Auchincruive.

p. 19 "Is there no more to be said about it? No!" A typical, sardonic, Dreiserian *No!* A common feature of his conversation.

4 MATERIAL BASE OF FORM

p. 26 The Black Grouper figures in a key, metaphoric passage at the close of Dreiser's novel *The Titan*, balancing the introductory parable of lobster and squid. See also *Notes on Life* I 22, p. 153.

p. 29 Eye magnetism fascinated Dreiser. His right eye impaired from birth and virtually useless to him, he believed he himself had become mystically endowed with eye magnetism at the moment of his mother's death. He ascribes it to his most dynamic male protagonists, along with his own blue-gray eye color. Cf. *Dawn*, pp. 446, 516–517; *The Financier*, pp. 157, 164; *Letters of Theodore Dreiser*, ed. Robert H. Elias, III:999.

5 THE FACTOR CALLED TIME

p. 34 Sir Isaac Newton (1642–1727), English mathematician, physicist, and astronomer. A temperament akin to Dreiser's in his fascination for the metaphysical.

p. 37 Train wrecks held a macabre fascination for Dreiser. As a young reporter in St. Louis he gave graphic news coverage to a major train wreck (See *Newspaper Days*, chapters 26 and 27). Dreiser's sister Theresa was killed by a train in Chicago in 1897. Acting on a premonition, in the 1920's, Dreiser once refused to board a train traveling between New York and Philadelphia. An hour later it was wrecked with heavy loss of life.

7 WEIGHTS AND MEASURES

p. 48 "He weigheth the waters" (Job 28:25).

p. 48 "He made a decree for the rain" (Job 28:26).

p. 48 "The very hairs of your head are numbered" (Matt. 10:30).

p. 48 "He marks the sparrow's fall" (Matt. 10:29).

p. 48 "Behold the nations are counted as the small dust of the balance" (Isa. 40:15).

p. 48 "What is man that thou art mindful of him" (Job 14:1–2). Quoted in full in *Notes on Life* II 7, p. 323.

p. 49 "In my Father's house are many mansions" (John 14:2).

p. 49 "God is a spirit. You shall worship him in the spirit of truth" (John 4:24).

p. 49 "This day, you shall be with me in paradise" (Luke 23:43).

p. 49 "Come unto me all ye that labor and are heavy laden, and I will give you rest" (Matt. 11:28).

8 THE MECHANISM CALLED MAN

p. 50 Certain *Notes* were evaluated by the late William Gailmore, a writer and editor on medical subjects and an authority on sports medicine, which concerns itself with the functioning of a healthy body. Gailmore, impressed with Dreiser's speculations, concluded that he was ahead of his time.

p. 53 Daniel Defoe (1659–1731), English novelist and dissenter. In *An American Tragedy*, Dreiser's protagonist, Clyde Griffiths, while awaiting execution, reads Defoe's *Life and Adventures of Robinson Crusoe* (1719), which is, if we may take the word of Wilkie Collins' Gabriel Betteredge in *The Moonstone*, the gospel of the self-reliant man.

p. 56 Jacques Loeb (1859–1924), physiologist and model for Dr. Gottleib in Sinclair Lewis's *Arrowsmith* (1925). Loeb saw man as a chemical mechanism. Dreiser read Loeb's books and Loeb read Dreiser's books. They corresponded with one another for two years before they met in the winter of 1922–23 at the Rockefeller Institute, where Loeb was director of the division of experimental research. Dreiser was especially delighted that the chemical trail which he had blazed in *Sister Carrie* under the influence of Elmer Gates gathered support from Loeb's inquiries. To Loeb, all living things are chemical machines, their workings to be accounted for in the same way we account for the workings of all machines made of inert matter. Tropisms were an area of special concentration for Loeb, and Dreiser was early interested in his *Heliotropism of Animals* (1890). He also read Loeb's *Mechanistic Conception of Life* (1912). In the winter of 1935, at the start of serious work on *Notes on Life*, Dreiser launched his reading program with three Loeb titles, *The Organism as a Whole from the Physicochemical Viewpoint* (1916), *The Dynamics of Living Matter* (1906), and *Forced Movements, Tropisms, and Animal Conduct* (1918), and monographs by him in experimental biology relating to parthenogenesis.

p. 57 Ivan Petrovich Pavlov (1849–1936), Russian physiologist, notable for his work on the digestive glands and the conditioned reflex. In 1904, Pavlov received the Nobel Prize in medicine.

p. 57 "Even now I have the strangest feeling of life within lives (George Fox, John Woolman)." The celebrated passage in the *Journal* of John Woolman in which Woolman has a sense of Christ living within him, and supplanting him, greatly appealed to Dreiser. His treatment of it in the penultimate chapter of *The Bulwark* has much importance in that narrative.

p. 57 George Fox (1624–1691), founder of the Society of Friends. Fox's *Great Journal* (1694) was a Dreiser favorite.

p. 57 John Woolman (1720–1772), American Quaker and pioneer abolitionist. The impact of Woolman's noble *Journal* (1774) is manifest in Dreiser's *Bulwark*. Of the *Journal* Emerson said: "I find more wisdom in these pages than in any other book written since the days of the apostles. There is a true philosophy—a clear insight—a right estimate of things." Emerson's mentor, William Ellery Channing, called it "beyond comparison the sweetest and purest autobiography in the language."

9 PHYSICAL AND CHEMICAL CHARACTER OF MAN'S ACTIONS

p. 61 Calvin Blackman Bridges (1889–1938), American geneticist who formulated the theory of genetic balance. Dreiser spent the summers of 1928 and 1929 at Woods Hole, Massachusetts, visiting almost daily the Marine Biological Laboratory, where Bridges, his close friend, worked. Visiting Marguerite Tjader at Nantucket in the summer of 1929, Bridges and Dreiser discussed the wonders of science, and of biology in particular, for hours, looking out over the ocean and speculating on the forces regulating the life-process. During the summer of 1937, Bridges, who worked in California in winter, carried on research at the Cold Spring Harbor Laboratory on Long Island. Dreiser consulted with him there and scrutinized Nature through the telescope. At this time he wrote Miss Tjader: "It is so charming over here. These people! These scientists! How sincere! How self-sacrificing! A lovely, clean, courteous world of thought."

10 Mechanism Called Mind

p. 64 Vannevar Bush (1890–   ), American scientist and administrator. Beginning in 1930 Bush directed the activities of a team which perfected in 1942 the Bush Differential Analyzer, a machine for solving quickly complex mathematical problems, the forerunner of analog and digital computers. During all of World War II, Bush directed the U.S. Office of Scientific Research and Development and had the overall responsibility for development of the atomic bomb.

p. 65 Dreiser's naturalistic theory of chemisms is used to account for the downfall of George Hurstwood in *Sister Carrie* and for Carrie's rise to renown. Dreiser was introduced to it by its original formulator, Elmer Gates, in January 1900. In Dreiser's *Hand of the Potter* (1918), Isadore Berchansky, a psychopathic child murderer, is described as "badly chemically compounded."

p. 69 "[Wherefore] by their fruits ye shall know them" (Matt. 7:20).

p. 69 "I and my Father are one" (John 10:30).

p. 71 "hewer of wood and a drawer of water" (Josh. 9:23).

p. 73 "I am in my Father and my Father in me" (John 17:21).

11 The Emotions

p. 81 "Sorrow is for the night but joy cometh in the morning" (Ps. 30:5).

12 The So-called Progress of Mind

p. 86 Sir James Hopwood Jeans (1877–1946), English astronomer and mathematician. Jeans's *Universe Around Us* (1929) is addressed to the lay reader. Writing to H. G. Wells in 1931, Dreiser opined that, given human limitations, Jeans's "enormous calculations" in this book had about them an "airy unsubstantiality."

13 Mechanism Called Memory

p. 88 Dreiser often would sit in front of shorter *Notes*, such as this one, brooding over them, till he decided where to fit them in. Some such *Notes*, though he intended to use them, he never incorporated into the main body of his material. Because of their originality they can stand alone, leaving the reader to brood about their relevance. This is as Dreiser wished. As he often said, he wanted to surprise and shock the reader into coming to his own conclusions. Remarking on Nature's practice of sowing acorns in profusion when only a few would develop into oaks, Dreiser likened to this phenomenon his own practice of producing *Notes* in abundance though only a small sum of the total might be used finally. To him this was Nature's method— the true process of Creation.

p. 90 George Washington Crile (1864–1943), American surgeon. As early as 1920 Dreiser had read Crile's *Origin and Nature of the Emotions* (1915) and *Man, An Adaptive Mechanism* (1916). In 1936 he wrote to Crile to congratulate him on *The Phenomena of Life*, newly published. Crile here ascribes to life a mechanistic origin and sees electricity as responsible for life. In *The 'Genius'* (1915) and in *The Titan* (1914) Dreiser used both electrical and solar imagery to emblemize the vitality of dynamic characters.

14 Myth of Individuality

p. 92 Upanishads. Books of Hindu philosophy and metaphysical speculation, dating from 600 B.C.

p. 93 Gustav Strömberg (1882–1962), Swedish born American astronomer, on the staff of the Mount Wilson Observatory, 1917–46. The New York World's Fair, 1940, carried Strömberg's name on its Wall of Fame among those citizens of foreign birth who had made notable contributions to American culture. Strömberg's areas of interest included stasis, brightness of stars, stellar motions, and the philosophy of science. Dreiser read Strömberg's *Soul of the Universe* (1940), expressed an interest in Strömberg's wave system, and sought him out to discuss with him his belief in limited Free Will.

16 Myth of Free Will

p. 103 The question of whether or not man's will is free endlessly tormented Dreiser. Indeed, his whole philosophy centers around this speculation, regarding it from all angles. His evolution from acceptance of a blind determinism to a belief that the process of life is guided by a superior Creative Force can be followed through these *Notes* and perhaps is implied in the modesty of the final title he chose for his book of philosophy.

A handwritten note to himself is found among Dreiser's other pages. It carries the double heading "Myth of Free Will" and "The Emotions." It reads: "I will not trouble to [use] arguments to prove the absence of Free Will. Instead I will confine myself to series of convincing illustrations of its absence in, so far as man is concerned, almost every situation and direction. T.D."

17 Myth of Individual Creative Power

p. 111 Huebaldus. Dreiser means Guido Aretinus, a French Benedictine (995–1050) attached to the monastery of Arezzo in Italy, where Guido took up residence after his brother monks at the monastery of St. Maur outside Paris protested his musical innovations. Guido invented the system of staff notation still in use. Moreover, he advanced incipient polyphony by advocating contrary motion of the voices against the then customary parallelism.

p. 112 Arthur James Balfour, first Earl of Balfour (1848–1930), British prime minister, 1902–05. As foreign secretary in 1917, Balfour issued the declaration stating that Britain favored establishment of Palestine as a national homeland for the Jews.

p. 114 Albert Abraham Michelson (1852–1931), American physicist, recipient of the 1907 Nobel Prize for physics. Michelson's experiments with the velocity of light gave Einstein his starting point for his theory of relativity. Mirrors and a tank of mercury were part of the apparatus which Michelson used.

19 Myth of Individual Responsibility

p. 134 William Beebe (1877–   ), American zoologist and oceanographer.

p. 134 "What, then, did the hand of the Potter shake?" The line is not from Amos, as Dreiser suggests, but from Edward Fitzgerald's "Rubaiyat of Omar Khayyam," stanza 86. Possible Biblical passages which Dreiser may have had in mind are found in Isa. 45:9 and Jer. 18:6. The line provided Dreiser with a title for a controversial play.

21 THE FORCE CALLED ILLUSION

p. 142 Dreiser's fascination with cities, which began in his youth, is reiterated in each of his novels. Of his protagonists only Jennie Gerhardt and Solon Barnes are not beguiled by the beckoning excitements of the urban world. The genesis of this feeling is found in Dreiser's accounts in *Dawn*, *Newspaper Days*, and *The Color of a Great City* of the impact which cities had on him personally, especially in the period of his youth. Every phase and aspect of man's life in the city interests Dreiser, yet he is at his most authoritative when he undertakes to describe youth in its first ecstatic contact with the urban environment.

p. 143 Herbert Spencer (1820–1903), British philosopher. Dreiser's encounter in 1894 in Pittsburgh with Spencer's *First Principles* (1862) introduced him to the concept of mechanism.

p. 145 The nomadic style of Dreiser's early life, dictated by family need, made him both envious and scornful of American domesticity. This ambivalence about "home" receives its most extended treatment in Dreiser's works in *The 'Genius'*, but Dreiser returns to it again in *A Hoosier Holiday* and *Hey Rub-A-Dub-Dub* as well as in the autobiographical volumes and in *An American Tragedy*. During his active years, Dreiser seems to have found the idea of a settled existence antipodal to the doctrine of change. By the time he wrote *The Bulwark* (1945), he could concede that a state of inertia lay beyond change and at last, with tolerance and implied approval, conceded a place to the concept of domestic stability.

p. 149 "There is nothing either good or bad, but thinking makes it so." *Hamlet*, act 2, sc. 2, line 259.

22 VARIETIES OF FORCE

p. 153 Parable of the sower (Matt. 13:18–23).

p. 157 Claude Bernard (1813–1878), French physiologist who did pioneering work on the functioning of the liver, pancreas, and sympathetic nervous system. His public funeral was the first such honor accorded a scientist by the government of France.

p. 158 William Harvey (1578–1657), English physician and anatomist. In 1616 Harvey discovered the circulation of the blood.

p. 159 Joseph Banks Rhine (1895–   ), American parapsychologist. Appointed director of the parapsychology laboratory at Duke University in 1935. An authority on extrasensory perception.

p. 160 Hamlin Garland (1860–1940), pioneer American realist. Garland's long time interest in the occult led to publication of his *Forty Years of Psychic Research* in 1940. Dreiser knew him but did not esteem him.

p. 160 Isidor Isaac Rabi (1898–   ), American physicist, winner of the Nobel Prize for physics in 1944.

p. 160 Alexis Carrel (1873–1944), French surgeon and biologist, awarded the Nobel Prize (medicine) in 1912. Carrel worked at the Rockefeller Institute as a coworker of Loeb's. His *Man the Unknown* (1935) disturbed Dreiser because of its rejection of mechanism.

p. 161 D. H. Lawrence (1885–1930), British novelist and poet. He discusses Nathaniel Hawthorne's *Blithedale Romance* (1852), a dystopian novel based on Hawthorne's stay at the transcendental community of Brook Farm in 1841, in his *Studies in Classical American Literature* (1923).

p. 163 Amos Alonzo Stagg (1862–1965), dean of American football coaches. Stagg was director of athletics at the University of Chicago from 1892 to 1933 and coached football at the College of the Pacific and elsewhere till his ninety-eighth year.

23 TRANSMUTATION OF PERSONALITY

p. 165 "Canst thou not minister to a mind diseased." *Macbeth*, act 5, sc. 1.

p. 170 Ernest Orlando Lawrence (1901–1958), American physicist. Lawrence invented the cyclotron, isolated uranium 235 (used in the atomic bomb), made possible the use of the neutron for cancer therapy and the medical use of radio isotopes. He was awarded the Nobel Prize (physics) in 1939.

p. 174 John Hunter (1728–1793), Scottish surgeon who did the first scientific study of teeth, classifying them as molars, bicuspids, etc., and was the originator of forced feeding by stomach tube.

p. 175 Donald Culross Peattie (1898–1964), American botanist and writer. His poetic responsiveness to Nature places him in the tradition of Thoreau. *Green Laurels* (1936), which Dreiser read, recounts the lives and achievements of great naturalists.

p. 175 Oscar Riddle (1877–   ), American biologist, staff member, department of genetics, Cold Spring Harbor Laboratory, Long Island, during the period of Dreiser's visit. He retired in 1945.

24 THE PROBLEM OF GENIUS

p. 177 Dreiser often returns to the view that "all good things are gifts." See *A Hoosier Holiday*, p. 253; and *A Gallery of Women*, "Ida Hauchawout," p. 365.

p. 177 Congress in 1972 agreed to the installation of electronic vote-counting equipment.

p. 178 "Who produces a perfect work is obedient to laws yet unexplored." Here Thoreau might seem to acknowledge a mechanistic bias. Dreiser knew that Thoreau, as a transcendentalist, had implicit faith in free will, but perhaps thought that here Thoreau did not grasp fully the implications of his own insight.

p. 178 Marie Sklodowska Curie (1867–1934), Polish born French physicist, codiscoverer in 1902 with her husband Pierre of radium. In 1903 the Curies shared the Nobel Prize in physics with Henri Bequerel. In 1911 Marie Curie won a second Nobel Prize, this time for chemistry.

p. 178 Hans Friedrich Geitel (1855–1923), German physicist, who originated the concept of atomic energy and formulated the law of radioactive fallout. Geitel built the first cathode tube.

p. 178 Harvey Brace Lemon (1885–   ), American physicist. Dreiser visited Lemon at the University of Chicago in April 1935, and Lemon gave him an inscribed copy of *From Galileo to Cosmic Rays* (1935). His views on the physics of protoplasm interested Dreiser.

p. 180 "The Man with the Hoe" (1899), a poem written by Charles Edwin Markham (1852–1940). Based on a painting of that title done by France's Francois Jean Millet, it won Markham world renown. It exalted the worker and the dignity of labor.

NOTES ON LIFE II

1 The Theory that Life is a Game

p. 184 The "life is a game" concept was in Dreiser's mind at least as early as January 26, 1935. At that time, in a letter to George Douglas outlining his plans for a work which was to evolve into *Notes on Life*, Dreiser told him: "I look on life as a progressive game that is being played for some purpose, probably for self-entertainment. I hold that there is no evidence to show that this game, as played here, is planned to solve anything" (*Ltrs.* II:719).

p. 186 Edward Lee Thorndike (1874–1949), American psychologist and educator, noted for developing various tests measuring individual achievement and skills.

2 Special and Favoring Phases of the Solar System

p. 192 Clifford Cook Furnas (1900–   ), American educator and research administrator. Furnas was at Yale from 1931–42. His books include *The Next Ten Years* (1936); *Man, Bread, and Destiny*, with S. M. Furnas (1937); *The Storehouse of Civilization* (1939).

3 The Necessity for Contrast

p. 200 Henry Leslie Garabedian (1901–   ), American mathematician, principal physicist at Oak Ridge National Laboratory, 1946–48.

4 The Necessity for Limitation

p. 205 Paul Ehrlich (1854-1915), German bacteriologist. In 1908 Ehrlich shared half the Nobel Prize for physiology and medicine. In 1909 he discovered salvarsan, the first synthetic chemotherapeutic agent, a treatment for syphilis.

p. 205 "They also serve who only stand and wait." John Milton, Sonnet XV ("On His Blindness").

5 The Necessity for Change

p. 208 "Beyond which memory runneth not to the contrary." William Blackstone, *Commentaries* I, 1, p. 18.

p. 208 "He giveth his beloved sleep" (Ps. 127:2).

p. 208 "I am the vine and ye are the branches" (John 15:1).

p. 208 "In my Father's house are many mansions" (John 14:2).

p. 213 Dreiser's own varietistic impulses and his disappointments in marriage often are his subject in *The 'Genius'* and in *Free, Chains,* and other volumes of short stories, anticipating the revolt from the village as encountered in Sherwood Anderson's *Winesburg, Ohio* (1919) and Sinclair Lewis's *Main Street* (1920).

7 The Necessity for Ignorance

p. 215 "Seek and ye shall find, knock and it shall be opened unto you" (Matt. 7:7). Yet another quotation from Matthew, supporting the claim of his wife, Helen Richardson Dreiser, that he preferred this gospel to the others and found the essence of true religion concentrated in it.

10 Scarcity and Plenty

p. 226 Sir William Matthew Flinders Petrie (1853–1942), a major founder of Egyptology. Flinders Petrie established enviable precedents in accurate measurements and in immediate reporting of field work.

p. 226 Albert Francis Blakeslee (1874–1954), American botanist. Blakeslee drew important conclusions about chromosome behavior, genic balance, and species evolution. He was an associate in genetics at Columbia, 1940–1942. From 1943 on he was director of the Smith College genetic station. With A. G. Avery he wrote *Method of Inducing Doubling of Chromosomes in Plants* (1938).

11 Strength and Weakness

p. 231 "Thrice is he armed who hath his quarrel just." *King Henry VI*, Part II, act III, sc. 2, line 233.

12 Courage and Fear

p. 234 "Black-Birds and Fear." This passage survived as a penciled manuscript, evidently written by Dreiser toward the close of his life to record an incident which had taken place in his garden on King's Road in Hollywood.

p. 235 David Hume (1711–1776), Scottish philosopher and historian. Hume denied the existence of reason, favoring as an explanation habitual associations of sensations or experiences.

13 Mercy and Cruelty

p. 239 Dreiser's vast compassion, which conspicuously contradicts the naturalistic ideal of clinical detachment, is nowhere better seen than in his constant efforts to account for pain and suffering in the world. See *Hey Rub-A-Dub-Dub*, p. 125 and *Living Thoughts of Thoreau*, pp. 23–24.

p. 239 "a divine far off event." In Tennyson's "In Memoriam," Conclusion, stanza 36, the poet refers to "one far-off divine event."

p. 240 "red in claw and beak." In "In Memoriam," part LVI, stanza 4, Tennyson refers to "Nature, red in tooth and claw."

p. 241 On May 11, 1919 Dreiser was knocked down in Columbus Circle, New York City by a car. One wheel passed over his midsection. He was hospitalized with two fractured ribs and extensive contusions and treated as well for scalp lacerations and shock. At forty-eight, Dreiser seems to have been more hurt by the words of a girl onlooker who cried out, "Oh, the poor old man!"

14 Beauty and Ugliness

p. 243 At the close of *The Stoic*, the final volume of the trilogy of desire, Dreiser concludes that the search for beauty is merely a search for the divine design behind all forms. Dreiser came to this view after a quest that had gone on through the whole of his literary lifetime. See *Sister Carrie*, p. 418; *Living Thoughts of Thoreau*, p. 14.

p. 244 Ernest Heinrich Haeckel (1834–1919), German biologist and natural philosopher. Haeckel believed God to be identical with eternal, all-inspiring energy, that God and matter are one, and that the will of God is seen in all physical and psychical phenomena. He rejected the concept of a personal God. Dreiser liked Haeckel's *The Riddle of the Universe at the Close of the Nineteenth Century* (1900). In January 1921, however, he wrote to a journalist friend, Edward H. Smith, saying that while he had read Haeckel for years "with unwearied interest," he rejected "completely, his conclusion that such forces as we sense, make in the ultimate, for either the good, the true, or the beautiful." (*Ltrs.* I:337).

p. 248 Lao-tze (604?–531? B.C.), pre-Confucian Chinese philosopher, founder of Taoism.

16 GOOD AND EVIL

p. 254 "lead us not into temptation" (Matt. 6:13).

p. 254 "For evil needs must come, but woe to him by whom the evil cometh" (Matt. 18:7).

p. 256 William James (1842–1910), American philosopher and psychologist, advocate of pragmatism. His *Pluralistic Universe*, from which this passage is taken, was published in 1909.

17 THE PROBLEM OF KNOWLEDGE

p. 258 "From everlasting [and] to everlasting" (Ps. 41:13).

18 THE EQUATION CALLED MORALITY

p. 267 "He is of eyes too pure to behold evil" (Hab. 1:13).

p. 269 "Do unto others" (Matt. 7:12).

p. 269 "An eye for an eye" (Matt. 5:38).

p. 269 "They that live by the sword" (Matt. 26:52).

19 THE COMPROMISE CALLED JUSTICE

p. 273 "Rain falleth on just and unjust" (Matt. 5:45). Dreiser included this phrase in a tribute to Sherwood Anderson which was read at Anderson's funeral by Stanley Young.

p. 275 "With what measure ye mete, it shall be measured to you" (Mark 4:24).

p. 275 "Are not two sparrows sold for a farthing" (Matt. 10:29).

p. 276 Remy De Gourmont (1858–1915), French critic, essayist, moralist. One of the first critics to recognize the importance of Mallarmé, Huysmans, and Nietzsche. His *Physique de l'Amour* (1903) undertakes to the rid the philosophy of love of all mystical and romantic elements, to view it as a biological operation.

20 THE SALVE CALLED RELIGION

p. 277 Dreiser's often cited animosity toward structured religion was directed less against honest faith than that narrow dogmatism which makes of religion an exercise in mental and moral inertia. See *A Hoosier Holiday*, pp. 182, 183.

p. 278 "The Lord giveth, the Lord taketh away" (Job 1:21).

p. 280 Edward Jenner (1749–1832), an English physician, conquered smallpox with the first effective vaccination technique (1798).

p. 280 Sir Ernest Rutherford (1871–1937), New Zealand born British physicist, winner of the Nobel Prize for chemistry in 1908.

p. 280 Louis Pasteur (1822–1895), French chemist and bacteriologist whose demonstration of the germ theory of disease opened the way to modern medicine.

p. 282 The reference is from Thoreau's essay "Wild Apples," under the section headed "How the Wild Apple Grows." See *Excursions* (Boston, 1893), pp. 372–375.

21 The Problem of Progress and Purpose

p. 290 Arthur Holly Compton (1892–1962), American physicist. For his studies of x-rays and cosmic rays, Compton shared the Nobel Prize in physics with C.T.R. Wilson in 1927. Dreiser conferred with Compton at the University of Chicago in April 1935.

p. 290 Robert Andrews Millikan (1868–1953), American physicist who in 1923 won the Nobel Prize (physics) for isolating and measuring the electron. Millikan also worked on cosmic rays, a subject which fascinated Dreiser. In March 1935, Dreiser sought to initiate a correspondence with Millikan, soliciting his views on the subject of chaos in the universe. His belief in an "ordered universe" interested Dreiser. That summer he visited with Millikan and Bridges at Cal. Tech.

p. 290 Sir Arthur Stanley Eddington (1782–1844), English astronomer and physicist. His most important scientific work dealt with the evolution and motion of stars. He was a popularizer of science.

p. 290 Sir Arthur Keith (1866–1955), British anthropologist, noted for his success in reconstructing prehistoric man from fossil fragments.

p. 290 Sir Julian Sorrell Huxley (1887–   ), British biologist.

22 The Myth of a Perfect Social Order

p. 298 James Bryce, first Viscount Bryce (1838–1922), British statesman, jurist, and author of the classic *The American Commonwealth* (1888).

p. 298 Alexis de Rocqueville (1805–1859), French writer, statesman, and author of the renowned work *Democracy in America* (1835). In 1849 deTocqueville was France's minister of foreign affairs.

p. 300 In a *Note* entitled "Will Democracy Endure?" Dreiser says: "American democracy is not quite a frail flower. It may not be the most beautiful that the world has yet developed, but most certainly it has proved to be a slow growing, tough-fibred thing." In *A Hoosier Holiday* Dreiser says: "I am in favor of the dream of democracy, on whatever basis it can be worked out" (pp. 78, 279). Yet in *Tragic America* Dreiser asked finally for a fundamental change in government; or its disestablishment (pp. 84, 201, 316).

23 Laughter

p. 302 "And the loud laugh that spoke the vacant mind." A line (121) from Oliver Goldsmith's "The Deserted Village" (1770).

p. 303 Immanuel Kant (1724–1804), German philosopher, author of *Critique of Pure Reason* (1781). His thought, as developed by Hegel, is the foundation on which Marxist socialism was built. It also provided some basic concepts to Emerson, Thoreau, and their fellow transcendentalists.

24 MUSIC

p. 312 "We are grateful when we are reminded by *internal* evidence." Once again Dreiser finds support in Thoreau's quasi-mechanistic submissiveness to the decrees of Nature.

27 THE PROBLEM OF DEATH

p. 319 (Ilia Ilich Mechnikov) Elie Metchnikoff (1845–1916), Russian bacteriologist who formulated the theory of phagocytosis and discovered phagocytes. Author of *Etudes sur la Nature Humaine,* published in English as *The Nature of Man* (1903). In 1908, Metchnikoff, with Paul Ehrlich, received the Nobel Prize for medicine and physiology for his work in immunity.

28 MY CREATOR

p. 327 The original manuscript of "My Creator" was signed "Theodore Dreiser, Hollywood, November 1943." Dreiser meant to publish it as a separate article. In *My Life with Dreiser,* Helen Dreiser says that Dreiser got the idea to write the essay one day while spading in his garden, in the shade of an avocado tree, outside his stucco villa on King Street in Hollywood. He wanted it to be, she said, "an appreciation of the life processes as expressed by the creative force working in nature" (p. 291).

p. 328 Sir Oliver Joseph Lodge (1851–1940), English physicist whose interests centered on electrical and magnetic phenomena. After 1910 Lodge became a leader in psychical research, communicating with the dead, and reconciling science and religion.

p. 328 Sir William Crookes (1832–1919), English chemist, physicist. Crookes invented the Crookes tube, which led to Röntgen's discovery of x-rays, and discovered selenocyanides, thallium, and the repulsion resulting from radiation. He was interested in spectral phenomena and his opinions on the subject carried weight because of his scientific reputation.

p. 328 Karl Augustus Menninger (1893–   ), American psychiatrist, cofounder of the Menninger Clinic at Topeka, Kansas.

p. 329 Piltdown Man was the name which science gave to fossil fragments allegedly found at Piltdown, East Sussex, by amateur anthropologist Charles Dawson in 1911. They were believed to be remains of a primitive man, Eoranthropus, who lived more than half a million years ago. In 1953 chemical tests established that claims made for these bones were fraudulent.

p. 333 The concluding portion of "My Creator" echoes sentiments found in a statement which Dreiser circulated among friends in July 1940. This statement was written as a reply to a college student, Dorothy Payne Davis, who had asked Dreiser for a summation of his philosophy (*Ltrs.* III:886–890).